NEW TESTAMENT EPISTLES

1 & 2
THESSALONIANS

A CRITICAL AND EXEGETICAL
COMMENTARY

by

GARETH L. REESE

HEAD OF NEW TESTAMENT DEPARTMENT
CENTRAL CHRISTIAN COLLEGE OF THE BIBLE
MOBERLY, MISSOURI

Scripture Exposition Books, LLC
803 McKINSEY PLACE
MOBERLY, MISSOURI
65270

Acknowledgments

The Scripture quotations contained herein, unless otherwise noted, are from the New American Standard Bible, copyrighted 1960, 1962, 1963, 1971, 1972, 1975, 1977, 1995 by the Lockman Foundation. Used by permission.

Suggested Cataloging Data

Reese, Gareth L., 1932-
New Testament Epistles: 1 & 2 Thessalonians, a critical and exegetical commentary / by Gareth L. Reese. Moberly, MO: Scripture Exposition Books, 2020.

[vi], 269 p.; 26 cm. – (New Testament Epistles)
Includes bibliographical references and index.
ISBN 099-845-186X

1. Bible. N.T. Thessalonians, 1st & 2nd – Commentaries.   I. Title   II. Series.

BS 2723.53 R259

DEDICATION

To all who have loved the first appearing on earth
Of our great God and Savior Jesus Christ

And who patiently await His return in glory with all
His holy ones

And who, in the meantime, seek to live in a manner
worthy of the heavenly calling to be His followers.

TABLE OF CONTENTS

PART FOUR: SPECIAL STUDIES

Commentary On

1 Thessalonians

CONCISE INTRODUCTION TO
1 THESSALONIANS

One of the earliest apostolic letters to be preserved

Chronologically, 1 Thessalonians has the distinction of being the first of the letters signed by the apostle Paul which has been preserved. (A letter written to the churches in AD 51 at the close of the Jerusalem Conference is included in Acts 15.)

Perhaps one other New Testament epistle, that of James, antedates 1 Thessalonians. This commentator has suggested that just after the Jerusalem Conference is a likely time when the epistle of James was written. At that Jerusalem Conference, some Pharisees who pretended to be Christians (Galatians 2:4) misused the example of James as an argument against Christian liberty. A date of AD 51 for the writing of the epistle of James thus makes that letter a wonderful rebuttal to the claims of the Pharisees who had been misusing James' name and example.

Today, some European scholars have proposed that Galatians was written prior to the Jerusalem Conference. However, such proposals are contradicted by Galatians 4:13 which has Paul visiting Galatia twice before this letter was written to them. Paul did not visit the churches of Galatia a second time until his visit during the second missionary journey, which post-dated the Conference at Jerusalem.

Authorship

Three names occur in the signature – Paul, Silas, and Timothy (1 Thessalonians 1:1) – and throughout the letter the verbs used tend to be plural ("we"). However, in one or more places, Paul does indicate his own personal concerns (2:18).

Destination

The destination given in the epistolary opening is "to the church of the Thessalonians." According to Acts 17:1-9, the church at Thessalonica was founded by Paul and Silas during Paul's second missionary journey, which we date AD 51-54.

Place of Writing

From the history recorded in Acts, after the planting of the church in Thessalonica, it was in Corinth when the three men whose names appear in the signature were next together (Acts 18:5). The subscription found in the KJV, which has the letter written from Athens, is in error.

Date

About AD 51, or perhaps early AD 52, the church at Thessalonica was planted (Acts 17:1-4). From Thessalonica, Paul went to Berea and Athens (Acts 17:10,16). Probably several months after leaving Thessalonica, Timothy was sent back from Athens to Thessalonica (3:1,2). Several months more would intervene before Timothy could return to Paul at Corinth. This letter was written after Timothy's return. It is therefore probable that the letter was written late AD 52 or early AD 53, perhaps a year after the congregation was planted.

Purpose

Written only a short time after the congregation at Thessalonica was started, this letter was called forth by the trials and needs of a young congregation of Christians. Paul and Silas had been forced to leave the city by an uproar stirred up by Jews. Shortly after their departure, the persecution which had driven them away turned upon the church (2:14, 3:3).

When Timothy returned from Thessalonica (3:6), he reported that the new Christians were being persecuted by both Jewish and Gentile adversaries. There were also some matters of practical Christian living that needed emphasis. The missionaries who planted the congregation wanted desperately to visit again (2:18), but were prevented. The next best thing was to write such instructions as they would have given had they been present in person.

Contents

B.W. Johnson has succinctly stated that "the letter is full of comfort, instruction, and encouragement." Two chapters especially emphasize events that will take place at the second coming of Christ, so the letter is often characterized as having an eschatological emphasis.

Outline of 1 Thessalonians

Epistolary Opening – Signatures, Address and Greeting.   1:1

I.   Thanksgiving for the Thessalonians' Faith and the Reasons for the Thanksgiving. 1:2-10.

II. The Writers' Vindication of Their Lives and Ministry among the Thessalonians.   2:1-16

III. The Writers' Desire to Visit Thessalonica Again.   2:17-3:13

IV. Calls to Action.   4:1 - 5:22
  A. Exhortations About Living to Please God.   4:1-12
     1. An exhortation to improve their keeping of the instructions learned from their missionaries.   4:1-2
     2. An exhortation to sexual purity.   4:3-8
     3. An exhortation to brotherly love.   4:9-12
  B. Exhortations Concerning the Second Coming of Christ.   4:13 -5:11
     1. Encouraging words concerning Christians who have already died.   4:13-18
     2. Further instruction about the day of the Lord.   5:1-11
  C. Exhortations to Aid Preparation for the Lord's Return.   5:12-22
     1. Concerning responsibilities to congregational leaders.   5:12,13a
     2. Concerning the responsibility to live in peace with one another.   5:13b-15
     3. Concerning responsibilities to oneself.   5:16-18
     4. Concerning responsibilities during public worship.   5:19-22

V.   Some Final Prayers and Requests.   5:23-27
  A. More wish-prayers for the Thessalonian Christians.   5:23,24
  B. Three things requested from the Thessalonians.   5:25-27

Epistolary Closing.   5:28

THE EPISTLE OF
1 THESSALONIANS

Epistolary Opening. Signatures, Address & Greeting. 1:1

1:1 -- *Paul and Silvanus and Timothy, to the church of the Thessalonians in God the Father and the Lord Jesus Christ: Grace to you and peace.*

Paul and Silvanus and Timothy – Writers of ancient letters signed their names at the beginning of the letter. In this epistle there are three men's names included in the signature. For those familiar with the books of the New Testament, little needs to be said about the man whose name heads the list, "Paul." Acts 9-28 is filled with information about this man's call to be an apostle of Jesus and of his subsequent ministry, especially to the Gentiles. "Silas" (such is the Greek spelling of the man's name in Acts) is a shortened form of "Silvanus," which is the regular Roman transliteration of the man's Jewish name in Paul's letters. Silas was a Jewish Christian (Acts 15:22, 16:20) and was, like Paul, a Roman citizen (Acts 16:37,38). He was chosen by Paul to accompany him on what is known as Paul's second missionary tour (Acts 15:40). He was a New Testament prophet (Acts 15:32), so his input into the content of this letter would be as inspired as was the apostle Paul's. "Timothy" was recruited by Paul to accompany him and Silas on that second tour (Acts 16:1-3). If Timothy served as the amanuensis in the composition of this letter,[1] his input, too, has the possibility of being inspired since Paul had imparted a special gift to Timothy by the laying on of hands (2 Timothy 1:6). All three men were known to the readers to whom the letter is addressed. Paul and Silas were instrumental in planting a new church in Thessalonica during that second missionary tour (Acts 17:1-9). Timothy evidently was sent to Thessalonica after Paul and Silas left (1 Thessalonians 3:2), and he has joined the other two men before this letter was composed and sent.[2] The only time we know these three men were together after the planting of the church at Thessalonica is when they were in Corinth (Acts 18:5). So we determine this first letter to the Thessalonians was written from Corinth, about AD 52.[3]

To the church of the Thessalonians – The address is the second element in the opening of ancient letters. A "church" (*ekklēsia*) is a local assembly of Christians. The word translated "church" did not refer to a building in which the Christians assembled, but to the meeting or congregation of those who had been "called out" of the world into fellowship

---

[1] Perhaps the reason Timothy is named third is because he was the amanuensis. Perhaps it is also true that of the three men named, Timothy's name is third because he is the youngest.

[2] See the Detailed Introduction to 1 Thessalonians for a full reconstruction of Timothy and Silas' travels during this period when the church at Thessalonica was planted.

[3] For details concerning the time and place of writing, see the Detailed Introduction to 1 Thessalonians.

with Jesus Christ. The assembly, or church, in the city of Thessalonica consisted of a group of baptized believers (implied in the fact they had received the Holy Spirit, 1 Thessalonians 4:8), with a recognized leadership (1 Thessalonians 5:12,13), which met together regularly, at which meetings the apostolic epistles were read as inspired scripture (1 Thessalonians 5:27) and folk greeted each other with a holy kiss (1 Thessalonians 5:26).

In God the Father and the Lord Jesus Christ – Since God's Old Testament people could be called a "church" (Acts 7:38) and since "called out" meetings for conducting city business could be called a "church" (Acts 19:41), this phrase serves to identify in particular the "assembly" in the city of Thessalonica to which this letter is addressed. It is not a pagan or non-religious assembly (cf. "God the Father"); it is not a Jewish assembly (cf. "the Lord Jesus Christ"). It is a congregation of God's new people. Here the church is not called "the church *of* God" but the church "*in* God." This is an unusual expression in Paul's writings. Perhaps the preposition "in" has an instrumental force; the church was brought into being by God the Father. Or perhaps it is a dative of sphere; God and Christ are the sphere in which the church exists. There is also need to call special attention to what all three words, "Lord Jesus Christ," are saying to us. "Lord" is not a title added to Jesus' name. "Lord" was the word the Jews said when they came to the four-letter sacred name of Yahweh. To call Jesus "Lord" is to affirm His deity. The modern insinuation that no one called Jesus "Lord" (i.e., attributed deity to Him) until the close of the 1st century is contradicted by most every book in the New Testament. Before 1 Thessalonians was written where He is called "Lord," the Gospels record that even during Jesus' earthly ministry they called Him "Lord." "You call me Lord, and that is right. That is who I am" (John 13:13). "Jesus" is the earthly name of the One who became incarnate at Bethlehem (Matthew 1:18-23), coming to earth on a mission to save people from their sins. "Christ" tells us that this incarnate One was the long-promised Messiah, God's specially anointed one.

Grace to you and peace – The greeting or salutation was the third element in the opening of ancient letters. These words of greeting are in the form of a prayer.[4] The usual Greek salutation was *chairein* ("greeting," cf. James 1:1, Acts 15:23). By a slight change of spelling, the word of salutation becomes *charis* ("grace"), a word full of spiritual connotation. "Grace" is God's attitude of loving-kindness; in the LXX, *charis* translates the Hebrew *chesed* ("loving-kindness"). "Peace" may refer to a right relationship with God and man. "Peace" signifies spiritual well-being in its widest sense. To a persecuted congregation like at Thessalonica, "peace (to you)" may be a prayer for cessation of hostilities from the persecutors.

---

[4] Commentators whose writings are based on the KJV have an additional phrase in verse 1 ("from God our Father and the Lord Jesus Christ") that is not found in the NASB. When that phrase is added, this prayer is that God and Jesus will grant grace and peace to the readers.

I. THANKSGIVING FOR THE THESSALONIANS' FAITH AND THE REASONS FOR THE THANKSGIVING. 1:2-10.

1:2 – *We give thanks to God always for all of you, making mention* of you *in our prayers;*

We give thanks to God always for all of you – Ancient letters usually included a word of thanksgiving to deity for blessings received. In most of Paul's letters, he thanks God for what the readers are doing, though in 1 Corinthians he thanks God for what God has done for the Corinthians, and he has no word of thanksgiving in the letter to the Galatians for disappointment and indignation ruled out any thanksgiving. Paul's thanksgivings usually anticipated the major topics to be covered in the body of the letter. Verses 2-5 form a single sentence in Greek. The main verb "we give thanks" (present tense, continuous action implied, "we keep on giving thanks") is followed by three participial phrases: "making mention" (verse 2), "bearing in mind" (verse 3), and "knowing" (verse 4). These detail some of the things for which the writers are thankful. All three men ("we") who signed the letter are giving thanks for the same things. "Always" does not mean Paul and his companions prayed around the clock without ceasing; it rather says that every time they prayed for the Thessalonians, they give thanks for all the Christians at Thessalonica for all the reasons about to be enumerated. "All of You" reflects the fact that a "great multitude" of Thessalonians had turned to the Lord (Acts 17:4 KJV). The note of thanksgiving is sounded over and over in the first part of this letter, as far as 1 Thessalonians 3:13.

Making mention *of you* **in our prayers** – This first of three participial phrases tells how Paul and his fellow workers expressed their thanks. They did it in their prayers.

A reminder of recent events will help us get the feel of this thanksgiving. A few months earlier, the stay of Paul and Silas in Thessalonica had been cut short by opposition to them from Jewish antagonists. They had been forced to leave town suddenly (Acts 17:5-10), and such a hasty departure under cover of darkness undoubtedly might make some people wonder whether they were just another set of fast-talking, fast-moving religious con-men. Paul devotes much of the first three chapters of 1 Thessalonians to assuring these Christians that their preachers were not con-men, and in fact neither God nor their preachers had abandoned them, nor forgotten them. Paul was anxious to know how the new converts were handling the persecution they were facing. He had been so anxious that he sent Timothy to see how the Thessalonian Christians were doing and to encourage them (1 Thessalonians 3:1-8). Timothy has returned from his mission, and upon hearing from Timothy that they were strong and unfaltering in their faith, the hearts of Paul, Silas and Timothy overflowed with gratitude, and that in turn led them to express thanks to God for the Thessalonian believers.

1:3 – *constantly bearing in mind your work of faith and labor of love and steadfastness of hope in our Lord Jesus Christ in the presence of our God and Father,*

Constantly bearing in mind – Paul calls attention to three things in particular about the Thessalonians' spiritual progress that constantly came to mind as they gave thanks to God in their prayers for the Thessalonians. Paul and Silas constantly thought back to the time they were with the Thessalonians.[5] As they thought about the Thessalonian converts, they "recalled how their faith had led them to work, their love had led them to labor, and their hope had made them steadfast."[6] Paul and Silas have recurring pleasant memories of the Thessalonians' response to the gospel.

Your work of faith – First of all, Paul and Silas remembered how the Thessalonians did what Jesus wanted them to do. Their faith expressed itself in action. They put their faith into practice. Their new life in Christ was characterized by faith and prompted by faith.

> Faith is a dynamic force in life as may be seen from the verbs with which it is associated in the book of Hebrews. There it is stated that by faith men and women prepared, went out, offered up, sojourned, received, gave, refused, chose, forsook, kept, passed through, subdued kingdoms, wrought righteousness, obtained promises, stopped the mouths of lions, quenched fires, escaped the sword, and waxed valiant.[7]

It is not surprising that Paul indicates that genuine faith results in action. Elsewhere in his writings he emphasizes the obedience of faith (Romans 3:20,21,28; Romans 4:4-6; Galatians 5:6). In numerous places faith and practice are interchangeable terms (e.g., Galatians 3:11,12; Hebrews 10:36, 38; Romans 10:5,6). It has been a mistake to interpret "not as a result of works" at Ephesians 2:9 to mean that mental assent is all there is for faith to be genuine, and then it is an even greater mistake to array Paul against James when the latter demonstrates the absolute necessity of works accompanying faith to authenticate its validity (James 2:14-26).[8]

And labor of love – Just as the genitive in the phrase "work of faith" is almost equivalent to a very emphatic adjective, "faithful activity," so the genitive here is equivalent to "loving labor." The Greek word translated "labor" (*kopou*) implies more than work, for it includes the notion of toil, fatigue, and hard work that results in bone-tired weariness. The Thessalonians' love for their brethren prompted them to go beyond ordinary effort and to endure hardship and discomfort, in order that they might minister to the needs of their

---

[5] Some attach *adialeiptōs* ("constantly," "without ceasing") to the previous clause, making it say they prayed without ceasing. If we attach it to verse 3 as the NASB does, it does not mean that they thought of nothing but the Thessalonians. Rather it is a way of showing continued and intense interest in the Thessalonians.

[6] Orrin Root, *Standard Lesson Commentary 1984-85* (Cincinnati: Standard Publishing Company, 1984), p.90.

[7] S. Edward Tesh, *Standard Lesson Commentary 1973-74* (Cincinnati: Standard Publishing Company, 1973), p.347.

[8] Faith that saves includes knowledge, assent, confidence, and obedience. See the Special Study on "The Faith that Saves" in the author's commentary *New Testament History: Acts* (Moberly, MO: Scripture Exposition Books, 2002), pp.598-610.

brethren (cp. 1 Thessalonians 2:9). This is the second thing for which Paul and Silas give thanks as they remember how the Thessalonians put the gospel into practice.

And steadfastness of hope – The third thing for which Paul and Silas give thanks is that the Thessalonians' hope led them to be steadfast. The word translated "steadfastness" is *hupomonē*, which at times is also translated endurance or perseverance. The KJV translation "patience of hope" is misleading since the word "patience" suggests to the present-day reader a totally passive attitude. The real meaning is that of an aggressive and courageous Christian quality; namely, making the best of their circumstances even though times were hard, and then ministering to others based on the learnings from their own experiences. If Paul's thanksgiving anticipates ideas that will be developed later in the letter, then the hard times faced by the Christians were the result of persecution by their unconverted neighbors. "Hope" triggered their steadfastness and perseverance. "Hope" is a rather complex emotion, involving both the expectation of a future event and a confident waiting for that event. What is that future event? Later in this letter, Paul will emphasize the promises of God concerning the future coming of Christ (cf. 1 Thessalonians 2:19; 3:13; 4:13; 5:8).[9]

In our Lord Jesus Christ – It is a debated question among commentators whether this clause is to be tied to all three clauses earlier in this verse (making Jesus the object of their faith and love and hope), or whether it is tied only to the last clause (making the Lord Jesus Christ[10] the one in whom their hope rests). Paul calls Jesus "our" Lord. He and Silas and Timothy and the brethren at Thessalonica all have the same Lord and the same hope. Because of Jesus, their Lord and Messiah, they had the unfailing hope of eternal life and happiness, and that hope gave them endurance in their troubles.

In the presence of our God and Father – It is uncertain how much of the preceding verse is to be taken together with this phrase. If it is tied with the participle "bearing in mind," then this clause introduces one of the concerns that will be covered in this letter, namely that someone has been questioning the motives of Paul and Silas as they dealt with the Thessalonians. Paul would be affirming that their evangelistic work in Thessalonica had all been done in the watchful presence of God. He knows there were no questionable motives on the part of the preachers. If this clause is tied with "faith, love, and hope" then those qualities exhibited by the Thessalonian Christians were not merely such as would pass as genuine before men, but would pass as genuine "in the sight of God," the Searcher of hearts. "In the presence of" calls to mind the picture of a subject facing his King to give an account for deeds done in the body, whether good or bad (2 Corinthians 5:10). Whether it be Paul and Silas or the Thessalonians, when we think of God we are reminded to reflect on the fact that we must soon stand before him. In fact, the same phrase occurs at 1 Thessalonians 3:13 where it is closely associated with the thought of Christ's return.

---

[9] In this first letter written by Paul we are introduced to the great triad (faith, hope, and love) which appears in many of his letters. Though not always in the same order, the triad occurs in 1 Corinthians 13:13; 1 Thessalonians 5:8; Galatians 5:5,6; Ephesians 4:2-5; Colossians 1:4,5; Hebrews 10:22-24; 1 Peter 1:21-22. Perhaps "hope" is placed emphatically last in the triad here in 1 Thessalonians because of the emphasis in the whole letter on the second coming of Christ.

[10] See comments at verse 1 on "Lord Jesus Christ."

1:4 – *knowing, brethren beloved by God, His choice of you;*

Knowing, brethren beloved by God – Still in the midst of the single, long sentence that began in verse 2, Paul now offers a the third participial phrase modifying "we give thanks." This one expresses a further cause for the thanksgiving which Paul and Silas and Timothy give to God, and it affirms two things concerning the Thessalonian Christians. The first is that they are brothers whom God loves. "Behold what manner of love the Father has given us, that we should be called sons of God!" (1 John 3:1). The perfect tense verb "beloved" pictures not only God's attitude to them in the present, but the long continuance of it in the past.[11] 'God loved you in the past, and He still does.' Paul knows about God's love from God's revelation of Himself.[12]

His choice of you – As part of this participial phrase, Paul affirms a second truth concerning the Thessalonian Christians for which the writers of this letter give thanks. "Choice" translates *eklogēn*, which the KJV translated "the election of God." Here for the first time in Paul's epistles we are introduced to the doctrine of divine election or choice. "Election" (KJV) is a term that has resulted in much doctrinal controversy. When placed alongside other Scriptures, such as Acts 10:43 ("of [Jesus] all the prophets bear witness that through His name everyone who believes in Him receives forgiveness of sins") and Ephesians 1:4,5 ("[God] chose us in [Christ] before the foundation of the world, that we would be holy and blameless before Him"), the best explanation of God's election is that back in eternity, as He was planning His creation, God elected (i.e., He decided) that all who are in Christ would be His chosen people. Whether or not a person is "in Christ" depends on his or her free-will response to the gospel. "God's 'elect' do not believe because they were chosen; rather, they are chosen because they believe."[13] Verses 5-10 explain how Paul knows the Thessalonian Christians are among the "elect." It is because of their response to the gospel of Christ which Paul and his companions preached.[14]

1:5 – *for our gospel did not come to you in word only, but also in power and in the Holy Spirit and with full conviction; just as you know what kind of men we proved to be among you for your sake.*

---

[11] Perfect tense verbs denote past completed action with present continuing results.

[12] The word "knowing" translates the verb *oida* which refers to knowledge that comes by book learning. By contrast, *ginōskō* is knowledge that comes by experience.

[13] Jon Weatherly, *Standard Lesson Commentary 2003-04* (Cincinnati: Standard Publishing Company, 2003), p.283.

[14] We would not word it that "election, or choice, denotes the action of God according to which He has predetermined from eternity certain individuals to be believers in Christ," nor would we word it that "God has foreknown our belief from all eternity past, and that foreknowledge is how He can decide in advance who will be in Heaven, and who won't." Rather we would word it that God chose (i.e., He determined ahead of time) that those who would be "in Christ" as a result of their own free-will response to God's call and invitation through the gospel would be the ones who become His adopted family members. Whether or not we are in Christ is our own choice, not the result of His unconditional and absolute predestination. He does not arbitrarily decide who will believe and who will not.

For our gospel did not come to you in word only – "For" represents the Greek word *hoti* and here it means "because."[15] The writers recognize the Thessalonian Christians are among God's "chosen people" because of two historical facts: the preachers had divine guidance in their preaching the gospel (verse 5), and the Thessalonians' response to that gospel was whole-hearted (verse 6ff). For Paul and Silas to call their preaching "our gospel" does not imply that their preached message was different from the gospel preached by other apostles. What Paul and Silas preached at Thessalonica and elsewhere was equally well called "the gospel of God" (1 Thessalonians 2:8), "the gospel of Christ" (1 Thessalonians 3:2), or "the gospel of our Lord Jesus" (2 Thessalonians 1:8). It was the very gospel which had been given to them by God in trust (1 Thessalonians 2:4).[16] Paul and Silas do not call attention to themselves as messengers, but to the message as demanding men's attention. When Paul and Silas came to Thessalonica (Acts 17:1-3) they were the first to bring the *euangellion* ("good news" or "gospel") to that town. Bible scholars are still searching for the reason why the Christian message came to be called "good news" or "gospel." Perhaps it is because Isaiah 40-66 used *euangelizesthai* to describe the good news of Zion's future restoration once the Babylonian captivity was over. Isaiah 52:7 is quoted at Romans 10:17 with reference to the message Christian preachers would preach, and Isaiah 61:1 is likewise applied at Luke 4:18 to the salvation that Christ came to bring. The last three words of this clause ("in word only") refer to the fact that the preachers spoke words as they delivered the good news. But Paul goes on to affirm that several other things were happening as they preached, and those things were evidence that God wanted these Thessalonians to become numbered among His chosen people.

But also in power and in the Holy Spirit and with full conviction – It looks like there were three elements that accompanied the preaching at Thessalonica, all of which show that what was happening there was in harmony with God's eternal plan for some men to become His adopted family members. Since this verse continues by calling attention to how the preachers behaved while they were in Thessalonica, we presume that all three elements named in this clause are related to God's messengers rather than to the Thessalonian listeners. "Power" may refer to miracles wrought by Paul and Silas while they were in Thessalonica, or it may be another way of stating what we read in Romans 1:16 that the gospel is "the power of God unto salvation to all who believe." "In the Holy Spirit" reflects the truth that when the gospel is preached, the Holy Spirit goes to work to produce conviction and obedience (1 Corinthians 12:13). "Full conviction" (if it speaks of the preachers) says the preachers had full conviction of the truth of their message. Recall that just prior to their coming to Thessalonica, the preachers had been horribly mistreated at Philippi (Acts 16:22-24) because of their preaching. The fact that they spoke with "full assurance" when they got to Thessalonica speaks volumes about their conviction concerning the truth of what they were preaching.

---

[15] Treating *hoti* as causal ("because") rather than epexegetic, verses 5 and 6 are not a statement of what "election" consists, but of the historical facts from which "election" may be inferred.

[16] It borders on wresting of Scripture to affirm that "our gospel" means Paul's message was different from the gospel of Christ preached by Jesus and the other apostles of Christ. Nor should "our gospel" be pressed to mean that the message originated with Paul and Silas.

Just as you know what kind of men we proved to be among you for your sake – Keep in mind that we are still looking at evidence by which the Thessalonians themselves can know that they are now God's "chosen people" (verse 4).   Paul and Silas call attention to how their own lives were consistent with the message they preached.   The preachers were conscious of their responsibility to live what they preached.   They imitated Christ so their listeners would have an example that was tantamount to following Christ Himself.   We can account for the zeal and diligence and bravery the preachers exerted, even in the face of opposition in Thessalonica (1 Thessalonians 2:1,2), when it is understood they were seeking to benefit the Thessalonians, not themselves.   The attitudes and actions of the preachers had been completely unselfish because that is how God's plan for folk to become "chosen people" now works.   "The holy life of a preacher goes far to confirm the truth of the religion which he preaches, and is among the most efficacious means of inducing men to embrace the gospel."[17]

1:6 – *You also became imitators of us and of the Lord, having received the word in much tribulation with the joy of the Holy Spirit,*

You also became imitators of us – "You also" introduces a new point in the writers' explanation of how they knew the Thessalonian Christians were among God's elect. "You" is emphatic and is contrasted with what the preachers had done (verse 5).   The Thessalonians had made a ready response to the message the preachers proclaimed. Hearing the gospel from Paul and Silas, the Thessalonians followed in the footsteps of these Christian missionaries in that they too became followers of the Lord.[18]   Their complete change of lifestyle from what it was before the gospel came to them is that to which Paul can point and say now that they are among God's "chosen people."

And of the Lord – That the Thessalonians imitated the Lord tells us that the previous clause cannot be interpreted to mean Paul and Silas set themselves up as the heads of a peculiar sect nor as unconventional models to be followed.   What is here written about being imitators is in total harmony with Paul's claims in 1 Corinthians 11:1 that he was an imitator of Christ.   When the Thessalonians became converts, they, too, lived not only like their teachers who imitated the Lord, but they were living in harmony with how the Lord lived.   How encouraging this must have been to the Thessalonians "to be told they were walking in the very steps of the Lord.   How bold of the Apostle, and what a good conscience he kept, that he could identify following himself with following Christ."[19]

---

[17] Albert Barnes, "Thessalonians - Philemon," in *Barnes' Notes on the New Testament* (Grand Rapids, MI: Baker Book House, 1955), p.12.

[18] The Greek word "imitators" suggests an adult pupil's relationship with his teacher.   In the 1st century, education was not limited to formal instruction during fixed hours, but involved the sharing of a way of life.   (Paul Ellingworth & Eugene A. Nida, *A Translator's Handbook on Paul's Letters to the Thessalonians* [New York: United Bible Society, 1976], p.11.)

[19] George G. Findlay, "The Epistles to the Thessalonians" in *The Cambridge Bible for Schools and Colleges* (Cambridge: At The University Press, 1898), p.54.   "'Lord' always means Jesus Christ in Paul's writings, unless the context clearly indicates otherwise."   (Ellingworth & Nida, *ibid.*)

Having received the word in much tribulation – One way in which the Thessalonian Christians imitated their teachers was in their shared experience of persecution. Living enthusiastically for Christ, they, too, suffered persecution for their newfound faith just as had Paul and Silas (Acts 17:5-13). In this context, where "the word" is a synonym for the "gospel" which was preached by Paul and Silas, "received" is essentially equivalent to "believed" as it is at John 1:12. "Tribulation" can include various kinds of hardship which Christians may be called on to endure because of their faith and witness. The historical record in Acts tells us how the unbelieving Jews at Thessalonica stirred up the heathen rabble and raised a persecution against Paul and Silas. As a consequence, Paul and Silas had to depart from Thessalonica (Acts 17:4-10). After the preachers had left the city, it would appear that the persecution, far from abating, rather increased, and that Gentile inhabitants united with the unbelieving Jews against the Christians. We're told that the Thessalonian converts suffered "much tribulation" from their own countrymen as well as from the Jews (1 Thessalonians 2:14). The idea being developed since verse 4 is that the Thessalonian Christians are God's New Testament "chosen people." Since Jesus had indicated His followers would be persecuted, their persecution because they had become Christians is evidence they are among God's chosen ones.

With the joy of the Holy Spirit – The Holy Spirit's activities are introduced in 1 Thessalonians 1:5,6 as something well-known by the Thessalonian Christians. While verse 5 spoke of the Spirit's work through Paul and Silas, verse 6 introduces His work in the lives of the Christians. Only those who are immersed into Christ receive the indwelling Holy Spirit. We are still looking at the evidences the Thessalonians are among God's "chosen people." The Holy Spirit made them able to rejoice while being persecuted. Perhaps the joy the Thessalonians experienced was like that produced as a result of Philip's preaching in the city of Samaria (Acts 8:8). Perhaps their joy was like that of the Ethiopian whom Philip immersed (Acts 8:39). Most likely, the joy here in view is the joy which the Holy Spirit can prompt when believers are in the midst of persecution. Paul alludes to this in Romans 5:3-5 when he writes, "We rejoice amid our tribulations ... because the love of God is poured out in our hearts through the Holy Spirit who has been given to us."

1:7 – *so that you became an example to all the believers in Macedonia and in Achaia.*

So that you became an example to all the believers in Macedonia and in Achaia – "So that" tells us what happened next when the Thessalonians became God's chosen people. Just as Paul and Silas had been models of Christlikeness to the Thessalonians, so now the Thessalonians have become the same to others. Verses 6 and 7 read "you" plural, but the better manuscripts read "example" (singular).[20] The congregation as a whole became a

---

[20] Commenting on the KJV which reads "ensamples" (plural) Frank H. Marshall wrote, "It probably does not mean that every member of the church was an outstanding Christian, active and efficient enough to inspire those of other churches. There were always some in every congregation who would not attain to the high standard. But it does indicate that there was a goodly number of workers there who were an inspiration to those in other cities." (Frank H. Marshall, *Standard Lesson Commentary 1958* [Cincinnati: Standard Publishing Company, 1958], p.91.)

model or pattern to be imitated. "Believers" here is a synonym for Christians. The only believers in the provinces of Macedonia and Achaia before the folk at Thessalonica became Christians were those at Philippi in Macedonia.[21]   So this verse must mean that the past conduct of the Thessalonians is an example to all believers who were now to be found in those provinces at the time Paul and Silas wrote this letter.   By the time 1 Thessalonians was written, there were Christians not only in Philippi, but also in Berea, Athens, Corinth, and other areas of Achaia.

1:8 – *For the word of the Lord has sounded forth from you, not only in Macedonia and Achaia, but also in every place your faith toward God has gone forth, so that we have no need to say anything.*

For the word of the Lord has sounded forth from you – Verses 8-10 form a single sentence in the Greek text. "For" tells us this sentence is intended to introduce several ways the believers at Thessalonica were examples for others.[22]   The perfect tense Greek verb translated "sounded forth" pictures a loud trumpet blast whose sound hangs in the air for long while after it sounded out.   Exactly what is signified by the phrase "the word of the Lord" is not easy to determine.   If it is treated as the equivalent of a prophetic utterance from the Lord (cp. Isaiah 38,4,5), the verse says that already the Lord has used some of the Thessalonians as missionaries.   Or if instead of a message *from* the Lord, the Greek means a message *about* the Lord, this verse might be understood as describing the spreading of the gospel message (cp. Acts 8:25, 16:32), so that the verse pictures the Thessalonian congregation as being mission-minded from the beginning.   Or perhaps Paul and Silas are not lauding the Thessalonians' vigorous propagation of the gospel; perhaps Paul and Silas are continuing to express delight with how the example of the Thessalonians has influenced Christians in other areas.   This verse goes on to relate how the remarkable change in the lives of the Thessalonians was news that had spread around the region like wildfire.   If this is the emphasis, the "word of the Lord" is news about how the Lord Jesus had changed their lives for the better.

Not only in Macedonia and Achaia – The word of the Lord has sounded forth in Macedonia where the Thessalonians were, and in Achaia where Paul and Silas were as this letter was being written.

But also in every place your faith toward God has gone forth – "Faith toward God" is an expression we don't often meet in Scripture.   The Thessalonians had become believers

---

[21] A look at the map will show that Macedonia was the region of northern Greece in which Philippi, Thessalonica, and Berea are found.   Achaia was the region of Greece just to the south of Macedonia that included the important cities of Athens and Corinth.   "There had been times when the name Achaia was applied to the whole of Greece, but at the time Paul wrote, Macedonia and Achaia were two Roman provinces whose boundaries corresponded to those of no modern state.   Together, they covered almost the whole area of modern Greece and Albania, and also the southern part of Yugoslavia, which is still called Macedonia."   (Ellingworth & Nida, *op. cit.*, p.12.)

[22] It is also possible to see in this sentence another evidence that the Thessalonian Christians are God's chosen people.

in the true God, rather than continuing to be devotees to idols. In this context, "in every place" would be regions other than Macedonia and Achaia. That the Thessalonians, as a result of the preaching of the gospel, had relinquished idolatry was something that came to be much talked about, not only in Macedonia and Achaia but also in many other places.

So that we have no need to say anything – Paul and Silas had no need to tell folk they met about the new Christian faith and life embraced by the Thessalonian converts. That news had already spread without Paul and Silas calling attention to the wonderful thing that had happened.

1:9 – *For they themselves report about us what kind of a reception we had with you, and how you turned to God from idols to serve a living and true God,*

For they themselves report about us what kind of a reception we had with you – Verse 8 began with "for" and explained verse 7. So now verses 9-10, which also begin with "for," explain verse 8. "They themselves" are the inhabitants of the regions Paul and Silas have visited since leaving Thessalonica. Travelers going from Thessalonica to distant destinations carried the news of what had happened in Thessalonica. The travelers reported both sides of the story. They reported how Paul and Silas had come to Thessalonica, what they had preached, and how they had so lived as to set an example for Christ. They also reported how the Thessalonians had welcomed the preachers and their message. "You" in this clause reminds us Paul is not writing to the whole population of Thessalonica, but this is a letter addressed to the church there. Chapter 2 of Thessalonians will fill in more details concerning the preachers and the reception of their message.

And how you turned to God from idols – In Acts 17:6, the preachers of the gospel were accused of turning the world upside down. That is an apt way to describe the kind of radical change in lifestyle when one abandons the worship of idols and turns to the living God. It looks like Paul and Silas preached a similar message in pagan Thessalonica that Paul and Barnabas earlier had preached in idolatrous Lystra. They pleaded with folk to turn from "these vain things (worshiping idols) to serve the living God" (Acts 14:15). The 1st century world was filled with idolatry. Every region had its own local god. Even trade guilds and businesses had patron deities that they worshiped. Most people in Paul's day believed that if worshiping one god was good, then worshiping several was better. Men were in rebellion to the one true God, and this rebellion was most obvious in the worship of idols and in the licentious lifestyle that often was part of that worship. To turn from serving idols to God meant a striking change in their faith, attitude, and life, and even one's pagan neighbors were bound to talk about the change.

This verse leaves the clear impression that the congregation addressed at Thessalonica consisted predominantly of converted pagans. It also corroborates the idea that the ministry of Paul and Silas in Thessalonica was longer than the three weeks that they were welcome in the Jewish synagogue as Acts 17:1-9 relates. This verse, which speaks of turning from idols, prompts us to believe that Paul and Silas carried on evangelistic work among the non-Jewish population when they were no longer welcome in the synagogue.

To serve a living and true God – Two infinitives ("to serve" and "to wait") suggest to us the new purpose of mind that characterizes what it means to "turn to God from idols." "To serve" indicates the converts considered themselves as the property of and at the absolute disposal of a new master. The new master is the "living" God, which is in stark contrast to the lifeless idols they once worshiped, and "true" means He is the only being who is really God and who deserves men's obedience and worship, as contrasted with the idols and demons who are behind them (1 Corinthians 8:4-6, 10:20). "To serve" is a present tense infinitive suggesting a willingness to serving Him always, habitually and continually.

1:10 – and to wait for His Son from heaven, whom He raised from the dead, that is Jesus, who rescues us from the wrath to come.

And to wait for His Son from heaven ... that is Jesus – When they became Christians, not only did the Thessalonians turn from idols to serve the living God, but they also began to wait and continue to wait (i.e., it is a present tense infinitive) for the return of Christ. Jewish folk understood that to call Jesus the "Son" of God was a claim that Jesus was equal with God (John 5:18). This description explains where Jesus is now. The Greek word for "heaven" in this place is plural, indicating, as the plural generally does, the place where God is.[23] Since His ascension to heaven, Scripture elsewhere shows Jesus sitting at the right hand of the Father (Hebrews 1:13; 8:1). While it could be said of an observant Jew that he "served the living and true God," this expectation of Christ's return separated the church of Thessalonians from the synagogue. Christians recognize that Jesus is the Messiah (Acts 17:3), that He is the Son of God (Mark 1:1), that He arose from the dead, and that He is coming again. On at least two different occasions, Christ himself promised that He would return from heaven, (Matthew 16:27; John 14:3). The angels, likewise, who appeared at the time of His ascension solemnly promised that He would come back "in just the same way as you have watched Him go into heaven" (Acts 1:11). It is clear from this first phrase in verse 10 that the return of the Lord Jesus to this world was a prominent subject in the preaching of Paul and Silas while they were in Thessalonica.[24] Thus, this phrase also introduces a theme which will be discussed in greater detail in 1 Thessalonians 2:19, 3:13 and 4:13-5:11, and which will be one of the two main subjects of the second letter to the Thessalonians.

Whom He raised from the dead – The living God demonstrated that He is living by His raising of Jesus from the dead. Just as all three members of the Godhead were involved

---

[23] 2 Corinthians 12:2 makes reference to three heavens. One is the atmosphere where the birds fly, one is the starry heavens, and the third is the place where God dwells. In Paul's writings and sermons, he sometimes uses the singular ("heaven") and sometimes the plural ("heavens"). A brief examination of the passages seems to suggest that when he wishes specially to emphasize God's abode, he uses the plural.

[24] Paul's preaching about the Second Advent is no different from that of other Christian leaders of the first generation. See Acts 3:19-21, 1 and 2 Peter, as well as Jesus' eschatological discourses.

in the original creation (Genesis 1:1,2; Colossians 1:16), so all three – Father (Acts 2:24), Son (John 10:18) and Holy Spirit (Romans 8:11) – were together responsible for Jesus' resurrection from the dead.   Just as the resurrection of Jesus from the dead was part of the apostolic preaching at Athens (Acts 17:18,24-31), so we may conclude that the resurrection of Jesus was part of the message Paul and Silas preached at Thessalonica.

Who rescues us from the wrath to come – At Athens the resurrection of Jesus was used as proof of the judgment to come (Acts 17:31).   Here in Thessalonians, the resurrection of Jesus makes it possible for Jesus to rescue us from the wrath to come.   (For the first time in this letter, "us" includes not only Paul and Silas, but the Thessalonian believers, too.) The "wrath to come" (or, as it is better translated, "which is coming") is the divine judgment to be poured out on the wicked at the time of the end.   In the letter to Colossae, the Colossians were told "the wrath of God will come upon the sons of disobedience" (Colossians 3:6).   Unlike men's wrath which is sometimes triggered by unholy thoughts of revenge, or long-nursed memories of ancient hurts unfairly suffered, God's wrath is His settled displeasure against sin, and it grows out of His very nature (which is holiness). There is nothing selfish or momentarily out of character in God's wrath.[25]   Various explanations have been proposed to explain the present tense verb "rescues."[26]   Perhaps there is an allusion to an Old Testament Messianic prophecy, "and the deliverer shall come for Zion's sake, and shall turn away ungodliness from Jacob" (Isaiah 29:20[27]), where the same present-tense Greek participle (*rhuomenos*) occurs and is translated "the deliverer." Perhaps the present tense indicates that the deliverance is a continuing process.   The Lord is presently interceding on behalf of the saints (Hebrews 7:25), and supplies grace to help in the time of need, thus delivering them from the power of sin and temptations, and so preserving them in a state of salvation (Hebrews 4:15,16).   His delivering work continues until, at last, at the final judgment, it will be consummated on "the day of wrath and revelation of God's righteous judgment" (Romans 2:7).   The way the topic is alluded to here indicates that the Thessalonians already were acquainted with it, and thus it is implied that the deliverance work of Jesus as well as the final judgment were another of the important doctrines taught by Paul and Silas when they were in Thessalonica.

---

[25] Even among men, not all anger or wrath is sinful. Do we not speak of a 'righteous anger'? So God's wrath can be in perfect harmony with His righteous character, His holiness, and His love.

[26] Reference to 2 Corinthians 1:10, or 2 Timothy 4:17-18, where the same verb is used, will show that it signifies rescue rather than redemption. (Findlay, *op. cit.*, p.60.)

[27] This translation of Isaiah 29:20 comes from *The Septuagint Version of the Old Testament and Apocrypha with an English Translation* (London: Samuel Bagster and Sons Limited, nd), p.894.

II. THE WRITERS' VINDICATION OF THEIR LIVES AND MINISTRY AMONG THE THESSALONIANS. 2:1-16

2:1 – *For you yourselves know, brethren, that our coming to you was not in vain,*

For you yourselves know, brethren – It seems most likely that this "for" is like the one in 1:5. In that verse Paul was unfolding how he knew the Thessalonians were among God's chosen people, for it was God who had sent and empowered the missionaries to minister in Thessalonica. We may thus think of 2:1-16 as being an expansion of the previous mention of the missionaries' conduct in Thessalonica. Emphatically placed first in the sentence, "you yourselves" implies an understood contrast between the readers (here, again, called "brethren"[1]) and other persons who were making attacks on the missionaries and their message. To protect the new saints in Thessalonica from the slanderous attacks being made by Paul's opponents, Paul reminds his readers that, if they drew from their own memory and experience, they could easily certify that the teachers of the gospel were men of integrity, and known to be speakers of truth.[2]

That our coming to you was not in vain – "Our" continues to identify Paul and Silas as a team, while "coming to you" refers to their original evangelistic visit to Thessalonica (Acts 17:1-9). "In vain" (Greek, *kenos*) is a word whose meaning has received much discussion. If the idea being expressed was that their short mission to Thessalonica accomplished very little, or was a failure, that idea would have been better expressed by the Greek synonym *mataios*. As a matter of fact, much was done in the lives of the converts. In the verses that close chapter 1, Paul has said that several marvelous changes had occurred in the lives of the Thessalonian believers. Since *kenos* can denote "empty," Hendriksen has suggested that Paul uses *kenos* as a denial that the missionaries came with empty hands, expecting a handout.[3] As verses 2-8 will explain, "the missionaries did not come with hands outstretched to receive material benefits; they came bearing gifts of themselves and the gospel."[4] The perfect tense verb translated "was" indicates that what was true at the time of their visit to Thessalonica remains true. They are still offering themselves and the gospel.

2:2 – *but after we had already suffered and been mistreated in Philippi, as you know, we had the boldness in our God to speak to you the gospel of God amid much opposition.*

---

[1] See comments on "brethren" at 1 Thessalonians 1:4.

[2] An appeal made to the recollections and experience of the readers is characteristic of these Thessalonian letters. See 1 Thessalonians 1:5; 2:2,5,10-11; 3:3,4; and 2 Thessalonians 2:6; 3:7.

[3] William Hendricksen, "Exposition of I and II Thessalonians" in *New Testament Commentary* (Grand Rapids, MI: Baker Book House, 1955), p.60.

[4] Edwin V. Hayden, *Standard Lesson Commentary 1996-97* (Cincinnati: Standard Publishing Company, 1996), p.235.

But after we had already suffered and been mistreated in Philippi – The strong adversative "but" (*alla*) marks a contrast to "in vain" (verse 1). It took boldness to dare to preach in Thessalonica what had cost them so much in Philippi. Paul and Silas recall what had happened to them at Philippi just before they came to Thessalonica. As described in Acts 16:12-40, Paul and Silas were arrested, dragged into the marketplace before the rulers, falsely accused, flogged, and imprisoned, with their feet fastened in stocks. In the morning the magistrates of Philippi realized their mistake and wanted to release them. But Paul and Silas, both being Roman citizens, demanded and got an apology for their mistreatment before leaving the city. It was not pride that prompted Paul to demand an official apology. He and Silas had been convicted of no crime, and they wanted no undeserved blot on their record. This was important, for Paul's enemies were going about slandering him and his ministry. Their treatment in Philippi was outrageous whether they were Roman citizens or not.

As you know – If we read this with what precedes, it says the Thessalonians had heard about what happened at Philippi. News about it may have traveled down the Egnatian Way from Philippi to Thessalonica, or Paul and Silas themselves informed the Thessalonians what had recently happened to them as they explained how there came to be welts on their bodies. If we read this clause with what follows, then it says that the Thessalonians knew that God gave the preachers courage to tell the good news.

We had the boldness in our God to speak to you the gospel of God – After what happened at Philippi, most people would have refrained from repeating a message that had led to such violent treatment, but not Paul and Silas. "Boldness" denotes both speaking with boldness (Ephesians 6:20) and also acting with boldness and confidence. The "gospel" is good news about the redemption from sin made possible by the mission of Jesus to earth, while "of God" says that God the Father is the original author of the plan, and "in our God" says the missionaries were confident that when they preached God Himself exerted power unto salvation (Romans 1:16). The boldness of Paul and Silas was evidence that they knew the divine source of their message.[5]

Amid much opposition – The Thessalonian Christians had not only heard about the problems Paul and Silas had at Philippi, but when Paul came to Thessalonica to preach the gospel in their midst, it was not long before the Thessalonians had seen and experienced a similar conflict. The Greek word translated "opposition" in this verse is *agōnia*, from which we get our English word "agony." The word was used of the contests in Grecian games where each participant had to put forth strenuous effort against their opponents. Like athletes intent on winning, as active contenders Paul and Silas plunged into the contest for the hearts of the Thessalonians. From the information we have, it seems that unconverted Jewish activists precipitated the opposition faced by Paul and Silas during this

---

[5] Though three names (Paul, Silas, and Timothy) occur in the signature of this letter (1 Thessalonians 1:1), since the immediate context alludes to the initial preaching of the gospel at Thessalonica, we treat the plural "we" in this context as a reference to Paul and Silas. Timothy did not come to Thessalonica until later.

timeframe of their ministry. That was true at Thessalonica (Acts 17:5), at Berea (Acts 17:13), and at Corinth (Acts 18:12-17).[6]

2:3 – *For our exhortation does not* come *from error or impurity or by way of deceit;*

For our exhortation does not *come* **from error** – Since "for" tells us the topic is still the boldness of the missionaries in speaking the gospel of God at Thessalonica, the "exhortation" alluded to must be the appeals those preachers made for the Thessalonians to embrace the gospel. Verses 3-7 are concerned with the motives behind their preaching and their behavior as they went about their work. Paul and Silas had spoken openly and fearlessly because they had no unworthy motives to hide. Both verse 3 and verse 5 begin with "for," and are immediately followed by verses introduced with "but" (verses 4 and 7). We are thus led to realize that Paul and Silas are not only giving an explanation of their boldness in God to speak the gospel, but at the same time are refuting the kind of charges being brought against them and their preaching since they left Thessalonica. From 1 Thessalonians 1:6 and 2:14-16, we learn that the young church at Thessalonica was under attack. We may imagine the opponents ridiculed the new converts as being deluded followers of crafty and deceptive foreigners who had brought ridiculous tales of a Jewish cult leader called Jesus. Then, these so-called preachers had skipped town when the pressure became too much for them, probably even taking considerable cash from their followers. It is not surprising this has happened, the opponents could claim, for the Roman world was full of such wandering "philosophers," who were, in reality, swindlers who victimized their followers. What would happen to the cause of Christ in and around Thessalonica if such charges were left unanswered? For the sake of Christians young and immature, in Thessalonica and elsewhere, it was necessary for Paul and his companions to vindicate their integrity, and at the same time to champion the absolute validity of their message. 1 Thessalonians 2:3-8 give assurance to the new Christians that they were not a band of deluded sheep trailing after self-serving hireling shepherds, but were instead a company of substantial believers who had heartily embraced an established gospel. We may also infer that each of the negative terms stressed in these verses reflects something the opposition had charged.[7] The NASB translation "not from error" treats the word *planē* as being in contrast with *alētheia*, the truth (as in 1 John 4:6 where "spirit of truth" is contrasted with "spirit of error").[8] In Romans 1:27, "error" (*planē*) refers to the idolatrous perversion of Monotheistic worship. The message Paul and Silas preached was

---

[6] Here in 1 Thessalonians 2:2, when Paul and Silas talk about opposition, it is opposition they themselves faced. At 1 Thessalonians 2:14-16, when Paul identifies the opposition being faced by the Thessalonian Christians, he identifies the opponents as "your own countrymen," while at the same time recalling that the early Christians at Jerusalem faced opposition from their own countrymen, the unbelieving Jews.

[7] While it is very possible to regard the terms *planē*, *akatharsia*, and *dolos* as simply characteristic of the 1st century traveling mountebanks with whom Paul and Silas have been compared, we think Timothy has reported to Paul and Silas that these very terms have been used at Thessalonica to discredit the gospel preachers. In any case, we treat Paul's response as taking the accusations personally and seriously.

[8] The KJV translation "not of deceit" treats the word *planē* as being indistinguishable from "guile" (*dolos*) with which this verse concludes.

not based on some departure from the truth of God, but was based on the established acts of Jesus' life, death, and resurrection.   Paul and Silas were sure their message was genuine.

Or impurity – Since the context deals with the motives of the preachers, it is very possible this word is intended to be a denial that their motive was greed (as 1 Thessalonians 2:5 will specify).   There were men of impure motive who supposed "that godliness is a way of gain" (1 Timothy 6:5), but Paul and Silas are definitely not to be numbered among them.[9]

Or by way of deceit – It seems likely the change of preposition (from "from" to "by way of") indicates a shift from motives to method.   "Deceit" translates a word (*dolos*) that originally described a fisherman's method of enticing his catch.   Paul and Silas used no methods that were designed to trick their listeners.   They did not "bait" their appeal with promises to potential converts of health, wealth, and happiness.   They did not try to hide some of the harsher aspects of following Jesus, such as the fact that believers would suffer persecution (1 Thessalonians 3:4).   They preached Christ in clear, straightforward terms, relying for success on the power of the Holy Spirit rather than on persuasive words of men's wisdom (cp. 1 Corinthians 2:1-5).

2:4 – *but just as we have been approved by God to be entrusted with the gospel, so we speak, not as pleasing men, but God who examines our hearts.*

But just as we have been approved by God to be entrusted with the gospel – Using the strong adversative "but" to repudiate the idea they used bad motives and methods, here Paul and Silas outline the basic motivation that compelled them to serve as they did.   Their ministry and message were "just as" (*kathos*), that is, "in conformity with," the omniscient God's approval and trust.   "Have been approved" is a perfect passive verb indicating past completed action with present continuing results.   That approval involved a process of testing, success in completing the tests, and a consequent state of endorsement by God.   Verse 2 has indicated that God the Father is the original author of the gospel, so "entrusted with the gospel" in this verse likely means that Paul and Silas were entrusted with the responsibility to deliver it just as God gave it to them.

So we speak – "So" translates *houtos*, an adverb describing the manner or rule according to which something was done.   Just like a bank messenger is accountable to deliver the items of great value entrusted to him, Paul and Silas were aware of their accountability before God to deliver the gospel message just as God gave it to them to deliver.   The present tense verb "we speak" expresses what was always their practice.

Not as pleasing men, but God who examines our hearts – Behind this denial that they did things superficially just to please men, we are likely hearing a refutation of another of the accusations made by the opponents.   What Paul has written elsewhere helps us to understand what he means when he denies   he and Silas were focused on "pleasing men."

---

[9] The word translated "impurity" (*akatharsia*) often denotes sexual debauchery.   We doubt that Paul and Silas have been accused of being sexual perverts.

Paul's adaptability, his readiness to "become all things to all men" for the gospel's sake (1 Corinthians 9:22), could easily have been misrepresented as the policy of a people pleaser, who adapted his message to suit his varying audiences.   Carefully notice that it was not the message that he varied, but, as the context in 1 Corinthians 9 shows, his behavior in matters of opinion.   1 Corinthians 10:31-33 ("whether, then, you eat or drink or whatever you do, do all to the glory of God.   Give no offense either to Jews or to Greeks or to the church of God; just as I also please all men in all things, not seeking my own profit but the profit of the many, so that they may be saved") shows very clearly in what areas Paul made an effort to please men.   When Paul was an unconverted Pharisee, there was a time he was trying to please men.   However, Galatians 1:10 (where Paul wrote, "If I were still trying to please men, I would not be a bond-servant of Christ") helps us understand that all that has changed now that he is serving his new Lord and Master.   As one whose overarching motive was to please God, Paul did all he could to win men, but he did not stoop to flattery, or simply to tickling peoples' ears (i.e., simply telling people what they wanted to hear) in order to get a commitment from his listeners.   Whenever it involved a choice between doing just what people wanted them to do or what was pleasing to God, Paul and Silas always came down on the side of pleasing God.   In case any of the opponents should ask, "How can you prove you are pleasing God," Paul's response is that God is one who searches the hearts of men.[10]   "The 'heart,' in the language of the Bible, is not the seat of the feelings alone; it is 'the inner man,' the real self, the center and meeting-point of all our thoughts, feelings, and resolves."[11]   The participle translated "examines" is the same root as that translated "approved" earlier in this verse, but now it is in the present tense, emphasizing the continuing aspect of God's testing and approval.   God, who is constantly watching, knows what the honest motives were that drove the preachers to preach and practice as they did.   What stronger proof could be given concerning the purity of their motives than the testimony of God Himself?

2:5 – *For we never came with flattering speech, as you know, nor with a pretext for greed –* *God is witness –*

For we never came with flattering speech – Verses 5-7 are one sentence in the Greek and are intended (as were verses 3 and 4) not only to give an explanation of the preachers' boldness in God to speak the gospel, but at the same time are refuting the kind of charges being brought against them and their preaching since they left Thessalonica.   "Never" ("not at any time"), whether while they were in Thessalonica or elsewhere, have Paul and Silas used flattering speech.   The word here translated "flattering" (*kolakeias*) occurs nowhere else in the New Testament, but it was the regular classical Greek word to describe the reprehensible behavior of those traveling charlatans who for purely selfish reasons made a practice of speaking flowery and extravagant words of adulation and praise in order to gain influence over others.

---

[10] It is often said to be an attribute of God that He tries or searches the hearts of people.   See 1 Chronicles 28:9, 29:17; Jeremiah 11:20, 17:10; Psalm 11:4; Romans 8:27.

[11] Findlay, *op. cit.*, p.64.

As you know – From their own personal experience, the Thessalonian Christians were fully aware that Paul and Silas were not among those who "by good words and fair speeches deceive the hearts of the simple" (Romans 16:18). The Christians did not have to wait on a word from God to know that this charge against Paul and Silas, made by the opponents, was patently false.

Nor with a pretext for greed – Another charge that Paul disavows is that he and Silas put on masks to cover up their greed. The idea in the word "pretext" is that of putting on a show of piety in order to cover up one's true motive. "Greed" is the desire to possess something that belongs to someone else, a desire to get more of something one does not have even if others must be exploited in order to obtain it. Paul could with perfect confidence appeal to the experience of his converts, and be known to be speaking the truth, when he said, "I have coveted no man's silver, or gold, or apparel" (Acts 20:33).

– God is witness – This solemn appeal to God as being one who could testify that there was no hidden inner motive of greed in either Paul or Silas is the strongest possible evidence that the charge against Paul and Silas was untrue. God is not going to give misleading or false testimony.

2:6 – *nor did we seek glory from men, either from you or from others, even though as apostles of Christ we might have asserted our authority.*

Nor did we seek glory from men, either from you or from others – Another false charge the opponents hurled against the preachers was that they were seeking the praise of men.[12] The charge is summarily denied. Neither at Thessalonica, nor elsewhere, did Paul and Silas ever seek personal fame or special adulation or honor or plaudits from their converts. One cannot seek the praise of men and at the same time have praise from God, Jesus said (John 5:44).

Even though as apostles of Christ we might have asserted our authority – It is easier to follow the thread of thought if we treat this clause as the beginning of a new sentence which continues in verse 7, rather than making it the conclusion of verse 6.[13] The title "apostles of Christ" is here applied to Paul and Silas.[14] The word "apostle" means one sent on a mission, and "of Christ" says that Paul and Silas were sent on their mission to Thessalonica by Christ Himself. Such a comment harmonizes with the verse that speaks of the "Spirit of Jesus" having something to do with where the missionaries went next (Acts

---

[12] The English word "glory" once had the connotation of praise, but that is a connotation that is not much recognized today. "Praise" is the better English word to represent the Greek *doxa*.

[13] Ancient manuscripts did not have punctuation marks. The punctuation marks in our Greek texts have been added by men. There is disagreement among the various editions of the Greek text and consequently among translations as to where verse 7 begins. The decision about punctuation at this place rests partly on the meaning assigned to *baros*, translated "authority."

[14] As earlier in this chapter, the reference is to the men who first preached the gospel in Thessalonica, and since Timothy did not arrive in that town until later, we limit the title "apostles" to the original preachers.

16:7), and with verses that make a distinction between apostles of Jesus (chosen and sent personally by Jesus) and apostles of churches (chosen and sent by some local congregation, e.g., 2 Corinthians 8:23, Philippians 1:25).   Since Jesus did teach that the worker is worthy of his wages (Luke 10:7), and since He ordained that those who preach the gospel should live off the gospel (1 Corinthians 9:14), it appears that *baros* ("authority")[15] has reference to the right which preachers of the gospel had to be financially supported by their converts. Paul here denies that he and Silas demanded financial support from the Thessalonians.[16] In the next verse he will affirm the very opposite – rather than demanding *from* their converts, they were giving of themselves lavishly *to* their converts.

2:7 – *But we proved to be gentle among you, as a nursing mother tenderly cares for her own children.*

But we proved to be gentle among you – "Among you" means while we were in your midst.   Not only did Paul and Silas choose to waive their right to receive wages from the Thessalonians, they also chose to adopt the most loving and kind and gentle methods in order to promote the spiritual growth of their new converts.   "Gentleness" is listed among the fruit of the Spirit (Galatians 5:23) and this likely explains why the verb translated "proved" is a passive voice verb with the connotation "we were made to be."   Gentleness, the opposite of austerity or harsh rigor, is a good contrast to "asserting one's authority."[17]

As a nursing mother tenderly cares for her own children – The comparison pictures the mother's special effort to protect and to provide for her child's every need, even to the extent of great sacrifice.   A nursing mother pours herself into the life of her infant without thought of advantage to herself.   She directs that life by her constant care and consistent teaching.   This was the kind of self-investment practiced by Paul and Silas as they ministered in Thessalonica.

---

[15] The word carries the connotation of "weight," "heaviness," "burden." In this clause the Greek contains a metaphor of weight which is well brought out by the translation, "We could have made you feel the weight of our authority." (Ellingworth & Nida, *op. cit.*, p.29.) Commentators who treat this clause as the conclusion of verse 6, which referred to the praise of men, have written that the clause means the apostles could have dealt heavily with the Thessalonians, making them acknowledge their apostolic dignity and demanding their praise and adulation.

[16] From Philippians 4:15,16 we learn that the Christians at Philippi sent offerings to their preacher friends when they were in Thessalonica, and again when the preachers got to Corinth (2 Corinthians 11:9). Paul did accept missionary offerings from churches after he left their town, but to demand financial support from the folk he was presently ministering to was a right which Paul chose not to exercise (cf. 2 Thessalonians 3:7-9; 1 Corinthians 9:3-18; 2 Corinthians 11:7-11).

[17] The Greek manuscripts have a variation at this place with some reading *nēpioi* ("babies") and some reading *ēpioi* ("gentle"). The modern editors (with the weighty exception of Westcott and Hort [see the Note in their *New Testament in Greek*, vol. II., p. 128] and UBS[4]), decide in favor of *ēpioi* – (1) because "gentle" better suits the context; and (2) because this Greek word occurs only one other time in the New Testament (1 Timothy 2:24), for copyists are prone to change an unfamiliar into any familiar word resembling it that gives a tolerable sense, and "babes" otherwise is a favorite expression of St Paul. If "babes" be the genuine reading – and it is difficult to resist the manuscript evidence in its favor – then it must be explained as it was by Origen and Augustine, and endorsed by Westcott: "like a nurse amongst her children, talking in baby language to the babes." (Findlay, *op. cit.*, p.67)

2:8 – *Having so fond an affection for you, we were well-pleased to impart to you not only the gospel of God but also our own lives, because you had become very dear to us.*

Having so fond an affection for you – Paul is continuing the metaphor introduced in the previous verse. The word here translated "having fond affection" (*homeiromenoi*), which occurs nowhere else in the New Testament, is "a term of endearment borrowed from the language of the nursery."[18] It conveys the fondness of a mother's love. The writers picture the Thessalonians as in the infancy of their Christian life, and themselves as nursing mothers who tenderly cared for them. The gospel is the milk which they fed them. It was a loving ministry which brought continual delight to the preachers. "Could the fondest mother carry her affection for her helpless infant further?"[19]

We were well-pleased to impart to you not only the gospel of God – The plural "we" still refers to both Paul and Silas. The imperfect tense verb translated "were well pleased" denotes a continual delight to be able to share the gospel with the Thessalonians, even though recent experience at Philippi indicated that such a boldness could bring persecution on the preachers. The divine origin of the gospel is again indicated by the genitive "of God."

But also our own lives – Not only did Paul and Silas find it a continual delight to share the gospel, but they also delighted in the opportunity to share their own lives with the Thessalonians. Involved in sharing one's soul (the word translated "lives" is *psuchas*) is "utter self-denial, spending and being spent in the interest of others."[20] The preachers learned from Jesus to be willing to lay down their lives for their converts. "We know love by this, that He laid down His life for us; and we ought to lay down our lives for the brethren" (1 John 3:16).

Because you had become very dear to us – This is why Paul and Silas were willing to lay down their lives for the Thessalonian Christians. The word translated "very dear" or "beloved" is *agapētoi*. Not only did the apostles have fond affection for them, but they had come to love Thessalonian Christians very much. All of Paul's and Silas' behavior was motivated by their love for the Thessalonians – even leaving town when failing to do so would have brought hardship on the Thessalonians like Jason who had provided the preachers with lodging while they were in town (Acts 17:9,10).

2:9 – *For you recall, brethren, our labor and hardship, how working night and day so as not to be a burden to any of you, we proclaimed to you the gospel of God.*

---

[18] David Williams, "1 and 2 Thessalonians" in *New International Biblical Commentary* (Peabody, MA.: Hendrickson Publishers, 1992), p. 41.

[19] Joseph Benson, "Romans-Revelation" in Vol. 5 of *Benson's Commentary* (New York: Lane & Tippett, 1847), p.388.

[20] F.F. Bruce, "1 & 2 Thessalonians" in Vol. 45 of *Word Biblical Commentary* (Waco, TX: Word Books, 1982), p.32.

For you recall, brethren, our labor and hardship – As 2:1 called attention to certain facts that supported the general principles already stated, facts the Thessalonians could well remember, so this verse calls attention to some easily remembered behaviors that support the truth that Paul and Silas were willing to and did share their lives with the Thessalonian brethren.[21]   The missionaries remind the church how they had worked to support themselves.   Paul often worked as a tent-maker or leather worker (Acts 18:3; 20:34; 1 Corinthians 4:12); perhaps Silas worked alongside him in the same trade.   Handling animal hair and skins to produce tent material was hard work.   "Labor" (the same word used at 1 Thessalonians 1:3) emphasizes the fatigue that manual labor causes on the human body, while "hardship" is the ordinary word for hard and painful labor.

How working night and day so as not to be a burden to any of you – The word used here for "working" is the regular word denoting work for wages.[22]   The word order "night and day" reflects the way both Jews and Greeks counted nightfall as the beginning of the day.[23]   We may presume that Paul and Silas were busy teaching and preaching during the daylight hours, and then worked at tent-making far into the night.   "Be a burden" comes from the same root as the word translated "authority" in verse 6.   It expresses the fact Paul and Silas worked to earn their own living wages rather than being a financial burden on the Thessalonian converts.   The preachers chose to work a double shift, night and day, in order to provide an example for others and to deprive their critics of any plausible basis for charging them with mercenary motives.

We proclaimed to you the gospel of God – "Proclaimed" translates the common Greek word used of an official herald making a public proclamation for the king.   A herald did not proclaim his message to entertain or to win approval, but to faithfully transmit the message that was entrusted to him.   In this case, the message is "the gospel of God."   This is the third time the designation "the gospel of God" has occurred in this letter (cp. 1 Thessalonians 2:2,8).

2:10 – *You are witnesses, and so is God, how devoutly and uprightly and blamelessly we behaved toward you believers;*

You are witnesses, and so is God – Verses 10-12 form a single sentence in Greek and serve as an emphatic summary of all the major ideas which had been written in the preceding paragraph (verses 1-9).   "You" is emphatic and reminds the Thessalonians that they had been personal witnesses of all that has been said about the conduct of the preachers.   The emphatic "you" likely is intended to counteract the charges made against the preachers by the opponents.   "You" know from your own personal experience that their charges of misconduct are false.   The confidence with which Paul and Silas call on

---

[21] Again, he calls them "brethren."   See at 1 Thessalonians 1:4.

[22] Cp. 1 Corinthians 9:6; 2 Thessalonians 3:10,12.

[23] The creation account in Genesis over and over again reads "evening and morning" as the days are counted off (and compare Acts 20:31) while Pliny, *Nat. Hist.* ii. 79, has the same order among the Greeks.

God as their witness is impressive.   While the preachers' outward conduct was something the Thessalonians could testify to from personal experience, Paul says that "God will corroborate what we have said about our inner motives, which are something that you cannot know about from personal experience."   This first statement in verse 10 recalls verse 5.

How devoutly and uprightly and blamelessly we behaved toward you believers – Three adverbs are used to describe the conduct of the missionaries. *Hosiōs* ("devoutly") denotes conduct that is in harmony with the God of the universe. *Dikaiōs* ("uprightly") refers to their conduct toward their fellow men. *Amemptōs* ("blamelessly") says that in neither of the first two aspects could any fault be found in the behavior of Paul and Silas as the lived among the new Christians[24] in Thessalonica. "Blamelessly" is not a claim to absolute perfection, but "it is a claim to consistency of character, and to faithfulness in duty, both to God and to man, a claim which every Christian should be able to make."[25]   This second statement of verse 10 summarizes verses 3-4.

2:11 – *just as you know how we* were *exhorting and encouraging and imploring each one of you as a father* would *his own children,*

Just as you know – "Just as" (*kathaper*) is a stronger word than the word translated "how" (*kathōs*) in verses 1 and 5.   The Thessalonians might not have as certain a knowledge of the missionaries' blameless behavior, but they certainly can recall what the missionaries did as they dealt with each one of them, as a father with his own children.

How we *were* **exhorting and encouraging and imploring each one of you** – The emphatic "each one of you" conveys the idea of dealing with each individual convert personally, on a one by one basis.   While "exhortation" (*paraklēsis*) in verse 3 had reference to the preachers' appeal to non-Christians, "exhorting" (*parakalountes*) here in verse 11 refers to the kind of motivation believers often need. "Encouraging" (*paramuthoumenoi*) can be comfort in times of affliction, or it can be encouragement to continue in a particular course of conduct.   "Imploring" is an attempt to convey the idea in *marturomenoi*, a word which carries a note of authority, as when a parent makes an urgent appeal to one of their children.

As a father *would* **his own children** – Whereas verse 7 pictured the preachers as cherishing their converts as a nursing mother cherishes her child, this verse changes the figure slightly, making reference to a father and his relation to his own children as he instructs and directs them because he is interested in their welfare.

2:12 – *so that you would walk in a manner worthy of the God who calls you into His own kingdom and glory.*

---

[24] "You who believe" is "a common description of Christians in the New Testament [cp. 1 Thessalonians 1;7]. This is not surprising, for faith (in Christ) is central to Christianity. It puts us into the way of salvation and is the key to our continuing relationship with God. The latter is especially in view here since Paul uses a present participle. (Williams, *op. cit.,* p.43.)

[25] Barnes, *op. cit.,* p.24.

So that you would walk in a manner worthy of the God – This phrase expresses the goal of the preachers' fatherly actions toward their spiritual children. "Walk" is a common figure of speech for conduct of life. A Christian's behavior should reflect "the God" whom they serve. The emphatic "the" before God reminds us that it was this God's message the apostles of Christ had brought to the Thessalonians (1 Thessalonians 2:2,9) and it was unto this God, "the living and true one," that they had turned when they abandoned their idols (1 Thessalonians 1:9).

Who calls you into His own kingdom and glory – This is the first passage in the Thessalonian epistles where the eschatological system accepted by the commentary writer may influence the comments that are offered to explain it. Each of the key words has proven a place where the commentator will claim evidence to support the eschatological system the writer believes the Scripture as a whole teaches.[26] While it has proven difficult to find an equivalent English term to translate *basileia*, "kingship" might be superior to "kingdom," for the Greek word refers to the king's reign, his rule rather than to His realm.[27] This "rule" (this "kingship" or "kingdom") is sometimes described as a present reality already in existence on this side of Christ's second coming (see Matthew 12:28; 13:1-52; Romans 14:17; 1 Corinthians 4:20; Colossians 1:13), and sometimes it is pictured as being yet in the future, with the "kingdom" held out as something the Christian will inherit (see 1 Corinthians 6:9,10; Galatians 5:21; Ephesians 5:5). In our Greek text, both here and again at 1 Thessalonians 5:24, the participle translated "calls" is a present tense participle.[28] Present tense participles indicate continuing action. If the present tense participle is what Paul wrote, it looks like we should treat "kingdom and glory" as future in this passage, something not yet realized by the Thessalonian Christians.[29] God's continual calls to this future kingdom and glory were heard as the preachers like Paul and Silas exhorted and en-

---

[26] By "eschatological system" we are referring to premillennialism, postmillennialism, amillennialism, and modern dispensationalism. It is likely that each of us comes to this passage with some already formed beliefs about the events likely to unfold in the future as the second coming of Christ occurs. What is difficult, but what is surely best, is to attempt to let this passage speak first, and then, if need be, to adapt our already accepted system to agree with it.

[27] The lexicons tell us the word *basileia* has three meanings – rule, the people ruled, the area ruled. The first meaning is most often correct in the eastern world, while in the western world, one of the last two is often emphasized first.

[28] In a few manuscripts the participle is an aorist tense, and would be translated "called." That would look back at the gospel invitation offered to folk to become a Christian. God invites folk to become Christians through the gospel (2 Thessalonians 2:14). With this reading, "kingdom" has been treated as here and now, and "glory" as hereafter, though Sharp's rule of grammar suggests "kingdom" and "glory" are two aspects of the same event. In fact, a comparison of the parallel passages at Mark 10:37 ("in your glory") and Matthew 20:21 ("in your kingdom") also suggests kingdom and glory are two aspects of the same blessed future kingship of Christ.

[29] To treat the "kingdom" and "glory" as future does not mean we must embrace either the eschatological system that insists the kingdom Jesus intended to set up when He came to earth the first time had to be postponed, nor must we accept the system that claims that a future millennial kingdom follows Christ's advent. If God's reign, His kingship, is the thing emphasized, then why not contemplate what His rule means both for the final and complete overthrow of Satan and for the restoration of humanity to a relationship with Himself?

couraged and implored, as verse 11 has indicated.[30] The day will come when "the kingdom of this world has become the kingdom of our Lord, and of His Christ, and He will reign for ever and ever" (Revelation 11:16). That is most certainly the future kingdom to which God continually calls His children. What "glory," the last of the key words in this passage, means is also the subject of controversy. Some suppose it refers to the glory Jesus will receive when the second coming occurs (1 Peter 4:13). Some see an allusion to the glorified bodies the redeemed will receive (1 Corinthians 15:43; Philippians 3:21). Ephesians 1:18 speaks about the glory of God's inheritance in the saints. Others call attention to the fact the New Jerusalem has the glory of God (Revelation 21:11). Still others call attention to "glory" as being something the Christian has to look forward to. Hebrews 2:10 has God "bringing many sons to glory," while Colossians 1:27 has the expression "the hope of glory," and 2 Timothy 2:10 speaks of "eternal glory."

2:13 – *For this reason we also constantly thank God that when you received the word of God which you heard from us, you accepted it not as the word of men, but for what it really is, the word of God, which also performs its work in you who believe.*

For this reason ... also – The Greek word *kai* appears twice as this verse begins. If we translate *kai ... kai* as "and ... also," as did the ASV, this verse introduces a new reason why Paul and Silas are thankful.[31] They had already thanked God (1 Thessalonians 1:2,3) for the Thessalonians' progress in the gospel, which was evidence they were among God's chosen people (1 Thessalonians 1:5-10). After drawing attention to the missionaries' part in the conversion of the Christians at Thessalonica (1 Thessalonians 2:1-12), Paul and Silas now offer thanks to God for the Thessalonians' own ready acceptance of the preaching as being the word of God. This reminder about their own ready acceptance was part of how the Thessalonians could know that the teachers of the gospel were men of integrity.

We ... constantly thank God – The "we," which is emphasized in the Greek, implies a contrast. Perhaps the "we" is in contrast to the Thessalonians themselves who are giving thanks. Perhaps the "we" is in contrast to "all the believers in Macedonia and Achaia" (1 Thessalonians 1:7). 1 Thessalonians 1:2 informed the readers that Paul and Silas always in their prayers thanked God for the Thessalonians' response to the gospel. Here we learn another thing for which Paul and Silas constantly gave thanks to God.

That when you received the word of God which you heard from us – As Paul and Silas preached the gospel in the city of Thessalonica, their spoken words had a divine source. "Of God" occupies an emphatic position in this clause. The Thessalonians, on their part, believed the instructions the preachers handed down by word of mouth. At John 1:12, "received" is a word synonymous with "believed."   We may compare Hebrews 4:2 for

---

[30] In passing, the question arises whether "the upward call of God in Christ Jesus," referred to in Philippians 3:14, refers to the same continual calling from God? This commentator thinks it more probable the "upward call" verse refers to the rapture of Christians, when Jesus will invite the redeemed to "come up here" (Revelation 11:12) to receive their crown of life.

[31] We are treating "for this reason" as looking forward to what is about to be written.

"word of hearing" and also Romans 10:17, which tells us that "faith comes by hearing."

You accepted *it* – The Thessalonians not only received (*paralabontes*) the word, they welcomed (*edexasthe*) it.

Not *as* **the word of men, but** *for* **what it really is, the word of God** – As the italics indicate, the words "it" and "as" are not actually in the Greek text. Throughout this whole verse, Paul is calling attention to the essential nature of what he and Silas preached, and what the Thessalonians understood they were hearing. What the preachers were saying were not words of human invention, but the word which God had appointed to be heard through the preaching of Paul and Silas.[32] There may also be an affirmation of Holy Spirit inspiration as the preachers delivered the "word of hearing." So the letter writers' now affirm that the Thessalonians' appraisal of what they heard was accurate. Paul elsewhere tells us he received his gospel by revelation from Christ (1 Corinthians 11:23, Galatians 1:12). *Kathōs* is the Greek word translated "what"; it tells us that their preaching was actually "just as" (*kathōs*) it had been described. Such a conviction about the gospel explains Paul and Silas' commitment to preaching it.

Which also performs its work in you who believe – Not only did the word of God have an effect on the preachers, it also worked in the lives of the hearers.[33] Romans 1:16 tells us the gospel is "the power of God unto salvation to everyone who believes." "Believe" is a present tense participle which pictures continuing belief. "Performs" is a present tense verb which pictures the word operating continually in the believer's life.[34] When it was at work in those "who believe" there was a change in behavior by the Christians and a constant fruitfulness of the Christians. This word still works when it is presented, accepted, and followed for what it really is – the Word of God.

2:14 – *For you, brethren, became imitators of the churches of God in Christ Jesus that are in Judea, for you also endured the same sufferings at the hands of your own countrymen, even as they did from the Jews,*

For you, brethren – "For you" (*humeis gar*) is an emphatic resumption of the verb "you accepted" in verse 13. If they hadn't accepted the word of God, they would not now be experiencing the persecution they are in fact experiencing. The frequent repetition of "brethren" (cp. 1 Thessalonians 1:4; 2:1,17) is a significant way for the writers to say to the readers that we are together in this new community of the followers of Jesus Christ.

---

[32] The words in the Greek read "the word of hearing of God," with emphasis on "God" as its ultimate source.

[33] The antecedent of "which" is "word," not "God."

[34] The KJV at this place reads "which effectually worketh." Calvinism posits both a general call and an effectual call, but this verse in Thessalonians is hardly a proof text for that doctrine. The KJV translators had a Calvinistic bias, and that bias sometimes shows through in their choice of words as they translated.

Became imitators of the churches of God in Christ Jesus that are in Judea – The past tense verb "became" indicates the Thessalonian Christians already have been persecuted before this letter was written to them. 1 Thessalonians 1:6 has alluded to how the readers were imitators of the apostles and of their Lord in their tribulations. Now the "churches of God in Judea" are given as another example of how folk who accept the gospel of Christ Jesus are persecuted by opponents of the gospel. Local congregations in any country are "the churches ... in" that country. Collectively the local congregations make up the "church of God" (singular) in that country. Since an assembly of Jewish people could be called a "church of God" (Deuteronomy 23:1-3; Nehemiah 13:1) the addition of "in Christ Jesus" distinguishes Christian congregations from those assemblies that were not followers of Christ. [35] Christian congregations in Judea and the Christian congregation in Thessalonica were all following the same pattern. Embracing Jesus as the Messiah brought persecution from those who did not become Jesus' followers, just as Jesus had predicted would happen (Mark 10:34; Luke 12:52,53).

For you also endured the same sufferings at the hands of your own countrymen – This clause explains wherein the imitation consisted. 'You Christians in Thessalonica were so like the Christians in Judea, who suffered persecution because of their new faith, that you, too, were persecuted.' Apparently, the way those early Jewish Christians handled themselves when persecuted had become widely known, even before Luke wrote Acts c. AD 63. When 1 Thessalonians was written about AD 51 or 52, the Christians in Thessalonica already knew about the persecution of the church in Judea. "Countrymen" translates *sumphuletōn*, which means belonging to the same tribe or ethnic group. Opinion is divided whether this means it was unconverted Jewish folk who persecuted the Thessalonians, or whether it was Gentile folk who persecuted the Thessalonians. The original persecution of the preachers at Thessalonica was led by Jewish opponents (Acts 17:5,13), but if "countrymen" refers to Jewish folk persecuting the church it would also require us to affirm that the majority of the converts were themselves Jewish. On the contrary, since Acts 17:5 indicates that Jewish troublemakers stirred up a mob of local people to attack the preachers, it seems most probable that "countrymen" here means Gentile unbelievers continued to persecute the church after the preachers had been driven out of town, with this also implying that the majority of the congregation were Gentile converts.

Even as they did from the Jews – The record in Acts indicates several persecutions instigated against Christians living in Judea by the unconverted Jews of Judea. It was their own "countrymen" in Judea who persecuted the Jewish converts. This letter to the Thessalonians represents accurately the history recorded by Luke in Acts, both as it concerns the church in Judea and as it concerns the church in Thessalonica.

---

[35] At the time 1 Thessalonians was written, the word translated "church" had not yet narrowed its meaning to the local Christian community (still less to the meaning of the whole body of Christians, which is not in question here). In AD 51, the word still carried many of its secular associations, like the ordinary English word "assembly." Thus, it was necessary to specify the "assembly" being addressed: first that these communities belong to God, and secondly that, in contrast to Jewish synagogues, they belong to Christ Jesus.

2:15 – *who both killed the Lord Jesus and the prophets, and drove us out. They are not pleasing to God, but hostile to all men,*

Who both killed the Lord Jesus – The nearest antecedent of "who" is "Jews" at the close of verse 14. Verses 15 and 16 contain four participles that state a four-fold indictment of the persecuting element among the Jews, ranging from what they did to Jesus, to what they continued to do to prevent His followers from preaching the gospel.[36] What we read in these verses is a straightforward indictment based on the actual historical facts. "Killing" is the first participle and the first charge in the indictment. The sheer enormity of what the persecutors did in Jesus' case is emphasized by the word order in the Greek. "The Lord" emphatically comes before both the verb "killed" and the object "Jesus." It would have been bad enough to falsely accuse and torture a mere human, but to so unjustly mistreat and dishonor "the Lord" is a terrible sin.

And the prophets – Jesus had spoken of how some Jewish folk had killed the Old Testament prophets who predicted beforehand the coming of the Messiah (Matthew 23:37), and He also had foretold how some Jewish folk would continue to persecute those whom Jesus Himself would send to them (Matthew 23:34). Stephen also made the same accusation which we now read here in Thessalonians when he said to his persecutors, "Which one of the prophets did your fathers not persecute? They killed those who had previously announced the coming of the Righteous One, whose betrayers and murderers you have now become" (Acts 7:52). Hundreds of years earlier, Elijah had complained that the sons of Israel had killed the prophets (1 Kings 19:10; Romans 11:3[37]).

And drove us out – This is the second of four participles in the Greek and thus is the second charge in the indictment against the persecuting element among the Jews. Paul and Silas wrote these words while the terrible treatment to which they had been subjected in Thessalonica (Acts 17:5-10) and Berea (Acts 17:13,14) was still fresh in their memory.

They are not pleasing to God – This is the third charge against the Jews. Speaking to the Twelve on the night before He was betrayed, Jesus warned them what to expect from those Jews who would oppose their work and message. He said, "They will make you outcasts from the synagogue, but an hour is coming for everyone who kills you to think that he is offering service to God. These things they will do because they have not known the Father or Me" (John 16:2-3). If one is a persecutor of Christ and His followers, that person is not just "not pleasing to God," he has made himself an enemy of God.

But hostile to all men – When God sent Messiah to reach all men, the persecuting Jews' stubborn resistance to admitting Jesus' Messiahship made them *ipso facto* hostile to all men. The historian Tacitus gives, as a characteristic of the race, "an attitude of hostility

---

[36] It is not all Jews as such who are indicted but those Jews who were actively involved in the crucifixion of Jesus, and their sympathizers who continued to oppose the spread of the gospel and thus showed themselves hostile to the best interests of mankind.

[37] It should be observed that when Paul refers to the death of the prophets in Romans 11:2-5, he is not blaming *all* Jews, but just those who had bowed the knee to Baal.

and hatred towards all others."[38]   Juvenal makes the same accusation.[39]   Paul was not condemning all his fellow Jews as did Tacitus and Juvenal.   But he did condemn the persecuting element among them on the grounds that their rejection of Christ had a detrimental influence on other Jews as well as on the Gentiles.

2:16 – hindering us from speaking to the Gentiles so that they may be saved; with the result that they always fill up the measure of their sins.   But wrath has come upon them to the utmost.

Hindering us from speaking to the Gentiles – This is the fourth charge, and the fourth participle, in the indictment against the Jews.   Here is how the hostility to all men, which Paul spoke about (verse 15), is expressed in every day behavior.   "Us" includes both Paul and Silas, if not other gospel messengers.   "Gentile" is a technical word used to identify a person who is not a Jew.[40]   The "speaking" which the persecutors are trying to hinder is the preaching of the gospel to the Gentiles, something the preachers have been commanded by the Lord to do.

So that they may be saved – "So that" expresses the purpose for the missionaries' preaching the gospel to the Gentiles.   It was in order that the Gentiles might have the forgiveness of their sins and everlasting salvation through belief and obedience to the message.   Had the preachers been hindered from preaching to the Gentiles, the Gentiles very likely would have missed their present opportunity for salvation.   No wonder the opponents are said to be hostile to all men.

With the result that they always fill up the measure of their sins – Instead of pleasing God, the result of the opponents' behavior is ominously pictured as filling up the measure of their sins.   "Always" is placed emphatically at the end of the clause in the Greek, and says that the opponents of the gospel preachers were acting as the persecuting element among the Jews had always acted – in the time before Jesus came, while Jesus was here on earth, and since.[41]   The Greek word translated "fill up" has a prefix added to it which may be intensive.   If so, the picture is that their cup of guilt was well on the way to being filled to the brim.   In God's mind there is a well-defined limit on how much sin will be temporarily tolerated.   When that limit is reached, when the cup is full, divine punishment becomes inevitable.

But wrath has come upon them to the utmost – At 1 Thessalonians 1:10 it was explained that God's "wrath" (*orgē*) is His settled displeasure against sin, that grows out of His very

---

[38] *Hist.* v. 5.2

[39] i. xiv. 103, 104.

[40] The Greek word *ethnē*, in its plural form as it is here, is sometimes translated "peoples" and is inclusive of Jews as well as other people groups.   But here in 2:16, where there is an explicit contrast with Jews, "Gentiles" is the correct translation.

[41] Compare Matthew 23:32, where Jesus, speaking to His enemies, said to them, "Fill up, then, the measure of the guilt of your fathers."

nature (which is holiness). In the epistle to the Romans it is taught that there is both a temporal wrath of God as well as a future wrath. Romans 1:18ff speaks of God's wrath being experienced by Gentiles in the present time as God gives them up (i.e., allows them to go on sinning, withdraws His gracious aid, and sends the appropriate punishment for their sins). Then, alluding to the final judgment, Romans 2:5-9 speaks of wrath, indignation, tribulation, and anguish being rendered upon every soul of men who habitually works evil, whether he be Jew or Greek. Hebrews 10:26-29 speaks of a fury of fire that those who have trampled underfoot the Son of God will experience at the final judgment. So the question here in verse 16 is whether it is temporal or future wrath that is in view. Because the verb translated "has come" is an aorist tense, some have argued for temporal wrath.[42] However, many Old Testament Messianic prophecies were expressed by past tense verbs, because the thing predicted was so sure to happen it could be spoken of as having already happened. It seems likely that something similar is done here and that it is best to understand that this reference is to future wrath. *Eis telos*, translated "to the utmost" in NASB, and "at last" in several English versions, then is understood to say that the issue is now settled. God's determination, that those who persist in persecuting Christ's followers will experience wrath, cannot be reversed.[43]

III. THE WRITERS' DESIRE TO VISIT THESSALONICA AGAIN. 2:17-3:13

2:17 – *But we, brethren, having been taken away from you for a short while – in person, not in spirit – were all the more eager with great desire to see your face.*

---

[42] Commentators have struggled to document what the temporal wrath might have been. (1) Attention has been called to a series of disasters that involved Jewish folk c. AD 49-51, including a massacre in the temple (Josephus, *War* 2.224-227; *Ant.* 20:105-112) and their expulsion from Rome (Suetonius, *Claudius* 25:4: cf. Acts 18:2). However, it can hardly be shown that the folk who so suffered were suffering because they had been persecuting Christians, which is something this passage in 1 Thessalonians is treating. ("Them" in verse 16 is not *all* Jews, but those who have just been described by the four participial phrases.) (2) Some interpret 1 Thessalonians 2:13-16 as a reference to the fall of Jerusalem in AD 70; in fact, some commentators treat these verses as an interpolation added to the text after the original letter was written. In the Detailed Introduction to 1 Thessalonians in this volume, the idea that 2:13-16 are a reference to the fall of Jerusalem in AD 70 was introduced and answered. Thus, if this verse is speaking of God's temporal wrath, it has certainly proven difficult to find a historical, completed fulfillment of this warning about wrath on the persecutors.

[43] Two other explanations have been proposed for this difficult phrase in verse 16. (1) The verb "has come" and the original expression *eis telos*, translated in our NASB as "to the uttermost," was understood by the ancient commentators as signifying that the wrath of God was coming upon the Jews, not for a few years, but for a long duration, even for many generations, "unto the end" (*eis telos*) of time. If this option, which treats God's wrath as being temporal, should be embraced, it must be kept in mind that not all Jewish folk down through the ages are threatened with wrath – only those who are the persecuting element among them. Indeed, unbelievers are cut off from the olive tree, but Romans 11 indicates that Jews who become believers in Christ will be grafted back into the olive tree. (2) Some premillennial writers think *eis telos* refers to the great tribulation, which their system occurs at the close of the church age, just before Christ's second coming. Even if we do have a future time when Jewish folk are severely persecuted, it is difficult to see how this passage in Thessalonians refers to that, for the persecutors here threatened with wrath have been long dead before that tribulation of folk then living occurs.

But we, brethren – Several commentators have observed that it would have been well if the chapter break to begin chapter 3 had been made before verse 17, since here the topic changes to the writers' desire to visit the Thessalonian Christians again. No longer do the writers reflect on their memories of the time when they were among them. Now the topic is their hopes and concerns for the Christians at Thessalonica since the missionaries were forced to leave town.

Having been taken away from you for a short while – Paul and Silas had not left town voluntarily, but because of persecution initiated by Jewish unbelievers. The verb *aporphanidzo*, translated "taken away from," is used of the mental anguish little children feel when they are left alone as orphans because of the death of their parents. It is used of the feeling of being deprived of something valuable that a bereaving parent experiences when a beloved child dies. It is also used of the longing a lover feels when separated from his or her beloved. It is a beautiful choice of words by the writers to express their strong affection for and attachment to the Christians they were forced to separate from. Though it has already been perhaps six months since they left Thessalonica, "for a short while" indicates that both Paul and Silas expected the separation to be short. But as it turned out, it has been much longer than they at first anticipated.[44] Accordingly, the writers go on to indicate that they endeavored to return, and Paul himself had actually made several attempts in that direction, but their desires had been thwarted by the devil's activities.

In person, not in spirit – Perhaps the persecutors have insinuated that the missionaries' continued absence was evidence of their lack of concern for the Christians in Thessalonica.[45] While they could not be present in person, their concern for the Thessalonians remained intense and constant. "My heart is with you" is the elegant and touching expression we still use to denote affection for an absent friend.

Were all the more eager with great desire to see your face – The preachers were not to blame for the separation. In fact, rather than the separation leading to a diminishing interest or affection for the Thessalonians, it had only whetted (*perissoterōs*) their eagerness to see their beloved Thessalonians face to face.

2:18 – *For we wanted to come to you – I, Paul, more than once – and yet Satan hindered us.*

For we wanted to come to you – In the better attested texts, verses 17 and 18 are linked by the Greek conjunction *dioti*, meaning "for" or "because." The point is being driven home that their continued absence had been unavoidable. It did not stem from a lack of concern or interest for the new Christians at Thessalonica. Having written a number of

---

[44] In Paul's case, it would be some five years, as far as we can tell, before he would see them again. This is an implication drawn from what is recorded between Acts 17:10 and Acts 20:1ff.

[45] The piling up of words in this verse and in chapter 3 to express their eager longing may reflect rumors that the preachers did not really care for the Thessalonians, and had no interest in coming back to them.

expressions denoting their strong desire to return, another is here added, as though the writers were not satisfied that they had conveyed the true state of their feelings.

– I, Paul, more than once – At this place, Paul expressly distinguishes himself from Silas and Timothy. 1 Thessalonians 3:1,2 indicates that Timothy had visited Thessalonica since Paul and Silas had been forced to leave. Silas had been left behind in Berea (Acts 17:14) where he appears to have stayed to evangelize and minister until he and Timothy joined Paul at Corinth (Acts 18:5). Paul may not be able to speak for either of those men during the time they were absent from Thessalonica, but he certainly can testify to his own strong desires to return to Thessalonica. The phrase, "more than once" is better taken with "I Paul" than with "we wanted to come." It indicates a plurality of occasions without exact specification.[46] The six months or so that intervened between his departure from Thessalonica and his writing of 1 Thessalonians was sufficiently long to allow for his wish to visit to be repeated.

And yet Satan hindered us – "Us" includes Paul and Silas as being the ones hindered from returning to Thessalonica. Timothy did visit Thessalonica (1 Thessalonians 3:1); he was not hindered by the activity of Satan. From Revelation 12:9 and 20:2 we learn that "Satan" and "devil" are both names by which God's ancient adversary is known. Elsewhere in the Thessalonian epistles he is called "the evil one" (2 Thessalonians 3:3) and "the Tempter" (1 Thessalonians 3:5). Satan is, throughout the New Testament (e.g., 2 Thessalonians 2:9; 1 Timothy 3:7, and Revelation 12:9), presented as a real personality, not just a figure of speech or a personification of evil. The Greek word translated "hindered" means literally "to cut a trench between one's self and an advancing foe, in order to prevent his further progress." Somehow, behind the scenes, Satan was opposing the wishes and attempts of Paul and Silas to revisit Thessalonica in as timely a manner as they had wished.[47] What form, in human terms, the hindrance took we can only guess. Human beings who assist the devil in his malicious attempts are called ministers of Satan (2 Corinthians 11:15). Perhaps Satan was been behind the lawless rioting instigated by the Jews (Acts 17:5) which forced the politarchs' hand. Perhaps Satan was behind the decision of the politarchs, who required Jason and other leading Christians to keep the peace by pledging themselves to prevent further preaching in Thessalonica by Paul and Silas.[48] Since at 2 Corinthians 12:7, the thorn in the flesh, a messenger from Satan, may

[46] The same expression occurs in Philippians 4:16. Morris, after rejecting the idea that *hapax kai dis*, (translated "once and again" in the KJV) is a Latinism, finds its source in the LXX. The English meaning most suitable for the idiom, he writes, is "more than once." (L. Morris, KAI HAPAX DIS, *NovTest* [1956], 1:205-208.)

[47] "In translating 'Satan hindered us,' it is important to avoid giving the impression that Paul and his colleagues required permission from Satan to do anything. It may be better to translate 'but Satan prevented us from doing so,' 'Satan made it impossible for us,' or 'Satan stopped us'." (Ellingworth & Nida, *op. cit.*, p.49.)

[48] William M. Ramsay, *St. Paul the Traveller and Roman Citizen* (Grand Rapids: Baker Book House, 1960), pp.230-231. In the parable of the tares Jesus points out that the tares were sown among the good seeds by the "enemy," the devil, while men slept. The reality of the devil's hindrance to the spread of the Word is quite pronounced in these vivid teachings of Jesus (Matthew 13:24-30,36-43). (James G. Van Buren *Standard Lesson Commentary 1977-78* [Cincinnati: Standard Publishing Company, 1977], p.381.)

be either a physical sickness of some kind or persecution, perhaps both Paul and Silas were temporarily incapacitated by some kind of physical sickness.[49]   Whatever the means used by Satan to hinder their actual return, at least it is beyond any doubt that Paul and Silas longed intensely to see the Thessalonian Christians.   The next verse explains one reason why.

2:19 – *For who is our hope or joy or crown of exultation?   Is it not even you, in the presence of our Lord Jesus at His coming?*

For who is our hope or joy or crown of exultation? – "For" introduces the reason why Paul and Silas were concerned about the Thessalonian Christians and wanted to come back. 'We are anxious that you hear Jesus' words of approval when the second coming occurs and the judgment takes place.'   "Hope" is an earnest longing for something in the future, coupled with an expectation that this desire will be satisfied.   Without the expectation, it is just wishing, not hope.   Paul and Silas' hope was that the Thessalonians would not be put to shame when the final judgment takes place, but would rather be found pure and blameless, as those who embraced the faith with eagerness, and heroically persevered in it in spite of all opposition.   The missionaries wanted to visit Thessalonica again, if by any way they might help the Thessalonians to be faithful.   Paul and Silas anticipated feeling great delight if the persons they had helped to know the Savior were to be welcomed into the presence of Jesus at His second coming.   In fact, "crown of rejoicing" says they could think of no greater delight than to see the Thessalonians so honored by Jesus.   It would be like the feeling of receiving a victor's crown at one of the Olympian Games.   To see the Thessalonians welcomed by Jesus would be lasting proof that they had not run in vain as they went about their evangelistic mission.

Is it not even you, in the presence of our Lord Jesus at His coming? – This question answers the question asked in the first part of the verse.   "Not even you" implies there will be other converts, in addition to the Thessalonians, whom Paul and Silas anticipate will be present with the Lord, because they, like the Thessalonians, have been faithful unto death. 1 Thessalonians 4:14-17 will detail some of what it means to be in the presence of the Lord at His coming.   Only then, in His presence, will Paul's achievements be truly assessed.   If the Thessalonian Christians are in the multitude of the redeemed, Paul and Silas will be more than delighted.   The Greek word translated "coming" is *parousia*.   This is the first time this word occurs in the Thessalonian letters, but it evidently was a familiar word to the readers.   It was the word used to describe a royal visit such as when a visiting dignitary arrived in town and games were held in his honor.[50]   Jesus Himself had used the word when He talked about His second coming (Matthew 24:37-39).   Following Jesus' example, the New Testament writers picked up the term and continued to use it often when writing about His second advent.

---

[49] In God's providential government of His people and His world, Satan is sometimes permitted to inflict bodily suffering upon men (Job 2:7; Luke 13:16; Acts 10:38; 1 Corinthians 5:5).

[50] A. Deissmann, *Light from the Ancient East,* (London: Hodder and Stoughton, 1927), p.372.

2:20 – *For you are our glory and joy.*

For you are our glory and joy – This verse offers an emotional affirmation to the answer given to the question posed at the beginning of verse 19. Not only will the faithful Christians be the missionaries' glory and joy when Christ returns; they are already so right now. "Glory" here is used in the sense of "that in which one takes pride" (cp. 1 Corinthians 11:7).

We may perhaps draw some implications in addition to what has been specifically affirmed in these verses. It is implied that Paul and Silas will recognize their converts when the second advent occurs and redeemed folk are with the Lord. It is also implied that we will recognize one another in heaven. And it is also implied that some peculiar award or honor will be conferred on those who have been instrumental in the conversion of sinners, as Daniel 12:3 long ago indicated.

All the loving expressions of interest in the Thessalonians spiritual welfare, which we have just covered, would certainly silence the insinuations made by some that the reason Paul and Silas had not returned to Thessalonica was that they really had no concern for their converts.

III. THE WRITERS' DESIRE TO VISIT THESSALONI- CA AGAIN.   2:17-3:13 *(continued)*

3:1 – *Therefore when we could endure it no longer, we thought it best to be left behind at Athens alone,*

Therefore when we could endure it no longer – As was noted in comments at 2:17, it would have been well if the chapter break to begin chapter 3 had been made before verse 17, rather than where it currently is located since the opening verses of what is now numbered as chapter 3 of this letter are closely connected with the immediately preceding verses (2:17-20). The opening particle *dio*, translated "therefore," shows that what is being introduced – i.e., the fact that Timothy had been sent to them – is another proof of the writers' affection and concern for the Christians at Thessalonica.

The use of the plural pronoun "we" throughout this letter has created some hard questions for interpreters, and never more so than in these opening verses of chapter 3. Generally, the use of "we" in this letter is taken literally, as referring to Paul and Silas (and occasionally including Timothy, too), rather than being treated as an editorial "we" (and thus simply the equivalent of "I").   In chapter 3, decisions must be made as attempts are made to explain the change from the plural "we could endure no longer" and "we thought" and "we sent" in verses 1-4 to the singular "I could endure no longer" and "I sent" in verse 5, which certainly means Paul alone. Furthermore, complicating the decision-making is the related historical material contained in the book of Acts, which must likewise be fitted together with what is written in 3:1-5. If we treat "we could endure it no longer" as being a real plural, verse 1 indicates that all the missionaries were anxious about the welfare of the brethren to whom this letter is addressed.[1]

We thought it best to be left behind at Athens alone – The expression "left alone" seems to refer to Paul himself being left behind by himself as the other team members went to their various mission stations. The word "alone" helps us feel something of Paul's apprehension about being left alone in a foreign city where there was little or no Christian fellowship. But his concern for the welfare of the brethren was so great he was not willing to gratify himself at the expense of the Thessalonians. Their need for Timothy's ministry had to take precedence to his own needs.

The wording "we thought" and "at Athens" raises a considerable challenge when we try to reconstruct the travels of Paul and Silas and Timothy. Luke's account (Acts 17:15,16) of their travels at this point in history has Silas and Timothy left behind at Berea when Paul fled the city to go to Athens. When he arrived at Athens, the Berean Christians who accompanied him are given a command to convey to Silas and Timothy that they are

---

[1] The word picture in the Greek word "endure" is that of the keeping out or keeping in of water or another fluid (e.g., of a watertight barrel or of a ship that does not leak). We must supply a noun to explain what was being held in or held out, and in light of the context it is evidently anxiety that the missionaries could not keep out of their minds.

to join him as soon as possible. `Luke tells us that "Paul waited for them at Athens" (Luke 17:16), but he does not say whether they ever arrived in Athens. Luke's history then further states that, after Paul had remained some time at Athens, he went to Corinth, where he was joined by Timothy and Silas, who came to him "from Macedonia" (Acts 18:5). In this commentator's judgment, this is how the travels are to be reconstructed.[2] If we take the "we" as a real plural, and "at Athens" as the place where the decision was made, it looks like all three did get together in Athens.[3] When anxiety about the welfare of the church at Thessalonica became hard to bear, we suppose the decision was made that Silas would return to Berea, while Timothy would go to Thessalonica. This would explain Paul's being left alone at Athens, and it also explains how in Acts 18:5 both Timothy and Silas come from Macedonia to Corinth.

3:2 – *and we sent Timothy, our brother and God's fellow worker in the gospel of Christ, to strengthen and encourage you as to your faith,*

And we sent Timothy – The aorist tense "sent" indicates that this mission of Timothy to Thessalonica was over and done before 1 Thessalonians was written. "We" says that Paul and Silas together concurred in the need to send Timothy to Thessalonica. In our reconstruction of the travels of these three men, it appears that before he was sent from Athens to Thessalonica, Timothy had never been to Thessalonica. If that is true, he can now go there without endangering Jason's bond that dealt just with Paul and Silas. Paul would have been left alone in Athens if, simultaneous to Timothy's departure for Thessalonica, Silas departed for Berea.

Our brother and God's fellow worker in the gospel of Christ – This is the first separate reference to Timothy in this letter, and some have thought it surprising to have this accumulation of Timothy's qualities listed in a letter to folk who already knew him. In fact, his mission to Thessalonica had already been completed and he had already reported the results of his mission back to Paul (1 Thessalonians 3:6). Perhaps this language reflects the possibility that Timothy is the bearer of this letter to Thessalonica, and is returning to serve there as evangelist/minister. This would account for this strong recommendation of Timothy.

The better attested Greek text (as translated in the NASB) uses two expressions to describe Timothy.[4] "Our brother" identifies Timothy as a fellow Christian. "God's fellow worker in the gospel of Christ" says Timothy has a reputation for hard laborious work in preaching the gospel. Just as Paul and Barnabas reported how God had worked

---

[2] In the Detailed Introduction to 1 Thessalonians, we outline how the church at Thessalonica began, attempting to harmonize the Acts record with what we read here in this letter to the church at Thessalonica.

[3] Luke's history is not inaccurate at this point, but it does omit certain events – such as Paul's intermediate trip to Corinth (2 Corinthians 12:14; 13:1), and the fact that Paul wrote any letters at all – which we learn about separately from Paul's epistles.

[4] Some copyists, apparently hesitant to give Timothy such a bold designation as "fellow-laborer," omit the word. Some manuscripts omit the words "of God," which results in Timothy being described as a co-worker with other humans. Some copyists (followed by the KJV) add a third description, calling him a "minister of God" as well as a "fellow worker."

with them during what is known as Paul's first missionary journey (Acts 14:27), and just as 1 Corinthians 3:9 indicates that God works along with His messengers in the building of a church, so "God's fellow worker" pictures God as working alongside Timothy as he goes about his work as evangelist. Not just any speaking will do to achieve such a result as God working with the speaker. It is when men are speaking the gospel of Christ that God is pictured as working side by side with them. This high recommendation of Timothy may be intended to convey the idea that the Thessalonians should not be disappointed that it is Timothy rather than Paul and/or Silas who is coming to Thessalonica. Timothy is God's fellow worker. He is a good man for the job.

Thus far in this letter the gospel has been called repeatedly "the gospel of God" (2:2,5,9) and once "our gospel" (1:5). Now it is called "the gospel of Christ" since the heart of the message is good news concerning the Messiah whom God sent into the world.

To strengthen and encourage you as to your faith – This clause explains what Timothy's first assigned mission to Thessalonica was intended to accomplish. It was more than just the wish of Paul and Silas to keep in touch with them. "Strengthen your faith" is important because recent converts need to be firmly grounded in the truth so their faith will continue to grow. The next verse goes on to describe what Paul and Silas were most worried about, namely, that afflictions might cause them to become disheartened.[5] "Faith" (in this context) might be either the body of doctrine that makes up the Christian religion, or it might refer to each individual Christian's personal convictions which would be taking a pounding when opponents of Christianity began to question and attack the new converts for their beliefs. "Encourage you" reflects the fact the believers at Thessalonica were being persecuted. Timothy's job was to come alongside the brethren and give them aid and support so they will continue in their belief in Jesus as the Savior. To strengthen and encourage folk in their faith was something Paul himself usually did (Acts 14:22; 15:32). But since Paul for the moment could not come personally, Timothy was sent because it was something that Timothy could also do.

3:3 – *so that no one would be disturbed by these afflictions; for you yourselves know that we have been destined for this.*

So that no one would be disturbed by these afflictions – This clause states one of the purposes behind Timothy's mission to Thessalonica. The Thessalonian Christians were suffering persecutions at the hands of their fellow townsmen (1 Thessalonians 1:6, 2:14). The verb *sainō* ("disturbed") occurs nowhere else in the New Testament. In Homer's writings it was used of dogs wagging their tails in fondness, but in later papyri it was used to describe the gradual detachment of a person from his resolution, thus he was wavering or was disturbed mentally. Either of these meanings could be used of the Thessalonians. They might have become fond of the position their persecutors favored, or they might have been in danger of wavering in their faith in Christ. The noun *thlipsis*, here translated "afflictions," is sometimes translated "tribulations," or the "pressure" of persecution. The

---

[5] Some wonder why they should have been concerned about the faith of those who life and witness were an example to believers elsewhere (cf. 1 Thessalonians 1:7,8). The anxiety stemmed from lack of information about the Thessalonian Christians before Timothy and others came bringing good reports.

trials Paul refers to are part of the past and present experience of the Thessalonian Christians. The Scriptures may predict a final tribulation of God's people before the second coming of Christ, but this verse (3:3) should not be used to refer to that coming affliction.

For you yourselves know that we have been destined for this – "In the world," said our Lord, "ye shall have tribulation" (John 16:33, KJV). Like Jesus Himself had warned His followers to expect persecution (Matthew 5:11,44; John 15:20), Paul must have regularly told new Christians that trials and persecutions are an inevitable part of Christian experience (verse 4; cp. Acts 14:22). When Timothy was sent to Thessalonica on his now-completed trip, he was to reinforce this warning as he ministered to the brethren. Forewarning about persecutions will be a preventive to aid folk not to be disturbed or waver. It is probable that "we" refers to Christians in general, not just to Paul and Silas who are writing this letter, nor even just to Paul, Silas and the Thessalonians. The idea seems to be that all Christians are exposed to persecution and cannot hope to avoid it. Persecutions are the product of the prince of this world's special targeting of the Christian. "Destined for this" should not cause us to think that God Himself had purposely planned or even organized the persecutions against the Christians in Thessalonica, but rather in His overall plan for the redemption of mankind God allows the persecutions and trials to occur because the testing of our faith produces perseverance (James 1:2).

3:4 – *For indeed when we were with you, we kept telling you in advance that we were going to suffer affliction; and so it came to pass, as you know.*

For indeed when we were with you – This verse tells how the Thessalonian believers knew that they could expect afflictions. During the few weeks or months they were evangelizing in Thessalonica, Paul and Silas had warned the Thessalonians to expect persecution for their faith.

We kept telling you in advance that we were going to suffer affliction – "Kept telling" is an imperfect tense verb in the Greek. It pictures repeated warnings, not just a single occurrence. The missionaries plainly and candidly told their potential converts that they could expect opposition and persecution if they embraced the Christian faith. "Suffer affliction" translates the infinitive form of the same word translated "afflictions" in verse 3. It is a present tense infinitive which indicates the converts will suffer ongoing or repeated afflictions. The fact that Paul and Silas had given them advance warning did not lesson the pain of their suffering, but the fact the converts expected it should lessen the temptation to abandon their faith when they actually had to experience that suffering.

And so it came to pass, as you know – "As you know" indicates the Thessalonians could testify from personal experience that what Paul and Silas predicted had happened. The suffering had begun while Paul and Silas were still with them, and the preachers naturally were anxious to know if the Thessalonians had been able to endure this form of temptation by Satan in their absence. We are not told how Paul and the others learned about the persecution which the Thessalonian church had to endure after their departure, but it would not have been difficult for a message to be sent to them in Berea or in Athens.

3:5 – *For this reason, when I could endure it no longer, I also sent to find out about your faith, for fear that the tempter might have tempted you, and our labor would be in vain.*

For this reason – "For this reason" points to what follows. 'Since I knew you were being persecuted, and since I feared that some might be turned from the truth by this opposition.'

When I could endure it no longer – "Endure" the suspense speaks of Paul's intense longing for information about the new Christians back in Thessalonica. 1 Thessalonians 3:1 indicated that Paul, Silas, and Timothy were all concerned about how the Thessalonian Christians were handling the persecution they faced. However, Paul ("I"), speaking only of himself at this point, indicates he finally took the lead in sending Timothy to Thessalonica. By writing "I" Paul especially calls attention to his own personal interest in the matter.

I also sent to find out about your faith – Timothy is the one who was sent (3:2). While "faith" in 3:2 might be either a body of doctrine or Christians' personal faith, in this verse there can be little doubt that "faith" refers to personal faith. *Pistis* could well be translated "faithfulness" at this place. Paul is here concerned about whether the Thessalonian Christians were continuing to be faithful to Christ.

For fear that the tempter might have tempted you – Paul here states the first of two reasons he was anxious about their faithfulness. The Greek behind "the tempter" is a present participle, thus describing Satan as one who tempts people constantly.[6] While it was the Thessalonian Christians' own "countrymen" (2:14) who persecuted them, Paul recognizes that the devil's activity led to the persecutors' actions. "Tempted" is an indicative verb; the way the Greek sentence is written shows that Paul had no doubt the Thessalonians had been tempted, for persecutions can produce a serious temptation to become unfaithful to Christ. What Paul did not know, before Timothy reported back to him, was whether or not the tempter's solicitations had been successful.

And our labor would be in vain – Here is the second reason for his anxiety about their faithfulness. If the Thessalonians' faith had collapsed, the missionaries' hard work (*kopos*[7]) in preaching the gospel to them would have been empty in terms of lasting results. "The faithfulness of the Thessalonians was Paul's hope and joy and crown of rejoicing at the coming of the Lord Jesus (1 Thessalonians 2:19,20). Thus, Paul's anxiety about their bearing up so that all his work would not be fruitless also made Timothy's trip important."[8]

3:6 – *But now that Timothy has come to us from you, and has brought us good news of your faith and love, and that you always think kindly of us, longing to see us just as we also long to see you,*

---

[6] Matthew 4:1-3 shows that the devil, Satan, is the one who is indicated by "the tempter."

[7] The Greek word here translated "labor" is the same one used at 1 Thessalonians 1:3 and 2:9.

[8] James G. VanBuren, *Standard Lesson Commentary 1981-82* (Cincinnati: Standard Publishing Company, 1981), p.438.

But now that Timothy has come to us from you – In the first six verses of this chapter, we have had the account of Timothy's being sent to Thessalonica. Now, we begin Paul's account of Timothy's return, in which we have the message he brought and the effect of that good news upon the apostle. Paul was in Athens when Timothy was sent to Thessalonica (3:1). At Acts 18:15, we learn that Timothy, in company with Silas, joined Paul at Corinth, and brought information concerning the state of the Thessalonian church. "Now" translates *arti* – "just now." Immediately after Timothy's arrival, it seems, Paul wrote this epistle, while his joy was fresh because the report Timothy brought was the opposite of what he feared might have happened to the Christians at Thessalonica.

And has brought us good news of your faith and love – The "good news"[9] Timothy brought concerned three things: their faith, their love, and their pleasant memories of the missionaries. As in verse 5, we would suggest translating it as "your faithfulness." "Your love" picks up "your labor of love" which Paul commended at 1 Thessalonians 1:3. They were continuing to put their faith into practice as they expressed their love to God, to man, and to Paul.

And that you always think kindly of us – "Us" includes Paul, Silas, and Timothy. Timothy's report of the kindly feelings of the Thessalonians toward Paul and the others assured Paul that they had not written him off as an exploiter, disinterested in their welfare, and this was true notwithstanding all the efforts which had been made to alienate their affections from him.

Longing to see us just as we also long to see you – Timothy has reported that their memories of the missionaries were so pleasant that they had an intense longing[10] for the missionaries to return. Such a longing was not one-sided. The missionaries, too, had a desire to revisit the brethren in Thessalonica. Paul here reiterates what he had already indicated in 2:17-18.

3:7 – *for this reason, brethren, in all our distress and affliction we were comforted about you through your faith*

For this reason, brethren – In verse 5, the phrase *dia touto* ("for this reason") pointed to what follows. Here in verse 7, it looks back to what was just said. Because of the good news that Timothy's report contained, Paul tells them that the mental anxiety he and his

---

[9] Paul uses here the verb *euangelizomai*, which generally in the New Testament is used to refer to the preaching of the gospel. As it also does in Luke 1:19 (i.e., the good news that Zechariah and Elizabeth are to have a son) and in Revelation 14:6 (where it speaks of good news respecting Christ's second coming), *euangelizomai* here has the meaning which is usual in secular Greek writings: that of bringing any kind of good news.

[10] The participle translated "longing" is present tense – i.e., an ongoing action – and denotes a very strong emotion. The adverb *pantote* ("always") further strengthens the idea of an ongoing emotion.

colleagues once felt had been relieved. Williams writes that Paul highlights four points to fill out why Timothy's report was so comforting. First, the good news came at a time the writers were in distress and affliction. Second, it was about the Thessalonians. Third it was because of their faithfulness. Fourth, the report was like a breath of fresh air (verse 8).[11]

In all our distress and affliction – "Distress" translates *anangkē*, and "affliction" translates *thlipsis*. Perhaps "distress" refers to inner feelings, while "affliction" results from pressure without, perhaps resulting from persecution.[12] We have no concrete information concerning the possible events in Corinth that might have led to some of the disturbing feelings Paul references. Acts 18:6 does record that the Jews had resisted and blasphemed, perhaps expelling him from their synagogue, and Acts 18:12 relates how the Jews rose up against him and dragged him before the Roman proconsul, Gallio. But both these events occurred *after* Timothy's return and report (Acts 18:5). If "our" includes Silas as well as Paul, then we must look to their worries about the state of the Thessalonian believers as being the cause of their disturbed emotions.

We were comforted about you through your faith – "We were comforted" is the main verb in the long sentence that makes up verses 6-8. The Greek phrase "your faith" is identical with that of verse 5. "Faithfulness" in the lives of converts to Christ is always a matter of serious concern. Paul expresses similar words of comfort in 2 Corinthians 7:3-7. Those words were written in response to the good news brought to him by Titus about the spiritual health of the Corinthian Christians, after a long period of great anxiety concerning them. Paul's tone has changed from painful suspense to relief and joy because of the good news Timothy has brought from Thessalonica.

3:8 – *for now we really live, if you stand firm in the Lord.*

For now we really live – "Now" covers not only the time of writing, but also into the future. To Paul and Silas, the good report was like they had been given a new lease on life. Distress and affliction can leave a person discouraged. Discouragement can bring all activity to a halt. Could Christianity take root in a large city like Thessalonica or like Corinth? Yes! If the Thessalonians were standing firm, then the ministry in Corinth might be potentially viable. Now, the possible reasons for being discouraged are gone. Paul and Silas can go back to work for the Gospel with renewed energy.

If you stand firm in the Lord – The "if" has the half-future sense, as though Paul was indicating that the continuance of this "life" was contingent upon their continued steadfast-

---

[11] Williams, *op. cit.*, p.62.

[12] Consult the notes on *thlipsis* in 1 Thessalonians 1:6 and 3:3.

ness.[13]   There is perhaps little difference of meaning between this phrase "in the Lord" and the more common "in Christ" or "in Christ Jesus."   Their continuing union with the Lord Jesus gives the missionaries great joy and motivation.

3:9 – *For what thanks can we render to God for you in return for all the joy with which we rejoice before our God on your account,*

For what thanks can we render to God for you – The conjunction "for" ties this verse together with the strong declaration he just made in verse 8 that the good news brought by Timothy was like a new lease on life.   Here he says there is nothing greater for which they could give thanks to God than the news that the Thessalonians were remaining steadfast in their faith.   Eight times in four verses Paul has written "you."   The Thessalonian Christians were the cause of his joy and delight!

In return for all the joy with which we rejoice before our God on your account – Paul and Silas' joy respecting the Thessalonians arose first from their conversion and then from their perseverance in the faith amidst great temptation and persecution.   "Before God"[14] suggests that God is a witness to the joy that fills the hearts of Paul and Silas.   Because the sentence continues on in the next verse – which speaks of prayers being offered – "before God" pictures how when praying Paul and Silas thought of themselves standing in the presence of God.

3:10 – *as we night and day keep praying most earnestly that we may see your face, and may complete what is lacking in your faith?*

As we night and day keep praying most earnestly that we may see your face – Along with thanksgiving and rejoicing (verse 9), Paul and Silas payed that providentially they would be allowed again to see the Thessalonians face to face.   "Praying" translates *deomai*, the Greek word for prayer that implies a sense of dependence on God.   "Night and day"[15] indicates the extreme frequency of the petitions about to be highlighted. "Earnestly" (*huperekperissou,* a double compound adverb in the comparative degree), helps convey with the greatest possible emphasis the intensity of this request being made to God.   This is the second time (see 2:17) Paul has used the Hebrew idiom "to see your face."   The anxiety about the Thessalonians has been removed, but this longing to see them personally is greater than ever.

---

[13] It is rare to find *ean* ("if") followed by a present indicative such as *stēkete* ("stand").   [Among the manuscripts, there is a weakly attested present subjunctive form here.]   Paul's choice of a present indicative rather than a more normal aorist subjunctive after *ean* has the effect of expressing anticipation that his readers will continue to stand firm from this point on.

[14] A few manuscripts read "Lord" rather than God.

[15] See on 1 Thessalonians 2:9 concerning the order of words.

And may complete what is lacking in your faith? – The earnest prayers of the writers also included this second petition. When we recall that Paul and Silas were able to do evangelistic work in Thessalonica for but a comparatively short time before they were compelled to depart to Berea, it is understandable that there were many subjects which called for further instruction. While the report Timothy brought when he returned from Thessalonica removed Paul's and Silas' anxiety, it also made them still more aware of the need of this young church for further instruction. The verb translated "complete" is used of mending fishing nets (Matthew 4:21) and is translated "fully trained" at Luke 6:40 and "prepared" at Romans 9:22. We have no way of knowing in detail what the Thessalonians' faith lacked, but it seems likely that what is written in chapters 4 and 5 are examples of the kind of instruction still needed. We may even assume that Paul thinks it necessary to provide the teaching in this letter since it was not likely there would be an opportunity in the near future for him and Silas to be able to return to Thessalonica in order to give the instruction face to face. This written word is the same content as would have been in their spoken word.

3:11 – *Now may our God and Father Himself and Jesus our Lord direct our way to you;*

Now may our God and Father Himself – "Now" translates the conjunction *de*, and might well be translated "and" since it serves to connect the prayer requests in verses 11-13 to the prayer of thanksgiving recorded in verses 9-10. Verses 11-13, a single sentence in the Greek, are a prayer which expresses some wishes,[16] both for the missionaries and for the Thessalonians. The wish-prayer for the missionaries is that God and Jesus together may make it possible for them to pay another visit to Thessalonica. The emphatic pronoun "Himself," which stands first in the sentence in the Greek, seems intended to mark a contrast, either with their own attempts at returning or to Satan's hindrance of those attempts. It also is very likely that "Himself," both here and at 2 Thessalonians 2:16-17, refers both to Father and Son. If so, it implies the one essence of these two persons of the Godhead.[17] Recall that Jesus Himself, on the day of great questions (Matthew 22:34-45), tried to help folk see that the *Shema* (Deuteronomy 6:4) did not teach there was but one person in the Godhead.[18] Given this fuller understanding of the Godhead that came from Jesus' teaching, people like Paul, who were nurtured on the truth that there is one God, could, without ceasing to believe that truth, now pray to God as Father and Son. The verb

[16] These requests are called wishes since the verbs in these three verses are in the optative mood. Each verb is translated with the helper "may" to aid English speakers catch the thrust of the Greek optative mood.

[17] "Our God and Father Himself and our Lord Jesus" is the compound subject of a singular verb (*kateuthunai*, "may [He] direct"). While it is true that the verb following a compound subject usually agrees with the nearest antecedent, it is also very likely that the construction here is a clear indication of the unity of the Godhead. Jesus Himself taught that He and the Father were one (John 5:17,19; 10:30,38), and because of that oneness that it was His prerogative to hear and answer prayer (John 14:13,14).

[18] After saying "another just like it" (Matthew 22:39), when Jesus asks about whose son is Messiah, the thrust of His question, connected with His answer to the question about the greatest commandment, is that just as there can be the Father in heaven, there can be another "just like Him" on earth. Messiah was predicted to be one of the members of the Godhead in the flesh.

"direct" reflects the idea that divine providence is active in directing human actions. Perhaps verses like Psalm 37:23 which says, "The steps of a man are established (LXX, "directed") by the LORD, and He delights in his way," were in Paul's mind. At present there were barriers to the missionaries' return to Thessalonica. Their prayer asks both Father and Son together[19] to have a part in removing those barriers so the missionaries can come straight to the Christians without having to take a round-about course or deal with a multitude of detours or false starts. We have no direct information whether this wish-prayer was ever realized. Paul most likely did visit Thessalonica when passing through Macedonia on his third missionary journey (Acts 19:21 and 20:3). But there is no record that he and Silas together ever had the opportunity to return there to complete what was lacking in new Christians' faith. A possible reconstruction of events has the evangelist Timothy being given the responsibility for delivering the second letter to Thessalonica, and then staying at Thessalonica to carry out the needed further teaching.

3:12 – *and may the Lord cause you to increase and abound in love for one another, and for all people, just as we also* **do** *for you;*

And may the Lord cause you to increase and abound in love – Paul's first wish-prayer was for the missionaries to be able to return to Thessalonica. Here begins their wish-prayers for the Christians themselves at Thessalonica. Since Jesus was called "Lord" in verse 11, we may assume that He is the Lord of this verse as well.[20] This verse has every appearance of being a prayer addressed to Jesus.[21] The Thessalonians already are known for their love (1 Thessalonians 4:9,10), but the writers wish for them to love more and more. The two verbs "increase" and "abound" picture first a progress of growth in love, and then of a state of overflowing abundance to which that progress will bring them.

For one another, and for all people – "One another" would be fellow Christians, and "all people" would be all mankind in general. The New Testament places a special emphasis on loving our Christian brothers and sisters (John 13:34,35; Romans 13:8; 1 Thessalonians 4:9; 1 Peter 1:22; 1 John 3:11,23). But it is also true that if God so loved the world (John 3:16), His children should do likewise. Jesus certainly taught a broad concept of who is one's neighbor (Matthew 5:43-48; Luke 10:25-37) when He taught His followers to love their neighbors.

Just as we also *do* **for you** – We mentally supply the verb "abound" to complete this clause. The missionaries' Christlike devotion to the Thessalonians constituted an example of the love they recommend the Thessalonians to emulate.[22]

---

[19] The Pauline view identifies Jesus as "Lord," who is now exalted to the right hand of the Father. As "Lord" He is involved in the government of the world, ordering everything for the promotion of His kingdom.

[20] Because the Holy Spirit is called "Lord" at 2 Thessalonians 3:5 and 2 Corinthians 3:17, the commentaries by Jamison, Fausset, and Brown propose that the third member of the Godhead is intended at this verse.

[21] Jesus indicated that prayers would be addressed to Him (John 14:14), and at Acts 1:24 and 7:59 we have two specific examples of prayers addressed to Jesus.

[22] Hayden, *op. cit.*, p.243.

3:13 – *so that He may establish your hearts without blame in holiness before our God and Father at the coming of our Lord Jesus with all His saints.*

So that He may establish your hearts without blame in holiness – "So that" indicates that this verse is intended to highlight the goal of this wish-prayer for the Thessalonians. If they abound in love for the brethren and for all men, they will be ready for the accounting which they must make to God at the final judgment. "As in 2:4, the heart is not only the seat of understanding and will, but the place where the hidden motives of life and conduct take shape."[23] "Without blame" indicates there could be no sustainable "charge" or "accusation" against them about a lack of holiness. *Hagiōsunē* ("holiness") conveys the idea of being set apart for sacred service. Such sacred service, motivated by love, was practiced in ministry to the sick, the sorrowing, the hungry, and the homeless (Matthew 25:31-46). Where love is lacking, selfishness drives a person's life, and there are no such practical expressions of love as would allow Jesus, at the final judgment, to treat that person as blameless in holiness. "Establish as blameless" is something Jesus does. *Stērixai* ("establish") is an aorist optative; it pictures a one-time act. It seems to say that at the final judgment (at the *parousia*) Jesus, as the judge, will have the privilege of speaking to the Father about the Christian being without blame in the matter of holiness.

Before our God and Father – The day when it will be vitally important to be "without blame in holiness" is the final judgment, which Paul here says will take place in the personal "presence of our God and Father." 2 Corinthians 5:10 tells of the "judgment seat of Christ," and at Matthew 25:34 Jesus indicated that He would be the judge. This passage in Thessalonians has the Father involved at the judgment. These are not contradictory ideas. The unity of Father and Son just indicated in verse 11 makes it possible for Father and Son both to be involved in concert at the judgment.

At the coming of our Lord Jesus with all His saints – The "coming" (*parousia*) of the Lord has already been introduced at 1 Thessalonians 2:19. At this coming, the degree to which Christians have attained blamelessness in holiness will be divinely scrutinized. But that is not all that will occur at the "coming". The next two chapters of Thessalonians will unfold some of the events connected with Christ's *parousia*. "With all His saints" pictures Jesus as being accompanied by "the saints" when His kingly visit (*parousia*) occurs.

"All the saints" translates *pantōn tōn hagiōn*. *Hagiōn* ("holy ones") is a plural masculine gender adjective. But since there is no noun to specify who the holy ones are, great caution is required as comments at this place are studied.

(1) In the Old Testament (Deuteronomy 33:2 compared with Hebrews 2:2 and Acts 7:53) "holy ones," (*kadoshim* in the Hebrew, *hagioi* LXX) refers to angels. Thus, one interpretation affirms that "holy ones" here in Thessalonians refers only to angels. But defenders of another view insist that in the New Testament the designation "holy ones" without any qualifying noun never refers to angels.

[23] Bruce, *op. cit.*, p.72.

(2) Another interpretation affirms that the "holy ones" are Christians who have died and gone to be with the Lord. Compare 1 Thessalonians 4:14 ("those who have fallen asleep in Jesus") and 1 Thessalonians 2:19 (which has the Thessalonian Christians present with Jesus at His coming). Defenders of a different view insist that "holy ones," if it applies to the redeemed at all, must include *all* of them – Old Testament and New Testament "holy ones" alike.

(3) A third interpretation notes that Scripture elsewhere has Jesus accompanied by both the holy angels (Mark 8:38; 2 Thessalonians 1:7) and by the souls of the redeemed (1 Thessalonians 4:14) as He returns. 2 Thessalonians 1:7-10 also has both angels and saints present when the Lord is revealed from Heaven at His second advent.

It appears most likely that the "holy ones" who accompany Christ at His *parousia* include both saints and angels.[24] Indeed, the angels will be involved in gathering from the four winds the elect who are then still living on earth (Mark 13:27). It looks like Paul is picturing the Thessalonians, for whom he is praying, as being among the "holy ones" who accompany Jesus when He returns.[25]

---

[24] In Revelation 19:14, the armies of heaven who accompany Jesus when He returns may include both saints and angels.

[25] Both this verse (3:13) and 1 Thessalonians 4:14-17 seem to be strong evidence there is a serious flaw in certain modern premillennial reconstructions of events at the end of this church age. Many modern premillennial interpreters follow W.E Blackstone's scenario (*Jesus is Coming*, p. 75) which has a *parousia* coming followed later by a *revelation* coming (the Greek word for "revelation" is *apokalupsis*). At the *parousia* coming, according to Blackstone's scenario, Jesus is said to come *for* the saints, and then He comes "*with* His saints" at the later *revelation* coming. What is faulty is that Blackstone uses 1 Thessalonians 3:13 when he speaks of the *revelation* coming, even though "coming" in that verse is *parousia*, not *apokalupsis*. Further, in 1 Thessalonians 4:14-17, when the saints come *with* Christ, the word translated "coming" again is *parousia*.

If it be insisted that we make a distinction between Christ's coming *with* the saints and His coming *for* the saints, a plausible explanation is that at the *parousia* Jesus comes *with* those of His saints who have died in Christ and whose souls have been with Jesus in heaven before the *parousia* (2 Corinthians 5:8) while at the same time He is coming *for* those saints still living on earth who are going to be caught up to meet the Lord in the air. It is this commentator's studied conclusion that the Scriptures present but one second coming of Christ.

IV. CALLS TO ACTION.   4:1 - 5:22

A. Exhortations About Living to Please God.   4:1-12

1. An exhortation to improve their keeping of the instructions learned from their missionaries.   4:1-2

4:1 – *Finally then, brethren, we request and exhort you in the Lord Jesus, that as you received from us instruction as to how you ought to walk and please God (just as you actually do walk), that you excel still more.*

Finally then, brethren – "Brethren" is in the vocative case.[1]   The following exhortations are addressed to the Christians at Thessalonica. "Then" (*oun*, "therefore") shows that what is about to be written is logically dependent on what has already been written. Because the writers desire that the readers will be found to be blameless in holiness (3:13) they now urge them to be still more earnest in their pursuit of Christian virtue.   More is needed than the prayers of the writers to accomplish this goal.   Careful observance of the exhortations which follow will help the readers to be blameless in holiness.   "Finally" may not be the best choice for an English equivalent for the Greek *loipon*, especially since we are just now in the middle of this letter to the Thessalonians.   "What remains [to be said]" or "Let me add this" (TLB) would be a better choice.

We request and exhort you in the Lord Jesus – "Request" translates a verb which means "to ask," and it looks as if the writers are asking this as a personal favor. "Exhort" is a stronger word which makes an appeal to the will of the person being spoken to. "In the Lord Jesus" might speak of the readers being united with Christ and thus it would be equal with "because you are Christians."   "In the Lord Jesus" might also be connected to the verb "exhort," in which case the writers are speaking these words of counsel as fellow-members of the body of Christ.[2]

That as you received from us instruction as to how you ought to walk and please God – When they were in Thessalonica, Paul and Silas had given verbal instructions to their converts.   Several times in this chapter (verses 1,2,6, and 11) reference is made to this previous on-site verbal instruction, which is now being repeated in written form.   The missionaries' teaching dealt with the kind of everyday living that will prepare one for the day when Jesus returns. "Ought" (*dei*) is a strong word which means "must" or "it is necessary."   There was no question of this walking and pleasing God being a matter of choice.   Rather, it is part and parcel of what it means to be a Christian.   When we surrender our lives to Christ, we take on the obligation to be like Him.   The figure "walk"

---

[1] The vocative case is used when making a direct address to someone.   "Brethren" was explained in comments at 1 Thessalonians 1:4.

[2] Some Bible readers suppose "in the Lord Jesus" speaks of the authority the missionaries have to lay down rules, but we judge that we should wait until verse 2 to speak about the authority that lies behind the missionaries' teaching.

(a present tense infinitive) suggests the Christian life should be marked by continual progress (i.e., spiritual growth).[3] "The Christian life is a *walk* because it is progress in a given direction."[4] "Please God" is another present tense infinitive, also picturing continuous action. Christians must conduct themselves in a holy manner if they wish to please and continue in the favor of the living and true God.[5]

(just as you actually do walk) – This parenthetical note guards against the readers drawing the false inference that they are being censured by what is here being exhorted. The writers are aware the Thessalonians are mindful of the instructions they had already received, and the present tense verb "do walk" indicates they are behaving accordingly. Perhaps this awareness of the Thessalonians' continuous Christian living stemmed from the report Timothy has brought, and perhaps that same report also indicated there were serious temptations to revert to old heathen lifestyles. This would account for this exhortation now given, urging the Thessalonians to keep working on bringing their lifestyle into harmony with the holiness that pleases God.

That you excel still more – "Excel" is a good choice to translate the present tense verb. It calls on the Thessalonians to keep making more and more effort to live in a fashion pleasing to God by following the directions they have learned from their Christian teachers. In the matter of living to please God there is no room for complacency or being satisfied with past accomplishments. There must be continual improvement.

4:2 – *For you know what commandments we gave you by* **the authority of** *the Lord Jesus.*

For you know what commandments we gave you – This verse, beginning with "for," is intended to give a reason why they should do even more when it comes to following the directions given them by Paul and Silas. The "commandments"[6] referred to in this context are concerned with Christian living. "You know" serves to call on the Thessalonians to recollect what they had heard the missionaries teach.

By *the authority of* **the Lord Jesus** – This clause indicates that the instructions given by Paul and Silas did not originate with themselves, but there is some uncertainty concerning exactly what is being claimed. The NASB translators added the words "the authority of" because they understood the phrase to mean that when the missionaries spoke they spoke

---

[3] The verb "walk" being used to refer to one's behavior has been explained at 1 Thessalonians 2:12.

[4] Don DeWelt, *Standard Lesson Commentary 1972-73* (Cincinnati: Standard Publishing Company, 1972), p.60.

[5] The abiding necessity of pleasing God is the controlling thought behind several passages in 1 Thessalonians. At 1 Thessalonians 2:4 Paul spoke of himself and Silas as governed in their work by the thought of "pleasing God." In 1 Thessalonians 2:15, the condemnation of certain Jewish opponents is found in the fact that they were "not pleasing God."

[6] *Parangelias* ("commandments"), often used in a military context, signifies the public deliverance of an order being passed from one to another (cf. Acts 5:28; 16:24; 1 Timothy 1:5,8).

with the authority of Christ who sent them. The translators of the ASV made the phrase to read simply "through the Lord Jesus" because they understood the Greek construction (*dia* followed by a genitive case) to refer to Jesus being the agent who acted for God in the transmission of the orders from God to the missionaries, who in turn delivered them to the Thessalonians.

2. An exhortation to sexual purity. 4:3-8

4:3 – *For this is the will of God, your sanctification;* **that is,** *that you abstain from sexual immorality;*

For this is the will of God, your sanctification – "For" serves to introduce a needed example of the instructions which Paul and Silas wish them to recall. Since "your sanctification" stands in apposition to "this," the translation could well read "For this, namely your sanctification, is the will of God." "Sanctification," which is one of the "commandments ... through the Lord Jesus" (verse 2), is here called "the will of God," i.e., it is a thing which God wills.[7] The fact that in the Greek there is no article before *thelēma* ("will") indicates there is more to what God wills than the one area of sanctification being indicated here. "Sanctification" translates the Greek word *hagiasmos*.[8] If "holiness" (*hagiosunē*, 3:13) is the state of being holy, "sanctification" (*hagiasmos*) is the process that results in being holy. In Romans 6:22 it is affirmed that the outcome of "sanctification" is eternal life. In Hebrews 12:14, the exhortation to Christians is to "pursue sanctification without which no one will see the Lord." 1 Thessalonians 4:3-6, which form a single sentence in the Greek, contains four infinitive phrases which highlight some of the specific behaviors involved in this "sanctification."

That is, **that you abstain from sexual immorality** – The Greek verb translated "abstain," a present tense middle voice infinitive, is the first of these specific behaviors involved in this process of "sanctification." The present tense calls for continuing action (i.e., total abstinence) and the middle voice makes this something the Christian does for his own benefit. "You" is plural in the Greek and so includes each and every reader addressed in this letter. "Sexual immorality" is a glaring opposite of sanctification. The Greek word here translated "sexual immorality" is *porneia*, a word covers all types of sexual sins. In fact, the word is the basis for our term "pornography," which depicts and promotes *porneia*, both mentally and physically. Such *porneia* was a major component of pagan religion, not only in Corinth, the city from which the letters to Thessalonian were written, but in most ancient towns and cities. Christians may not for a moment compromise with this im-

---

[7] "The will of God may be seen at two levels: what He *determines* and what He *desires*. We cannot change what He determines, but we can thwart His desires for us by our own rebellious choices." (Hayden, *op. cit.*, p.244.)

[8] *Hagiasmos* was sometimes translated as "holiness" and sometimes as "sanctification" in the KJV, but in the NASB is translated "sanctification" (Romans 6:19,22; 1 Corinthians 1:30; 1 Thessalonians 4:7; 2 Thessalonians 2:13; Hebrews 12:14), or "sanctity" (1 Timothy 2:15), or "sanctifying" (1 Peter 1:2).

moral lifestyle.   When Paul and Silas emphasized this behavioral standard as they evangelized Thessalonica, they were carrying out a Spirit-led mandate.   About a year previous, the Holy Spirit (Acts 15:28) had led apostles at the Jerusalem Conference to set forth God's expectations of Gentile converts, and one of these expectations was to avoid sexual immorality (Acts 15:20,29).   Paul was one of the apostles who helped promulgate that decree, and Silas was one of the two prophets appointed by the leaders at Jerusalem to carry the letter containing this decree to the church at Antioch and to others.

4:4 – *that each of you know how to possess his own vessel in sanctification and honor,*

That each of you know how to possess his own vessel – By changing from the plural "you" of the previous verse to the singular "you" here, the exhortation about to be stated is made extremely personal.   The infinitive "know" indicates that the behavior now being emphasized is something that can be learned; this is the second of the specific behaviors involved in this process of "sanctification."   "Possess his own vessel" is the third of these infinitive phrases which describe the "sanctification" process, and through the years this phrase has been given two interpretations.   (1) In classical Greek, the verb *ktaomai* in the perfect and pluperfect tenses means "to acquire."   So it is proposed that the infinitive here, *ktasthai*, may be translated "acquire," and then with 1 Peter 3:7 in mind, which speaks of the wife as being the "weaker vessel," "vessel" here in Thessalonians has been explained as meaning "wife."   The verse then becomes Paul's instructions about how a man should acquire a wife for himself, rather than going the route of immorality to satisfy sexual desires.[9]   (2) The second interpretation, which this commentator judges to be correct, calls attention to the fact that *ktasthai* in the present tense does have the meaning "possess." The present tense also conveys the idea that there is a process involved in gaining possession, or gaining control.   Then, with 2 Corinthians 4:7 ("this treasure in earthen vessels") in mind, the word "vessel" is interpreted to mean the physical body which is a vehicle for the inner self.   This verse then becomes a general instruction to both men and women as to how they should conduct themselves sexually.[10]   They are to learn to gain control of the desires of their bodies and not resort to immorality.

In sanctification and honor – "Sanctification" translates *hagiasmos,* and as in verse 3 it is a process of making holy.   A man or woman who considers that the physical body is a vessel that is to be consecrated to the service of the Lord will dread polluting it in any way. It is implied that Christians do not become "saints" (in the popular sense) overnight; rather, sanctification is something to be worked at as long as we are in these physical bodies. Romans 6:19 encourages Christians to present their bodily members as slaves to righteousness, which will result in sanctification.   Christians also understand they are to honor God with their bodies, and not be involved in "dishonoring their bodies with one another" (Ro-

---

[9] TEV's translation, which reads "each of you men should know how to live with his wife ...," thrusts at the English reader an interpretation which the Greek does not actually say.   *Ktasthai* hardly means "live with," and it is not easy to justify the addition of "men."

[10] The NIV at 1 Thessalonians reads 4:4 "that each of you should learn to control his own body ...." This appears to be the better way to understand the verse.

mans 1:24).   Hebrews 13:4 affirms that "marriage is to be held in honor among all, and the marriage bed is to be undefiled; for fornicators and adulterers God will judge."   A Christian's body belongs to the Lord, and must be used in a way that glorifies Him (1 Corinthians 6:20).

4:5 – *not in lustful passion, like the Gentiles who do not know God;*

Not in lustful passion – Both words here translated as "lustful passion" occur in Galatians 5:24: "Those who belong to Christ Jesus have crucified the flesh with its passions (*pathēmasin*) and desires (*epithumiais*)."[11]   Romans 7:5 describes "sinful passions" as being "at work in the members of our body" and the verse also says that they "bear fruit for death."   Christians are called on to master those desires and passions.   This "not … passioning" is involved in the "sanctification and honor" that is part of "possessing" our vessels correctly.

Like the Gentiles who do not know God – The Gentiles are pictured as being mastered by their sexual passions and desires, exercising little self-control.   The unconverted Gentiles behaved as they did because they do not know the "living and true God" (1 Thessalonians 1:9).   "Their behavior is explained by their ignorance but it is not excused by it.   In Romans 1:28, the heathens' ignorance of God is not due to any lack of data but to their deliberately ignoring God (cf. 2 Thessalonians 1:8)."[12]

> In a society filled with various abuses of God's precious gift of sex, the gospel called men and women to lives of purity and faithfulness, both to God and to spouse.   Needless to say, Paul's teaching possesses great relevance to modern society, which seems obsessed at times with "passionate lust."   This is an area where Christians must determine to live differently from those who know not God.[13]

4:6 – *and that no man transgress and defraud his brother in the matter because the Lord is the avenger in all these things, just as we also told you before and solemnly warned you.*

And that no man transgress and defraud his brother in the matter – Since verses 3 to 6 are one long sentence in the Greek, the topic of this verse would be the same topic as in the earlier verses, and "the matter" is thus the same one that has already been under discussion, namely the matter of sexual relationships.   The Greek word translated "transgress" pictures crossing a boundary – here of going beyond the bounds of what is right in the eyes of God.   The word translated "defraud" is sometimes translated "to covet" for it means to want something one has no right to take or possess.   In this context

---

[11] The KJV translators chose "lust of concupiscence" to translate the Greek at this place. "Concupiscence" comes from the same word that is the basis of the name Cupid, the Roman god of sexual love.

[12] Williams, *op. cit.*, p.73.

[13] Hayden, *op. cit.*, p.244.

it speaks of lusting for sexual relations with a person who belongs to someone else.[14] "Brother" is often used to indicate a fellow Christian, but in this context it may be a brother in Adam, for it would hardly be correct to limit it to a fellow Christian and then to affirm that a Christian could act toward a pagan in this matter in a way different from how he acted toward his brother or sister in Christ. "Not ... transgressing" is the last of the specific behaviors involved in the process of "sanctification" Paul highlights in verses 3-6.

Because the Lord is the avenger in all these things – The sentence begun in verse 3 closes with a warning which at the same time serves as a reason for complying with the standards set forth in verses 4-5. The use of the word "avenger" reflects the Biblical idea of retributive justice, whereby the person guilty of a sin was punished in proportion to the crime which had been committed. This warning about the Lord being the avenger likely refers to what will occur at the final judgment, when the Lord Jesus has a role in dealing out God's justice (2 Thessalonians 1:7,8). At that time, one of the things Jesus will take account of is sexual morality. He will act on behalf of the persons who have been cheated, and also in reprisal for the commandments violated.

Just as we also told you before and solemnly warned you – This teaching about the coming judgment and the fact that sexual morality was one of the things to be judged was not new to the Thessalonians. It was part of the instruction given to them when Paul and Silas were preaching in their city. In fact, the two verbs here used ("told before" and "solemnly warned") indicate it was a topic that was emphasized. It is not true that sinners will escape eternal punishment simply because they can "get away with it" on the earth.

4:7 – *For God has not called us for the purpose of impurity, but in sanctification.*

For God has not called us for the purpose of impurity – It looks like verses 7 and 8 (which begin with "for" and "so") are intended as a reason why the Thessalonians should respond in a positive fashion to this appeal for sexual purity. "Impurity" (*akatharsia*) here is moral laxity or immoral behavior.[15] The aorist tense verb "called" points back to the time of their conversion. God calls us to become Christians through the gospel (2 Thessalonians 2:14). When God invites us through the gospel to become Christians, it is not an invitation to a life of immorality. It is rather an invitation to leave the old immoral lifestyle behind.

But in sanctification – "Sanctification" here is the same one translated "sanctification" in verse 3. It denotes a process carried on during the Christian's whole life here on earth. Sexual license is one behavior that is diametrically opposite the sanctification God looks for in His children. Sexual license stifles and stops sanctification from happening.

---

[14] Greek terms cognate to the verb translated "defraud" occur in close association with words denoting fornication or impurity at Ephesians 4:19 and 5:3,5.

[15] The use of the word "impurity" in this verse indicates the subject is still sexual and tends to confirm the conclusion in verse 6 that the subject there ("defraud") is sexual behavior rather than covetousness for material riches.

4:8 – *So, he who rejects* **this** *is not rejecting man but the God who gives His Holy Spirit to* **you.**

So, he who rejects *this* -- The emphatic Greek compound particle *toigaroun* introduces the serious consequence of rejecting what has just been written about sexual purity. The verb translated "rejects" means to treat as insignificant, to disregard, to treat as of no account. The verb was sometimes used of disregarding or annulling legal documents such as a will (Galatians 3:15). What is being rejected, in this context, is what has just been written in verses 3-6 about avoiding immorality.

Is not rejecting man – Paul and Silas were men, but here is a claim that when they spoke or wrote words such as we have in this letter, they were speaking by inspiration of the Holy Spirit. They were acting as God's mouthpieces when they wrote what they have just written.

But the God who gives His Holy Spirit to you – God is the giver of the commands about sexual immorality. Thus, to despise or reject the command against sexual irregularity is to flout God, not simply to disregard man. The NASB translators have left untranslated the conjunction *kai*, which in this case means "also." The conjunction stands between the words "who" and "gives." Not only did God give the Holy Spirit to Paul and Silas so they could speak by inspiration, but He *also* gave the Holy Spirit to the readers to help them live the Christian life.[16] One of the ways the Spirit works to help Christians is through the Word. If the Thessalonians disregard what has been written by God's messengers, they are hindering the Spirit from giving the help and guidance He otherwise could give in this matter of Christian living. The present tense verb "gives"[17] matches the truth that when each person becomes a Christian, he or she receives the Holy Spirit (Acts 2:38). Such giving by God goes on all through the church age. 1 Corinthians 6:19 tells us that the Christian's body (the very "vessel" with which sexual sin is committed) is the dwelling place of the Holy Spirit. The word "holy" in the Greek text is very emphatically put: "Who also gives His Spirit, His *Holy* Spirit, to you." This word order brings out the startling contrast between using the body for foul purposes and the holiness of the indwelling guest who is anxious to help each Christian progress toward sanctification. Romans 6:12,13,22 speak to the same wonderful truth that careful living as the Spirit prompts results in sanctification.

3. An Exhortation to brotherly love. 4:9-12

4:9 -- *Now as to the love of the brethren, you have no need* **for** anyone *to write to you, for* *you yourselves are taught by God to love one another;*

---

[16] The Greek manuscripts which read as the KJV does, "hath also given unto us His holy Spirit," makes this whole verse a claim to inspiration. However, that reading is not as well-attested as the one which reads "to you." The uncials Vaticanus and Alexandrinus omit the *kai* and thus some recent UBS Greek texts enclose the word in brackets.

[17] The better attested text has a present tense verb, rather than the past tense "hath given" found in the Received Text behind KJV.

Now as to the love of the brethren – For some reason the writers now return to a subject initially introduced in 3:12 – the practice of Christian love.   The Greek words *peri de* are here translated "now"; at 1 Corinthians 7:1 the same Greek words are translated "now concerning".   In that place they take up a subject about which the Corinthians had asked in a letter sent to Paul.   Perhaps in this Thessalonian passage they represent a question that Timothy, as he reported to Paul, has indicated the Thessalonians were asking.   The word for "love of the brethren" is *philadelphia*, and is a different kind of "love" than the *agapē* written about in 3:12.   Brotherly love is the special affection Christians have for other Christians, who are members of the same family.   When we take into consideration how this short exhortation (verses 9–12) is concluded, it begins to look like some of the Thessalonians were taking advantage of their Christian family's love by expecting them to supply living necessities when, instead, the folk making such demands should have been working to support themselves and others.

You have no need *for anyone* **to write to you** – The virtue of brotherly love is regularly taught in Scripture (Romans 12:10; Hebrews 13:1; 1 Peter 1:22; 2 Peter 1:7; 1 John 3:14).[18] The Thessalonians had no need for such instruction because they had already been made aware of God's expectation that they practice brotherly love; indeed, they were actively practicing it (4:10).   Still, the question arises, If folk are taking advantage of your brotherly love, how long and how far is the Christian expected to go?   Some guidelines to help the Thessalonians decide such questions are about to be given by the writers.

For you yourselves are taught by God to love one another – Here is explained why there is no need for Paul and Silas to write on the subject of brotherly love.   This is the only occurrence of *theodidaktos* ("taught by God") in the New Testament.   In fact, this is the word's earliest occurrence in Greek literature, suggesting that perhaps Paul coined the word.   The present tense verb "are" suggests this is a recurring experience for the Thessalonians even after Paul and Silas left Thessalonica.   It is difficult to decide if "God" in *theodidaktos* is a reference to Jesus (who taught His followers to love their brethren) or if it is a reference to the Holy Spirit (whose work was just alluded to in verse 8).[19]   The word for "love" in this clause is *agapē*, not *philadelphia*.   *Agapē* love is the willed behavior that deliberately does what is spiritually best for the other person.

4:10 – *for indeed you do practice it toward all the brethren who are in all Macedonia.   But we urge you, brethren, to excel still more,*

For indeed you do practice it toward all the brethren who are in all Macedonia – The

---

[18] A few manuscripts read "we have no need to write to you" while the better attested reading requires us to supply something like "for us" or "for anyone" as the subject of the infinitive "to write."

[19] "Taught of God" does not necessarily mean that God had spoken to them directly.   They had received God's teaching through the preachers who had labored among them.   Even 1 John 2:20,27 do not teach the direct operation of the Holy Spirit on men's hearts, but rather the word translated "anointing" emphasizes the *result* of an anointing, such as the apostles received which enabled them to speak God's words as He wanted them spoken.

nearest antecedent to "it" indicates that it is *agapē* love that the Thessalonian Christians have been practicing. This phrase seems to say the Thessalonian Christians have made efforts to provide the necessities of living to their Christian brethren in the province of Macedonia, many of whom were poor (2 Corinthians 8:2).

But we urge you, brethren, to excel still more – "To excel" is a present infinitive. To excel at love such as verses 9 and 10 have described is, like sanctification (3:13), a process susceptible to constant improvement. "A few years later, Paul would write to the Christians in Corinth, calling their attention to the relatively poor churches in Macedonia who were demonstrating an overflowing generosity toward their still poorer brethren in Judea (2 Corinthians 8:1-7). The writers' exhortation toward continual growth in love was not in vain."[20]

4:11 – *and to make it your ambition to lead a quiet life and attend to your own business and work with your hands, just as we commanded you,*

And to make it your ambition to lead a quiet life – "And" plus the infinitive "to make it your ambition" tie verses 11-12 to the verb "we urge you." The infinitive *philotimeisthai* ("make it your ambition") could also be translated "make it a point of honor" or "consider it a matter of honor." Three infinitive phrases follow, each of which identifies a goal on which they should set their ambition. The first infinitive phrase, "to lead a quiet life," likely means "to avoid taking advantage of brother-love." Perhaps the disquiet was triggered by some idle Christians who were demanding that others take care of them.[21] Constant demands for financial help might be the opposite of a "quiet life." Bad conduct by any individual in the congregation can make brotherly love more difficult to practice for the person who is being taken advantage of.

And attend to your own business – This is a second goal which the Thessalonians were to make a point of honor. Another present tense infinitive indicates "attending to your own business" was to be their constant practice. To "mind your own business" is an idiom of wide meaning. Here it is an appeal to Christians to take responsibility for their own financial support, rather than expecting others always to take care of them.

And work with your hands – All the infinitives in this verse, *lead*, *attend*, and *work*, like *do* in verse 10, imply activity over a period of time. Working with their own hands to earn a living so they will not have to depend on others for their needs and also to be able to help those who are unable to provide for themselves, is what is here encouraged. Paul does not present the Christian life as one of withdrawn contemplation. None who are physically able to support themselves have a right to expect others to provide their needs.

---

[20] Hayden, *op. cit.*, p.245.

[21] The plea for quietness in 2 Thessalonians 3:12 may show that 2 Thessalonians 3:6-12 is the place to go for an information concerning what caused Paul to give this exhortation.

Just as we commanded you – When they were in Thessalonica, Paul and Silas had already commanded the same three things he has just written about self-reliance and employment. Greek culture tended to downgrade manual labor. Had Paul and Silas observed a tendency among the new converts to let others do the hard work? The verb translated "commanded" is from the same family of words as "commandments" in 1 Thessalonians 4:2. Paul and Silas were passing along commands from their great commander Jesus Christ.

4:12 – *so that you will behave properly toward outsiders and not be in any need.*

So that you will behave properly toward outsiders – At least two desirable results would come from the kind of daily diligence just prescribed. "Behave properly" is an attempt to translate the Greek adverb *euschēmonōs* which literally means "in good form." It means to live in such a way as to bring honor or credit to Christianity. Christians endeavor to live winsome lives so folk outside the Christian brotherhood will be more likely to respect what they see the Christians doing. If outsiders saw that Christianity led to sloth and poverty, Christianity quickly would be discredited in their estimation.

> The special point being stressed here, of course, is what has just gone before in verse 11. The industry, restraint, and integrity of the Christian is the kind of action that cannot be criticized and must bring appreciation. The idea that any follower of Christ should have a poor credit rating is unthinkable. All obligations of a business and financial nature that a Christian freely assumes ought to be unfailingly met – unless, of course, some catastrophic illness or tragedy intervenes. It is important to be respected by non-Christians. However, it is wrong to make that respect such a number-one priority that we qualify or play down aspects of our Christian commitment. When their respect is gained because of our reliability, honesty, modesty, courtesy, etc., this is right. Respect achieved by faithfulness is to be commended, while popularity won by compromise is to be deplored.[22]

And not be in any need – This is the second desired result of Christians being industrious. The Greek can be translated either "that you may have need of no one" or "that you may have need of nothing."[23] If the word is masculine it is an abuse of brotherly love that is being condemned. (Note, Paul is not talking about a person who has fallen prey to illness or accident who must depend on others for help.) If the word is neuter, then what Paul writes here is similar to what he will write in a later letter to Ephesus, in which he urges Christians to work with their hands at what is a good job, so that they will have something to share with those who are in need (Ephesians 4:28). Working with one's own hands will put the Christian in possession of what is necessary for life, whereas idleness necessarily involves poverty and dependence on others. The Christian must not be a parasite, taking his living from the labors of others.

---

[22] VanBuren, *1977-78*, p.388.

[23] *Mēdenos* can be either masculine or neuter.

B. Exhortations Concerning the Second Coming of Christ. 4:13 - 5:11

1. Encouraging words concerning Christians who have already died. 4:13-18

4:13 – But we do not want you to be uninformed, brethren, about those who are asleep, so that you will not grieve as do the rest who have no hope.

But we do not want you to be uninformed, brethren, about those who are asleep – Although this subsection is not introduced by *peri de* like those immediately preceding and following (4:9; 5:1), its contents make it highly probable that it is dealing with a question which Timothy has reported (3:6) was troubling some of the members of the church at Thessalonica. The correct reading at this place is the plural pronoun "we" rather than the singular "I" found in the KJV. Paul and Silas are in harmony as they write on the following subject. It is difficult to decide whether "we do not want you to be uninformed" is an attempt to correct false impressions (as the expression likely means in Romans 11:25; 1 Corinthians 10:1; and 12:1) or whether the verses following are introducing new pieces of information (as is likely the meaning in Romans 1:13). Either way, the expression tends to emphasize that what follows is something important for them to know. The use of "sleep" or "asleep" as a euphemism for physical death was commonplace in Bible times. In the Old Testament one reads the expression "slept with his fathers and was buried" (1 Kings 2:10), and Jesus Himself spoke of Lazarus being asleep when He was telling His disciples about that man's physical death (John 11:11-14). The present-tense participle translated "are asleep" pictures that from time to time, since the missionaries left Thessalonica, some Christians had died physically.[24] When the missionaries were in Thessalonica, they had talked about Christ's second coming (1 Thessalonians 2:19), but perhaps in that short time no Christians had died, so the question of what happens to the Christian dead was never raised.

So that you will not grieve as do the rest who have no hope – Here is the reason Paul and Silas want the readers to be informed. Christians have a hope of life beyond the grave, something the unbelievers in general ("the rest") do not have. As most pagans saw it, there was no hope at all for the dead body, and no substantial hope for the departed soul. Without hope of life beyond the grave, people viewed death as a sleep from which there is no awakening. Their poets and playwrights spoke of "one unending night to be slept through"[25] or "one unbroken night of sleep."[26] With a correct understanding of what happens to those who are asleep, when their loved ones die the Christian will not sorrow

---

[24] There is a manuscript variation here. The Textus Receptus has a perfect tense participle, but the older manuscripts have a present tense participle. "This figure of speech [asleep] is suggested by the similarity in appearance between those sleeping people and dead bodies. It does not imply that the dead have no consciousness beyond the grave, what some call 'soul sleep.' Paul will make that clear in verse 14 and other passages (2 Corinthians 5:1-10; Philippians 1:20-23)." (Weatherly, *op. cit.*, p.291.)

[25] Catallus 5:4-6.

[26] Aeschylus, *Eumenides* 651.

or grieve like folk who have no hope sorrow and grieve at such times. Not all sorrow or mourning when friends or loved ones die is forbidden to the Christian, but the fact that it is not a hopeless sorrow or mourning changes its tenor.

> Paul's remark about "sorrow" must be carefully understood. He does not criticize the Thessalonians Christians for the natural sadness that they feel over the death of fellow Christians (cf. Philippians 2:27). Rather, their grief is not to be like the grief of pagans, who have no hope of ever seeing their deceased loved ones again. When Christians lose a fellow Christian to death, they will grieve the loss as they feel the void that has been left in their lives. But their grief will be tempered by the assurance that God will reunite them.[27]

4:14 – *For if we believe that Jesus died and rose again, even so God will bring with Him those who have fallen asleep in Jesus.*

For if we believe that Jesus died and rose again – "For" introduces the reason Christians should not grieve as non-Christians do. That reason rests on the events of Jesus' death and resurrection and return. The New Testament language has two words for "if." The word Paul uses here expresses a positive assumption. His meaning is, "Since we believe" or "If we believe – and we do – that Jesus died ...." Jesus' death has already been alluded to in 1 Thessalonians 1:10 and 2:15, and His resurrection has already been mentioned in 1:10. Both the death and the resurrection of the Messiah were predicted by the Old Testament prophets (1 Corinthians 15:3,4), and in his first recorded sermon Peter affirmed that what was predicted had happened to Jesus the Christ (Acts 2:23,24). What is written about Jesus in this letter to the Thessalonians simply summarizes what had been known and publicized for over 20 years,[28] and is presented as irrefutable. Within a Greek world in which denials of any resurrection of dead bodies were common (cf. 1 Corinthians 15:12), whether writing to the Thessalonians or to the Corinthians, the Scripture writers spoke of Jesus' death and resurrection as being actual recognized historical facts. "Jesus did rise from the dead. That fact is so well-established that it cannot be doubted. See Paul's review of the evidence in 1 Corinthians 15:3-8, or read it in the closing chapters of the four Gospels and the opening of Acts."[29]

Even so God will bring with Him those who have fallen asleep in Jesus – Several profound truths are encapsulated in these few words. In the Greek, the word "God" stands

---

[27] Weatherly, *op. cit.*, p.291.

[28] The verb translated "raised" at 1 Thessalonians 1:10 was *egeiro*, while the verb used here in 4:14 for "rose" is *anhistēmi*. Just because the New Testament writers used two different verbs (*anhistēmi* and *egeiro*) when telling about the resurrection, this should not cause the facticity of the resurrection to be questioned. This is especially true where the verb is *anhistēmi*. *Anhistēmi* is the verb used when we are told (John 20:9 and Luke 24:46) the Scriptures taught He would rise from the dead. Furthermore, since Jesus Himself used *anhistēmi* when referring to His own resurrection (Mark 9:9), scholars are ill-advised to call attention to the different verbs used as they try to construct an argument questioning whether or not Jesus' dead body was raised from the dead. Nor should we be quick to postulate that, because *anhistēmi* occurs here, the writers are quoting some early creedal statement of the church.

[29] Orrin Root, *Standard Lesson Commentary 1984-85* (Cincinnati: Standard Publishing Company, 1989), p.67.

in the emphatic position. What God is doing is emphasized. "Even so" says God raised Jesus and God will do some wonderful things for the dead in Christ. God will see to it that these dead Christians will not miss the *parousia*. It is Christ's *parousia* coming (as introduced at 1 Thessalonians 3:13) that is in view in these verses here in chapter 4. Just as 3:13 had the holy ones accompanying Christ at His *parousia*, so "with Him" here in 4:14 pictures the souls of the dead in Christ as accompanying Him as He returns in His *parousia*. "Fallen asleep" (a euphemism for physical death) is an aorist tense participle which looks back at what happened before *parousia*. "With Him" also assumes the souls of the Christian dead and the risen Christ were together in the same place before it came time for His return. It is assumed that when the dead body is buried, the person's soul and spirit are not entombed with the body. "The body returns to the dust it was, the spirit to the God who gave it" (Ecclesiastes 12:7). For the Christian, to be "absent from body is to be at home with Lord" (2 Corinthians 5:8). Paul and Silas are telling their readers that Christians who have died physically are still real persons who are alive and active. The verses following here in 1 Thessalonians inform us that the disembodied souls who accompany Jesus at His *parousia* will be united quickly ("in a flash") with their glorified bodies after the resurrection of dead bodies has occurred. In their glorified bodies they will then be caught up to meet the Lord in the air, to remain with Him forever. The words "in Jesus" translate the preposition *dia* and the word "Jesus" in the genitive case. *Dia* and the genitive express the intermediate agent through whom something is done. Jesus is the intermediate agent whom God uses as He carries out His eternal plan. All through Scripture, what happened to Jesus becomes a model for what will happen to Christians. "Those who, in faith and repentance, were baptized into Christ share all things with Him. They share his death, His burial, His resurrection (Romans 6:3,4), His sufferings, and His glory (Romans 8:17). All who go with Him through all these experiences are with Him also in His return."[30] There is life after death. Some wonderful things are going to happen to those who have died physically before Christ returns. What has just been written is the kind of information that keeps Christians from grieving over lost loved ones like pagans who have no hope grieve.

4:15 – *For this we say to you by the word of the Lord, that we who are alive and remain until the coming of the Lord, will not precede those who have fallen asleep.*

For this we say to you by the word of the Lord – The beginning word in this clause, "for," indicates either that this verse is a reason for having no grief, or that it is an explanation which unfolds the details of what was claimed in verse 14. "This" points to the details which follow, while the "we" points again to Paul and Silas and Timothy (cf. 1:1). Though "Lord" is likely a reference to Jesus, we do not have enough information to decide what was being claimed when they write "by the word of the Lord."[31] (1) Perhaps the information here summarized can be found by appealing to such passages in the Gospels as Matthew 24:30,31; 25:1; 26:27; and Luke 14:14. (2) It could refer to something

---

[30] Tesh, *op. cit.*, p.363.

[31] It is certainly a mistake to search in apocryphal writings for the source of the words about to be written. Such writings would not have the irrefutable authority behind them which this context in 1 Thessalonians requires.

Jesus said during His earthly ministry but which is unrecorded elsewhere. (Cp. Jesus' words, "it is more blessed to give than receive," which were unrecorded elsewhere until Luke wrote Acts 20:35.) John 20:30 tells us that Jesus' teachings were far more extensive than the written records we possess in the canonical gospels. (3) It could refer to a special revelation given by Jesus, similar to those related in 2 Corinthians 12:1, Galatians 1:12 and 2:2. Paul was an apostle, and Silas was a prophet. Both would have had revelations directly given to them by the risen Lord. The fact of the divine origin of the truths about to be expressed was important to the Thessalonians' peace of mind.

That we who are alive and remain until the coming of the Lord – Beginning with this phrase and continuing probably through verse 17 we can read the teaching of "the word of the Lord" introduced in verse 15a.

One thing the word of the Lord indicated would be true is that there would be folk living on earth when the coming (*parousia*) of the Lord takes place. But just who is included in the "we" has been a matter of serious dispute.

- Before this verse, the plural "we" in 1 Thessalonians has most often been explained as meaning Paul and Silas and Timothy, though at 1 Thessalonians 3:4 "we" was used to refer to the Thessalonian Christians to whom this letter is addressed.
- Many commentators limit the "we" in this clause to the writers and readers, and then affirm that the writers and original readers were mistaken about the time of the second coming, thinking it would occur within their lifetimes. To draw such a conclusion from what is here written is replete with objectionable features.[32] Before accepting the suspicion that Paul may have written some mistaken ideas about the time of the second coming, there are some thoughts to consider. A fundamental rule of Biblical interpretation is to avoid taking any passage in isolation; rather, it is important to take all the verses on a subject. To suppose that in verse 15 Paul is affirming the second coming to be in his lifetime is an idea not readily harmonized with what is written just a few verses later in this same letter (5:1,2), where Paul insists on avoiding date-setting. In 4:15ff the writers are relating the contents of a special revelation from the Lord, so we would assume this revelation to be in harmony with what the Lord Himself said about not knowing the date or the hour of His coming (Matthew 24:36), which is the same point 1 Thessalonians 5:1 makes. Later in this same letter we have the phrase "whether we wake or sleep" (5:10), language which indicates Paul did not know whether the second coming would be in his lifetime or not. Indeed, in Paul's other writings, there is evidence that he did not know the time of the second coming. He sometimes writes as though he might be among the living (1 Corinthians 15:51), and sometimes among those who have died before the Lord returns (1 Corinthians 6:14; 2 Corinthians 4:14; 2 Timothy 4:6). Even 2 Thessalonians 2 does not leave the impression the return of the Lord is going to be soon after these letters were written.
- The likely explanation to be advocated is that the "we" in this passage refers in general

---

[32] To assert Paul here writes something that later history has shown was mistaken or in error impinges on the doctrine of inspiration and the authority and veracity of all his teaching. If Paul was wrong about the time of the second coming, it becomes appropriate to wonder how much else that he wrote is in error.

to folk like "us Christians."   Lightfoot noted that Paul's words could be paraphrased "When I say 'we,' I mean those [Christians] who are living, those who survive to that day."[33]   This would be in harmony with Jesus' parable of the wheat and tares which has righteous people living on earth when it comes time for the harvest at the end of the age (Matthew 13:29).
- The folk in view ("we") here in verse 15 are among the redeemed since verse 17 speaks of them being caught up to meet and then ever be with the Lord.

Will not precede those who have fallen asleep – With an emphatic double negative (*ou mē*) this phrase asserts that the Christians who have died are in no wise at a disadvantage to those who are living when the *parousia* occurs.   We suppose the reason the living have no advantage is because the old pagan philosophical ideas (verse 14) of what happens to body and soul are not true.   Instead, exactly what happens to those who have died is further elaborated in verses 16 and 17.

4:16 – *For the Lord Himself will descend from heaven with a shout, with the voice of the archangel and with the trumpet of God, and the dead in Christ will rise first.*

For – Verse 16 begins the explanation that the Christians living at the time of the second coming certainly have no advantage over those who have died.   Verse 16 explains what happens to those who have died, and then verse 17 tells what happens to those who are living.   There will be an order of events at the *parousia*.   Following are some of the events in that order.

The Lord Himself will descend from heaven – When God determines it is time for the *parousia*, it is King Jesus Himself who will be making the descent from heaven where He is now seated at the right hand of the majesty on high.   This descent is visible (Revelation 1:7, "every eye will see Him"), audible (1 Thessalonians 4:16,17), and majestic (2 Thessalonians 1:7, "with His mighty angels in flaming fire").   Other events will follow His descent: the resurrection, the rapture, the judgment (Matthew 25:31-46).   If the words "He shall so come in like manner as you beheld him going into heaven" (Acts 1:11) may be interpreted somewhat broadly, it would seem that the actual descent (as distinguished from the suddenness and unexpectedness of Christ's initial appearance) will be characterized by a kind of majestic leisureliness.

With a shout – The Greek word translated "shout" pictures the order which an officer shouts to his troops, or a hunter to his dogs, or a charioteer to his horses, or a ship-master to his rowers.   It is a command given by someone in authority.   Like Jesus called out with a loud voice at the resurrection of Lazarus (John 11:43), so the descending Jesus gives a shout that will literally wake the dead.[34]   John 5:25 tells us, "the dead shall hear the voice of the Son of God, and those who hear shall live."

---

[33] J.B. Lightfoot, *Notes on the Epistles of St. Paul* (Grand Rapids: Zondervan, 1957), p.66.

[34] Contrary to some modern premillennial scenarios concerning the *parousia* coming, it is certainly not a secret coming.

With the voice of the archangel – The word "archangel" (which means an angel who is ruler over other angels) occurs nowhere else in the New Testament, except in Jude 1:9, where it is applied to Michael. The Greek is indefinite, "an archangel" (rather than "the archangel"), which implies there is more than one archangel. In Daniel 10:13, Michael is called "one of the chief princes," and Jewish apocryphal literature gives the names of seven chief angels, who are called "watchers" – Uriel, Raphael, Raguel, Michael, Sariel [or Saraqael), Gabriel and Remiel [or Jeremiel].[35] Of these seven names, two are named in canonical Scripture – Michael and Gabriel.[36] A possible conjecture is that the "voice" is the order given by one of the rulers of the angels to the subordinate angels to "gather the harvest" (cp. Matthew 24:31).

With the trumpet of God – This phrase is united in the Greek with the previous one, so that, evidently, an archangel both speaks and sounds the trumpet. In the Old Testament times, when God "came down" as it were to meet his people, this meeting was announced by a trumpet blast (Exodus 19:16-19). Jesus Himself had spoken about this trumpet blast that would announce His return from Heaven at the second coming (Matthew 24:31). Paul gives further details in 1 Corinthians 15:51,52, "Behold, I tell you a mystery; we will not all sleep, but we will all be changed, in a moment, in the twinkling of an eye, at the last trumpet; for the trumpet will sound, and the dead will be raised imperishable, and we will be changed." In Revelation 11:15, the seventh of the angels "who stand before God" blows his trumpet, and there were loud voices in heaven, saying, "The kingdom of the world has become the kingdom of our Lord and of His Christ; and He will reign forever and ever," and that the time has come "for the dead to be judged."

And the dead in Christ will rise first – Far from those who have died being excluded from the *parousia*, their souls will accompany Jesus as He descends (4:14), and they will be the first participants in that grand event after the trumpet sounds. The contrast introduced by the adverb "first" is between those Christians who have died and those who are still living on earth (verse 17) when the Lord returns.[37] The same sequence of events is carefully observed in 1 Corinthians 15:52, "the trumpet will sound, and the dead will be raised imperishable, and we will be changed." Instead of what pagans thought happens to body and soul when a man dies, the Thessalonians are informed that the "word of the Lord" has made it explicit that the souls that have accompanied Jesus will be clothed upon

---

[35] 1 Enoch 20:1-7; 22:3; 4 Ezra 4:36. Since angels are called "spirits" in Hebrews 1:14, some Bible students have supposed that the "seven spirits" before the throne in Revelation 1:4 and 4:5 are archangels.

[36] Michael, the prince of the Jewish nation, is named at Daniel 10:13; 10:21; and 12:1. Gabriel, who stands before God, is named at Daniel 8:16; 9:21; Luke 1:19 and Luke 1:26.

[37] While "the dead in Christ will rise first" seems to describe the same thing as the "resurrection of the righteous" referred to in Luke 14:14, it is a misuse of the adverb "first" to immediately begin speaking about the resurrection of the wicked being a thousand years after the resurrection of the righteous (an idea some millennial scenarios have tried to force upon Scripture because of how they read Revelation 20:4-6). In this Thessalonians passage there is no contrast between the dead in Christ and the dead not in Christ. All that is here asserted is that the dead in Christ shall rise before the living in Christ shall be changed. In this passage there is no contrast between the dead in Christ and the dead not in Christ, nor any allusion to the resurrection of the wicked.

with glorious new spiritual bodies (see this in detail in 1 Corinthians 15:41-44[38]) before the believers who survive on earth will be changed into their glorified bodies (as vividly described in 1 Corinthians 15:51-53) and ascend to meet the Lord. Instead of those who have died in Christ being behind the survivors in advantages, it is the survivors who will have to wait a moment, as it were. And instead of the soul being in a dismal place like Hades, as some pagans thought, it has been with the Lord!

4:17 – *Then we who are alive and remain will be caught up together with them in the clouds to meet the Lord in the air, and so we shall always be with the Lord.*

Then we who are alive and remain – *Epeita* ("then") marks a succession in time, so that verse 17 tells us what will happen next in the order of events after the dead in Christ have risen from the dead. As explained at verse 15, "we who are alive and remain" indicates there will be Christians living on earth when the Lord returns in His *parousia*. What happens to the living, at the time of the second coming, is as much a truth taught by "the word of the Lord" as was what happens to the dead in Christ. Following the raising of the dead in Christ in their glorified bodies, the living Christians will be similarly "changed," and will no longer be subject to decay and death (1 Corinthians 15:51-53).

Will be caught up together with them – Christians still living when the *parousia* occurs and the dead in Christ who have been raised are on equal footing. The dead in Christ have not missed anything. Because the Greek word translated "caught up" was translated in the Latin version as *rapere*, this catching up has been given an English equivalent name, "the rapture." "Caught up" is a passive voice verb. The redeemed do not just float up of their own accord. Some power is exerted on them to cause them to rise. Perhaps the power by which all the redeemed are caught up is a result of the ministry of the angels who are sent to gather them (Matthew 13:30).

In the clouds to meet the Lord in the air – The word for meeting is the standard word used in the ancient world for a royal reception or a royal welcome given a returning conqueror or visiting dignitary. The Greek (*eis* plus an infinitive) shows this meeting is the purpose of being caught up. "In the air," as well as the numerous verses (Daniel 7:13; Matthew 24:30, 26:64; Acts 1:11; Revelation 1:7) which speak of Jesus coming on or in or with the clouds, seems to indicate that the meeting takes place in the region of the clouds, rather than indicating that the redeemed are grouped in such numbers as they ascend that they resemble clouds. Once the meeting has taken place, whether the returning Lord ever sets His foot on earth at all is a topic not covered in this passage. The analogy of escorting dignitaries on the remainder of their journey (cp. Matthew 25:6 where the bridal party meets the bridegroom in order to escort him to the bridal hall) might suggest that those who were caught up (namely, the redeemed newly raised from the dead and those who were still

---

[38] The bodies in which the souls of men live in this present world are described as "natural" bodies in 1 Corinthians 15:44. The Greek word translated "natural" is *psuchikon*. That is, men's bodies are suitable for a soul (*psuchē*) to inhabit and animate. The resurrection body is called "spiritual" (*pneumatikon*). That is, it is a body suitable for a spirit (*pneuma*) to inhabit and animate.

living on earth) will escort the Lord on the remainder of His journey to earth.[39]   On the other hand, Daniel 7:13 has the Lord going from the clouds to the throne of God.[40]

And so we shall always be with the Lord – The main thrust of this passage is that once the meeting has taken place, the believers and the Lord will never be separated.   Wherever Jesus is, there the believers will be!   Those who have died in Christ are at no disadvantage when compared with the survivors.   All will share the glories God has to offer through Jesus Christ.   "What a beautiful statement!   It is not to be for a time, or for a season, but forever.   Here is our hope of joy, fulfillment, victory, peace."[41]

4:18 – *Therefore comfort one another with these words.*

Therefore comfort one another with these words – The passage has now turned full circle.   Having begun with the objective that the readers not grieve hopelessly (verse13), the readers are now urged to use this information to encourage and comfort one another.[42] "One another" (*allēous*) is a reciprocal pronoun.   One Christian needs comfort today, another needs it tomorrow.   In proportion as we bear each other's burdens we all will encourage and comfort each other.   With these words from the Lord we not only comfort one another in our grief, we also encourage one another to live today in the assurance of eternity.

> "There's going to be a meeting in the air, in the sweet bye and bye,
> How I long to meet you over there, a way beyond the sky.
> Such singing you will hear, never heard by mortal ear,
> 'Twill be glorious I do declare.
> For God's own Son will be the honored one, at the meeting in the air."

---

[39] Zechariah 14:4 says "In that day His feet will stand on the Mount of Olives ...."   It is this commentator's conclusion that Zechariah 14:1-5 is an Old Testament prophecy of the AD 70 destruction of Jerusalem, rather than a reference to the second coming.   As Jesus had instructed them to flee (Matthew 24:16; Luke 21:21), the Christians fled over the Mount of Olives as they left the city.   We nowhere read in Scripture that Christ and the glorified believers will reign on the earth during a coming Millennium. Revelation 5:10, which has saints ruling on (or over) the earth, more likely refers to the new earth (in which righteousness dwells, 2 Peter 3:12) which follows the renovation of the universe.

[40] Does the whole retinue ascend to heaven or return to the earth?   Any answer given to this question will depend upon the total interpretation of New Testament eschatology adopted by the one giving the answer.   For example, Pre-tribulationists posit an ascension to heaven at the time of the *parousia* coming with a subsequent return to earth, seven years later, at what is alleged to be a "revelation" coming of the Lord.   Post-tribulationists hold that a descent to earth immediately follows this reunion of the believers with Christ.   The sequence of events highlighted here in 1 Thessalonians 4, that the saints will all experience, omits some details: the instantaneous change of the living into their glorified bodies, and a specific reference to the final judgment which follows the meeting in the air.   Nor does it tell where Jesus and the saints will be.

[41] VanBuren, *1977-78*, p.389.

[42] The word *parakaleō* has a range of meanings.   Both "comfort" (NASB) and "encourage" (ASV) have been found suitable in this context.

2. Further instruction about the day of the Lord.   5:1-11

5:1 – *Now as to the times and the epochs, brethren, you have no need of anything to be written to you.*

Now as to the times and the epochs, brethren – A natural question arises as we finish reading 4:14-17. "When is all this (i.e., the *parousia*, the rapture, the meeting in the air) going to take place?" It is likely that "times and epochs" is a Hebraism meaning, "How long until this happens?" and "Are there any precise events that will signal that the time for the *parousia* has arrived?"

You have no need of anything to be written to you – The reason nothing needs now to be written is not because the Thessalonians already knew when the Lord would come, but because when Paul and Silas were with them, they instructed the new believers that no one save the Father – not Paul, not Silas, not Jesus Himself – knew the time of Christ's return. The next verses give a short review of what they had been taught when the missionaries were still in Thessalonica.

5:2 – *For you yourselves know full well that the day of the Lord will come just like a thief in the night.*

For you yourselves know full well – "Full well" translates *akribōs*, a word that speaks of precision or exactness. The teaching given about the matter of the unknown time when the day of the Lord would come had been adequate, definite, and specific.

That the day of the Lord – As is usual in the New Testament, "the Lord" here means Jesus Christ. The expression "day of the Lord" maybe understood as a proper title. This designation occurs first in Joel (1:15; 2:1-2; and verses following) and then was used by Isaiah (2:12) and Ezekiel (13:5) to denote the epoch when God intervenes in history to judge Israel's enemies and vindicate His people. In verse 2, there is no "the" in the Greek, though there is an article at 2 Thessalonians 2:2.[1] The absence of the article tends to give a qualitative emphasis to the phrase – it is a day when who the Lord is will be made exceedingly obvious. He will be the One prominently in view by the host of the redeemed and prominently in view by those left behind when the rapture occurs (2 Thessalonians 1:10).[2] "*Day* of the Lord" here and elsewhere (1 Corinthians 1:8; 3:13; 2 Corinthians 1:14; Philippians 1:6,10; 2:16; and "that day," 2 Timothy 1:18) is not to be understood as a 24-hour day, but as a certain period of time. Scriptures indicate that not only the *parousia* and the resurrection and the rapture occur in this time, but many more events, including a renovation of the universe and the final judgment (Acts 17:31; 2 Peter 3:7,10-13), are involved.

---

[1] When one reads 2 Thessalonians 2:1,2 together, it seems to require that we treat the article ("the") in 2 Thessalonians 2:2 as an article of previous reference. That passage is dealing with the same "day of the Lord" that 1 Thessalonians 5 does.

[2] What happens to those left behind is vividly described in Revelation 19:11-21.

Will come just like a thief in the night – While He was on earth during His earthly ministry, Jesus Himself used this comparison to illustrate the unexpectedness of His coming (Matthew 24:43). In fact, over and over again as we read Jesus' eschatological sermon in Matthew 24:29-25:13, we hear Him saying that men will not know the day nor the hour the Lord is going to return.[3] It is probable that, when they were with the Thessalonians, Paul and Silas had repeated to them Christ's very words, including His injunction to be ready, because at such an hour when men are not thinking about it is when the Son of Man comes (Matthew 24:44). The verb *erchetai* translated "will come" is a present tense verb ("is coming") in the Greek. The present tense characterizes the coming as certain and as already on its way in God's management of history.

5:3 – *While they are saying, "Peace and safety!" then destruction will come upon them suddenly like labor pains upon a woman with child, and they will not escape.*

While they are saying, "Peace and safety!" – The contrast between "you, brethren" (verse 4) and "they" of this verse indicates that it is unbelievers who are saying "peace and safety." Perhaps "peace" speaks of no internal disquiet and "safety" speaks of a feeling of external security. "It is ungodly people who are saying in essence, 'peace and safety,' for all seems to be well. Their health seems good, their investments safe, and they and their friends are enjoying life. They give no thought whatsoever to the spiritual aspect of life, thinking that life will forever go on as it is now going."[4] Jesus pictured the false sense of security this way. He said (Matthew 24:37ff) that the world in general will be eating and drinking, buying and selling, building and planting, marrying and giving into marriage, when it is time for Jesus to come again. In themselves such things are not wrong, but when higher, spiritual needs are neglected, they are a curse and no longer a blessing.

Then destruction will come upon them suddenly – "The ungodly will not be caught up to meet the Lord in the air, as His people will be. They, the unbelievers, will find no hiding place when the earth and its works will be burned up (2 Peter 3:10). Sudden destruction will overwhelm the whole world, and they shall not escape."[5] "Will come" in this place translates *ephistatai*, a verb that means to close in upon. It, too, is a present tense whose meaning is similar to the present tense verb in verse 2. "Destruction" translates *olethros*, a word which in the New Testament always refers to destruction or depriva-

---

[3] This commentator has been accustomed to say that in contrast with the signs that preceded the near approach of the AD 70 destruction of Jerusalem (Matthew 24:4-26) there are no signs by which to predict the near approach of the second coming. 2 Thessalonians 2 will detail a few of the momentous things that must occur before the second coming, but not even these will help us to calculate on our calendars when Christ's return will be. As we read on here in 1 Thessalonians 5, we find in verse 3 that it is the ungodly who are surprised by the return of the Lord, while in verse 4 Christians who are not in darkness are not surprised. Perhaps when we say there are "no signs" for the near approach of the second coming, we mean no signs the wicked will pay attention to.

[4] Tesh, *op. cit.*, p.365.

[5] Root, *1984-85*, p.99.

tion or ruin caused by supernatural power.   The day of the Lord will be a disaster for those who do not believe in Him and do not await him expectantly.   In 2 Thessalonians 1:9 "destruction" is qualified by the prepositional phrase "*away from* the presence of the Lord." "Suddenly" translates *aiphnidios*, which means unforeseen or unexpected.   The only other time *aiphnidios* occurs in the New Testament is in Luke 21:34 (KJV), "Lest that day come upon you unawares."

Like labor pains upon a woman with child – The point of this comparison is its unavoidableness.   A woman with child knows her labor is coming.   It cannot be avoided. What will happen to the wicked cannot be avoided.

And they will not escape – The desperate attempt of the wicked and unprepared to escape punishment is also vividly portrayed in Revelation 6:12-17.   No one escapes!   The Greek has a double negative (not ever, never), emphasizing that unredeemed persons absolutely will not escape the destruction.

5:4 – But you, brethren, are not in darkness, that the day would overtake you like a thief;

But you, brethren, are not in darkness -- Now the Thessalonian Christians ("brethren") are told openly what has been implied previously.   The fearful aspects of Jesus' return exist only for unbelievers.   "Darkness" is used figuratively in this verse to describe spiritual ignorance that results from a failure to hear and heed what God has revealed through His Son Jesus Christ.

That the day would overtake you like a thief – Beginning with *hina* ("that") this clause expresses what would be the result if Christians were in darkness.   The day of the Lord would come on them as unexpectedly as it will on the unbelieving world.[6]   Christians are aware of the clear promises of Jesus' coming, and they prepare for it.   If He comes today, they are ready.

5:5 – for you are all sons of light and sons of day.   We are not of night nor of darkness;

For you are all sons of light and sons of day – "For" indicates this verse gives a reason why the day of the Lord will not suddenly overtake the believers like it will the wicked. "You ... all" continues the contrast between the believers with the ungodly.   "All" gives reassurance that none of the believers are excluded.   The fainthearted among them may take heart, as may those who have been confused about what happens to the "dead in Christ" at the *parousia*.   In its figurative usage in the Bible, to be "sons of" or "children of" means to be characterized by something.   I.e., Christians are characterized by the light

---

[6] In this context, the verb *katalambanō* ("overtake") means to come suddenly upon, to surprise. There is a manuscript variation here, with two uncials reading "as thieves" (plural) rather than the better attested singular reading "as a thief."   Perhaps the plural form arose when a scribe accidentally copied the -*as* ending found on the preceding pronoun *humas,* thus giving us the plural spelling *kleptas* rather than the singular *kleptēs.*

of God's truth.[7]   By following the light of God's truth Christians have been born again, and are members of God's family (John 1:12).   Therefore, they have great privileges, and they also have great responsibilities.   God's truth tells them how to live so they will be prepared for Jesus' return.   It is much easier to see where one is going in the daytime than it is at night.   While "day" earlier in this passage had reference to "the day of the Lord," the thread of the language in the verses immediately following leads us to explain "sons of day" as a Hebraism meaning folk whose lives are characterized by behavior synonymous with the bright daylight of the gospel.   Verse 8 will give some specific examples of what it means to be living in the light of "day."

We are not of night nor of darkness – By a deliberate change from "you" to "we," the writers place themselves alongside their readers in needing to accept the following exhortation.   "Night" and "darkness" are the inverse opposites of "day" and "light." Because of their relationship with Jesus, Christians endeavor to avoid living in ignorance or rebellion to God's revealed truth.

5:6 – *so then let us not sleep as others do, but let us be alert and sober.*

So then let us not sleep as others do – "So then" introduces an inescapable obligation that rests on all Christians.   "Let us ... sleep," a subjunctive verb, is an exhortation.   The Bible tells little about when Jesus will come again, but it tells much about what we are to do while we are waiting.   It is clear that the terms "sleep," "alert," and "sober," are used metaphorically in this verse.   The "others" are who are sleeping are the people described in verse 3, the people who falsely think they are secure even while destruction hangs over them.   Folk who are asleep are insensitive to and unconscious of spiritual truth.   They live as if there will never be a judgment day.   Folk who are alert and sober are responsive to the certainty of Christ's return and the stern reality of God's coming judgment.

But let us be alert and sober – Again, the subjunctive verbs translated "let us" are exhortations written to Christians, and being in the present tense the verbs call for continuous action.   Exhortations are an appeal to the will.   The person being exhorted has to decide whether or not to comply with the exhortation.   The word picture "be alert" is that of a sentinel on duty, who is guarding against a surprise attack.   For the Christian to be alert means to be prepared for and looking for the return of the Bridegroom (Luke 12:35-40).   The verb "be sober" when used figuratively in the New Testament, has the meaning "be self-controlled," "exercise self-restraint," or "avoid excess."   Being spiritually sober results in the believer's living a sane, sensible, and holy life (cf. Luke 21:34-36 and 1 Peter 4:7).

5:7 – *For those who sleep do their sleeping at night, and those who get drunk get drunk at night.*

---

[7] If "darkness" (verse 4) is figurative for ignorance of what is going to happen, then "light" (verse 5) is figurative for the information available in the gospel of Christ.   Jesus said, "I am the light of the world; he who follows Me will not walk in darkness, but will have the light of life" (John 8:12).

For those who sleep do their sleeping at night – Intended to give a reason why Christians need to be alert and sober, what is written in verse 7 also may be an attempt to help the readers grasp the significance of the figurative language "sleep" and "sober" and "night" used to describe the conduct of the "others" (verse 6). Night and sleep, literally, are not evil; but in the figurative sense in which the terms are used here, they represent the opposite of Christian conduct. Since Christians are no longer living in the dark night of ignorance about spiritual things, there is no excuse for insensibility to divine things. There is no excuse for a failure to be alert and sober.

And those who get drunk get drunk at night – This is true both literally and figuratively. There are those who go out for "a night on the town" and drink alcoholic beverages until they sink into a drunken slumber. And there are also those who run recklessly into sin until their foolish heart is darkened. In this state of spiritual slumber there is little or no thought of the coming day of the Lord and of the need to be prepared for it.

5:8 – *But since we are of the day, let us be sober, having put on the breastplate of faith and love, and as a helmet, the hope of salvation.*

But since we are of the day – After the parenthetical explanation of verse 7, the exhortation begun in verse 6 concerning how to be ready for Christ's return now continues. "Sons of day" repeats what was written in verse 5. Since Christians are not living in spiritual darkness, they know what needs to be done to get ready for the day of the Lord.

Let us be sober – As in verse 6 this exhortation calls for self-control. This verse goes on to explain several things that are part and parcel of how to be "sober."

Having put on the breastplate of faith and love – The aorist participle *endusamenoi* ("having put on") indicates that the action of putting on the breastplate and helmet precedes the action called for in the verb "let us be sober." Several times in Scripture a Christian's spiritual resources are compared to the arms and armor of ancient soldiers (Romans 13:12; 2 Corinthians 6:7; Ephesians 6:13-17). Breastplates were intended to help protect the wearer from the arrows and spear thrusts of the enemy.[8] Made of leather, bronze, or iron in antiquity, breastplates were ancient pieces of armor made of two parts which covered both the front and back sides of the body from the neck down to the waist. The Christian who tries to fight life's battles without faithfulness[9] to Christ will suffer defeat. A determination to be faithful results in the believer's submission to God's truth, confident that God is right in all that He says. Whether we understand "love" to be love for God that leads us to do His will, or love for our fellow-men that leads us to help them in any way we can, love will guard the Christian from indulging selfish fleshly desires.

---

[8] Bullet-proof vests are the modern descendant of breastplates.

[9] The word here translated "faith" is translated "faithfulness" in the NASB at Matthew 23:23; Romans 3:3; and Galatians 5:22.

And as a helmet, the hope of salvation – Ancient helmets, some made of leather and some of metal, were worn to protect the soldier's head. What answers to the spiritual helmet that protects the Christian's head (or mind) is the hope of salvation. "Salvation" is a rather broad term. In the sense that it refers to forgiveness of sins, it is something the Christian enjoys in this life. But in this verse "salvation" that is yet hoped for refers to something that will be experienced when Christ returns. "Hope," as we learned at 1 Thessalonians 1:3, is a rather complex emotion, involving both the expectation of a future event and a confident waiting for that event. In verse 8, Paul explains that hope for the salvation to be revealed at the second coming is an impetus to loving a sober life. Peter, also, wrote of a connection between hope and sober living. He worded the idea this way: "Therefore, prepare your minds for action, keep sober in spirit, fix your hope completely on the grace to be brought to you at the revelation of Jesus Christ. As obedient children, do not be conformed to the former lusts which were yours in your ignorance, but like the Holy One who called you, be holy yourselves also in all your behavior; because it is written, 'YOU SHALL BE HOLY, FOR I AM HOLY'" (1 Peter 1:13-16).

5:9 – *For God has not destined us for wrath, but for obtaining salvation through our Lord Jesus Christ,*

For God has not destined us for wrath – *Hoti*, translated "for" in our version, could also be translated "because." Verse 9 thus gives a reason why Christians may confidently entertain a hope of salvation. It is because this idea of future salvation rests on what God has planned for the believer. For the Christian to have hope of salvation is not unreasonable. "Destined," or "appointed" (as *etheto* is translated in the ASV) is the word used regularly for God's sovereign determination of events. Before the creation of the world, when God formulated His eternal plan for His creation, He decided or determined that if folk chose to rebel against Him they would experience His wrath. Those who chose to love Him would not experience eternal wrath. What was before called "destruction" (verse 3) is here called "wrath," because God's wrath produces it, and is manifested in it.

But for obtaining salvation – This is the positive side of God's eternal plan or purpose for His creation. Those who choose to love Him are destined for salvation. Romans 8:28-30 reveals several details included in God's plan. "Whom He foreknew" says that when He made His plan, God determined that He would approve those who, by their own choice, are in Christ. "Predestined" says that God determined that certain things would happen in order that those who chose to be in Christ might reach the destiny He planned for them. Men would be called or invited to become part of God's spiritual family. His Son, Jesus Christ, would be a vital component of carrying out the plan. Because Jesus died and rose from the dead, it would be possible for men to be forgiven of their sins and to rise to walk in newness of life. Those who respond positively to God's invitation would be justified – they will be treated as forgiven and thus having a right standing in God's sight. The day would come when those who have been justified would be raised from the dead in a glorified body just like the one Jesus now has. This is what God has destined for Christians to obtain. "Obtaining" this salvation implies that the believer has an active response to make.   In this context, this future salvation is acquired or won or gained by obeying the admonitions written in verses 6 and 8.

Through our Lord Jesus Christ – "Through" (*dia*) indicates that Jesus is the intermediate agent through whom God has provided salvation.   God's plan of salvation is effected in the Lord Jesus Christ[10] and by the Lord Jesus Christ; there is no salvation in any other (Acts 4:12).   The flock of God was purchased by the blood of Christ (Acts 20:28).[11]

5:10 – *who died for us, so that whether we are awake or asleep, we will live together with Him.*

Who died for us – In his first recorded sermon (Acts 13:27-39), Paul had preached that the death of Christ was the means of procuring men's salvation.   Now, in this verse in the first of his letters which are included in our New Testaments, he explains that the death of Christ is the specific means by which salvation is provided by God for men.   The preposition *huper* (translated "for") indicates Christ died on our behalf, for our benefit.[12]

So that whether we are awake or asleep – "Awake" and "asleep" here are figurative for "alive" and "dead" at the time of Christ's second coming.   What was written in chapter 4 is here repeated in abbreviated form.[13]   "In this verse those who are 'asleep' are those who die (4:13) to be raised when Jesus comes again (4:15,16).   Those who are 'awake' are those who are living on earth until Jesus comes (4:15).   All of us who are faithful, whether we are awake or asleep, will be caught up to be with the Lord (4:17).   This outcome means a lot to Jesus – so much that He died for us in order to bring us to live together with Him."[14]

We will live together with Him – As 4:17 promised that all the redeemed would be with the Lord, the word "together" here promises that those who "are awake or asleep" would together be with Him.   The Thessalonians are being assured that whatever their physical condition (i.e., dead or alive) when Jesus returns, they will not be disadvantaged.   The outcome for all believers will be the same; they will be with Christ.

---

[10] On the full title "our Lord Jesus Christ" see note at 1 Thessalonians 1:3.

[11] The verb translated "purchased" in Acts 20:28 is the same verb translated "obtaining" earlier in verse 9.   When it comes to the salvation of souls, everywhere in Scripture God's part and man's part in this acquisition are both emphasized.

[12] *Anti*, which is the preposition that says Christ died in our place as our substitute, occurs at Mark 10:45 and in composition at 1 Timothy 2:6.

[13] In chapter 4 the verb for "asleep" was *koimasthai*.   Here in chapter 5, a different word, *katheudō*, is used.   This word is used less frequently for physical death than the other, but it occurs in this sense often enough to establish that it was indeed so used (Mark 5:39; John 11:11; and in Psalm 87:6 and Daniel 12:2 in the LXX).

[14] Root, *1989-90*, p.69.

5:11 – *Therefore encourage one another and build up one another, just as you also are doing.*

Therefore encourage one another and build up one another – "Therefore" (*dio*) refers to the promise just stated, that whether dead or alive, believers together would share the blessings of the second coming of the Lord. "Encourage one another" repeats the exhortation found in 4:18. "Build up one another" indicates that by instructing one another and by encouraging one another with the information in these paragraphs, the believers will be doing very valuable personal work. They will be building up the temple of God! "One another" after the verb "encourage" is the same reciprocal pronoun *allēlous* used in 4:18. However, the "one another" following the verb "build up" is *heis ton hena* ("each other"), which expresses individual responsibility in the job at hand of helping each other to grow.

> We build one another in knowledge by teaching God's Word and discussing how to apply it in our lives. We build one another in courage and strength by supporting and helping and praising. We build up leaders by offering them our high esteem and faithful following (1 Thessalonians 5:12,13). If brethren are inclined to fall, we build them up by warning them (verse 14a). We build up one another by being patient rather than exasperated (verse 14c) no matter how exasperating some of our brethren may be. We build up one another by setting a good example of right living (verses 15-22).[15]

Intense involvement in building up one another is not just the task of the congregational leaders; it is the responsibility of each member of the body, as is so powerfully set forth in Ephesians 4:12-16.

Just as you also are doing – Here we have another example (cf. 1 Thessalonians 4:1; 4:10) of the writers' courtesy and tact. They are careful to recognize the Thessalonians' attainments, even while encouraging them up to further efforts.

C. Exhortations to Aid Preparation for Lord's Return. 5:12-22

1. Concerning responsibilities to congregational leaders. 5:12,13a

5:12 – *But we request of you, brethren, that you appreciate those who diligently labor among you, and have charge over you in the Lord and give you instruction,*

But we request of you, brethren – The writers have just directed their readers generally to "encourage and edify each other." At the same time, they must not ignore the services of their congregational leaders or deem their oversight and teaching needless. Paying proper respect to the guidance offered by their leaders will help the Christians to be better prepared for this mutual ministry they have just been encouraged to keep doing. "Breth-

---

[15] Root, *1989-90*, p.70.

ren" indicates this request is made to the whole congregation. "We request" translates *erōtaō*, a word which can mean either "to ask a question" or "to ask someone to do something." By using this rare word for making a request, the writers are asking the readers to do something, as it were, as a personal favor to them.

That you appreciate those who diligently labor among you – The Greek verb translated "appreciate" is literally "to know," in the sense "to know their worth." Three present tense participles ("labor," "have charge," and "give instruction") describe the persons who are to be appreciated. These three participles are governed by one article (translated "those"), which indicates that one group of people who perform three specified services is in view; the writers are not referencing three different groups. It seems obvious that, when the missionaries who planted the church had to leave, the new congregation at Thessalonica was not left without appointed or recognized persons as congregational leaders.[16] The newly appointed leaders at Thessalonica were necessarily new converts, and this fact may have been the reason they were being treated with less respect than they should have been.[17] The verb translated "diligently labor" (*kopiaō*) means they work hard, that they work until they are tired out. This verb is a cognate of the noun used at 1 Thessalonians 2:9 where the Thessalonians were reminded of the wearisome labor Paul and his fellow workers unselfishly did in order to support themselves while sharing the gospel with the Thessalonians. 1 Timothy 5:17 uses the same word for the "labor" that is involved in preaching and teaching.

And have charge over you in the Lord – *Prohistēmi* (translated "have charge over") has a range of meanings, from having authority over others (cf. Romans 12:8; 1 Timothy 5:17) to caring for others by doing good works (cf. Titus 3:14). Taking charge, or ruling, or presiding in a Christian way entails a sincere interest in the welfare of those who are ruled (cf. Matthew 20:26-28). 1 Peter 5:2,3 tells us how the leaders are to shepherd God's flock. It is important to notice that such leadership authority was not vested in one person. "Those" who have charge over you is plural. The qualifying phrase "in the Lord" distinguishes Christian leaders from civil leaders. The phrase also indicates the origin of the leadership office (it is from the Lord by institution), the leader's position (under the authority of the Lord), and the style of leadership they are to practice (it reflects how the Lord Himself would do it).

And give you instruction – This phrase describes a third area of the congregational leaders' hard work. The present tense participle pictures an ongoing task. Only at 1 Cor-

---

[16] The congregations started on Paul's first missionary journey soon had elders appointed in every congregation (Acts 14:23). The church at Ephesus had elders (Acts 20:17), as did the new churches on the island of Crete (Titus 1:5). There were overseers and deacons at Philippi not long after the church had begun (Philippians 1:1). If we are guided by these examples there is every reason to believe that similar leaders were appointed in every newly established congregation of Christians.

[17] In congregations not recently established, the men chosen to be leaders are not to be new converts (1 Timothy 3:6). Newly established congregations may pick the best men they have to be leaders, and then train them to do the task to which they have been selected.

inthians 10:11, Ephesians 6:4, and in this verse in the NASB is the verb *noutheteō* translated "instruction." Most often this verb is translated "admonish" or "admonishing" (Romans 15:14; 1 Corinthians 4:14; Colossians 1:28, 3:16; 1 Thessalonians 5:14; 2 Thessalonians 3:15). *Noutheteō* literally means to put in mind, to warn, entreat, or exhort, and that can be done by word or deed. *Noutheteō* indicates it is a part of the work of a congregational leader "to put his people in mind of the truth; to warn them of danger; to exhort them to perform their duty; to admonish them if they go astray."[18]

5:13a – *and that you esteem them very highly in love because of their work.*

And that you esteem them very highly in love – Not only are the Christians to appreciate their congregational leaders (verse 12), they are also to love them with the highest degree of love they can muster. Actually, the words in the Greek carry such an emphasis as cannot well be expressed in English. Perhaps the adverb "very highly"[19] is intended to modify the verb "esteem," in which case it means "hold them in the highest regard," or "show them how important you think they are."[20] Perhaps the adverb is intended to modify "in love," in which case it means "consider them to be worthy of the strongest love you can offer." "The book of Hebrews tells us such leaders are concerned about our souls. They want us to be alert and busy so that we can greet our Lord gladly when He comes. We ought to love them sincerely because of their work on our behalf. The best way to encourage our leaders is to follow so well and so joyfully that they will find joy and not grief in their leadership (Hebrews 13:17)."[21]

Because of their work – This is the reason for loving the leaders with the highest degree of love the members of the congregation can muster. "Their work" summarizes all the ways the leaders help the members of the congregation to be ready for the Lord's return. As verse 12 has highlighted, "their work" involves labor until they are tired out, plus the tremendous responsibility of taking charge and presiding, plus the very demanding and difficult task of admonishing each of the members of the congregation.

2.   Concerning the responsibility to live in peace with one another. 5:13b-15

5:13b – *Live in peace with one another.*

---

[18] Barnes, *op. cit.*, p.57.

[19] "Very highly" translates *huperekperissou*, a double compound adverb in the comparative degree. It is strongest intensive possible in the Greek language, conveying the greatest possible measure.

[20] Ellingworth & Nida, *op. cit.*, p.117.

[21] Root, *1984-85*, p.100.

Live in peace with one another – Bible students who attempt to outline 1 Thessalonians have debated how to handle this final phrase in what is numbered as verse 13. The question of whether it should be read with what precedes or with what follows requires that a decision be made concerning what was the original reading of the text at this place. Did the verse read "with them"[22] rather than "with one another"?[23] If "with them" is determined to be the correct reading, then this phrase is an exhortation to the readers to be at peace with their congregational leaders. Do not give them a hard time when they are trying to help you. If "with one another" is determined to be the correct reading, then it is more likely that this exhortation begins a new paragraph and refers to maintaining good relationships with all in the Christian community. Verse 14 then details some of the specific occasions where working to keep the peace will be especially important. "Live in peace" is the first of a whole series of present tense imperative verbs. Make it a practice to live at peace.

5:14 – *We urge you, brethren, admonish the unruly, encourage the fainthearted, help the weak, be patient with everyone.*

We urge you, brethren – The Greek verb translated "urge" (*parakaloumen*) is a stronger, more authoritative word than the word translated "request" in verse12. Except for the verb used, the beginning of this verse is exactly parallel to the beginning of verse 12, so it is likely that "brethren" in both verses refers to the same addressees, all the Christians in the congregation at Thessalonica.[24] As introduced by verse 13b, verse 14 calls attention to some special situations in the life of the congregation where obeying the command to live at peace needs to express itself.

Admonish the unruly -- The noun translated "unruly" is found only here in the New Testament, but a related verb and adverb are found in 2 Thessalonians 3:6-7,11, where the context makes it quite clear that Paul is speaking of a refusal by able-bodied persons to work in order to support themselves and their dependents. The Greek word *ataktous* (translated "unruly" or "disorderly") is a military term which described soldiers who were

---

[22] The reading *autois* ("with them") is supported by the uncial manuscripts Sinaiticus and Claromontanus, as well as by the Latin Vulgate and Peshitto Syriac versions.

[23] The reading *heautois* (here translated "one another") s supported by the uncials A, B, D³, K, L as well as the Coptic and Gothic versions. While most modern Greek texts accept *heautois* as the true reading, it requires translators to treat a reflexive pronoun as being equal to a reciprocal pronoun when they offer the translation "one another." A literal translation of *en heautois* would be "in yourselves." See the same phrase at Matthew 16:7 and 21:38, where it is also debated whether the construction should be treated as reflexive rather than reciprocal.

[24] Some early church fathers, beginning with Chrysostom, interpreted the commands in verse 14 as being addressed to the church leaders who were spoken about in verse 12. If that is true, then "brethren" ("brothers") becomes a special term almost equivalent to a leadership title. In light of the fact that (1) Jesus discouraged the use of special titles (Matthew 23:8-11) and that (2) a similar set of commands (Romans 12:15-17) is directed to the whole congregation, not just its leaders, it appears best to take these admonitions as addressed to all the members of the church at Thessalonica, leaders as well as people. All are responsible to fulfill these commands.

out of rank or who deserted their post and so were not performing their duty as soldiers. Apparently, there were some members of congregation at Thessalonica who were not merely not working (*argos*, "idle," Matthew 20:3,6) but who refused to work (cf. 2 Thessalonians 3:10, who were "not *willing* to work"). Since the missionaries had already warned against idleness when they were in Thessalonica (2 Thessalonians 3:10), before there was any confusion about the nearness of Christ's return, it is implied that the refusal to work did not stem from mistaken eschatological ideas but from a general attitude against work found in their society. Christians are to have a different work ethic than that of their townsmen who refused to work.[25] "Admonish" translates the same Greek word translated "instruction" in 1 Thessalonians 5:12. Living at peace in the congregation means being concerned about the welfare of our brothers and sisters in Christ, reminding them, if need be, of the standards expected of Christians. Admonition includes a note of disapproval of their disorderly conduct plus an exhortation to mend their ways by working to support themselves and helping meet the needs of others.

Encourage the fainthearted – This is the only place the word "fainthearted" appears in the New Testament. In this place it may refer to those who feel inadequate, who need to be made to feel they are someone who counts. It may refer to those who are conscious of some great sin, and who feel they may never be forgiven. Or it may refer to the folk who were troubled about their Christian friends who have already died (4:13). The word translated "encourage" was used at 1 Thessalonians 2:11, where we learned it can mean comfort in times of affliction or encouragement to continue in a particular course of conduct. Encouraging the fainthearted is something each church member can do. Because fainthearted people may be intimidated by a rigorous rebuke or by vigorous urging, what is called for is more gentle words of comfort or encouragement.

Help the weak – Judging from Romans 14:1-15:6 and from 1 Corinthians 8-10, the "weak" are those who do not have the courage to stand for their convictions when peers criticize or ridicule them for their convictions and tempt them to waver. They are weak in their own personal faith. When a weak brother is encouraged to violate his or her conscience on a matter, that violation is sin. When strong brothers are with their weaker brothers, and the weaker brother indicates he or she has a conscience about the matter at hand, the strong waives his rights lest he cause the weaker brother to behave in such a way as to violate his conscience. This temporary waiving of a right is how the strong brother "helps" or "takes hold of" the weaker brother in order to support him or her. There are times and differing matters when any Christian may be the weak brother. Then other Christians voluntarily bear the infirmities of the weak (Romans 15:1).

Be patient with everyone – There are two Greek synonyms for patience. One, *hupomonē*, means putting up with things. The other, *makrothumia*, the one used here, means putting up with people. This kind of patience is one of the fruit of the Spirit (Galatians 5:22). "Everyone" includes both those outside and inside the church. "Every-

---

[25] For the Christian expectation that able-bodied folk will work, see Ephesians 4:28 and 2 Thessalonians 3:6.

one" is not limited to the "unruly," the "fainthearted," and the "weak," though treating each of these certainly requires the exercise of patience because the erring and misguided so often refuse to respond immediately to constructive counsel. It also takes special care lest we Christians become short-tempered toward those outside the brotherhood who act in unreasonable and perverse ways toward us.

5:15 – *See that no one repays another with evil for evil, but always seek after that which is good for one another and for all people.*

See that no one repays another with evil for evil – The plural imperative "see"[26] and the singular "no one repays" calls for the Thessalonians to watch over both themselves and each other lest anyone fall for the temptation to get even when either brethren or outsiders have caused injury or done them wrong. In ancient society, retaliation was accepted as the norm. In this matter, Christians are expected to have a different lifestyle, because a prohibition against seeking revenge was something Jesus taught (Matthew 5:44-48; Luke 6:27-36). Both Peter and Paul, in almost identical terms (cp. 1 Peter 2:19-23; 3:9 with Romans 12:17), show the influence of Jesus' teaching. "It may be right to defend our lives and the lives of our friends; to seek the protection of the law for our persons, reputation, or property, against those who would wrong us; to repel the assaults of calumniators and slanderers, but in no case should the motive be to do *them* wrong for the evil which they have done *us*."[27]

But always seek after that which is good – "Always" is emphatic, meaning "do this all the time." The present tense imperative verb translated "seek" is plural, so this intense pursuit is something expected of all Christians.[28] The Christian ethic requires more than avoiding the evil. They are to constantly make it a matter of earnest and deliberate effort to do something good[29] even to those who are wronging them.[30] The Thessalonian church was a persecuted church, so what is here commanded was not an easy assignment. In fact, such a positive behavior is something that must be cultivated.

For one another and for all people – The duty of pursuing that which is good is not limited to fellow Christians ("one another"[31]) but extends to those outside the church ("all

---

[26] The subject of the plural imperative verb is the "brethren" specifically addressed in the previous verse. Only if "brethren" in that verse can be limited to church leaders would it be proper to indicate that it is only church leaders who have the responsibility here set forth in verse 15. "See" is used in the metaphorical sense of taking care or making sure the motive for revenge is overcome.

[27] Barnes, *op. cit.*, p.58.

[28] The verb translated "seek" is *diōkein*, which means to pursue or follow. It is the word used of hunting for food, and that hunt is intensive when the hunter is hungry. Figuratively, this command directs Christians to employ the same energy for doing good that they use when seeking food.

[29] Greek dictionaries commonly distinguish between the words for good used here and in verse 21. The word used here tends to mean "morally good" or "physically sound," while the word used in verse 21 tends to mean "good to look at, attractive, beautiful." (Ellingworth & Nida, *op. cit.*, p.120.)

[30] Compare Matthew 5:44-48; Romans 12:20,21; 1 Peter 3:8,9.

[31] Galatians 6:10 stresses doing good for fellow Christians. "So then, while we have opportunity, let

people"). It may be more difficult to do good to "all people," for those outside the church may be enemies of the Christian. But those outside the church are the ones who need the Lord the most, so the Christian aims to display a winsome behavior toward them.

3. Concerning responsibilities to oneself. 5:16-18

5:16 – *Rejoice always;*

Rejoice always – The paragraph which begins in verse 16 lists a number of essential activities Christians are to be doing for themselves in order to prepare for the Lord's return. The presence of this list suggests two thoughts. First, Paul delineates these qualities to remind his readers that such qualities do not appear automatically in any Christian's life; rather, the Christian's inner man is developed only through careful and intentional cultivation. Second, Christians will need to possess the qualities highlighted in verses 16-18 if they are to fulfill their responsibilities to their congregational leaders (verses 12-13a) and their responsibilities to live in peace with one another (verses 13b-15).

Joy or rejoicing is a feeling of delight which arises from the possession of present good, or from the anticipation of future happiness. The Christian rejoices in the hope of the future that has been unfolded in chapters 4 and 5. "Joy" is the second word in the list of fruit of the Spirit (Galatians 5:22). Romans 14:17 indicates one thing that is important in the kingdom of God is joy in the Holy Spirit. In his letter to the Philippians, Paul explicitly instructs those Christians to "rejoice *in the Lord* always" (Philippians 4:4). Indeed, the believer who is living for Christ has abundant reason to rejoice constantly, whatever may be his or her present earthly circumstances, for there is an awareness that God is causing all things to work together for good to those who love Him (Romans 8:28).

> Many of the sorrows of mankind are our sorrows, but we Christians have a joy that lives with sorrow. We belong to God's family. Our sins are forgiven. We are assured of eternal life with our Father. Because of this we feel a joy that pain cannot cancel. A Christian does not rejoice because he has lost his job, or because he has a broken leg, or because a dear friend has died. But in the midst of suffering he rejoices because nothing can separate him from God's love (Romans 8:35-39). And in the experience of suffering he learns that suffering can make him strong, and in that also he finds joy (James 1:2-4; Romans 5:1-5).[32]

5:17 – *pray without ceasing*;

Pray without ceasing – This exhortation does not say that Christians should be engaged in prayer to God twenty-four hours a day, never stopping to sleep or to work or to eat. "Without ceasing" means is that Christians are to be persistent in prayer, like the persistent widow (Luke 18:1-8). Paul's own letters are an example. They are full of prayers for

---

us do good to all people, and especially to those who are of the household of the faith."

[32] Root, *1984-85*, p.101.

his readers. "Pray" (*proseuchomai*) is a general term for prayer to God, and such prayers may be requests, praises, petitions, and intercession for oneself and others. One may pray silently when starting or finishing a task, or whenever some difficulty arises. Spontaneous prayers may be offered while one is doing something else, whether it be housework, or driving a tractor, or while waiting in a check-out line. Perhaps in this context the prayers are for wisdom or guidance to carry out the exhortations given in verses 12-15, or for developing the qualities listed in verses 16-18.

5:18 – *in everything give thanks; for this is God's will for you in Christ Jesus.*

In everything give thanks – Each of the verbs in this paragraph about personal development is in the imperative mood. In Romans 1:21, Gentiles are rebuked for not giving thanks to God. This imperative suggests that thankfulness is something that requires conscious effort or it will be neglected. The verse does not say, "Give thanks *for* everything," but "Give thanks *in* everything." In health or sickness, in prosperity or adversity, even in loss or disaster, Christians may still give thanks for the changeless love of God, for the strength that is gained by enduring trouble, for the fellowship of God and His people, for the certainty of eternal joy.

> "Start the day with a prayer, a prayer of thanks to God.
> Thank Him for keeping you through the night,
> Thank Him for sending the morning light ...
>
> For our blessings, dear Lord, we bow in thanks to Thee;
> Thank You for giving daily bread,
> Thank You for mercies around us spread ...
>
> At the close of the day, we bow in thanks to Thee,
> Thank You for wonderful saving power,
> Thank You for keeping us hour by hour ...."[33]

For this is God's will for you in Christ Jesus – Each word in this clause causes us to pause and meditate on possible meanings. For example, the word in the middle of the clause translated "for" is *eis*, and might well be translated "toward." It highlights the idea that God has some expectations for Christians beyond what ordinary men might do. In the Greek, "in Christ Jesus" follows immediately after "God's will." That might mean that the thing willed by God was taught by Jesus while He was on earth, or it might mean this is something God especially wants those who are Christians (i.e., those who are in Christ Jesus) to do. Does "this" point back only to giving thanks, or does it point back to all three imperatives (rejoicing, praying, and giving thanks)? "Will" means the thing willed, just as it did in 1 Thessalonians 4:3, while the absence of an article in the Greek before "will" indicates that giving thanks (or rejoicing, praying, and giving thanks) does not exhaust God's will, but are vital parts of it. When we encounter phrases in the New

---

[33] Blanche K. & Virgil P. Brock, *A Prayer of Thanks* (Winona Lake, IN: Rodeheaver Co., 1949).

Testament that are capable of more than one meaning, such as the case here, we treat all the meanings as true, unless a verse elsewhere in Scripture specifically rules out one of the possible options.

4. Concerning responsibilities during public worship.   5:19-22

5:19 – *Do not quench the Spirit;*

Do not quench the Spirit – There are five imperative verbs in verses 19-22, all of which apparently are describing proper behavior when the Christians meet together in their weekly public assembly. "Spirit" is likely a metonymy for miraculous spiritual gifts.[34] Such gifts were bestowed on some Christians by the laying on of an apostle's hands.[35] As at Corinth (1 Corinthians 12-14), so at Thessalonica, those who had spiritual gifts exercised them at the public assembly.   We find greater detail concerning the various manifestations of the Spirit in the public assembly in 1 Corinthians 12-14 than we find here in 1 Thessalonians 5. "Quench" is a common metaphor for putting out a fire, and "do not quench" (a present imperative with *mē)* is a command to stop doing something they have already begun to do. Since "prophecy" is specifically mentioned in the next verse, we may suppose that folks with gifts of the Spirit other than prophecy were encountering resistance in the public assembly.   Such throwing of cold water on the gifts of the Spirit was to stop.

5:20 – *do not despise prophetic utterances.*

Do not despise prophetic utterances – Prophecy means to speak by inspiration in the local language of the people, no matter the content of the message,[36] whereas the gift of speaking in tongues was to speak in a foreign language. This is clearly indicated in Acts 2, where groups of foreigners visiting Jerusalem heard the apostles speaking in the very dialect common back in the home country of the visitors. We may suppose that this appeal to the Thessalonians to stop despising prophetic utterances is similar to what we read in 1 Corinthians 14 where the gift of prophecy was to be preferred to the gift of tongues in the public assembly.   Tongues were permissible in the public assembly if there were foreigners present who might better be taught or evangelized if they were addressed in their native tongue, or if a translator were present who could tell the local folk what was being said in the foreign language by the tongues-speaker. The reason for preferring prophecy to tongues (as they were being misused at Corinth) is because when a message was delivered in the local language, the audience received instruction and edification and exhor-

---

[34] There are lists of such spiritual gifts in 1 Corinthians 12:8-11 and 12:29,30, and perhaps in Romans 12:6 ff.

[35] Acts 8:18; Romans 1:11; 2 Timothy 1:6; Hebrews 2:3,4.

[36] A well-known example of a prophetic message is recorded in Acts 11:27,28. However, a prophet was not limited to foretelling the future. Probably he more often gave guidance in Christian living and the management of the church (Acts 15:32).

tation and comfort (1 Corinthians 14:3-6). A message delivered in a foreign language which no one present understood allowed no one to even know when to say the "Amen." If there was a tendency at Thessalonica, as appears to have been the case subsequently in Corinth (cp. 1 Corinthians 14:19), for folk to value the more spectacular gifts of working miracles or speaking in tongues above prophecy, then this warning is immediately intelligible.

5:21 – *But examine everything carefully; hold fast to that which is good;*

But examine everything carefully – While the Thessalonians are to stop quenching the Spirit and to stop despising prophetic utterances, it is also imperative that they do not take as genuine all that which professes to be of the Spirit. In this context, "everything" is subject to the limitation of verses 19-20, i.e., the exercise of spiritual gifts.[37] The word here translated "examine" (*dokimadzete*) is one that was properly applicable to metals, referring to the art of the assayer, by which the true nature and value of the metal was tested. The reason for making such an examination is because some inspirations come from the devil (1 Corinthians 12:3; cp. 1 John 4:1, "Believe not every spirit, but try the spirits whether they are of God"). The means of examining or testing is not specified here in 1 Thessalonians, but elsewhere we learn of two tests of genuine prophecy: 1 Corinthians 14:29 suggests that prophets known to be true should judge the prophecies of others who claimed to be prophets. Another test or criterion is how the prophecy corresponds to "the Lord's command" (1 Corinthians 14:37,38). In addition, one of the spiritual gifts was the discerning of spirits (1 Corinthians 12:10). Folk so gifted could quickly pass judgment on whether or not the claimed spiritual gift was genuine.

Hold fast to that which is good – "Good" (*kalon*) has the sense of "genuine," and the reference may primarily be to prophetic utterances. Christians are not expected to be credulous and receive everything upon trust. They are to carefully examine what they hear in light of the word of God. Christians who have applied the proper tests and have found out what is divinely inspired truth are then bound to give that truth special attention, to embrace it and translate it into proper action. Christians are not at liberty to treat truth and falsehood alike.

5:22 – *abstain from every form of evil.*

Abstain from every form of evil – Verse 22 states in negative terms the same injunction written in verse 21. "Abstain" (avoid, or have nothing to do with) in this verse is the opposite of "hold fast" in the previous verse. "Evil" in this verse is the opposite of "good" in the previous verse.[38] Since this verse is a contrast to the previous verse, where it was

---

[37] It is preferable to treat *panta* ("everything") as neuter plural rather than accusative singular ("every person").

[38] The addition in this verse of the word "kind" has led scholars to discuss whether it is permissible to translate this construction as "evil kind" (which treats "evil" as being an adjective modifying "kind"), or whether "evil" is to be treated as a noun (as it is in the NASB's translation "form of evil"). In our comments we are following the lead of the NASB translators.

evidently prophetic utterances that were called good, what is "evil" here also refers to prophetic utterances. The Greek word *eidos*, which might be translated "form" or "kind," has been debated by the scholars.[39] It looks like Christians are being warned to avoid every "kind" of evil that may try to parade itself as a genuine manifestation of the Holy Spirit. The Greek word translated "evil" (*ponērou*) may be either masculine or neuter. Messages inspired by an unholy spirit are evil, and so are the men who deliver them. After examining everything carefully, messages inspired by the Holy Spirit were to be respected and obeyed, for such messages were the Word of God. Only when Christians have learned to accept what is valid and disallow what is not will they obtain maximum benefit for the body of Christ from their participation in the public assembly of the saints.

V. SOME FINAL PRAYERS AND REQUESTS (5:23-27)

A. More wish-prayers for the Thessalonian Christians. 5:23,24

5:23 – *Now may the God of peace Himself sanctify you entirely; and may your spirit and soul and body be preserved complete, without blame at the coming of our Lord Jesus Christ.*

Now may the God of peace Himself sanctify you entirely – The writers have indicated that they made mention of the Thessalonians in their prayers (1:2). Now we read a specific example of the kind of prayers that were offered for the Thessalonians. The NASB translators chose to translate the Greek conjunction *de* which opens this verse by the English word "now," but we judge that the ASV translators' choice of the conjunction "and" better helps us to see the connection between the prayer in verse 23 and what has been written earlier in the letter. Perhaps the intended connection is with what was just written in verses 21-22 about avoiding the bad and embracing the good. Perhaps everything advocated since 5:14 is intended. Perhaps the intended connection is with all that has been written since 1 Thessalonians 4:1. If the Thessalonians heed what has been written about sexual purity (4:3-8), brotherly love (4:9,10), personal independence (4:11,12), understanding the *parousia* (4:13-5:11), respect for leaders (5:12,13), love for other people (5:14,15), rejoicing, prayer, thankfulness, and positive participation in public worship (5:16-22), then they may expect something special from the God of peace. As was explained at 1:1, "peace" speaks of spiritual well-being, and "God of peace" says such well-being is something that God provides. The addition of emphatic pronoun "Himself" calls attention to something that only God Himself is capable of doing. In earlier passages, growth in sanctification or holiness was something each individual Christian was expected to demonstrate in his or her life. In this passage, God, not the Christian, is the one doing the sanctifying. The verb *hagiasai* ("sanctify") is an aorist optative, and speaks of a one-time act in the future. Earlier in this epistle (3:11-13, in what was the writers' first wish-prayer) it was indicated that at the final judgment Jesus would establish the fact that in His

---

[39] The English word "appearance," which was chosen by the KJV translators to explain *eidos*, has proven to be a misleading choice. It led to some very creative explanations concerning the avoidance of what may just look like evil, but most of those explanations ignored the context, especially when commentators talked about the appearance of evil in ourselves, rather than its appearance in others.

judgment the Christian was blameless when it came to holiness.[40]   This passage now
indicates that God also does something at that judgment following the *parousia*.[41]   When
God is the subject of the verb "sanctify," it often means that as the result of Christ's
propitiatory sacrificial sin-offering God is able to consider the person or object so cleansed
as being free from the guilt of sin,[42] and thus being suitable to be employed in special
service to God.   The word *holoteleis* ("entirely") is unique to this passage in the New
Testament.   It is comprised of two words, the one signifying wholeness, the other
completion.   It looks as though after Jesus establishes blamelessness in holiness (3:11-13),
God will then indicate that in His mind Christians are completely forgiven, treated as free
from the guilt of sin, and eligible to be invited to enter into eternal service for God.   Since
the word "entirely" modifies the pronoun "you," the prayer here being offered for each of
the readers is that God would, as has just been described, so treat them at the final judgment.
When Christians during this life have sanctified themselves in the ways indicated earlier in
chapters 4 and 5, Jesus can pass judgment that they are blameless in holiness, and when He
does that, then God can sanctify them, that is, treat them once and for all as pure and free
from the guilt of sin.

And may your spirit and soul and body be preserved complete – "May be preserved,"
also an aorist optative verb, makes this clause another wish-prayer for something to be
done in the future.   The verb is passive voice with God Himself as the implied subject who
does the preserving.[43]   The verb is singular and the adjective translated "complete" is
singular, indicating that a redeemed man (made of body, soul, and spirit) is pictured as
being an undivided whole.[44]   In the Greek, the verb "preserved" stands with emphasis at
the end of the sentence.[45]   Two highly disputed theological issues are raised by this verse:

---

[40] Such blamelessness is the result of being justified by faith; it is not the result of living a sinless-pure life.   Rather, the tenor of the justified person's life has been one of faithfulness to what the Lord has commanded.

[41] Both 3:13 and 5:23 make reference to the wish-prayers stated in the aorist optative verbs as being something that will take place at the "coming" (*parousia*) of Christ.

[42] God (or Christ) is the subject of the verb "sanctify" in passages such as 1 Corinthians 6:11 and Ephesians 5:26.   In those passages the truth being referenced is also the idea of being purified, or being treated as free from the guilt of sin.   Hebrews 10:10 specifically makes mention of the offering of the body of Christ as the sin offering which makes sanctification possible.

[43] The words "I pray God," which help the readers to see that this is a wish-prayer, included at this place in the KJV are not found in the Greek.   It would have been better if the insertion had been "we pray God," since Silas and often Timothy, too, are included in the numerous first-person plural verbs found in this letter.

[44] The KJV translation "your whole spirit" treated the adjective *holoklēron* as modifying the word "spirit."   The ERV, ASV, and NASB, which put the words "entire" or "complete" at the end of the clause, treat all three nouns as being governed by the adjective.   It is explained that the Greek adjective usually agrees in gender, number, and case, to its nearest antecedent in compound clauses.   Thus, *holoklēron* is neuter because "spirit" is neuter.

[45] Instead of "preserved" (*tērēthein*) a few inferior manuscripts read "may be found" (*heurethein*).   It is conjectured that the scribe who first made the change correctly recognized that the final judgment was the occasion being referred to, and "found" would better assist the readers to see that.

(1) It certainly appears that man is trichotomous, made of body, soul, and spirit.[46]   (2) If the righteous are preserved "spirit, soul and body," it appears to be implied that lost men, following the judgment, may lose one or more of their constituent parts.[47]   Care must be exercised here, since extended studies of these disputed points, if undertaken here, can lead to an overshadowing of the main idea expressed in the wish-prayer.[48]

Without blame – *Amemptōs* (translated "without blame" in the NASB) is an adverb in the Greek and should have been translated "blamelessly."   While the adverb might modify the adjective "complete," it is much more likely intended to modify the verb "preserved." Since God is the implied subject of the verb "preserved," this clause seems to be saying that no blame can be attributed to God for what He does with man at the judgment.   The idea is similar to the one written in Romans 3:25, where God is described as being both "just and justifier of the one who has faith in Jesus."   Because of the sacrificial death of Jesus, God can justify those who have faith in Jesus and at the same time not be accused of being a crooked judge.   He can justify both in this life and at the time of the final judg-

---

[46] Proponents of dichotomy have adopted various expedients to make this passage match their doctrine.   Some emphasize that elsewhere Paul merely divides man into two parts, visible and invisible, "body and spirit" (1Corinthians 6:20; 7:34).   The King James translation, which speaks of "the whole spirit" followed by "soul and body" has been interpreted to mean man is two parts, immaterial ("spirit") and material ("soul and body").   Some critics have tried to defend the untenable idea that this depiction of tripartite nature of man is evidence that Paul did not write this verse, and if that is true, then it need not be thought that the Bible teaches trichotomy.

When reading the Greek, what catches one's attention is the symmetrical arrangement of three nouns with their articles and the two conjunctions ("and") that tie them together.   This becomes a "distinct enunciation of three component parts of the nature of man" (Charles J. Ellicott, *Commentary on the Epistles of St. Paul to the Thessalonians* [Grand Rapids, MI: Zondervan Publishing House, 1957], p.84).   If we read the Scriptures through trichotomous glasses, a number of verses suddenly make sense which do not when those same verses are read from a dichotomous viewpoint.   Take the following brief synopsis as an example.   In this earthly life, man's body, made of flesh, bone, and blood, is the house (or "vessel," 1 Thessalonians 4:4) in which the soul and human spirit dwell.   The soul is the thing that animates the body. The spirit (man's human spirit) is the part that God intended should give directions to the soul, which in turn animates the body.   When a man begins to sin his spirit dies (Ephesians 2:1,5); that is, it ceases to function as God intended.   Such folk are described as "soulical," or "fleshly."   They have died "*spirit*ually." The new birth affects the spirit (John 3:6).   The spirit is restored to its God-intended function.   When physical death occurs, the soul and spirit leave the body (James 2:26).   The body is buried (returning to the dust it was), while the soul and spirit go to be with the Lord (Ecclesiastes 12:7).   As 1 Thessalonians 4:14 has indicated, the souls of the redeemed will accompany Christ when He makes His *parousia* return, and then will get their new, glorified bodies (1 Corinthians 15:35-48).

[47] Do the wicked lose their glorified bodies?   Daniel 12:2, Romans 5:14-18, and 1 Corinthians 15:22 indicate that all (both righteous and wicked) will be raised from the dead.   Yet at least two Scripture passages picture the wicked as being "consumed" (Hebrews 10:27; James 5:3).   While we rightfully reject the theory that the wicked are totally annihilated, we could rightfully speak of their souls and spirits as continuing to exist, even if their bodies were not "preserved" in the way that this wish-prayer in verse 23 speaks of the bodies of the righteous being "preserved."   Likewise, just as physical death is a separation of soul from body, might we not suppose that the "second death" (Revelation 20:6) also is a separation of soul from body?

[48] Robert L. Thomas (in "1 Thessalonians" in Vol. 11 of *The Expositor's Bible Commentary* [Grand Rapids: Zondervan, 1978], pp.294,295) has a very readable discussion of the issue involved in "body, soul, and spirit."   Older presentations of dichotomy are J.T. Beck, *Outlines of Biblical Psychology*, and John Laidlaw, *Bible Doctrine of Man*.   Older defenses of trichotomy include F. Delitzsch, *System of Biblical Psychology*, and J.B. Heard, *Tripartite Nature of Man*.

ment. The judgment thus becomes the final vindication of God for the rewards and punishments already in part bestowed to men,[49] both in this life and in the intermediate state between men's deaths and the time of the judgment.

At the coming of our Lord Jesus Christ – Both the "sanctifying entirely" and the "preserving blamelessly" occur at the *parousia*[50] of Jesus Christ. There is to be a judgment which occurs at the time of Christ's second coming.[51] "The coming of our Lord Jesus Christ" is in the thoughts of the writers both at the beginning and end of this letter. That is the goal toward which all of history moves. When that day comes it is those who have acknowledged Jesus as Lord who will receive God's favorable verdict.

5:24 – *Faithful is He who calls you, and He also will bring it to pass.*

Faithful is He who calls you – The previous verse has specified some things that, at the *parousia* and the final judgment, God has promised to do for believers in Christ. This verse gives a reason why the Thessalonian believers can confidently look forward to receiving what has been promised. One of God's characteristics is faithfulness. He keeps His word, He does what He has promised He will do. The beginning of their lives as believers in Christ resulted from God's invitation to them through the gospel to become believers (2 Thessalonians 2:14). "Calls," a present tense participle in the Greek, indicates something that God continues to do over and over again throughout the church age. He keeps inviting men to become obedient to His Son, Jesus Christ.[52]

And He also will bring it to pass – Romans 8:28 assures us that in harmony with the plan God made back in eternity, He "causes all things to work together for the good of those who love Him." Romans 8:30 identifies a series of actions which God does for the redeemed which terminate in their glorification. In 1 Peter 5:10, the apostle Peter voices

---

[49] Righteous people may experience blessings in this life, and wicked people may receive temporal punishments for sin. Then in the intermediate state, there are rewards and punishments, but not as wonderful or as terrible as will be experienced in eternity after the judgment has been completed.

[50] Events that transpire in connection with Christ's *parousia* have been noted in comments at 1 Thessalonians 1:1, 1:3, 2:19, 3:13, and 4:14-5:10.

[51] The KJV has mistakenly translated *en tē parousia* as "*unto* the coming." The preposition *en* means "in" or "at," not "unto." As a result of that mistranslation, comments based on the KJV have treated the sanctifying and preserving as something that happens during this life, rather than at the time of the second coming of Christ. The prayer is not that they might be kept entirely holy until the Lord Jesus should come; it speaks of what takes placed *at* the *parousia*. This verse is not a proof text for the perseverance (preservation) of the saints, as though God does the keeping.

[52] When we recall that some commentaries, based on verse 23 in the KJV, speak of God's being continually involved in making men holy in this life ("*unto* the coming of the Lord"), that causes those same commentators to put forth the idea that "calls" here in verse 24 refers not only to His calling the unbeliever to initial faith, but also continually calling the believer to holiness. That maybe more than this verse is intended to affirm.

a conviction similar to the one the writers of this letter here affirm.[53]   Peter worded it this way, "After you have suffered for a little while, the God of all grace, who called you to His eternal glory in Christ, will Himself perfect, confirm, strengthen and establish you."   The wish-prayer expressed in verse 23 was offered precisely because of the conviction of the writers that God is faithful.

B. Three Things Requested from the Thessalonians.   5:25-27

5:25 – *Brethren, pray for us.*

Brethren, pray for us – As they close this letter, the writers request that the Thessalonians do three things.   The first request is that the Christians ("brethren") will remember their missionaries in prayer, just as the missionaries have been praying for the Thessalonians (1 Thessalonians 1:2, 3:10-13).   "Pray" is a present tense imperative verb.   In the same confidence that God will answer their prayers for the Thessalonians (5:24), the missionaries ask the Thessalonians to pray constantly for them: 'Make us and our evangelistic work the subject of your prayers.'   Paul will make the same request in his epistles to Romans, Ephesians, Philippians, Colossians, Philemon, and in Second Corinthians.

5:26 – *Greet all the brethren with a holy kiss.*

Greet all the brethren with a holy kiss – The writers envision this letter being read in the public assembly of the Christians in Thessalonica.   Though this directive in other places is worded "greet one another ...," it is doubtful that the different wording of the command here in verse 26 is intended to indicate this command is addressed just to the congregational leaders.   Rather, the picture is that all the brethren who hear the letter being read aloud in the public assembly are to show their solidarity with all the other believers in Christ.[54] They are to do it by means of giving all their brothers a holy kiss.   In the Eastern world, a kiss on the cheek, men kissing men, and women kissing women, was the common sign of affection amongst kindred and near friends, both when they met, and when they parted from each other.   As a result of commands to so greet one another, giving one's Christian kinfolk a holy kiss became a universal practice in the primitive Christian assemblies in the Eastern world.   J.B. Phillips' "Give a handshake all around the brotherhood" represents what has been called "a brave attempt to find an equivalent custom in a western culture."[55]

---

[53] Care must be exercised lest this verse be treated as a promise of unconditional eternal security. It must be remembered that the writers have already expressed their fear lest the Thessalonians should be so overcome by Satan's temptations that their labors with them might be in vain (1 Thessalonians 3:5). If their heavenly Father is faithful, then His children also need be faithful if they would inherit the promises.

[54] See 1 Thessalonians 1:4 and 2:1,14, where it has been explained that Christians are spiritual brothers because they have the same Heavenly Father.

[55] This free translation of the verse by J.B. Phillips, in his *The New Testament in Modern English* (New York: Macmillan, 1958), is so characterized in the United Bible Society's handbook on 1 Thessalonians. (Ellingworth & Nida, *op. cit.*, p.128.)

5:27 – *I adjure you by the Lord to have this letter read to all the brethren*.

I adjure you by the Lord – The first-person singular verb makes this verse one of the few places in this letter in which Paul distinguishes himself from his fellow missionaries. It may be that Paul took the pen from the hand of the amanuensis and wrote these last few lines with his own hand. The personal pronoun "you" is plural, but we cannot determine for certain whether this third request is addressed to the congregational leaders or whether "you" includes all the members of the congregation. The verb "adjure" means to cause someone to take a solemn oath. It makes this command more than a request; it makes it a solemn obligation. "By the Lord" indicates it is not just Paul who wants the letter read, it is the Lord Jesus Christ. He is the one to whom the folk addressed in this letter will have to answer if they do not carry out this command.

To have this letter read to all the brethren – The Greek verb "read" has the meaning of "to read aloud," so this command likewise envisions something to be done in the public assembly on the Lord's day. Since 1 Thessalonians is the first of the apostolic epistles to be written, this command likely introduced into the Christian congregations the custom of publicly reading the apostolic writings during the Sunday meetings of the brethren. If great pains were to be taken to make sure "all the brethren"[56] heard what was in this letter, does that indicate that some might be absent from the assembly on any given Lord's day? Or might it indicate there were several house churches in Thessalonica, but all alike were to hear what is herein written? Was the letter delivered first to the leaders of the congregation, and they were to see to it that all the members heard the letter? Or were individual members, each of whom had a responsibility to encourage others to love and good works (Hebrews 10:24), responsible to see that each and every one heard the instructions and commands in this letter? Or are each of these options true? "All the brethren" might possibly include more than just the Christians in Thessalonica, so that the saints in Thessalonica were being given the responsibility of seeing that other congregations in Macedonia also had access to this letter. Whatever our conclusions to these questions, one key implication is obvious. The solemnity of this command indicates Paul was conscious of the weighty importance and far-reaching significance of the contents of this epistle. One would hardly write such a command unless he were aware of Holy Spirit inspiration being at work in its production.

EPISTOLARY CLOSING.   5:28

5:28 – *The grace of our Lord Jesus Christ be with you*.

The grace of our Lord Jesus Christ be with you – The wording of this closing benediction is similar to Paul's customary benedictions in letters later written by him.   He

---

[56] The KJV reads "to all the holy brethren," but the word "holy" apparently does not enjoy integrity. So no conclusion should be drawn that there may have been some brethren in Thessalonica who would be unconcerned about the contents written herein.

substitutes "grace" (*charis*) for the usual epistolary "farewell" (*charein*).[57]   These words are a prayer: "I pray that the Lord Jesus Christ will continue to show you His loving-kindness."[58]

****

Readers familiar with the KJV find several more words at the close of this letter. There is an "Amen," and a subscription which reads "The first *epistle* unto the Thessalonians was written from Athens."

The absence of *amēn* ("amen") from reliable representatives of both Alexandrian and Western text types indicates it likely was added to later manuscripts to indicate to the audience listening to the public reading of the letter when it was appropriate to express their agreement with what had just been read.

None of the subscriptions found in the KJV are as old as the epistles themselves; these subscriptions were subsequently added by scribes.   There are even manuscript variations in the wording of this one.   The oldest subscriptions simply repeat the title "To the Thessalonians 1."   Three different wordings ("from Athens," "from Corinth," and "from Laodicea") are found designating the place of writing.   In the Detailed Introduction to 1 Thessalonians, Corinth has been defended as the likely place of origin for this letter.

---

[57] *Charein* served both as the introductory and farewell greetings in ancient letters.   See notes at 1 Thessalonians 1:1.

[58] See comments at 1 Thessalonians 1:1 for the import of "Lord Jesus Christ."

Commentary On

2 Thessalonians

CONCISE INTRODUCTION TO
2 THESSALONIANS

The circumstances connected with the beginning of the church in Thessalonica were reviewed in the concise introduction to 1 Thessalonians. Some special needs the new Christians faced led to the writing of 1 Thessalonians. Some of the same issues covered in that letter are emphasized again in this second letter to the church at Thessalonica.

Authorship

Three names occur in the signature of this letter – Paul, Silas, and Timothy – and they are the same three names given in 1 Thessalonians.

Destination

The destination "to the church of the Thessalonians" is the same as in 1 Thessalonians.

Place of Writing

The only time we know about when the three men named in the signature were together after the church at Thessalonica was planted is during the years Paul was in Corinth (Acts 18:1-11).

Date of Writing

An interval of only a few months had passed since 1 Thessalonians had been sent to the church. That the second letter to Thessalonica followed soon after the first is indicated by (1) the fact that the three writers are still together, and (2) almost the same state of affairs at Thessalonica is described in each.

It is therefore probable that the letter was written late AD 52 or early AD 53, perhaps a year after the congregation was planted.

Occasion and Purpose of Writing

A report has reached Corinth concerning some troublesome new developments in the life of the congregation at Thessalonica. Someone, using forged evidence alleged to be from the missionaries themselves, has been teaching that the day of the Lord had already begun. That mistaken idea needed correction. Hence, the writers indicated that certain great events must precede that day, and insisted that these events were still future. Some unruly and undisciplined brethren were still refusing to work to support themselves; these ones needed to repent and become productive. The working Christians are directed both to quit enabling the unruly ones to continue in their undisciplined lifestyle and to take measures to lead the unruly to repentance.

Outline of 2 Thessalonians

Epistolary Opening – Signatures, Address and Greeting.   1:1,2

I.   Previous Commendation of the Christians at Thessalonica Reaffirmed.   1:3-12
   A. Commendation for Steadfastness.   3,4
   B. Explanation About Persecution.   5-10
   C. Prayer for Continued Spiritual Growth.   11,12

II. The Rebellion, The Man of Lawlessness, and The Restrainer.   2:1-17
   A. Reasons to Reject the False Teaching that the Day of the Lord had Already Dawned.   2:1-12
   B. Further Thanksgiving for, Assurance and Encouragement to, and Prayer for the Readers.   2:13-17

III. Practical Admonitions Concerning Practical Behavior.   3:1-15
   A. Prayer Requested.   3:1-5
      1. Paul and his helpers are in need.   1,2
      2. The Lord is sufficient for all needs.   3-5
   B. Idleness by Christians in Thessalonica is Rebuked.   3:6-15
      1. Avoid the unruly brother.   6
      2. Follow the example they had observed.   7-9
      3. An important principle.   10
      4. A command addressed to the idle brothers.   11,12
      5. Continue doing what is right.   13-15

IV. Two Final Wish-Prayers.   3:16

Personalized, Authenticating Greeting and Benediction.   3:17,18

THE EPISTLE OF
2 THESSALONIANS[1]

Epistolary Opening.   Signature, Address, Greetings. 1:1,2

1:1 – Paul and Silvanus and Timothy, to the church of the Thessalonians in God our Father and the Lord Jesus Christ:

Paul and Silvanus and Timothy – These three missionaries who dispatched the first epistle to Thessalonica are again together when this second letter is written. As indicated in comments at 1 Thessalonians 1:1, the only time we know these three were together after the congregation at Thessalonica was planted was when they all were at Corinth in the middle of Paul's second missionary journey (Acts 18:5). Paul's ministry in Corinth lasted a year and six months (Acts 18:11). 2 Thessalonians could have been written anywhere from several months to a year after 1 Thessalonians was written. 1 Thessalonians 3:1-6 indicated Timothy had made a trip to Thessalonica and reported back to Paul before 1 Thessalonians was written. Since someone had to carry that first epistle to Thessalonica, it seems to be a reasonable scenario that Timothy delivered the first letter to the church and then returned to Paul, and reported concerning the church's reception of 1 Thessalonians. The scenario continues that Timothy was then given this second letter to deliver, and he journeyed to Thessalonica with it. The 18 months stay of Paul in Corinth would give time for these several trips. Where has Silas been in the interval between letters? Was he with Paul in Corinth all the time, or did he perhaps make a trip to Berea and then back to Corinth between the times when the two letters were written? We have little information to help us decide. After Silas and Timothy both joined Paul at Corinth (Acts 18:5) about the time 1 Thessalonians was written, we have no further record of Silas' travels or ministry provided in the book of Acts. However, he is named in 2 Corinthians 1:19 as being known for his preaching in Corinth. His only other mention in the New Testament is years later when he is named as Peter's amanuensis (1 Peter 5:12).

To the church of the Thessalonians in God our Father and the Lord Jesus Christ – These words of address are almost entirely the same as the address at 1 Thessalonians 1:1.

---

[1] The letter we know as 2 Thessalonians must have been written after 1 Thessalonians. 2 Thessalonians 2:15 indicates a letter had been sent from Paul to Thessalonica before the one now being written. Before the 4th century when the Western church adopted Jerome's arrangement of the Pauline letters by length (i.e., the order made familiar to us by the arrangement of the books in our English Bibles), the letter we call 2 Thessalonians was already uniformly known as 2 Thessalonians, both in titles attached to it in the ancient manuscripts and in references to the letter in early Christian literature (see the Detailed Introduction to 2 Thessalonians). As a result of this determination of the order in which the two letters were written, comments offered for certain verses in 2 Thessalonians will reflect the assumption that what we can read in 1 Thessalonians forms a background for what we read in this second letter.

The addition of "our" in the phrase "God our Father" makes it clear that God is being presented as the Father both of the writers and of His people who specifically are the church at Thessalonica, rather than as the Father of Jesus. The missionaries who sign this letter claim a familial relationship with the Christians at Thessalonica when they speak of God as "our" Father. They are God's children because they have all been born again.

1:2 – *Grace to you and peace from God the Father and the Lord Jesus Christ.*

Grace to you and peace – The salutation may well be the Christian form of greeting in Greek and Jewish terms. "Grace," or favor, is a Christian variation of a common Greek greeting of good wishes. It was indicated at 1 Thessalonians 1:1 that grace is an attitude of loving kindness. "Peace" is the traditional Jewish greeting (the Hebrew word is *shalom*) and both words of greeting are a prayer for the readers' spiritual well-being in its widest sense.

From God the Father and the Lord Jesus Christ – The fact that grace and peace are to come from both God the Father[2] and the Lord Jesus Christ[3] indicates clearly that the writers have something more in mind than a mere perfunctory "greetings to you." There is a strong implication of Jesus' divine status in the fact that He is linked with God the Father as the source of the grace and peace that the Christian readers may enjoy.

I. PREVIOUS COMMENDATION OF THE CHRISTIANS AT THESSALONICA REAFFIRMED. 1:3-12

A. Commendation for Steadfastness. 3,4

1:3 – *We ought always to give thanks to God for you, brethren, as is only fitting, because your faith is greatly enlarged, and the love of each one of you toward one another grows ever greater;*

We ought always to give thanks to God for you, brethren – Twice in this letter (here in verse 3 and at 2:13), and nowhere else, the writers express a feeling of obligation to express

---

[2] Older English Bibles read "God our Father" at this place as well as in verse 1. Recent editions of the Greek text print the word "our" in brackets, since the manuscript evidence for or against its inclusion is about equally divided. It is more difficult to explain its omission if it originally were in the text than it is to explain its addition by a later copyist who wished to make this phrase match the one in verse 1.

[3] For the titles "Lord," "Jesus," and "Christ," see notes at 1 Thessalonians 1:1.

gratitude to God. "Ought" expresses a moral obligation, not just a duty. It looks like the writers are insisting they do have an obligation to give thanks to God for the Thessalonians. This strong affirmation may imply that the Thessalonians had protested that the commendation given them in the first letter (1 Thessalonians 1:2-10) was excessive. The writers, therefore, here insist that the Thessalonians well deserved all the thanksgiving with which the writers' hearts were filled on their account. "Brethren" indicates the readers are thought of as fellow believers by the writers. In 1 Thessalonians 1:2 the writers used the word "always," and they use it again here. All the time the writers felt the obligation to express their gratitude for the Thessalonian Christians.

As is only fitting – The thanksgiving was rightly warranted, and the following verses give some solid reasons why this was so. Verses 3-10 in the Greek form a single complex sentence in which several reasons for thanksgiving are highlighted.

Because your faith is greatly enlarged – This clause assigns one reason for saying that it was "fitting" for them to give thanks to God. "Greatly enlarged" is a metaphor taken from the observable rapid growth one can see in the animal or vegetable kingdom. Such growth causes delight in the eyes of the beholder.

As was true at 1 Thessalonians 3:2, so here, "faith" can be understood either subjectively as faithfulness, or objectively as the body of teaching. In 1 Thessalonians 3:10, the writers spoke of the Thessalonians' deficiency of faith in the latter sense, indicating that in some areas they needed further instruction. If this verse is speaking of faith in that sense again, "greatly enlarged" indicates they were now better instructed. On the other hand, the next verse here in 2 Thessalonians will speak of perseverance and faithfulness in the midst of persecutions. This, too, was a matter of concern at the time when 1 Thessalonians was written (1 Thessalonians 3:7). That Paul and Silas are aware of the delightful growth in faith among the Thessalonians implies that they have heard a report to that effect. It is reasonable to assume that the same report also contained information about the error which prevailed among them respecting the time of the second coming of the Lord Jesus, which led to the writing of what is contained in 2 Thessalonians 2.

And the love of each one of you toward one another grows ever greater – This clause gives a second reason the writers were bound to give thanks. In 1 Thessalonians 3:12 the writers prayed that the Thessalonians' love for one another and for all people might "increase" (*pleonadzō*, the same verb as used in this verse) and "abound." The two Greek verbs here in 2 Thessalonians 1:3 are in the present tense, indicating that their faith and love were still growing. This welcome bit of information that their prayers have been answered must have also been included in the report that has come from Thessalonica to the writers. There is also the very likely possibility that the emphasis on "each one of you" means the differences which had called forth such passages as 1 Thessalonians 3:12, 4:6-10, and 5:12-14 had apparently all ceased, and that as a result mutual love was multiplying.

Paul had commended the brethren in 1 Thessalonians 1:3 for their faith, love, and hope. "Hope" is missing from the commendations here in 2 Thessalonians, because their hope, especially in expectation of Christ's immediate return, needed some additional sharpening and training. But thanks be to God, they were growing in faith and love.[4] In fact, the measure of their growth in these two areas was impressive because it came despite hardships that the church members faced.

1:4 – *therefore, we ourselves speak proudly of you among the churches of God for your perseverance and faith in the midst of all your persecutions and afflictions which you endure.*

Therefore, we ourselves speak proudly of you among the churches of God – "Therefore" indicates that the boasting here alluded to is a result of the spiritual growth evident in the lives of the Christians at Thessalonica. The verb "speak proudly" governs two phrases: one specifies the object of boasting, and the other specifies the place where the boasting is done. To speak proudly about something, one must have a high estimation of the thing, rejoice in it, offer high commendation of it, and applaud the part the boaster had in it. "We ourselves" includes all three men named in the signature of this letter – Paul, Silas, and Timothy. Commentators have struggled to explain why the word "ourselves" was added since it lays stress on the fact that Paul and his companions were thus boasting.[5] Is this stress on boasting intended to be a contrast with the Thessalonians own self-evaluation, reflecting again the supposition that the Thessalonians were protesting that the commendation given to them in the first letter was excessive? Or is the stress on boasting intended to express the idea that the missionaries' boasting was not self-praise? After all, since they had been instrumental in planting the congregation, their boasting might be mistaken for self-praise. Or is the stress on boasting an allusion to the fact that, while others in the region knew of the remarkable change in the lives of the Thessalonians (1 Thessalonians 1:8,9), the missionaries themselves boasted about it?

Another debated question concerns which congregations, this early in church history, might be involved in what here are called "the churches of God"? In 1 Thessalonians 2:14

---

[4] These references to the satisfactory outcome of earlier matters of concern and prayer are corroborating evidence that both letters were addressed to the same people and written in their present sequence. (See the Detailed Introduction to 2 Thessalonians concerning the authenticity of 2 Thessalonians and the sequence of the letters.)

[5] There is a variation in word order in the Greek, some reading *hēmas autous*, and some reading *autous hēmas*. The former reading tends to affirm that such boasting was not the usual custom of the speakers. The latter reading tends to say that the praise of others concerning the Thessalonians was not sufficient for the writers. They had to express their joy by speaking proudly of the Thessalonians.

the Christian congregations in Judea were called "churches of God," but unless there was communication between the missionaries and those congregations, they hardly are the ones who are hearing this boasting about the Thessalonians. Perhaps the best answer to this question is that there were other congregations in both Macedonia and in Achaia besides those at Thessalonica and Corinth. 2 Corinthians 1:1 speaks of multiple congregations in Achaia. There was certainly one in Cenchrea (Romans 16:1).

This boasting likely gives us insight into the methodology employed by Paul, Silas, and Timothy. The missionaries held up the Thessalonians as an example to be emulated by other congregations, just as, on another occasion, the Corinthians were held up as an example to the churches in Macedonia (2 Corinthians 9:2).

For your perseverance and faith – This clause identifies what the missionaries were speaking proudly about. The verse will go on to say the readers are facing persecution and suffering. These words indicate the victorious way the Thessalonians are dealing with that persecution and suffering.

Another debate among commentators is whether the words "perseverance" and "faith" indicate one action or two.

- Some commentators appeal to 1 Thessalonians 3:5, where Paul had expressed misgivings about how the Thessalonians might respond to the tempter's tempting by persecution. Would they continue to be faithful to Christ? Those commentators see 2 Thessalonians 1:4 as a statement that they were faithful.

- However, rather than weakening the terms here in 1:4 into a Hebraism meaning "your patient faith," we think it best to treat them as separate ideas. (1) "Perseverance" (*hupomonē*) is the word used of Job at James 5:11, "You have heard of the perseverance of Job," and at Revelation 14:12, where perseverance is explained as "keeping the commandments of God and their faith in Jesus." The NASB margin, which offers "steadfastness" as an alternate equivalent of *hupomonē,* reflects the fact that no English word is quite strong enough to express the active courage and resolution implied here by *hupomonē.* (2) In order for steadfast endurance to be of any value in the sight of God, it must be combined with faith in Christ Jesus.

In the midst of all your persecutions and afflictions which you endure – Making a clear distinction between persecutions and afflictions is difficult.[6] One suggestion is that persecutions resulted in more physical suffering than afflictions do. Another suggestion is that

---

[6] In 1 Thessalonians 2:14 (cp. Acts 17:5-9) reference was made to the Thessalonian Christians being persecuted, while 1 Thessalonians 1:6 and 3:3-4 made reference to tribulations (*thlipsis*). In Acts 14:22 Paul and Barnabas warned believers they would face "many tribulations" (*thlipseōn*) on their way to heaven.

the persecutions are more the result of organized efforts by certain persons than are afflictions. The present tense verb *anechesthe*, which could be translated "are enduring," in this verse compares markedly with the past tense verb at 1 Thessalonians 2:14. It looks like one persecution ended before 1 Thessalonians was written and another round of persecutions has begun before 2 Thessalonians is written.

B. Explanation About Persecution.   5-10

1:5 – This is *a plain indication of God's righteous judgment so that you will be considered worthy of the kingdom of God, for which indeed you are suffering.*

***This is* a plain indication of God's righteous judgment** – From thanksgiving (verses 3,4), the writers turn to words of encouragement (verses 5-10) based on the prospect of the vindication Christians will receive on the day of the Lord for the suffering they are having to presently endure. Like David (Psalm 73:1-14) and Jeremiah (Jeremiah 12:1-4), the righteous are often perplexed when the wicked prosper in this world while the godly suffer. To prevent such thoughts from being discouraging, the Thessalonians are instructed to concentrate on how things will be set right at the final judgment.

The Greek is very concise. Even when the ASV translators added the words "which is," while the NASB translators added "this is," it still is not easy for the English reader to tie the verses together and follow the thread of thought. The word "plain indication" stands in apposition, though it refers back not to any single word in verse 4, but to the general sense of persecutions and afflictions about which the whole latter part of the verse 4 was occupied. The writers are saying that the persecutions the readers are enduring should be viewed as proof that there will be a final judgment, at which time the righteous who were persecuted will be rewarded and wicked men, like those doing the persecuting, will be appropriately punished by God. "Righteous judgment" is a positive answer to the question, "Will not the judge of the earth do right?" Quite clearly, the similar expression "righteous judgment" at Romans 2:5 points to the final judgement rather than to some temporal judgment that God enacts in this earthly lifetime.

So that you will be considered worthy of the kingdom of God – It is likely that "so that" indicates a result. The writers are promising the readers that "as a result" of their faithfulness in the midst of persecutions and afflictions, they will be "considered worthy."[7]

---

[7] The exact relation between present and future events in verses 5b-10 raises both theological problems and problems for Bible translators. These problems are not made any easier by the fact that, although many of the expressions used in this passage seemingly have a future meaning, it is not until verse 9 that a future tense verb is used.

The context requires that this consideration is something that takes place in the mind of the righteous Judge at the final judgment. It reflects the fact that God has revealed certain conditions that must be met in this life if one would, at the final judgment, receive the commendation, "Well done, good and faithful servant" (Matthew 25:21,23).[8] Since the "kingdom of God" in this passage is something that follows the righteous judgment of God, it seems to follow that the "kingdom" in this verse is not different than "the kingdom which Jesus hands over to the God and Father" at the *parousia* and the consummation of earth's history (1 Corinthians 15:24). Nor is this kingdom different than the one spoken about in Acts 14:22 where early Christians were apprised of the fact that "through many tribulations we must enter the kingdom of God."[9] The "kingdom of God" here is identical with the "kingdom and glory" into which God had called the readers (1 Thessalonians 2:12).[10] "Considered worthy of the kingdom" is synonymous with "those who are considered worthy to attain to that age and the resurrection from the dead" (Luke 20:35).

For which indeed you are suffering – The Greek word *kai*, translated by the NASB as "indeed," is translated "also" in the ASV. The ASV translation shows that other Christians (including the writers of this letter) besides the Thessalonians are suffering persecution. What was happening to the Thessalonians was not something strange or unexpected. The present tense verb ("are suffering") indicates that the Thessalonian Christians are suffering persecutions and tribulations at the very time the letter was written to them. It might be asked, "How can someone be suffering now for some future result (i.e., to be "considered worthy of the kingdom")?" The answer is in one of Jesus' beatitudes. He said, "Blessed are you when people insult you and persecute you, and falsely say all kinds of evil against you, because of Me. Rejoice and be glad, for your reward in heaven is great" (Matthew 5:11,12). Jesus' words about a "reward in heaven" refer to the same thing as do the words written to the Thessalonian Christians about being "considered worthy of the kingdom of God." Christians may and will suffer for the sake of righteousness while in this life, but at the final judgment "theirs is the kingdom of heaven" (Matthew 5:10). This promise be-

---

[8] The verb "considered worthy" has nothing to do with the debated theological question of merit. When Christians habitually fulfill the conditions of salvation, they are not earning or meriting salvation. Salvation is a gift of God (Ephesians 2:8). No discussion of earning salvation should be intruded by commentators who are purportedly explaining what here has been written.

[9] Care must be taken lest "kingdom of God" in this place is explained as being an anticipated earthly millennial kingdom. Some eschatological systems advocate the idea that the "kingdom of God" has reference to a thousand-year earthly kingdom, supposedly inaugurated after the second coming and consummating before the eternal state of heaven and hell begin. However, the idea that the kingdom spoken of here is a thousand-year period of time before the righteous are invited to heaven and the wicked are sent to hell cannot be harmonized with this context. This passage, after alluding to the final judgment, immediately goes on to talk about the wicked being punished with eternal destruction. No attempt should be made to use this "kingdom" passage in 2 Thessalonians as evidence there will be a millennial kingdom.

[10] In this connection, it may be useful to review the notes about "Kingdom" included at 1 Thessalonians 2:12.

came embedded in one of the faithful sayings, in the words, "If we endure, we shall also reign with Him" (2 Timothy 2:12).

1:6 – *For after all it is only just for God to repay with affliction those who afflict you,*

For after all it is only just for God to repay with affliction those who afflict you – The Greek word *eiper*, translated "for after all," introduces a truth that has been revealed by the Judge Himself. "Just" says God's justice is concerned not only with vindication, but also with condemnation. This theme is at least as old as the cry of Abraham, "Shall not the Judge of all the earth do right?" (Genesis 18:25). "Repay" is an emphatic word which suggests a reciprocal action, such as giving in return. Persecutors who cause Christians to suffer will be repaid by the Lord for their actions. "'I will repay,' says the Lord" (Romans 12:19) tells us that God is going to provide compensation for the injustices of this life. There is going to be a judgment just like verse 5 has indicated. Not only will the folk who have remained faithful to Christ despite their persecution be rewarded, but the persecutors of Christians will be properly recompensed for their outrageous behavior. The "affliction" (or tribulation) threatened in this verse is something that happens to the wicked after the final judgment,[11] and it differs significantly from the "afflictions" ("tribulations") the Thessalonians were then currently enduring (verse 4). The Greek word translated "affliction" both in verse 4 and here in verse 6 is *thlipsis,* a word that is elsewhere often translated "tribulation." While the term is not further defined at this point, verse 9 ("eternal destruction") details one of the consequences the persecutors will experience. It is the present lot of Christians to undergo many tribulations (Acts 14:22; 1 Thessalonians 3:4). For the non-Christians, tribulation will be future and it will be far greater in intensity. (See also what 1 Thessalonians 1:10; 2:16; and 5:9 said about God's wrath.)

1:7 – *and to give relief to you who are afflicted and to us as well when the Lord Jesus will be revealed from heaven with His mighty angels in flaming fire,*

And *to give* **relief to you who are afflicted** – This, too, is part of the righteous judgment of God. Not only will the wicked be punished, the sufferings of the righteous will be ended when Jesus returns. "Afflicted" pictures the hardships, the strain, the pain, that the person suffering persecution is forced to endure. "Relief" is a good choice of words to translate *anesis*,[12] for what is promised is the like the relaxation a soldier experiences after the hard-

---

[11] There may be a period of time known as "the great tribulation" just before the second coming (Revelation 7:14), but that is not the tribulation (or affliction) the persecutors of the Thessalonians are threatened with in this passage. The persecutors of the Thessalonians in the 1st century will have been long dead before the great tribulation occurs. In addition, the great tribulation occurs before the final judgment, not after, as does this affliction with which the persecutors will be repaid (verse 7).

[12] Some English versions use the word "rest" to translate *anesis* instead of "relief." Care must be taken lest Matthew 11:28 ("come unto Me, all you who are weary and heavy laden, and I will give you rest"), or Hebrews 4:1 ("a promise ... of entering His rest"), or Hebrews 4:9 ("there remains a Sabbath rest for the people of God") be used as cross references, for the three words translated "rest" in those passages are not *anesis*.

ships of a long and perilous march, or the relief one enjoys when pain no longer wracks the body. Such "relief" is not to be expected in its fullness until the judgment day.

And to us as well – Paul, Silas, and Timothy lived in the same world that the Thessalonian believers lived in, and they experienced similar persecutions and afflictions. They, too, were looking forward to the relief promised to the persecuted Christians.

When the Lord Jesus will be revealed from heaven – Both the repayment of the persecutors and the relief of the persecuted will occur at the time when the judgment introduced earlier in this sentence occurs. That judgment occurs, this verse says, when Jesus "is revealed from heaven." The Greek word used for Christ's second coming at 1 Thessalonians 3:13 and 4:15 was *parousia* ("coming"). This verse uses the verb form of *apokalupsis* ("revelation").[13] "Heaven"[14] is where the Lord Jesus now is, seated at the right hand of God (Hebrews 8:1; 10:12) and concealed from human view. "Will be revealed" indicates that the day is coming when He will no longer be concealed from human view. When He is revealed, every eye will see Him (Revelation 1:7). The last book in the New Testament, titled "Revelation," in numerous places describes what people will see when Christ comes in all His glory.

With His mighty angels – Literally, the Greek reads "the angels of His power." It is not the angels who are being described as mighty, though they are; rather, their presence and actions on His behalf will demonstrate Christ's power. Revelation 19:14 describes the returning Christ as being accompanied by the heavenly host, the armies of heaven, while Revelation 17:14 and 19:19 seem to indicate the armies take part in the battle against the harlot and the 8th beast and their armies. The angels also will be active participants in the

---

[13] The word *apokalupsis* literally means to unveil or uncover, such as is accomplished by removing the covering from a long-concealed work of art. Bible writers use several words as they portray Christ's second coming.

- *Epiphaneia*, "appearing" or "shining forth," is used in 2 Timothy 4:8.
- *Phanerosis*, "manifestation," is used in 2 Corinthians 4:2 and 1 John 3:2.
- *Parousia*, "coming" or "presence," is the word most often used, as at 1 Corinthians 15:23 and 1 Thessalonians 4:15.
- *Apokalupsis*, "revelation," is the word used at times, as in this text, in Luke 17:30, and in 1 Peter 1:7,13 and 4:13. (The verses in 1 Peter all highlight what the redeemed experience when Christ is revealed.)

It is this commentator's judgment that the different words are not intended to describe different comings; rather, the words convey different ways of looking at the same glorious return of the Lord. Attempts by some systems of eschatology to identify *parousia* as a coming which happens years before His *revelation* coming are mistaken. Angels are involved when Christ returns, whether it is described as His *parousia* (1 Thessalonians 3:13) or His *revelation* (2 Thessalonians 1:7). A judgment of both the righteous and wicked takes place whether it is His *parousia* (2 Peter 3:4-7) or His *revelation* (2 Thessalonians 1:6,7). It is difficult to think of a "*revelation*-coming" as a separate event occurring sometime after the *parousia* when 1 Corinthians 15:23-28 indicates the end of the age occurs at the *parousia*.

[14] See notes at 1 Thessalonians 1:10 and 4:16 concerning "heaven."

events of judgment, gathering the weeds for destruction and gathering the good grain for the Lord's use (Matthew 13:30,41). Christ's power is demonstrated as the angels are executors of His commands.

In flaming fire -- Most modern translations treat this clause as part of verse 7, making it a continuation of the description of Christ as He becomes visible to men on earth as His second coming occurs.[15]   In the Old Testament, "flaming fire" was a way of picturing the glory of God as He manifested Himself to men (Exodus 3:2; 19:18; 24:17; Daniel 7:9,10). This may be a figurative way of saying that when Jesus returns, men will see in Him "aspects of majesty unknown and inconceivable before."[16]

1:8 – *dealing out retribution to those who do not know God and to those who do not obey the gospel of our Lord Jesus.*

Dealing out retribution to those who do not know God – The description of what the Lord Jesus will do when His second coming occurs continues.[17]   *Didontos ekdikēsin* could well have been translated "giving punishment" or "giving justice," or perhaps even "inflicting punishment."[18]   This verse goes on to identify those who are going to receive the punishment.   Verse 6 indicated that the folk who were afflicting the Thessalonian Christians would be punished.   Here in verse 8 it is inferred that those persecutors were included among the two groups of folk[19] who would be punished after the final judgment.

---

[15] In the KJV this phrase is part of verse 8, which then reads "in flaming fire dealing out retribution to those who do not know God." This translation reflects a change in punctuation, inserting a comma after "angels" rather than after "fire." So punctuated, "flaming fire" becomes the instrument of punishment on the wicked. Writers commenting on the KJV often spoke of the phrase as referring to punishment in Hell.

[16] Findlay, *op. cit.*, p.132.

[17] The nearest antecedent to the participle *didontos* (translated "dealing out") is "the Lord Jesus" in verse 7.

[18] NASB's choice of "retribution" to translate *ekdikēsin* may be better than the KJV's "vengeance." Vengeance at times carries the connotation that the taking of revenge was a matter of settling a personal grudge. That may be too strong. In Luke 18:7 the same word occurs in a context where God brings about "justice" for the elect who have been oppressed by wicked men. That connotation of *ekdikēsin* would be suitable in this Thessalonian context. So is "retribution," for that word means a requital of punishment, a repaying someone for something they have done.

[19] The Greek word translated "those" (*tois*) is specifically repeated in the next phrase. According to Bruce (*op. cit.*, p.151), Lightfoot argued that the repetition of the word "those" before "do not obey" indicates two distinct classes or groups are meant. Bruce himself, however, held that, in verses 9 and 10, the repetition of *tois* "follows the parallelistic style of Old Testament prophecy and poetry," in which the two phrases are intended to be descriptions of the same group. Bruce's view is likely correct. Men, writing under the influence of Holy Spirit inspiration, whether they were Old Testament mouthpieces for God or New Testament apostles and prophets, were capable of employing a similar, exalted style of writing.

In vivid contrast to the Christians who know God, some of the persecutors were among the folk who do not know God. The verb "know" (*eidosin*) means to be intimately acquainted with, or to be in close relationship with. Those who do not know God may be either Gentiles (Psalm 79:6; Galatians 4:8; 1Thessalonians 4:5) or Jews (John 8:54,55).

And to those who do not obey the gospel of our Lord Jesus – In another vivid contrast to the Christians who have obeyed the gospel, the persecutors have not. As was true in the previous phrase, those who have not obeyed the gospel may be either Jews (Romans 10:16,21) or Gentiles (Romans 2:8,9; 11:30). "The gospel of our Lord Jesus Christ" can be either good news about Him, or good news of which He is the source.[20] That good news requires obedience to the commands contained in it. Jesus is the source of eternal salvation to all who obey Him (Hebrews 5:9). "Those who do not obey the gospel" is not referring to people who never had the opportunity of hearing the gospel, but rather to those who had the opportunity to hear it and did not respond. People who hear the gospel and refuse submission to it do so because they have deliberately decided to reject the Lord Jesus.

1:9 – *These will pay the penalty of eternal destruction, away from the presence of the Lord and from the glory of His power,*

These will pay the penalty of eternal destruction – "These" refers back to the both groups just described in verse 8. The awful words "pay the penalty" describe the retribution designed for godless people and rejecters of the gospel. The word translated "penalty" is a word that "normally means a penalty imposed by a court of law."[21] The verb translated "pay" implies that a price must be paid in return for their refusal to know and obey God. That price is described here as none other than "eternal destruction." The word translated "eternal" conveys the notion of unceasing duration, the express opposite of temporary (2 Corinthians 4:18).[22] The word translated "destruction" (*olethron*) is different from the word *kolasis* which occurs in Matthew 25:46 and is there translated "punishment." *Olethron* occurs at 1 Timothy 6:9 where it is translated "ruin" in the NASB. A thing which is destroyed or ruined does not mean it is annihilated, but rather that it is no longer useful for the purpose for which it was originally intended. Verse10 goes on to identify one important thing which the lost will not be able to do for Christ.

---

[20] See the notes at 1 Thessalonians 1:5 for the word "gospel" and at 1:1 for the word "Lord."

[21] Ellingworth & Nida, *op. cit.*, p.148.

[22] The Greek adjective translated "eternal" (*aiōnion*) occurs seventy-two times in the New Testament. For forty-four of these occurrences, the word is found in the phrase "eternal life." It is very difficult to suppose that "eternal" as used here in 2 Thessalonians 1:9 as part of the opposite combination "eternal destruction" somehow bears a restricted or limited sense.

Away from the presence of the Lord – In 1 Thessalonians 4:17 the life of the redeemed in the age to come was described simply as "we will always be with the Lord." Conversely, this verse explains part of what is involved in eternal destruction for the lost – it is to be separated from the presence of the Lord.[23] This phrase explains a reason why those suffering eternal destruction/ruin are unable to do for the Lord Jesus what the redeemed are privileged to do. They have been banished permanently from the presence (literally, "from the face of") of the Lord Jesus Christ.

And from the glory of His power – "The glory of His power" is a "metaphor from the courts of mighty Oriental kings, where only honored courtiers are admitted to spend their time in the immediate and familiar presence of the sovereign."[24] We learned in verse 7 that Christ's glory will be manifested when He returns. "Power" translates *ischuos*, a word that stresses power in action. That power in action will be one way Christ's glory hereafter is manifested. While familiar contact with Christ in all His power will be accorded to all the saved hereafter, the lost will be banished permanently from such familiar contact.[25]

1:10 – *when He comes to be glorified in His saints on that day, and to be marveled at among all who have believed – for our testimony to you was believed.*

When He comes to be glorified in His saints on that day – This clause indicates the time when the godless and unbelievers will pay the penalty (verse 9). It is when He comes again. The Greek word *hotan*, translated "when" or "whenever," carries an idea of indefiniteness. That indefiniteness does not refer to the event, but only to the time of the event, as was indicated in 1 Thessalonians 5:2. The coming of Jesus here referred to is His second coming, which is elsewhere described by the words *parousia* (1 Thessalonians 3:13) and revelation (2 Thessalonians 1:7). "That day" is a shorthand designation for "the day of the Lord" (cf. 2 Thessalonians 2:2; 1 Thessalonians 5:2, Isaiah 2:11,17). Coming at the end of the long sentence that in the Greek extends from verses 3 to 10, "on that day" is emphatic. That is the time when the righteous will get relief (verse 7) and the wicked will receive their coming retribution (verse 8).[26]

---

[23] "Lord" here in verse 9 is the same One identified as the "Lord Jesus" in verses 7 and 8.

[24] A.J. Mason, "The Epistles to the Thessalonians" in *Ellicott's Commentary on the Whole Bible* (Grand Rapids, MI: Zondervan Publishing House, 1959), p.153.

[25] The Greek preposition twice translated "from" in this verse is *apo*, which we have treated in both "from" clauses as expressing the idea of separation. Not all commentators agree that it implies separation in this second "from" clause. However, "if 'glory' be visible manifestations proceeding from His power, there is no problem in understanding how this expression also describes the anguish of separation." (Thomas, *op. cit.*, p.313.)

[26] If both righteous and wicked are sentenced on "that day," this passage seems to indicate there will be *one general judgment*. The godless and unbelieving are present, and will receive "retribution" and "penalty." Also present on the same day are the godly and believers, the righteous who will get "relief." The eternal destinies are contrasted, but those destinies are imposed at an identical point of time.

A number of questions must be answered as we try to offer an explanation of "to be glorified in His saints." (1) "To be glorified" is an infinitive which can indicate either purpose or result. Which shall we choose? (2) The words translated "in His saints" are written with the Greek preposition *en* followed by words in the dative case. Is it a dative of person, or a dative of sphere? (3) And who are included in *tois hagiois* ("His saints," "the holy [ones]")? This last issue is the same basic Greek wording and thus the same question that had to be answered at 1 Thessalonians 3:13.

This commentator has come to these conclusions. (1) It makes equally good sense if we say the purpose of Jesus' coming again is that He might receive glory and admiration, or if we say the result of Jesus' coming is that He receives glory and admiration. (2) If we choose to interpret the phrase as a dative of person, and translate using the preposition "by," the verse says Christ is glorified *by* all His saints. If we choose dative of sphere, and translate using the preposition "among," the verse says that Christ is glorified by what can be seen *among* the saints who are assembled in His presence. (3) We can draw the same conclusion as at 3:13. There may not be reason to limit "holy [ones]" to either redeemed men or to the angels.[27] If "saints" refers to redeemed men, what takes place *with* and *to* and *for* the saints as they rise from the dead in their glorified bodies (1 Thessalonians 4:16) and ascend to meet the Lord in the air will manifestly display the glory of Jesus' power. If "holy [ones]" refers to the angels of His power, what the angels do at Christ's command during His second coming will be a grand exhibition of the glory of Jesus' power. Either way, Jesus Christ gets the glory. The implications of Christ's second coming are far-reaching, not only on how it affects redeemed and lost men, but it also what it means for Jesus Himself.

And to be marveled at among all who have believed – "All who have believed"[28] pictures what happened back on earth before the second coming occurs. "All" indicates that no believer is excluded from this role. "Believed" is the opposite decision to those who disobey the gospel (verse 8). The prepositional phrase translated "among" in this clause is the same one in the previous clause. As was true there, so here; the Greek preposition *en* followed by the dative case can be either dative of person or dative of sphere. It is most likely the Greek phrase should be translated the same way in both clauses. English versions vary between "marveled at, admired, or honored" to translate the infinitive *thaumasthēnai*. Small things do not cause admiration or wonder. Jesus' power is so great that what He is doing is a cause of marvel or admiration.

---

[27] Bruce, who believes we have an example of Hebrew parallelism in these verses, argues that the parallelism between this "glorified" clause and the following "marveled at" clause strongly suggests the identity of the "holy ones" and the "believers" (*op. cit.*, p. 152). If Bruce is correct, just as those who are going to be punished are described by two parallel clauses, so the saved are described by two parallel clauses.

[28] There is a manuscript variation at this place. The Textus Receptus has a present tense verb "believe." The better manuscripts carry a past tense verb, "have believed."

– For our testimony to you was believed – The dash before this phrase indicates an ellipsis occurs in the Greek at this place. The NIV supplies the missing thought with these words, "This includes you." The Thessalonian Christians are being assured that they are numbered among those who have believed and who will marvel at Christ at His second coming. Why can such assurance be given by the writers of this letter? It is "because you believed our testimony (preaching) to you." Faith comes by hearing the word of Christ (Romans 10:17). The Thessalonian Christians had obeyed the gospel which had been preached to them.

C. Prayer for Continued Spiritual Growth. 11,12

1:11 – *To this end also we pray for you always, that our God will count you worthy of your calling, and fulfill every desire for goodness and the work of faith with power,*

To this end also we pray for you always – The writers have finished the long sentence begun in verse 3 in which they listed several reasons why they felt obligated to give thanks to God for the Thessalonian Christians. Now verses 11 and 12 are a summary of a prayer to God for the readers which the writers often offered ("we pray ... always") up to God. Having assured the persecuted readers that all things would be set right at the final judgment, the writers now inform their readers about their oft-repeated prayer that the Thessalonians might enjoy a full portion of the blessings prepared for the saints.[29]

That our God will count you worthy of your calling – The preposition "that" following a verb of praying indicates the content of what was said to God in their repeated prayers. This phrase states the first of two specific requests that were being made to God. "Our God" implies that both the writers and the readers were serving the same God. It seems most likely that the "calling" here referred to is the invitation which comes through the gospel to become a Christian.[30] To pray that at the final judgment God would count them worthy of that calling is an implicit reminder that faithfulness until death is part of the con-

---

[29] The antecedent of the Greek words translated "to this end" is not immediately apparent. Perhaps it is intended to include all that was promised to faithful believers in verses 5-10. Perhaps the antecedent is limited to what was stated in the first part of verse 10.

[30] The other possible option is to direct attention to the call to holiness that follows conversion (cf. 2 Peter 3:11ff). In harmony with this option, remember that at 1 Thessalonians 2:12 and 5:24 the verb there translated "calls" is present tense, speaking of a "calling" that follows conversion. Another option sometimes advanced says that in eternity before creation God called certain folk to be saved. If we were to accept this very dubious option, we then would be faced with the problem that teachers of the doctrine of unconditional eternal security find themselves wrestling with. Why are the writers praying for an item to happen which had already been settled in the unalterable will of God?

dition of being counted worthy.[31]   The writers' prayer for the Thessalonians is in harmony with what Paul later will write in Ephesians 4:1,2, "I ... implore you to walk in a manner worthy of the calling with which you have been called, with all humility and gentleness, with patience, showing tolerance for one another in love, being diligent to preserve the unity of the Spirit in the bond of peace."

And fulfill every desire for goodness – This rest of the verse specifies the second of two topics included in the prayers the writers continually send up to God for the readers.   The close proximity of this request to the first request strongly suggests that the two things highlighted in this second petition are the very things that will be examined when God sets out to determine whether or not they are worthy.   As "our God" was the subject of the verb "will count," so "our God" is the subject of the verb "fulfill."

In this clause, the difficult issue to settle is this: Is the desire for goodness God's desire, or is it the desire of the readers?   In this commentator's judgment "this clause presents what should be the resolute purpose of every sincere believer."[32]   The previous clause in this verse contains an implicit reminder that the readers need to be faithful if they would be counted worthy.   If the previous phrase refers to the readers' involvement, it certainly may well be supposed the same is true for this phrase.   Namely, it is the readers who have desires for goodness.[33]   "Goodness" (*agathōsunēs*) sometimes denotes moral goodness quite generally, and sometimes denotes a disposition to do good, to show kindness toward others.[34]   Paul afterwards tells the Romans how he is persuaded of them that they are "full of all goodness" (Romans 15:14).   Neither the Romans nor the Thessalonians would demonstrate such a quality unless they desired or resolved to do so.

And the work of faith with power – The subject and verb earlier expressed needs to be kept in mind here.   The whole idea is "may God fulfill ... the work of faith ...."   In an attempt to convey to English readers what "the work of faith" is, the NIV has "every act prompted by your faith."   Barclay has "the life that faith demands."   The words *en dunamei* ("with power" or "by power") come at the end of the verse in the Greek, but the phrase modifies the verb "fulfill."   The writers offer this prayer because Christians need

---

[31] Though TEV reads "We ask our God to make you worthy of the life He has called you to live," Lightfoot, (*op. cit.*, p. 105) long ago indicated it is doubtful that the meaning "make" for the subjunctive verb *axiōsē* is lexically demonstrable in New Testament usage.

[32] Hayden, *op. cit.*, p.253.

[33] Leon Morris ("The Epistle of Paul to the Thessalonians" in the *Tyndale New Testament Commentaries* [Grand Rapids, MI: Wm. B. Eerdmans Publishing Co., 1971], p.121) notes that the noun "goodness" (*agathōsunēs*) is never used of God elsewhere in the New Testament.   Though the KJV reads "His goodness" there is no word for "His" in the Greek.   George Milligan ("St. Paul's Epistles to the Thessalonians: Greek Text with Introduction and Notes" in *The International Critical Commentary*, London: MacMillan, 1908) suggested that it would be more natural to have a Greek article ("the") before "desire" (*eudokia*) if Paul were referring to God's desire.

[34] Thayer, *Lexicon*, p.3.

divine aid to accomplish their desires for goodness and for putting faith into practice. In Luke 1:35 the Holy Spirit is called the power of God. "Perhaps the power of the Holy Spirit to enable Christian living maybe compared with power steering in an automobile. The person at the wheel (the Christian) chooses to move in a direction pleasing to God; the machinery (the Holy Spirit) provides the energy to follow the chosen course."[35]

1:12 – *so that the name of our Lord Jesus will be glorified in you, and you in Him, according to the grace of our God and the Lord Jesus Christ.*

So that – This verse describes what will happen if the writers' prayers in the previous verse are fulfilled. "So that" indicates the ultimate purpose the writers had in mind that led them to pray for the Thessalonians as they did. They wanted glory to abound to the Lord Jesus Christ.

The name of our Lord Jesus will be glorified in you – "Name" in Biblical usage represents the essence of the person named. To honor the name is to honor the person. The theme of verse 10 about the Lord Jesus being glorified is repeated in this conclusion to which this chapter has been building. Verse 10 presented the idea Jesus would be glorified at the time of His second coming. Since the final clauses in verse 11 refer to the life the Thessalonian Christians are now living, perhaps this verse speaks of Christ being honored in this present life as well as at His coming.

And you in Him – When the glory of Christ becomes obvious at His second coming, as "every knee shall bow ... and every tongue confess that Jesus Christ is Lord" (Philippians 2:10), and His followers are welcomed into His presence forever, then it will be obvious to all that the Christians were right and wise to follow Him. The glorification will be mutual. Jesus will be glorified, and Christians, too, will be glorified.

According to the grace of our God and the Lord Jesus Christ – These closing words of chapter 1 indicate that positive answers to the prayer just offered will be in harmony with the grace (lovingkindness) of our God and the Lord Jesus. The language in this last clause of verse 12 repeats what was written about grace in the greeting (verse 2).

The NASB margin indicates that there is no "the" in the Greek before "Lord Jesus Christ." The marginal note in the NIV, based on the fact that one definite article governs both "God" and "Lord," offers another possible way the Greek can be translated: "our God and Lord, Jesus Christ." The translation offered in the text of the NASB treats the one article as drawing together the two persons of the Godhead as the source of the grace (lovingkindness). Grace has led both God and Jesus to act as they have in the divine plan of redemption offered to men.

---

[35] Hayden, *op. cit.*, p.254.

II. THE REBELLION, THE MAN OF LAWLESSNESS, AND THE RESTRAINER.   2:1-17

A. Reasons to Reject the False Teaching that the Day of the Lord had Already Dawned.   2:1-12

2:1 – Now we request you, brethren, with regard to the coming of our Lord Jesus Christ and our gathering together to Him,

Now we request you, brethren – "Now" translates the Greek conjunction *de*. In this place, it may be either adversative or explicative. If adversative, the translation would be "but." That is, the second coming of Jesus (2 Thessalonians 1:7,10) is a sure thing, *but* the readers must not entertain mistaken or unrealistic notions respecting it. "Now" treats the conjunction as an explanation. It says there is something about the second coming of Jesus and the day of the Lord that needs more explanation and clarification.

Paul used this same introductory phrase in 1 Thessalonians 5:12, so we should give this phrase the same meaning here in 2:1 as we did there. "Brethren" indicates this request is made to the whole congregation. "We request" translates *erōtaō*, a word which can mean either "to ask a question" or "to ask someone to do something." By using this rare word for making a request, the writers are asking the readers to do something; the writers are asking the readers, as it were, to do them a personal favor.

With regard to the coming of our Lord Jesus Christ – Just as the writers brought into view the purpose of writing the 1 Thessalonians letter after their opening words of thanksgiving, so here in 2 Thessalonians. After their words of thanksgiving, one specific object of this letter comes into view. That object concerns the timing of "the coming of our Lord Jesus Christ."[1] "Coming" translates the Greek word *parousia*, the same word used of Christ's second coming in 1 Thessalonians 2:19.[2] The specific thing about the coming of the Lord which the writers want the readers to focus on will be stated clearly in verse 3: namely, the wrong ideas the readers have begun to embrace concerning the timing of the day of the Lord need to be abandoned. How the writers learned about the problem we are not told. In 3:11 they speak of having heard a report that some in the church were idle. Did that report also tell about the wrong ideas about the timing of the day of the Lord?

---

[1] The preposition translated "with regard to" is *huper*. Since this preposition is never used of putting someone under oath, a translation that reads "by the coming" could be misunderstood. It is better to take the preposition *huper* in the sense of *peri*, "concerning."

[2] In comments at 2 Thessalonians 1:7 it was maintained that the words *parousia* and *revelation* are two words for one and the same coming. Here in 2:1, what was called Christ's revelation-coming at 1:7 and "that day" in 1:10 is now clearly designated as also being His *parousia*.

And our gathering together to Him – What is written here in 2 Thessalonians 2 deals with the same subject and the same time frame as did 1 Thessalonians 4-5. In the previous phrase and in this one there is an obvious allusion to what had been written in 1 Thessalonians 4:13ff, where the word "coming" (*parousia*) was used at verse 15 and the gathering together to Him was referenced in verses 16 and 17 ("the dead in Christ will rise first, then we who are alive and remain will be caught up together with them in the clouds to meet the Lord in the air, and so we shall always be with the Lord"). The verb corresponding to "our gathering together" was used by Jesus when He spoke of the angels "gathering together the elect from the four winds" (Matthew 24:31). While "our gathering together to Him" does picture both writers and readers as being among the Christians so caught up to meet the Lord, the following verses (which identify events that must happen before the Lord returns) make it clear that both writers and original readers are going to be among the dead who are raised first, before all the redeemed are caught up to meet the Lord in the air. Any notion that the words in 1 Thessalonians 4:15-17 might imply belief in an imminent return of the Lord must be abandoned; such a notion would be mistaken.

2:2 – *that you not be quickly shaken from your composure or be disturbed either by a spirit or a message or a letter as if from us, to the effect that the day of the Lord has come.*

That you not be quickly shaken from your composure – The sentence begun in verse 1 with "we request you" continues here in verse 2.[3] *Eis to* ("that") and the infinitive phrase "not quickly shaken" express the writers' concern about the Christians at Thessalonica. The rest of verse 2 indicates the Thessalonian Christians are in danger of believing, on insufficient grounds, that "the day of the Lord" had already come. "Quickly" has been variously interpreted. Some believe it means "so soon after our departure from Thessalonica," while others believe it means "so soon after what we taught you while we were with you." It may also be that "quickly shaken" means the Thessalonians are being "too easily disturbed."

The NASB marginal reading tells us the Greek translated "composure" is literally "from your mind." "Shaken" is a word used of sea travel when a ship is thrown off course by a storm. So the picture is that the brethren had a correct understanding about the day of the Lord coming like a thief (1 Thessalonians 5:2), but they were "thrown off the course of sound thinking and reasoning" about the matter. What was throwing them off course is identified in the next phrase.

Or be disturbed either by a spirit or a message or a letter as if from us – Teaching that purported to come from Paul and Silas and Timothy had been introduced by someone into the church at Thessalonica. The verb translated "troubled" (*throeisthai*) is used of soldiers

---

[3] Several English versions rearrange the word order so the verses read, "Now concerning the coming of our Lord Jesus Christ and our assembling to meet him, we beg you, brethren, not to be quickly shaken in mind ...."

who are surprised and agitated and filled with sudden alarm and worry by an unexpected rumor or bad news. Interestingly, the verb tense of the infinitive "be disturbed" differs in the Greek from the tense of the infinitive "be shaken." "Be shaken" is regarded as a single act while the feeling of trouble or being "disturbed" was a continuing or chronic condition.

The writers name three sources of the false information that had been introduced and were unsettling and alarming the Thessalonians.

(1) "A spirit" was the first of these. 1 Thessalonians 5:19-20 called attention to prophetic utterances in the public assembly. It is likely that "a spirit" indicates someone was telling the Thessalonians about an "inspired message" or a "prophetic voice" which he had received (or so it was claimed). "Prophetic utterances" may be prompted either by the Spirit of God or by unholy spirits (demons). 1 Thessalonians 5:21 directed the believers to examine everything, and 1 John 4:1 indicates it was necessary to test the spirits to see whether they are from God.

(2) "A message" is a second source of disturbing information. If we are correct in understanding that the words "as if from us" (at the close of the verse) modify both the last two sources of unsettling misinformation,[4] then it appears someone has misrepresented what they heard the writers actually say, or that someone was pretending to have been entrusted with a new message from the writers for the Thessalonians.[5]

(3) The third source of disturbing information is identified as "a letter as if from us." It is doubtful that the reference is to 1 Thessalonians. In light of 2 Thessalonians 3:17, this phrase seems to suggest that someone might have forged a letter purporting to be from Paul and Silas and Timothy which contained this unsettling idea that the day of the Lord was already here.[6]

To the effect that the day of the Lord has come – This clause identifies the mind-disturbing teaching that had recently been circulating among the Thessalonians. In Old Testament prophecies, the expression "day of the Lord" was sometimes used in a prediction of some temporal judgment about to be inflicted because of men's sins.[7] But in both 1 Thessalonians and here in 2 Thessalonians, "day of the Lord" refers to the final and great

---

[4] While "as if from us" certainly goes with "epistle" and perhaps also with "a message," it cannot modify "a spirit," for "a visionary would claim personal, not borrowed, authority for his revelation." (James Moffatt, "The First and Second Epistles to the Thessalonians" in *Expositor's Greek Testament*, ed. By W. Robertson Nicoll [Grand Rapids, MI: Eerdmans, 1967], p.47.)

[5] A word of caution is needed here. The language of this verse must not be pressed to mean that, since they left Thessalonica, the writers actually had changed their mind about the time of the coming of the day of the Lord. The letter as if from them might have so stated, but if it did so, it was a deliberate attempt at deception (verse 3). The writers had not changed their teaching.

[6] If this letter were being written today the writers "would have to add television to the list of things by which Christians are influenced to think the day of Christ is at hand" (W. Carl Ketcherside, cited in Root, *1984-85*, p.107).

[7] See the comments on "day of the Lord" at 1 Thessalonians 5:2.

day which is ushered in by the second coming of Christ the Lord.[8]   Several factors lead to this conclusion:

- In 1 Thessalonians 4 and 5, "day of the Lord" and the second coming of Christ described as His *parousia* were tied together.   In 2 Thessalonians 1 and 2, "day of the Lord" and the second coming of Christ described as His being revealed are tied together.
- The verb *enestēken* (translated "has come") means "is already present," or "has already come."   The older English versions which read "is at hand" (which can mean "is about to begin") do not precisely convey the idea which the Greek word means.[9]

It is difficult for us to understand how anyone might be led to believe that the day of the Lord had already come.   Was it not certainly obvious that what 1 Thessalonians 4 has described as happening when Christ comes again had not actually occurred?   How would what had been written there be interpreted to match a claim that the day of the Lord had already come?   Did the folk who circulated the mind-disturbing teaching spiritualize *parousia*, making it something other than Christ's personal appearance,[10] and did they claim, as Gnostics later did, that the resurrection had already occurred (2 Timothy 2:18)?   Certainly there had been no catching up of the living saints to be with the Lord, such as was described in 1 Thessalonians 4:17, nor had "the Lord Himself descended from heaven with a shout" as was described in 4:16.   Even when it is recognized that a complex series of events will occur on the day of the Lord, it still is hard to imagine how the Thessalonians allowed themselves to be deceived (verse 3) by the mind-troubling ideas which recently were being taught.[11]

---

[8] The presence of the Greek article "the" before "day" here in verse 2 (as compared with 1 Thessalonians 5:2 where there was no article before "day") is an article of previous reference. That is, the "day of the Lord" in 2 Thessalonians 2 is the same day introduced in 1 Thessalonians. This identification of the topic being discussed is obscured to readers of the KJV. The KJV, here in 2 Thessalonians 2:2, reads "day of Christ." However, "day of the Lord" is the better attested reading.

[9] There is a Greek term that does mean "is about to come." It is the word used by John the Baptist at Matthew 3:2 when He cried, "Repent for the kingdom of heaven is at hand (*ēngiken*)." In all the other places the New Testament uses *enestēken*, this word marks something already present (Romans 8:38; 1 Corinthians 3:22, 7:26; cf. Galatians 1:4; 1 Timothy 3:1; Hebrews 9:9).

[10] It certainly lies within the realm of possibility that the writers of 2 Thessalonians deliberately used "revealed" at 1:7 and *parousia* here in 2:1 to counteract any possibility of spiritualizing *parousia* into something other than a visible "revelation" of who Christ is. Furthermore, the terms used to describe the day of the Lord in these letters prohibit us from thinking that what happened to Jerusalem in AD 70 is the event being described in Thessalonians.

[11] We have no way of knowing whether or not the teaching about the second coming already given to the Thessalonians (2 Thessalonians 2:5) included the details we read elsewhere in the New Testament, about how the coming of the Lord Jesus to judge the world will produce great consternation and alarm. For example, Matthew 24:29-31 tell us "THE SUN WILL BE DARKENED, AND THE MOON WILL NOT GIVE ITS LIGHT, AND THE STARS WILL FALL from the sky, and the powers of the heavens will be shaken. And then the sign of the Son of Man will appear in the sky, and then all the tribes of the earth will mourn, and they will see the SON OF MAN COMING ON THE CLOUDS OF THE SKY with power and great glory. And He will send forth His angels with A GREAT TRUMPET and THEY WILL GATHER TOGETHER His elect from the four winds, from one end of the sky to the other." Revelation 1:7 adds that

2:3 – *Let no one in any way deceive you, for* it will not come *unless the apostasy comes first, and the man of lawlessness is revealed, the son of destruction,*

Let no one in any way deceive you – The wording of the prohibition given in verse 3, about not letting anyone even begin to deceive the readers, implies that the folk who were circulating the mind-disturbing teaching were either unconsciously or perhaps deliberately attempting to deceive the Thessalonians.[12] "In any way" points back to the variety of ways (verse 2) the deception was being presented. A.R. Faussett described some of the dangerous consequences if the mind-disturbing teaching were to be embraced. He wrote that the Thessalonians ...

> ... might be brought to question the truth of the whole gospel when [Christ's second coming] should not come to pass; they might be unprepared for the sufferings that were to come upon the church; their patience might fail in expecting this day, and their minds be doubting about the coming of Christ at all. This opinion also would much narrow their thoughts about Christ's kingdom, and the enlarging of the gospel among other Gentiles; and the profane might abuse it to sensuality, as 1 Corinthians 15:32.[13]

For *it will not come* **unless the apostasy comes first** – To guard the readers from being deceived about the time when the day of the Lord will happen, the writers identify three momentous things that, on God's calendar, must happen before that day comes. While 2 Thessalonians 2 is one of the most remarkable prophecies in the New Testament, there is a certain obscurity in the language which makes it difficult for us to state without hesitation what those three things are. We suppose the original readers did not labor under the handicap we do, for the Thessalonians had been previously instructed concerning the things here briefly outlined (2 Thessalonians 2:5).

Apostasia is one of three momentous things that have to happen before the day of the Lord comes. As we try to understand the first of these momentous things, observe that

---

when He comes on the clouds of heaven "every eye will see Him ... and all the tribes of the earth will mourn over Him." Revelation 6:12-17 unfolds yet more details: "There was a great earthquake; and the sun became black as sackcloth made of hair, and the whole moon became like blood; and the stars of the sky fell to the earth, as a fig tree casts its unripe figs when shaken by a great wind. The sky was split apart like a scroll when it is rolled up, and every mountain and island were moved out of their places. Then the kings of the earth and the great men and the commanders and the rich and the strong and every slave and free man hid themselves in the caves and among the rocks of the mountains; and they said to the mountains and to the rocks, 'Fall on us and hide us from the presence of Him who sits on the throne, and from the wrath of the Lamb; for the great day of their wrath has come, and who is able to stand?'"

[12] The Greek construction, *mē exapatēsē* (*mē* followed by an aorist subjunctive verb), is a third person prohibition, a construction familiar in some languages, but not in English. It prohibits even beginning to let the deception happen.

[13] A.R. Fausset, as presented in the *Jamieson-Fausset-Brown Bible Commentary* section at https://biblehub.com/commentaries/2_thessalonians/2-1.htm.

there are no words in the original Greek text that are represented by the phrase "it will not come," so our English versions print this phrase in italics. "Unless [literally, "if not"] the apostasy comes first" are the "if-clause" of a conditional sentence in the Greek text whose conclusion (the phrase printed in italics in English) must be mentally supplied by the reader. *Prōton* ("first") is an adverb; the translators have correctly understood that "the apostasy" precedes the day of the Lord.

A more difficult issue is to try to determine what the Greek word *apostasia* means. In ancient literature the word is used both of a "rebellion" against political authority[14] and of a religious defection (i.e., apostasy, a falling away from a previously held faith).[15] Interpretations based on each of these two separate meanings have been offered as being what the passage predicts. If the meaning "apostasy" is adopted, the discussion then turns to what religious defection it anticipates. Is it defection from Judaism, or is it defection from Christianity?[16] If the meaning "rebellion" is adopted, the discussion then turns to trying to identify the authority against whom the rebellion is directed. Is it some earthly government, or is it the law and authority of God Himself?

Perhaps the immediate context gives us some help in our understanding. First, observe that the KJV, which reads "*a* falling away," is a mistranslation. In the Greek there is an article ("the") before *apostasia*. The article "the" before *apostasia* indicates that the *apostasia* is one-of-a-kind. It is likely an article of previous reference, indicating the *apostasia* was either something already foretold in the Old Testament prophets, or something concerning which the readers had previously been orally instructed. In fact, both meanings are probably indicated by the article "the." Second, the lawlessness referenced in the phrases "man of lawlessness" and "mystery of lawlessness" (verse 7) may well speak of anarchy and rebellion against law and order. Third, the "man of lawlessness" (i.e., the leader of the rebellion) proclaims himself to be God. That certainly is rebellion against the God of heaven.

These considerations cause us to lean toward "rebellion" against God and His laws as being the first event that must occur before the day of the Lord comes.[17] That rebellion had not happened at the time 2 Thessalonians was written, so it was not right to believe that the day of the Lord was already present.

---

[14] *Apostasia* is used of rebellion against authority in Joshua 22:22; 2 Chronicles 29:19; Jeremiah 2:19; and also in Josephus, *Life* 43. Goodspeed, the RSV, NEB, and several other English versions read "rebellion" or "rebellion against God" here in 2 Thessalonians 2:3.

[15] Acts 21:21 is the only other place in the New Testament where the word *apostasia* occurs, and it could well be translated "rebellion" rather than "forsake."

[16] At the time of the Reformation, it was very common to identify the Roman Catholic Church as being the predicted apostasy from the Christian faith.

[17] A more detailed discussion of the history of the interpretation of this passage is included in a Special Study at the end of this volume on 2 Thessalonians.

And the man of lawlessness is revealed – The second momentous thing that must happen before the day of the Lord begins, the writers tell us, is the revealing of "the man of lawlessness." That had not happened as 2 Thessalonians was being written, so, again, it was not right for the readers to believe the *parousia* and day of the Lord were already present.

- The reading, "the man of *lawlessness*" has now been accepted as the true reading (see recent editions of Nestle's Greek text) rather than the reading "man of *sin*" (familiar to many because of the wording in the KJV).

- "Man of lawlessness" says the man is marked or characterized by lawlessness. The Law of Moses has been abrogated (Hebrews 7:12), so "lawlessness" must mean something other than merely opposition to the Law of Moses. If we allow verses 4 and 9-12 to be examples of what is involved in "lawlessness", *anomia* is the absence of respect for any authority, or rebellion against any law whatsoever.

- As was true in the previous clause where an article of previous reference appears, the presence of the article "the" before "man of lawlessness" apparently indicates that this event, too, either was something already foretold in the Old Testament prophets[18] or was something concerning which the readers had previously been orally instructed.

- 2 Thessalonians 2 contains a number of expressions describing this evil character. Two occur in this verse, "man of lawlessness" and "son of destruction." Several more descriptions occur in verses 4, 9, and 10. Yet even with all this information to guide us, the identification of who the man of lawlessness might be has proven elusive.[19]

- If "rebellion" is the meaning of the previous clause, then it would seem the man of lawlessness arises after the great rebellion begins, and then encourages further rebellion. In addition, 2 Thessalonians 2:8 indicates this "man of lawlessness" does not appear until shortly before the second coming of Christ, and will be slain when Christ returns.

It is a bit unexpected to find the same verb "revealed" used of both our Lord Jesus Christ (2 Thessalonians 1:7) and also of the man of lawlessness. The word may suggest that for a while when the man of lawlessness finally appears on the scene of history, his real identity will be hidden from his contemporaries, but who he really is will be made clear shortly before the Lord returns and the day of the Lord begins. The passive voice verb "revealed" implies God has a hand in making known the real identity of the man of lawlessness.

The son of destruction – The Greek word here translated "destruction" (*apōleias*) is not

---

[18] Of the prophecies recorded in the Old Testament Scriptures, the one about the "little horn" in Daniel 7:21-27 very likely is a prediction of the same person and events that 2 Thessalonians 2 says must happen before Jesus' second coming. In addition, it is most likely that the eighth beast of Revelation 17:10,11, who is called a "king," is another Biblical prediction of this same governmental figure.

[19] See the detailed discussion in the Special Study at the end of this volume. In that study we will examine whether or not other verses in the New Testament also describe this man of lawlessness.

the same Greek word that was used at 2 Thessalonians 1:9. When used of things at Romans 9:22 and Mark 14:4, *apōleias* means to destroy, to lay waste. In Acts 8:20 it is a general term meaning being laid to waste or perish. In Revelation 17:8,11 it likely is a reference to hell.[20] The expression "son of ..." indicates character, not destiny.[21] If one carefully looks at the man of lawlessness, what impresses is the waste and utter destruction his actions leave behind, something that is true of all that comes from the lower infernal regions.

2:4 – *who opposes and exalts himself above every so-called god or object of worship, so that he takes his seat in the temple of God, displaying himself as being God.*

Who opposes – The diabolic qualities which characterize the man of lawlessness are continued in this verse. The present tense participle translated "opposes" (*antikeimenos*) speaks of being an "adversary." Though the man of lawlessness is not the devil (2 Thessalonians 2:9), just as the devil is an adversary (1 Peter 5:8; Revelation 12:10) so the man of lawlessness is depicted as being a constant adversary of God, of God's law, and of God's people.

And exalts himself above every so-called god or object of worship – The middle voice verb "exalts himself" says this self-exaltation is for his own benefit. *Sebasma*, translated "object of worship," was used for temples, altars, and religious statues, and is closely related to *sebastos*, which is the Greek equivalent of the Latin *augustus*, the honorific title given to Octavian when he became Caesar Augustus.[22] The veneration given to the Roman emperor thus serves as an ancient example of the self-exalting acclaim which the man of lawlessness will demand of all the world's inhabitants. Paganism was bad with its false god, temples, altars, and worship of demons. The man of lawlessness promotes a worship worse than paganism. He recognizes only one god, namely, himself! In his own inflated opinion, no other being, imaginary or real, is to be revered on the level he wishes to be.

So that he takes his seat in the temple of God – It must be remembered that this is a prophecy of something that will happen just before the Lord Jesus returns. 2 Thessaloni-

---

[20] The English translators who chose "perdition" as the word to translate *apōleias* evidently have judged that this description of the man of lawlessness refers to his final destiny in hell.

[21] See the expression "sons of light" at 1 Thessalonians 5:5. Compare also the well-known "Son of God" used of Jesus Christ to indicate His deity. This Hebraism means "characterized by."

[22] The same expression denoting self-exaltation is found in Daniel 11:36,37. In this commentator's judgment, the only connection between the passage in Daniel 11 and this passage in 2 Thessalonians is that what the ruler in Daniel 11 did is an illustration of what the man of lawlessness will be like. We do not attempt to make the Daniel passage a reference to a future antichrist, but rather we agree with Philip Mauro that the person being depicted in Daniel 11:36ff is Herod the Great. (*The Seventy Weeks and the Great Tribulation* [rev. ed., Swengel, PA: Bible Truth Depot, 1944].)

ans 2:8 tells us that the man of lawlessness will be brought to an end at the very first moment Jesus becomes visible at His *parousia* coming. Living early in the 21st century, we stand at the same place the writers of 2 Thessalonians stood. The man of lawlessness has not appeared on the scene of history, nor has the day of the Lord dawned.

It is also true that the meaning of this prophecy has proven to be an eschatological battleground.

- The word translated "takes his seat" is an aorist infinitive, indicating one expressive act. If it is treated as figurative language, the idea is that the man of lawlessness presumes to be the supreme judge or ruler. The Greek preposition translated "in" is actually *eis* ("into"), which brings out the idea of an actual intrusion.
- The word translated "temple" is *naos*, a "sanctuary" where a deity dwells. It is not *hieron*, a place where a priest works, the entire temple complex with all its buildings and courts.
- Bible students have searched the Scriptures in an effort to identify what the language "temple of God" might signify and where the "temple of God" might be. Three possibilities have been proposed. (1) The expression "temple of God" is used in descriptions of heaven as it now is (Revelation 3:12; 11:1,19; 16:7; there will be no temple in heaven after the Lord returns per Revelation 21:22). It is difficult to imagine that heaven, God's throne room, is the place where the man of lawlessness is pictured as having seated himself. (2) The building in the city of Jerusalem that Herod the Great remodeled was known as the temple of God. Since that building was destroyed by the Romans in AD 70, some Bible students have theorized that a Jewish temple is predicted to be rebuilt in the years just before the return of Christ, and that this rebuilt temple is where the man of lawlessness would take his seat. However, it is not easy to document via Scripture that a temple is to be rebuilt in Jerusalem in the years just before the second coming of Christ.[23] This is a serious problem for this interpretation. (3) Another explanation is that "temple of God" is figurative language for the church (1 Corinthians 3:17, 2 Corinthians 6:16, Ephesians 2:20-22). Adopting this figurative interpretation, the prophecy of 2 Thessalonians 2 predicts a government figure, a political ruler, who tries to dictate to the church what to believe and practice. The "little horn" of Daniel 7:21-27, which speaks of a powerful political ruler who "wears down the saints," is very likely another prophecy of this person called the "man of lawlessness."[24] (4) Perhaps the best explanation of the phrase is to recall that "temple" translates *naos*, a sanctuary where a deity dwells. "He takes his seat in the temple (*naos*)" is a way of saying he declares himself to be God.

---

[23] Both 2 Thessalonians 2:4 and Ezekiel 37:26 speak of a temple, but the idea that it is a future rebuilt temple must be imposed on the passages.

[24] Since the "little horn" in Daniel 8:9 is a prediction of a political ruler who was to flourish before Christ's first coming, Daniel 8's "little horn" is a different powerful government official than Daniel 7's "little horn."

Displaying himself as being God – The Greek verb is used of a proclamation of an appointment to public office.   Marshall's interlinear translation of this passage has the man of lawlessness being proclaimed as "a god."[25]   However, if Daniel 7:25 ("He will speak out against the Most High") is a parallel prophecy, the man of lawlessness does not claim to be just any god, but the most high God.

2:5 – *Do you not remember that while I was still with you, I was telling you these things?*

Do you not remember that while I was still with you, I was telling you these things? – Paul's expectations for the Thessalonians have obviously been disappointed.   His question displays a tinge of reproof as he is in the midst of encouraging his readers to do better than to allow themselves to be distracted doctrinally by those who are obviously sounding forth a wrong message about the day of the Lord.   Maybe that is the reason why Paul, for the first time in this letter, distinguishes himself from Silas and Timothy by using the pronoun "I" as he reminds them of what he had himself repeatedly taught them during his ministry in Thessalonica.[26]   If they had only reflected more on what he taught them by word of mouth, they would not have been confused and unsettled by what they were hearing from some recently-arrived teachers.   "These things" certainly includes what is being written in this letter concerning such matters as the rebellion, the man of lawlessness, the restrainer, the coming of Christ, the rapture, and the day of the Lord. [27]

2:6 – *And you know what restrains him now, so that in his time he will be revealed.*

And you know what restrains him now – The NASB translators have correctly decided that the adverb "now" modifies the participle translated "restrains."   The Thessalonians know about the thing which "now" was holding up the revelation of the man of lawlessness.   The Thessalonians knew about the restraining because Paul also had taught them concerning this topic when he was with them in Thessalonica.   The basic argument of the passage is continued here: the man of lawlessness had not yet appeared on the scene of history and therefore the day of the Lord had not yet begun.   What the readers are being urged to remember is why the man of lawlessness has not yet appeared.   At the time 2

---

[25] Marshall's translation "a god" is also grammatically unlikely.   The noun *theos* ("God") is in the predicate position.   Colwell's rule of grammar says, "A definite predicate nominative has the article when it follows the linking verb; it does not have the article when it precedes the linking verb." (E.C. Colwell, *Journal of Biblical Literature*, 1933, lii.)

[26] The fact that Paul was an apostle and Silas was a New Testament prophet indicates Holy Spirit-inspiration was involved in their preaching.   We should recognize that when Paul was speaking, he was not remolding and/or reworking old Jewish ideas such as are found in uninspired Jewish apocalyptic literature and which were popular at the time.   Rather, he is speaking truth he received from God.

[27] That Paul had time to cover all these topics while ministering in their town reinforces the view that he was in Thessalonica for much longer than the three Sabbath days whose events are recorded in Acts 17.   The imperfect tense verb ("I was telling") indicates that more than once Paul had discussed these events.

Thessalonians was written, something [28] and someone [29] were already in operation preventing[30] the man of lawlessness from making his appearance.

So that in his time he will be revealed – Just as on God's calendar there was a "fulness of time" when Christ should appear (Galatians 4:4), so this verse seems to be saying there is a right time on God's calendar when it will be appropriate for "the man of lawlessness" to be revealed. The next verse suggests there is a series of events going on which will culminate in the revelation of the man of lawlessness.[31]   The question might be raised, "Why should a divine restraint be imposed on the advance of lawlessness and the appearance of the man of lawlessness?" The answer may involve the fact that when Thessalonians was written Christianity was in its infancy. Salvation had just begun to be offered to the Gentiles. Time was needed for Gentiles all over the world to have an opportunity to hear and obey the gospel until the "fulness of the Gentiles be come in" (Romans 11:25). We will be at the close of the church age and the dawning of the day of the Lord when it comes time for the restraining to be removed and the man of lawlessness to appear on the scene of history. Opportunities for salvation will be over when Jesus' *parousia* occurs. The passive voice verb "will be revealed" occurs three times (verses 3,6,8) and each time it refers to something God is going to do.

2:7 – *For the mystery of lawlessness is already at work; only he who now restrains* **will do so** *until he is taken out of the way.*

For the mystery of lawlessness is already at work – The "for" with which verse 7 begins indicates this verse is intended to be a further explanation of the statement just made "that in his own time he will be revealed." The reason the restrainer was already at work is because the mystery of lawlessness was already at work in the world. "Lawlessness" picks up the theme already introduced in verse 3. The term "mystery" is almost always used in the New Testament to speak of a truth which was unknown apart from divine special revelation, and which was only dimly foreshadowed in the Old Testament scriptures.[32] The New Testament apostles and prophets had the privilege of unfolding these hidden truths so New Testament people would know about them (Ephesians 3:5). In this explanatory verse the Thessalonians are being taught that the attitude of rebellion against God which already could be seen in the world, would in later times be carried to a great height by the man of lawlessness, just as was predicted in the Old Testament.

---

[28] The Greek here in verse 6 for "what restrains" is neuter.

[29] The Greek in verse 7 translated "he who restrains" is masculine.

[30] Arndt and Gingrich (William F. Arndt and F. Wilbur Gingrich, *A Greek-English Lexicon of the New Testament*, Chicago: University of Chicago Press, 1957, p.423) offer possible translations for the present tense participle *katechon* as "holds back, restrains, hinders, constrains."

[31] The comments on verse 3 offer an explanation what it means when it says the man of lawlessness is to "be revealed."

[32] Perhaps the "little horn" of Daniel 7 is one place where this mystery was dimly foreshadowed in the Old Testament.

Only he who now restrains *will do so* until he is taken out of the way – If the man of lawlessness is being restrained for the present time, and yet in time is going to be revealed (verse 6), this implies that the time will come when the restraint which keeps lawlessness from getting worse, and hinders the man of lawlessness from appearing on the scene of history, will no longer be operative. In fact, the writers tell us that the removal of the restraints on the man of lawlessness constitute the third momentous thing that must happen before the day of the Lord begins.

The Greek words at the close of this clause are *heōs ek mesou genētai*; literally, the clause reads "until out of the midst he goes." The verb is a deponent verb; i.e., it is irregular, or defective. Although the Greek words are written with middle or passive voice endings, the clause actually carries an active meaning.[33] The NASB elected to render the phrase with a passive meaning ("he *is taken* out of the way"). But a better rendering of the deponent verb tells us that God Himself is at work in the present restraining, and there will come a time when God Himself will remove the restraints He has been imposing.

Whereas verse 6 spoke of the *thing* which restrains (a neuter article and participle), in verse 7 it is a *person* who restrains (a masculine article and participle).[34] Because the change from neuter to masculine suggests that the restrainer can be spoken of as a thing or a person, attempts to identify the restrainer have proven to be challenging.[35] In fact it has

---

[33] *Genētai* in verse 7 is an aorist subjunctive form of the verb *ginomai*. The translations which give it a passive meaning, such as "he is removed" or "he is taken out of the way" can result in a wrong mental image of what is being said here. The Greek does not say that someone or something other than the restrainer is involved in removing.

According to J. Gresham Machen (*New Testament Greek for Beginners*, Toronto: MacMillan Company, 1923, p.61), "Many [Greek] verbs have no active forms, but only middle or passive forms, with active meanings. These verbs are called deponent [or defective] verbs." When students consult Greek dictionaries, they will find verbs with middle/passive personal endings, but the translations given are active voice verbs. For such deponent verbs, as is usual for active voice verbs in the Greek, the subject does the acting depicted by the verb.

[34] The use of the definite article "the" in both places in this verse, as was true of the use of the article in verse 3 earlier, suggests that the readers have heard of this restraining power or person already. The word "restrains" here has the same meaning the neuter form of the word had in verse 6.

[35] Early church fathers interpreted the restrainer to be the Roman Empire and its ruler, and taught that when the Empire was gone then an apostasy from the Christian faith would occur, or that when the Empire was gone there would be widespread anarchy (rebellion) affecting society. It would seem that history has proven this identification of the restrainer to be mistaken, for the Roman Empire has long since faded away, and the lawless one has not yet been revealed.

Modern Premillennial interpreters urge that the restrainer is the Holy Spirit. It is true that the Greek word for Spirit (*pneuma*) is neuter, but that the Holy Spirit is a person. In this, it is urged, we have the change of gender in verses 6 and 7 explained. For Premillennialism, the theory is that when the church is raptured at Christ's *parousia*, the Holy Spirit will leave the world too, and then with no more restraint on him by the Holy Spirit, the Antichrist will then be revealed. A serious flaw in this attempted identification is the fact that there are no Scriptures to commend the theory that the appearance of antichrist follows the *parousia* and rapture. On the contrary, even this passage in Thessalonians has the man of lawlessness active before the *parousia* and destroyed at the *parousia*.

been called "one of the most difficult questions in the entire Pauline corpus."[36] The most satisfying understanding of the verses is that "he who restrains" is God and "that which restrains" is the providential[37] outworking of His eternal plan.[38] Several lines of thought favoring this view can be marshaled:

1) The strongest objection to this identification is removed when the deponent Greek verb *genētai* is given its active meaning.
2) That God Himself is involved in the restraint is favored by verse 6 ("in his time") which spoke of things happening on a divine timetable.
3) Recall what the book of Romans affirms about God's hand in history, in the words "God gave them up" (Romans 1:24,26,28 ASV). In Romans 1 we not only see lawlessness growing worse and worse, but we also see how God withdraws His gracious providential aid as He removes restraints previously imposed against growing evil.
4) Acts 17:26 favors this view. It tells us that God determines when nations rise and fall, and how far their boundaries spread. God exercises an active hand in history, which is the idea being unfolded here in 2 Thessalonians 2:6,7.
5) Verse 11 of 2 Thessalonians 2 has reference to God's hand in His world.

2:8 – *Then that lawless one will be revealed whom the Lord will slay with the breath of His mouth and bring to an end by the appearance of His coming;*

Then that lawless one will be revealed – "Then" points to the time when God removes the providential restraint He has imposed on lawlessness and the appearance of the man of lawlessness. "Then," the Thessalonians are told, two things will happen: (1) the lawless one (the same "man of lawlessness" introduced in verse 3) shall be revealed[39] and (2) then the Lord will come and bring an end to the man of lawlessness.

Whom the Lord will slay with the breath of His mouth – The better-attested Greek text adds the word "Jesus" after Lord. The better-attested Greek text also has a verb that means

---

[36] Williams, *op. cit.*, p.126.

[37] "Providence" is defined as the care and preservation and government that God exercises over His creation so that it accomplishes the purposes for which it was made.

[38] According to 2 Timothy 1:9, before God ever began the work of creation described in Genesis 1, the members of the Godhead made a plan which they were going to put into operation. This "plan" or "resolve" or "purpose" is referred to in several New Testament texts. Romans 8:28 speaks of God working all things together for the spiritual good of those on earth who are called or invited to become Christians, in harmony with God's "eternal purpose." Ephesians 1:11 tells us that "according to His purpose [design, plan]" God works all things after the counsel of His will. Ephesians 3:11 indicates the inclusion of Gentiles in His plan of salvation was in "accordance with the eternal purpose which He carried out in Christ Jesus our Lord."

[39] This is the third time (see verses 3 and 6) in these verses that "revealed" is used of the man of lawlessness.

to "overthrow" rather than the verb meaning "consume" or "destroy" which is found in the text behind the KJV. When the divinely-decreed time comes for the restraint to be removed and for the man of lawlessness to come out on the scene of history, what follows will be the Lord's second coming which will bring down the man of lawlessness. Very likely Revelation 19:19,20 is John's description of this same decisive overthrow of the man of lawlessness. John describes the overthrow of the eighth beast and his kingly helpers (Revelation 17:11,12) in these words:

> And I saw the beast and the kings of the earth and their armies assembled to make war against Him who sat on the horse and against His army.[40] And the beast was seized, and with him the false prophet who performed the signs in his presence, by which he deceived those who had received the mark of the beast and those who worshiped his image; these two were thrown alive into the lake of fire which burns with brimstone. (Revelation 19:19,20)[41]

Analogy of Scripture can also be used to explain "breath of His mouth." Revelation 1:16 and Revelation 19:15,21 speak of the "sharp two-edged sword" that comes out of the mouth of the Lord, which is used to defeat the eighth beast and his armies. Appeal is also made to 1 Thessalonians 4:16 which spoke of a "shout" when the Lord begins to descent in His second coming. If the intended word picture is of the Lord blowing his breath on the enemies, it pictures the ease with which He is victorious over the man of lawlessness.

And bring to an end by the appearance of His coming – The verb *katargēsei*, translated "bring to an end," is a stronger verb than the one translated "slay" in the previous phrase. It likely is intended to indicate that the lawless one's whole program will wholly cease. The Greek word translated "appearance" is *epiphaneia*, and the one translated "coming" is *parousia*.[42] The ASV has "manifestation" and NIV has "splendor" as English equivalents of *epiphaneia*. The text says that the first gleam of Christ's advent (*parousia*) will be sufficient to abolish the lawless one, to put him out of commission.

---

[40] Christ is the rider on the white horse and He is accompanied by the armies of heaven (Revelation 19:11-16).

[41] The picture of the warrior Messiah has Old Testament precedent (Isaiah 11:4; 66:15,16; Malachi 4:1).

[42] Here in verse 8 we have a combination of two words which are elsewhere separately used to denote the second coming of Christ.

- *Epiphaneia* is used in 1 Timothy 6:14; 2 Timothy 4:1,8; and Titus 2:13. In these verses it is also translated "appearing" (or "manifestation" in the ASV) and refers to the brilliant display of Christ's power of judgment to be exercised at His second coming.
- *Parousia* was used to refer to Christ's second coming at 1 Thessalonians 2:19; 3:13; 4:15; 5:23; and 2 Thessalonians 2:1.

The use of these terms together here in 2 Thessalonians 2:8 makes it hard to justify the distinction made between the two terms by some Premillennial interpreters, as if they referred to two different comings separated by seven years (first the *parousia*, and then the *apokalupsis/epiphaneia* coming later).

2:9 – that is, *the one whose coming is in accord with the activity of Satan, with all power and signs and false wonders,*

That is, **the one** – The further description now introduced continues the description of the man of lawlessness already begun in verse 4,[43] with this difference: verse 4 pictured the lawless one's antagonism to the divine realm, while verse 9 sets forth the lawless one's relationship to the devil and his kingdom.   In 2 Thessalonians 2:9-12 …

1)   We are told of the activity of Satan, who will bring about the coming of the man of lawlessness and the means he will use to bring the lawless one to power (verse 9);
2)   Then we are told what happens to the deceived victims of the lawless one's ascent to power (verse 10);
3)   Then we are told about the temporal and eternal punishments which the victims will incur (verses 11,12).

Whose coming is in accord with the activity of Satan – The man of lawlessness and Satan are two different individuals, but both are of one purpose when it comes to opposing God and Christ.   The lawless one is an instrument used by Satan, who prompts and directs both the coming and the activities of the lawless one.   The word *energeian* ("activity") is reserved in the New Testament for supernatural activities.   "Coming" translates *parousia*. Just as Jesus will have His *parousia* (His "presence," or His "coming") into the world, so the man of lawlessness will have his *parousia* (his "presence" or his entrance into the world).   That *parousia* is used both of Christ's second advent and the coming of the man of lawlessness suggests the two events are linked together in terms of timing.   After all, the man of lawlessness is destroyed when Jesus first appears.   The present tense verb "is" describes the certainty of the coming in the future, a coming which is the logical and natural conclusion of the lawlessness already evident in Paul's day (verse 7).

With all power and signs and false wonders – "Power," "signs," and "wonders" are three terms used to indicate miracles, and are specific examples of the supernatural Satanic activity that will accompany the arrival of the man of lawlessness.   Since *pseudous* ("false") is a genitive singular adjective, the whole phrase could well be translated "with all power and signs and wonders of falsehood."   The word indicates the miracles are all counterfeit.[44]   They are lying miracles intended to deceive the folk who observe them into

---

[43] The genitive personal pronoun "of whom" which opens verse 9 picks up the "whom" of verse 8.   So verses 9 and 10 do not qualify the final clauses of verse 8, but look back to the subject of verse 8, namely, "the lawless one."

[44] Translators have struggled with how to translate this clause.   It is not easy to decide how many of the three terms the word "false" modifies.
- *Pseudous* ("false") is a genitive singular adjective.
- "All" is a dative singular adjective.
- "Power" is a dative singular noun.
- "Signs" and "wonders" are dative plural nouns.

Since "false" is the last Greek word in the clause does it go with just "wonders," as the NASB translators decided?   Since "false" is singular, can it in fact modify the last two nouns which are plural?

The NIV ("all kinds of counterfeit miracles, signs and wonders") has translated the dative singular

thinking the lawless one is someone whom he is not. The same words used of Jesus ("mystery," "revelation," "parousia," and "power and signs and wonders") are used of the lawless one as the devil empowers him to mimic all Christ does. The words used to describe the lawless one here in 2 Thessalonians lead us to identify the lawless one with the "antichrist" of 1 John 2:18, whether that name means opposed to Christ or in place of Christ.[45]

2:10 – and with all the deception of wickedness for those who perish, because they did not receive the love of the truth so as to be saved.

And with all the deception of wickedness – This clause, introduced as was the previous one by "with all," indicates a second form that the supernatural Satanic activity (verse 9) will take. The lexicon gives "wrongdoing, unrighteousness, wickedness, injustice" as possible meanings for *adikia*.[46] As the lawless one operates under the power given by the devil, he will use deceit to get the world's citizens to advance further and further into wickedness. With restraint removed the devil and man of lawlessness are free to use their full powers of deception. Such activity robs God of His glory.

For those who perish – It is not the Christians who are led astray, but those who will be on the way to punishment in hell.[47] The participle is present tense, suggesting that the process of perishing is already in operation when the man of lawlessness appears.

Because they did not receive the love of the truth – This clause states the reason they are already on the way to perishing.[48] The past tense "did not receive" pictures what hap-

---

"power" as though it were a plural, and has treated both "all" and "false" ("counterfeit") as though they governed all three terms.

Treating "false" as though it modifies all three terms for miracle is likely correct, which is why we have opted for the rendering "all power and signs and wonders of falsehood."

[45] It is also intriguing to study Revelation 13 as these verses in Thessalonians about the man of lawlessness are examined. Revelation talks about a beast out of the sea, which is likely a figure for antichristian government (Revelation 13:1-10), and a beast out of the land (Revelation 13:11-18), who is also called a "false prophet" (Revelation 16:13; 19:20; and 20:10). The beast out of the land influences dwellers on earth to submit to (worship) the beast out of the sea, and one of the tools used to convince earth dwellers are the "signs" he was given to perform (Revelation 13:13,14; 19:20).

[46] Arndt & Gingrich, *op. cit.*, p.17. "Wickedness" is another adjective for sin and is closely related to the word "lawlessness" used in verses 3 and 7.

[47] In Revelation 13:8, the beast receives worship from all the earth's inhabitants except those whose names have been written in the Lamb's book of life.

[48] "Because" translates *anth' hōn* which means "in return for which ...." Their liability to deception was just retribution for their having no love for the truth when it was within their reach. "The ones deceived are not excused because they are deceived. Their fate is their own fault. They are easily deceived because they did not receive the love of the truth" (Root, *1984-85*, p.108).

pened in the days just before the man of lawlessness appears. "Receive" is the same word (*dechomai*, which means "welcome") which was used in 1 Thessalonians 1:6 and 2:13 to describe the way in which the Thessalonians had responded to the preaching of the Christian gospel. "The truth" (note the definite article) here talked about, of course, is the gospel of Christ. This same gospel is called the message or the word of truth in Ephesians 1:13 and Colossians 1:5. The folk who were on their way to eternal punishment when the man of lawlessness appears had heard the gospel, but did not respond positively to it. "Love of the truth" is an unusual expression not found elsewhere in the New Testament. It describes a positive dedication to the gospel.

So as to be saved – "So as" may indicate either the purpose or the result of loving the truth. "Saved" ultimately has reference to eternal salvation. (Cf. "should not perish but have everlasting life" in John 3:16 and "in order that they may be saved" in 1 Thessalonians 2:16).

2:11 – *For this reason God will send upon them a deluding influence so that they will believe what is false,*

For this reason God will send upon them a deluding influence – Verses 11 and 12 describe the temporal and eternal punishments that will be inflicted by God on those who do not welcome a love of the truth. "For this reason" points back to "they did not receive the love of the truth." Certain spiritual laws come into play when the gospel is heard and rejected (see John 12:36-43). God's gracious gospel message calling men to repentance and obedience has always been so constituted that it will either harden or soften the heart of the hearer. The divine judicial punishment for refusing to obey has always been a hardening of the heart. God has so arranged things that there is always a penalty to be paid for rejecting the truth. The word translated "influence" (*energeian*) is the same word translated "activity" in verse 9, but with this difference: the supernatural operation in verse 9 is traceable to Satan, whereas the supernatural activity alluded to here in verse 11 is traceable to God.

So that they will believe what is false – What results when the temporal judicial punishment has been inflicted is that it is easier to get men to believe what is false. The Greek behind "false" reads "the lie." Apparently, the lie that men will believe is the lawless one's claim to be God (verse 4), and perhaps also the "deception of wickedness" (verse 10) by which the man of lawlessness gets men to rebel against the God of heaven. For the present moment, all that is keeping this evil and final rebellion from unfolding on the scene of history is the someone or something which restrains him. When the restraint is removed and the man of lawlessness finally appears, the next thing on God's calendar is the return of Christ and the final judgment.

2:12 – *in order that they all may be judged who did not believe the truth, but took pleasure in wickedness.*

In order that they all may be judged who did not believe the truth – The time spoken of is the final judgment. The ultimate consequence for those victims who are deceived by the man of lawlessness is condemnation[49] at the final judgment. As in verse 10, the "truth" here refers to the truth of the gospel. No one should claim that such judgment is unfair or unjust, for it has long been revealed to men that the result of disobedience to the gospel is eternal punishment. "All" who "did not believe the truth" in this passage are those alive at the time and who did not believe the message preached to them (verse 10).

But took pleasure in wickedness – "Wickedness" (or "unrighteousness," ASV) is the same word used in verse 10. The Greek verb *eudokēsantes* ("took pleasure") signifies both to take pleasure or delight in a thing and also to approve of it. This clause presents us with a reason why the gospel message was rejected. "If men find pleasure in sin, it is proper that they should be punished. There can be no more just ground of condemnation than that a man loves to do wrong."[50]

B. Further Thanksgiving for, Assurance and Encouragement to, and Prayer for the Readers. 2:13-17

2:13 – But we should always give thanks to God for you, brethren beloved by the Lord, because God has chosen you from the beginning for salvation through sanctification by the Spirit and faith in the truth.

But we should always give thanks to God for you, brethren beloved by the Lord – In stark contrast to the future awaiting the deluded victims of the man of lawlessness, verses 13-17 anticipate what is to come for those who love and obey the truth. The words which begin this verse repeat precisely the words found in 2 Thessalonians 1:3, and well could have been translated the same way. Again, Paul and his co-workers ("we") feel an obligation to give thanks to God as they look forward to the salvation which He makes possible both for the writers and their converts to enjoy.[51] In 1 Thessalonians 1:4 it says the Thessalonian Christians were "brethren beloved by God." Here they are also said to be "brethren beloved by the Lord." "Lord" in Paul's writings usually refers to Jesus. "Beloved" is a perfect tense participle which indicates that the love once shown them in the past by Christ (He went to Calvary for them) continues to enfold them as they strive to conduct their lives in righteousness.

---

[49] Rather than "judged," the word *krithōsin* would better be translated "condemned," for the context so requires.

[50] Barnes, *op. cit.*, p.92.

[51] Since they are spiritual brothers in Christ, it is implied that what is true for one is true for the other.

Because God has chosen you from the beginning for salvation – One reason Paul and his companions give thanks to God concerns God's hand in making sure the gospel came to Thessalonica. These are words of assurance to the believers in Thessalonica. If we adopt the slightly better attested textual reading which says "God has chosen you as firstfruits for salvation," it leads us to recall how a Macedonian call brought the missionaries to Philippi and then to Thessalonica early in Paul's second missionary journey (Acts 16:9-17:1). The Holy Spirit had been guiding them throughout their journey (Acts 16:6), and they knew that God had called them to go into Macedonia (Acts 16:10).

In the agricultural world, the "firstfruits" of any crop were a promise there was more harvest of that same crop yet to come. In the spiritual world, the firstfruits metaphor has the same connotation. If we are talking about some Christians being "firstfruits," the implication is that there are more to come. In God's management of history, His plan was that the gospel would go first to the Jews and then to the Gentiles. At James 1:18, James indicates that the Jewish-Christian readers to whom he was writing were "firstfruits" – the idea being that there were more Jewish folk who in the future would also become Christians. When the first Christian missionaries came to Thessalonica, it had only been about a dozen years since the gospel was first proclaimed to Gentiles at Cornelius' house (Acts 10:1-11:18), so the converts among the Gentiles at Thessalonica were very suitably declared to be like "firstfruits." The implication was that in the days and years following the conversion of Gentiles in the city of Thessalonica, Gentiles in numerous other cities and towns were envisioned as following in the footsteps of those first Gentile Christians.

"Chosen" is a middle voice verb that points to one time in the past. It suggests God made this choice for his own benefit.[52] "Unto salvation" is how the ASV translates the two Greek words *eis sōtērian*. 1 Thessalonians 5:8,9 have already used this word "salvation" to speak of the forgiveness of sin in this life (i.e., a rescue from sin's guilt, pollution, and punishment) and the future bliss of the redeemed after they have been invited into the joys of heaven. "Unto salvation" is the goal which Christian missionaries have in mind for their potential converts as those missionaries share the gospel with the lost.

Through sanctification by the Spirit – This clause describes one essential element or condition involved in God's way of making salvation available to men. "Sanctification" speaks of being set apart to sacred service, of being dedicated or consecrated to God. The debated issue here is whether to translate the genitive word *pneumatos* as "of spirit" or "of

---

[52] Because the Greek text represented in the KJV reads "God has chosen you from the beginning," and because the verb translated "chosen" is *heilato* (an aorist middle form of *haireō*) and not the usual verb (*eklegō*) used when God's choice of election back in eternity is the topic, commentators explaining this verse typically note that this is the only place in the New Testament where this verb is used of God's eternal election of some to salvation. Those commentators then often add, "The topic of God's election or choosing has already been covered in notes at 1 Thessalonians 1:4." When the better-attested Greek text "God has chosen you as firstfruits" is adopted, all such explanations prove to be irrelevant and unwarranted.

Spirit." What if we choose small "s" – i.e., "spirit"? Scripture elsewhere does speak of the importance of what happens to a man's spirit when conversion to Christ has taken place. Recall that in the new birth, the part of the man which is born again is spirit (John 3:6), and that 1 Thessalonians 5:23 spoke about man's spirit being preserved complete, without blame, unto the coming of our Lord Jesus Christ. What if we choose capital "S" – i.e., "Spirit"? Scripture elsewhere also indicates the Holy Spirit has an important role in helping a person to become and grow as a Christian. 1 Peter 1:2 refers to the pre-conversion work of the Holy Spirit. 1 Corinthians 12:13 indicates that in conversion the Holy Spirit has something to do with prompting a person to become immersed into Christ. Romans 8:1-14 indicates the indwelling Holy Spirit helps produce this sanctification (i.e., a process), whereby a person becomes increasingly detached from the world and attached to Christ, until His image is completely formed in that person.

And faith in the truth – This clause describes another essential element or condition involved in God's way of making salvation available to men. The translation in the ASV, "and belief of the truth," better reflects the Greek in which "truth" is in the genitive case. The "truth," the revelation of God and His way of salvation imparted in the gospel, is the same truth that verse 12 indicated was rejected by perishing men. "Habitually doing what God says" is a good way of explaining what faith or belief (in its Biblical sense) is. Such habitual behavior is a by-product of whole-hearted acceptance of the word of God as true because of the sufficiency of the evidence for its truthfulness.

2:14 – *It was for this He called you through our gospel, that you may gain the glory of our Lord Jesus Christ.*

It was for this He called you through our gospel – "This" is a neuter gender demonstrative pronoun. Since there is no neuter word in preceding verse to serve as the antecedent of "this," the proper conclusion to draw is that "this" is intended to include all the ideas – i.e., chosen to be firstfruits to salvation, sanctification of Spirit (or spirit), and belief of the truth – introduced in that verse. "Our gospel" is the gospel as preached by Paul, Silas, and Timothy when they were in Thessalonica.[53] It is identical with "the gospel of our Lord Jesus" (2 Thessalonians 1:8). God made the gospel the means of calling men unto salvation.

That you may gain the glory of our Lord Jesus Christ – One wonderful thing included in what was called "salvation" (verse 13) is here unfolded in detail. "Gain" translates the same rare verbal noun *peripoiēsin* translated "obtaining" in 1 Thessalonians 5:9, and again carries the same idea emphasized there: namely, that the believer has an active response to make to the call/invitation offered in the gospel. Verses 15-17 will highlight what some of those responses are. Scripture elsewhere offers several possible explanations of what

---

[53] The aorist tense verb "called" looks back to the time when the missionaries first visited Thessalonica and the call (invitation) of God was extended in what they preached. See comments at 1 Thessalonians 2:12 and 5:24 on the present tense verb "calls."

is involved in this "glory" that may be gained. In 1 Corinthians 15:43 and Philippians 3:21, "glory" is a reference to the glorified resurrection body which is received at the *parousia* of Christ. In Matthew 24:30 and Titus 2:13, "glory" speaks of the splendor and majesty and awesomeness that Christ will exhibit as He returns on the clouds of heaven. Romans 8:17,29 and 2 Thessalonians 1:12 indicate that Christians will share in Christ's glory. And the glory of Christ and His saints is a mutual glory. 2 Timothy 2:10 explained why Paul worked hard at his mission word. He affirms, "For this reason I endure all things for the sake of those who are chosen, so that they also may obtain the salvation which is in Christ Jesus and with it eternal glory." Colossians 3:4 promises "when Christ, who is our life, shall appear, then shall you also appear with Him in glory."

2:15 – *So then, brethren, stand firm and hold to the traditions which you were taught, whether by word of mouth or by letter from us.*

So then, brethren, stand firm – Here begins the writers' words of encouragement to the Christian brothers in Thessalonica. "So then" sums up what has already been written. Perhaps it refers to what was just written in verses 13 and 14, namely, that "the glory we are to share is worth waiting for and working for; and if we meet persecution as the Thessalonians did, it is worth suffering for."[54] Perhaps it refers to all that has been written thus far in chapter 2, namely, "now that you are reminded of the true doctrine about the Christ's second advent."[55] "Stand firm" is a military metaphor of a captain speaking to his soldiers, as he calls for them to maintain a firm persuasion of mind and a constant purpose of will. The present tense imperative verb means "keep standing firm"[56] whatever the present or the future might hold. It may be persecution because they are Christians, or it may be the pressures of increasing lawlessness all around them, but remaining faithful unto death is the price of the crown of life (Revelation 2:10).[57]

And hold to the traditions which you were taught – "Hold" translates another present tense imperative and means "keep holding." "Traditions" denotes a body of authoritative Christian teaching which is passed on by one generation to another.[58] These traditions

---

[54] Root, *1984-85*, p.109.

[55] Mason, *op. cit.*, p.159.

[56] The same verb, in the present tense indicative, occurred at 1 Thessalonians 3:8.

[57] Mason long ago reminded us that "such an exhortation is, in itself, conclusive against a theory of irreversible predestination." God may have chosen them as firstfruits for salvation and called them through the gospel to become Christians, still if they were going to gain glory, it was necessary for them to stand their ground. "If it were impossible for them to quit their ground, it would be needless to exhort them to maintain it. If it were possible for them to quit their ground, and yet be as well off after all, it would be needless also." (Mason, *ibid.*)

[58] Some cautions about the word "traditions" must be observed. (1) "The word 'traditions' has negative connotations for many Christians today. We tend to think of traditions as the things that the church has done for a long time without good, Scriptural reasons. That's not the meaning in this context" (Weatherly, *op. cit.*, p.300). (2) From the three passages (1 Corinthians 11:2; Colossians 2:8; 2 Thessalonians 2:15) in which "tradition" is used in a good sense, the Roman Catholic church has argued

had already been taught to the Thessalonians ("taught" is an aorist tense verb, indicating something done in the past). The Thessalonian Christians were not the only ones in the Jewish or Gentile mission areas to be instructed by word of mouth in matters of Christian truth and life. It is apparent that each community received the same instructions from Paul and his co-workers as were taught by the other apostles and New Testament prophets.

Whether by word of mouth or by letter from us – When he refers to traditions that came "by word of mouth," he is talking about preaching and teaching done in Thessalonica by Paul and his missionary companions. When he refers to traditions that came "by letter from us," the reference is to 1 Thessalonians, the only other Pauline letter written at the time 2 Thessalonians is penned.[59] In this exhortation, Paul and his fellow-laborers sum up what has been written thus far in this second letter with some simple advice: 'Keep doing what you know to be right. You have been taught well. You only need to continue to embrace what you learned from us.'

2:16 – *Now may our Lord Jesus Christ Himself and God our Father, who has loved us and given us eternal comfort and good hope by grace,*

Now may our Lord Jesus Christ Himself – Verses 16-17 give voice to the writers' prayer for the readers. Here again, as in 1 Thessalonians 3:11, prayer is addressed to Christ as well as to the Father. In 1 Thessalonians 3:11, the Father is mentioned first. In fact, it is a bit unexpected is to find Jesus mentioned first; the only other time this order occurs is at 2 Corinthians 13:13. Since both are members of the Godhead, might there be any theological significance to the variations in order? Perhaps the most that can be said is that since Jesus is mediator between man and God, calling on Him first might be an appeal for Him to act as mediator in getting a positive answer to this prayer.[60] "Himself" (*autos*) stands first in the Greek for emphasis, implying a contrast between divine power and the power unaided man is able to exert. In 1 Thessalonians 3:11 where "Himself" also stands first the conclusion was set forth that, since the compound subject "God and Jesus" is followed a singular verb, "Himself" points to a unity of essence or, better, a unity of action in which both members of the Godhead concur and work together to provide the answer to the prayer.

---

for her accumulation of uninspired traditions put forward as of co-ordinate authority with Scripture, yet which virtually override God's Word. That religious body basically ignores those passages (Matthew 15:2, 3, 6; Mark 7:3, 5, 8, 9, 13; Galatians 1:14; Colossians 2:8) which stigmatize man's uninspired traditions.

[59] Not many of the New Testament books (besides 1 Thessalonians) had been written at this early date, perhaps only Matthew's Gospel. Therefore, those early Christians of necessity would have had to rely on what was learned by authoritative oral tradition until written Scriptures supplanted the oral tradition as the continuing source of Christian truth.

[60] Rather than appealing to this word order to defend the deity of Christ as being equal with the Father, it would be better to find that argument in the designation "Lord Jesus Christ," the full significance of which was introduced in comments on "Lord Jesus Christ," at 1 Thessalonians 1:1.

And God our Father – To call attention to the fact that God is "our Father" is to underline what we can expect from Him.   Jesus told us that as Father, God gives His children exactly what they need (see Luke 11:11-13).[61]   It is also important to note that "and" indicates Jesus and the Father are separate personalities.

Who has loved us – The remainder of this verse reminds the Thessalonian believers why they can expect both Jesus and the Father to have every reason to answer this prayer. "Loved" is an aorist participle which looks back at one significant manifestation of that love.   While we are more familiar with verses that speak of God the Father's love for us (such as John 3:16 and 17:23), there are also verses that speak of Christ's love for us as being the reason He became incarnate and went to Calvary (John 15:23; Galatians 2:20; Ephesians 5:2,25).   While it might be argued that the nearest antecedent of "who" is "God the Father," the singular verbs that follow in verse 17 tend to reinforce the notion that the two together (i.e., Jesus and the Father) are acting as one when it comes to answering prayers like the one here being offered.

And given us eternal comfort and good hope – Here is another reason why the Thessalonians can expect a positive answer to this wish-prayer being offered to heaven for them.   "Given" is another aorist participle.   It, too, looks back to the cross as being the place where the Father and the Son have given us eternal encouragement.   "Us" means the Thessalonian Christians as well as the writers.   The Greek word *paraklēsin*, translated "comfort" in the NASB and "consolation" in the KJV, is better translated "encouragement" in this context.   What was accomplished at Calvary was intended to have far reaching consequences.   For all time, when men contemplate what happened back at Calvary, it is intended to encourage them to come to the conclusion that both Jesus and the Father are genuinely interested in them and have been at work for their everlasting welfare.   Not only that, but a contemplation of Calvary will also result in "good hope."   This hope is good because it both gives worth and joy to life, and "finds its fulfillment in eternal happiness and fellowship with God."[62]

By grace – Translators and exegetes both must make a decision concerning what it was that was done "by" or "in grace."   Moffatt chose to link "in grace" with verse 17 as he offered the translation "may the Lord Jesus and God the Father ... graciously encourage your hearts."   Most of our translations connect "by grace" to the verb "given" and explain that "grace" (lovingkindness in action) is what led to Calvary and thus resulted in the blessings of encouragement and hope.

---

[61] See comments at 1 Thessalonians 1:1 and 2 Thessalonians 1:1 about God being called "our Father."

[62] Enos Dowling, *Standard Lesson Commentary 1962* (Cincinnati: Standard Publishing Company, 1962), p.346.

2:17 – *comfort and strengthen your hearts in every good work and word.*

Comfort and strengthen your hearts – This verse is a continuation of the sentence which began in verse 16, so the subject of these singular aorist optative verbs is God, both the Son and the Father. Such optatives express a wish-prayer. These two verbs state the special items in the prayer of the writers for the readers. The writers are asking that divine help be given to the readers so they can fulfill the exhortation to "stand fast" given in verse 15. We may rightly understand that the verb "comfort" is connected to the "unending encouragement" of verse 16, while "strengthen" is connected to the "good hope" in that same verse. To "encourage" and "strengthen" the readers' "hearts" means to help those believers become firm in their convictions. Such a prayer ties together beautifully with the appeal to the readers in 2 Thessalonians 2:1-3 to use good sense and judgment. A comparison of what was written about "strengthen" in 1 Thessalonians 3:11 makes it obvious that this divine encouragement and strengthening occurs as the readers concentrate on what God's messengers have to say, rather than listening to uninspired messages that deceive and shake their faith.

In every good work and word[63] – "Good work" may be an intended contrast to the kind of lawlessness chapter 2 has highlighted. It is also the opposite of the disorderly conduct which is about to be treated in the next chapter. The writers know the Thessalonian Christians are busy in doing good (1 Thessalonians 1:3 and 4:10), and they will only continue to do that if they are firm in their convictions. "Good word" picks up the "word of truth" alluded to in 2 Thessalonians 1:10-13. Again, it is the words of the apostles, not the disturbing words of the false teachers, which will result in the maintenance of correct doctrine. The writers of this letter had a purpose in teaching about Christ's return and the day of the Lord here in chapter 2. They expected that with God's help the hearts/minds of the Thessalonians would correctly prompt them to the proper action and proper speech as they passed on the truths learned from Paul and his fellow missionaries.

---

[63] The KJV reads "comfort your hearts, and establish you in every good word and work." This reflects the Textus Receptus which has a "you" after the verb translated "establish." However, there is no "you" after this verb in the better-attested Greek text. The Textus Receptus also inverts the order (to "word and work") of the last three words found in the better texts. Commentaries explaining the KJV will have a different set of notes than commentaries based on the text as it reads in the ASV and NASB.

III. PRACTICAL ADMONITIONS CONCERNING PROPER BEHAVIOR.   3:1-15

A. Prayer Requested.   3:1-5

1. Paul and his helpers are in need.   1,2

3:1 – *Finally, brethren, pray for us that the word of the Lord will spread rapidly and be glorified, just as* it did *also with you;*

Finally, brethren – The writers introduce the practical portion of this letter in the same manner as they did in the first epistle.   And just as it did in 1 Thessalonians 4:1, "finally" does not imply that the end of the letter has been reached.   Rather, "finally" indicates that the last major subject is being introduced.   "Brethren" is in the vocative case in the Greek. That is, by using a form of direct discourse, the writers are signaling that what is yet to be written vitally concerns the Christian cause which is important both to the writers and the readers.

Pray for us – 1 Thessalonians 5:25 closed with a request that the Christians at Thessalonica pray for Paul, Silas, and Timothy ("us"), who at the time were involved in a challenging ministry in Corinth.   The verb in this request is a present tense imperative which means not just praying once but praying repeatedly.

That the word of the Lord will spread rapidly and be glorified – "That" introduces the first of two requests to God that the writers want the Thessalonians specifically to include in their prayers.   The "word of the Lord" is the gospel,[1] and this first request is concerned with the progress of the gospel.   "Spread rapidly" is a delightful representation of the Greek word *trechē*, which literally means, as the marginal note indicates, to run along. That is, they request prayer that the gospel may go on swiftly from person to person and place to place without any interruption.   "Be glorified" carries the idea of being received with honor.   In Acts 13:48, folk who "glorified the word" believed and obeyed it.   The gospel is, after all, "the power of God to salvation to everyone who believes" (Romans 1:16).   Both verbs are present tense verbs which point not to "a single great triumph but to a continuing progress – to 'keep on running and keep on being honored.'"[2]

---

[1] On "word of the Lord" see notes at 1Thessalonians 1:8.   The phrase can mean it is a message given to the preachers by the Lord, or it is a message about the Lord.   Both ideas are valid.

[2] Thomas, *op. cit.*, p.331.

Just as *it did* also with you – This is a very high commendation of the eagerness with which the Thessalonians accepted the gospel. Paul and his co-workers want the Thessalonians to pray that the work of the missionaries may be as successful in Achaia as it was in Macedonia. Just as the gospel sounded forth all over the neighboring region from Thessalonica (1 Thessalonians 1:5; 2:1), might it also be so in Corinth!

3:2 – *and that we will be rescued from perverse and evil men; for not all have faith.*

And that we will be rescued from perverse and evil men – This verse begins with "And that," indicating that what follows is the second of two requests to God that the writers want the Thessalonians specifically to include in their prayers. "Rescued" translates an aorist tense verb which likely points to one particular instance from which rescue or deliverance was being requested. Any attempt to identify what that instance may have been requires that several questions be answered.

1) What is the meaning of the verb translated "rescued"? This same verb occurred at 1 Thessalonians 1:10, where it was noted that "delivered" might be a better English equivalent than "rescued." The word "rescue" carries a greater connotation that the writers already were under the control of the evil men and so needed to be freed. "Delivered" may have a slightly more neutral connotation, leaving the reader to decide whether the danger was deemed as ominously imminent, versus being a circumstance that the writers were already experiencing at the time of writing.

2) Who were the "perverse and evil men"? We infer it was the unbelieving Jews who are described as being "perverse and evil." In Thessalonica it had been unbelieving Jews who brought an abrupt end to the work of Paul and Silas in that city (Acts 17:5). In Berea the Jews from Thessalonica again were instrumental in interrupting Paul's work (Acts 17:13). And in Corinth it again was unbelieving Jews who were the chief troublemakers (Acts 18:12). The word translated "perverse" (or "unreasonable," KJV) occurs in only three other places in the New Testament (Luke 23:41; Acts 25:5; Acts 28:6). In each instance it carries the connotation of doing "outrageous and harmful acts against others."[3] "Evil" translates the Greek synonym for "bad" that means more than being bad themselves. It indicates they are trying to get others to be evil just like they are. Men and women who oppose the spread of the gospel are properly characterized as being "perverse and evil."

---

[3] Thomas, *ibid.*

3) Is the pronoun "we" an editorial "we" or an actual plural? If, in this verse, it is an editorial "we" then Paul was asking for deliverance for himself. Under this scenario, the incident when Paul was brought before Gallio (Acts 18:12-17) may have been the situation for which petitions to God for His protection were being requested, and the outcome of that trial could be seen as the speedy answer to their prayers. If in this verse the "we" is a true plural,[4] then while we have no information in Acts about a particular dangerous crisis that involved all three missionaries when they were together in Corinth, we can surely sympathize with a request for providential protection so the missionaries can be relieved from anxiety rather than having to constantly look over their shoulders to see if more trouble is about to engulf them. "Here an element of personal safety enters into the request, but only for the sake of the gospel."[5]

For not all have faith – This is the reason perverse and evil men exist in the world. "Not all" is probably a deliberate understatement, for Jesus had said that "the gate is wide and the way is broad that leads to destruction, and there are many who enter through it" (Matthew 7:13). In light of the fact that Jesus warned His followers they would face persecution for their faith (Matthew 5:11; Luke 11:49) it is likely that "faith" (Greek, "the faith") here refers to the whole body of doctrine that makes up the Christian religion.[6]

2. The Lord is sufficient for all needs.   3-5

3:3 – But the Lord is faithful, and He will strengthen and protect you from the evil one.

But the Lord is faithful – This expression of confidence in the Lord to hear and answer prayer is likely intended as an encouragement to the Thessalonians to send up to the throne of God the petitions just requested in the first two verses of this chapter. The word order in the Greek is, "But faithful is the Lord," with the verb "is" being present tense. So the

---

[4] In the Detailed Introduction to 2 Thessalonians, the tentative decision was reached that all three named in the epistolary openings of these letters were involved in the composition of both letters. See especially the Authorship section of the Introductory Studies that identified the limited instances that likely use "we" in an editorial sense. All other uses of "we" or "us" in the Thessalonian letters likely are a true plural.

[5] Hayden, *op. cit.*, p.259. "Jowett observes that we have here the shrinking of the flesh from the dangers which awaited the apostle. But there is no trace of cowardice in these words; the apostle desires deliverance, not for his own sake, but for the sake of the free diffusion of the gospel." (P.J. Gloag, "II Thessalonians" in *The Pulpit Commentary*, Grand Rapids, MI: Wm. B. Eerdmans Publishing Co., 1950, p.62.)

[6] The suggestion that "faith" in this verse has the sense of the body of Christian teaching finds support in the ordinary usage of "the faith" in the New Testament (Lightfoot, *op. cit.*, p.125). Yet the idea of personal faith is not ruled out altogether by the context. If the persecutors had personally embraced the gospel they would no longer be "perverse and evil."

expression says the Lord is always faithful. "The Lord" likely designates, as has been consistently true in these letters, "the Lord Christ, Ruler and Defender of His people."[7]

And He will strengthen and protect you from the evil one – The promise is given that the same Lord who is being petitioned on behalf of the writers can also be counted upon to have a providential hand in the lives and welfare of the readers. "Strengthen" picks up the very verb used in 2 Thessalonians 2:17; that is, the writers express their confident assurance that the prayer offered for the readers at the end of chapter 2 would in fact be answered. The promise that the readers would be protected "from the evil one" echoes the prayer that Jesus taught His disciples (Matthew 6:13). In both Jesus' teaching and in this verse, the Greek words *tou ponērou* can be translated either "the evil one"[8] (masculine) or as "the evil [thing]" (neuter). So the phrase can apply equally "both to Satan and to his works – to evil in all its manifestations."[9] If we treat it as masculine, then "the implication is that the Evil One stands behind the activities of the wicked and evil men of verse 2."[10]

3:4 – *We have confidence in the Lord concerning you, that you are doing and will continue to do what we command.*

We have confidence in the Lord concerning you – This verse specifies what the writers expect to happen when the readers are strengthened and protected. The perfect tense verb translated "we have confidence" speaks of past completed action with present continuing results. "We have been persuaded and we still are persuaded." This confidence, or persuasion, began in the past at the time of their conversion, and continues on right up to the present.

That you are doing and will continue to do what we command – By "you" is meant the majority of the Thessalonian brethren, but not all of them, as is plain from 2 Thessalonians 3:11-14. "Command" is the same word used in 1 Thessalonians 4:2,11 where the missionaries are pictured (in a military metaphor) as passing on a command or charge from

---

[7] Findlay, *op. cit.*, p.146. Because a few late manuscripts (A, D, F, G) read "God," and because in 2 Thessalonians 2:16 both the Lord Jesus and God the Father were addressed in the writers' prayer for the readers, and because similar passages in 1 Corinthians 1:9 and 2 Corinthians 1:18 do read "faithful is God," Mason (*op. cit.*, p.136 cf. p.161) opted for the view that the word "Lord" is used here without distinct reference to any one person in the Godhead.

[8] In Matthew 13:38, 16:19; Ephesians 6:16; and 1 John 3:12 *tou ponērou* is treated as masculine and is one of the common names for the devil. (Compare 1 John 2:13,14 where *ton ponēron* is masculine.)

[9] Hayden, *op. cit.*, p.259. As in verse 2 ("rescue"), care must be exercised that there is no suggestion being made that the Lord will make it possible for the Thessalonians to avoid persecution completely.

[10] Williams, *op. cit.*, p.141.

their great commander Jesus Christ. This expression of confidence by the writers in the readers – that the Thessalonian Christians have been doing what the Lord has charged them to do and that they will continue to do so – is a powerful means of preparing the readers for the commands which are about to follow. The language used by the writers is a subtle claim of Holy Spirit inspiration as the source of the commands they deliver to the readers.

3:5 – *May the Lord direct your hearts into the love of God and into the steadfastness of Christ.*

May the Lord direct your hearts into the love of God – The thread of thought which ties this verse to what has gone before is that their being strengthened and protected from the evil one depends on their love of God and their steadfastness to their Lord. The optative mood verb translated "may [He] direct" makes this verse a wish-prayer. The mind is what is often meant by the Biblical word "heart." Of course, the Lord guides or directs men's minds through the word. "Into the love of God" is the first of two prepositional phrases which itemize and focus the precise ideas the writers want the Thessalonians' minds to concentrate upon. The practical way men show their love for God is by keeping His commandments (John 14:21; 1 John 5:3; 2 John 6).[11] Let the Thessalonians make such love for God one of their priorities.

And into the steadfastness of Christ – This is the second of the two prepositional phrases highlighting the precise ideas upon which the readers are to concentrate as the Lord directs their hearts. "Steadfastness" (*hupomonē,* a word also translated as endurance, or perseverance) "is the characteristic of a man who is unswerved from his deliberate purpose and his loyalty to faith and piety by even the greatest of trials and sufferings."[12] In James 1:3, which reads "The testing of your faith works endurance (*hupomonē*)," we learn that as Christians handle the trials and tests of their faith, they gain experience that helps them come to the aid of others when they have similar trials. This is how Christians put into practice steadfastness to Christ.[13]

---

[11] The context of Thessalonians calls for keeping those commands of God as were taught by Christ rather than Moses.

[12] Thayer, *Lexicon,* p.644.

[13] In the comments on these two prepositional phrases, a deliberate attempt has been made to treat the two genitive phrases ("of God" and "of Christ") in the same way, as objective genitives. That is, God is the object of the Christian's love, and the Christian practices steadfastness to Christ.

If we were to treat "of Christ" as a subjective genitive, then the comments would focus on some of the ways Christ's endurance and perseverance become a model for His followers (e.g., as are indicated in 1 Peter 2:19-24, 3:17-18, 4:1-2 and Hebrews 12:2-3).

In passing, the translation found in the KJV "into patient waiting for Christ" (i.e., steadfastly waiting for Him to return) may be in harmony with a theme of both Thessalonian letters, but it is likely an erroneous translation. If we compare 1 Thessalonians 1:10, the proper verb for "waiting for" is *anamenō* rather than *hupomenō.*

B. Idleness by Christians in Thessalonica is Rebuked.   3:6-15

1. Avoid the unruly brother.   6

3:6 – *Now we command you, brethren, in the name of our Lord Jesus Christ, that you keep away from every brother who leads an unruly life and not according to the tradition which you received from us.*

Now we command you, brethren – Having praised the Thessalonians for their obedience to commands from the Lord and having prayed they would continue that stellar behavior into the future, the writers now introduce two commands which they deem need special attention from the brethren.   In their first letter to the church (1 Thessalonians 4:10, 5:14), the writers used "we exhort you" (*parakaloumen*) when urging an important change in the behavior of the believers.   In this second letter, both here and earlier at 3:4, the writers use the stronger word "we command you" (*parangellomen*), the military vocabulary word meaning to pass along an order or command of the general.[14]   Likely the stronger word is used this time because there had been little response to the previous encouragement.   The details of the command take up several sentences (verses 6-12) as the writers share what the Lord Jesus commands the Christians to do concerning an important subject of the proper method of treating those brethren who were idle and disorderly in the church. "Brethren," in the vocative case, makes this command direct and personal, while "you" refers to those in the core of the congregation who were free from this fault of idleness. The exhortation in 1 Thessalonians 5:14, which also concerns members who were tending to live in idleness, was addressed to the leaders of the congregation.   This command is directed specially to the individual members personally.

In the name of our Lord Jesus Christ – By this formula the writers are asserting they are speaking on behalf of the Lord Jesus.   The Lord Jesus Christ is the commanding officer who has issued this command; after all, "all authority in heaven and earth" has been given unto Him (Matthew 28:18).

That you keep away from every brother who leads an unruly life – From the admonitions in 1 Thessalonians 4:11 and 5:14 concerning fellow-Christians who were "unruly,"[15] we have learned the reference is to able-bodied folk who were refusing to work

---

[14] Paul speaking as an apostle, Silas as a prophet, and Timothy as an inspired evangelist, were ones who were divinely authorized and equipped to issue such a command.   They expected Christians to heed this order.

[15] "Unruly" translates the same word used in 1 Thessalonians 5:14.   It is the military term picturing a soldier who is out of step (or who broke rank) with the rest of the troops.

to support themselves, with the result that they became dependent on others to take care of them. Instead, they should have been "working with their own hands" at a job that was honorable (Ephesians 4:28). Had they been working as the Lord expected them to do, they not only could have provided their own living expenses, but also would have had opportunity to help those brethren who, because of circumstances beyond their control, truly had needs.

The earlier admonition in 1 Thessalonians 5:14 was to "admonish" any such "unruly" brother. This passage, addressed to a continuing and perhaps worsening situation,[16] directs church members to "keep away" from any brother (fellow Christian) who was such an offender. The verb translated "keep away" is a nautical term used when sailors were warned to keep a safe distance from a certain port or destination. The command to "keep away" ("withdraw yourselves," KJV) does not mean to excommunicate or to break fellowship completely with the brethren in question, for in this same chapter (verse 15) such offenders are still called brothers. Further, if one were completely ostracized from the fellowship of the church, the Christians would hardly be in a position to "admonish him" as they are commanded to do in verse 15. So what is involved in keeping away from unruly brethren is to avoid enabling them to continue refusing to earn their own living while depending all the time on hand-outs, and to avoid any appearance of approving such unruly behavior.[17] "No one in the church is to coddle the offender with misplaced sympathy, thus creating division and destroying the corrective power of the action."[18]

And not according to the tradition which you received from us – The pattern of acceptable Christian behavior was established in the teaching delivered by the missionaries and by the example they set when they were in Thessalonica. The "tradition" of which this verse speaks was the divinely-inspired revelation of Christ that Paul and his co-workers had passed on to the Thessalonians, both by word of mouth (2 Thessalonians 3:10), and then in the first letter to the church there (1 Thessalonians 4:9-12; 5:14).[19]   "Which you

---

[16] The present tense of the participle "leads" indicates persistence in such undisciplined, irresponsible, and lazy conduct. In notes at 1 Thessalonians 5:14, it was proposed that originally the refusal to work did not stem from mistaken eschatological ideas, but from a general attitude against work among the populace of Thessalonica. Since then, if that disinclination to work was reinforced by a mistaken expectation that the end of the world would soon occur, we can readily see how the refusal on the part of some to work could become more aggravated. What need was there to work? Whatever might be earned would soon be left behind.

[17] Over a century earlier, J.A. Bengel (*New Testament Word Studies Vol. 2*, Grand Rapids, MI: Kregel Publications, 1971, p.501) called attention to the fact that Mendicant Orders, whose members regularly beg for handouts, have failed to heed the command given in these verses in Thessalonians. So have the folk who continue to give the beggars handouts.

[18] Hayden, *op. cit.*, p.260.

[19] For "tradition," see notes on 2 Thessalonians 2:15.

received"[20] indicates that both groups of the brethren, those who were now living unruly lives as well as those who were continuing to work, had all been taught clear instructions on this matter of conduct as well as doctrine. The idle brothers were blatantly disregarding what they had been taught.

2. Follow the example they had observed.   7-9

3:7 – *For you yourselves know how you ought to follow our example, because we did not act in an undisciplined manner among you,*

For you yourselves know how you ought to follow our example – "For" (*gar*) introduces this verse as a justification of the assertion that the brethren had received better teaching. "How" calls attention to the manner of living, and "ought" (*dei*) signifies "a compelling and often a divine necessity – something that springs from the will of God."[21]   What the missionaries taught and commanded, they practically exhibited by their own conduct, for they fully expected their converts to mimic or imitate their behavior.

Because we did not act in an undisciplined manner among you – "Because" (*hoti*) introduces the first of three reasons why the Thessalonian Christians can confidently and safely follow the example set by the missionaries.   The first reason is the missionaries did not live an idle, unruly, undisciplined life like many at Thessalonica were doing.[22]

3:8 – *nor did we eat anyone's bread without paying for it, but with labor and hardship we kept working night and day so that we would not be a burden to any of you;*

Nor did we eat anyone's bread without paying for it – This is the second reason why the conduct of the missionaries was a safe example to follow.   "To eat bread" is a Hebraistic expression that can cover not only food of any kind, but also living expenses.[23]

---

[20] The UBS[4] text now reads *parelabosan* ("they received").   Even the reading *parelabon* ("you received") is better attested than the reading *parelaben* ("which he received from us") found in the Textus Receptus and KJV.   The latter reading has no very old manuscript authority behind it.

[21] Williams, *op. cit.*, p.145.

[22] The word translated "undisciplined" is from the same root as the word translated "unruly" in an earlier verse.

[23] "In the Bible, the phrase 'eat bread' means to earn or get one's living, earn one's livelihood.   Adam was told, 'In the sweat of thy face thou shalt eat bread' (Genesis 3:19).   Amaziah told Amos, 'Go, flee thee away into the land of Judah, and there eat bread, and prophesy there' (Amos 7:12).   Amaziah was implying that Amos was preaching for a living" (Tesh, *op. cit.*, p.372).

The Christian missionaries did not depend on others to supply them with free food,[24] and the example they set says their converts should not do so, either.

But with labor and hardship we kept working night and day – The remainder of this verse is the third reason why they Thessalonians could safely follow the missionaries' example. Paul, Silas, and Timothy had worked hard when they were in Thessalonica living among the folk there.[25] Berry tells us that *kopos* ("labor") denotes the weariness which results from toilsome labor, while *mochthos* calls attention to how hard and often painful work can be.[26] "Working night and day" does not mean twenty-four hours around the clock, but rather suggests the missionaries worked a double shift, one shift preaching and teaching those who came for instruction during the daylight hours, and then a second shift at night to earn an income.

So that we would not be a burden to any of you – This clause states the purpose behind the missionaries' actions. They recognized that to expect others to provide all their food and shelter while they did nothing would be to put an unacceptable load on the new Christians and their charity. There is a not very subtle side glance at the idlers, who were doing exactly what the missionaries had refused to do. They were leaning too heavily on their working brother's charity.

3:9 – *not because we do not have the right to this, but in order to offer ourselves as a model for you, so that you would follow our example.*

Not because we do not have the right to this – The Thessalonians should not misconstrue the missionaries' refusal to ask the Thessalonians for food and lodging. They had a right (*exousian*, authority) taught by Christ Himself that "a worker is worthy of his support" (Matthew 10:10). A few years later at Corinth there were some detractors who likely argued from Paul's refusal to ask for food and lodging expenses that the real reason he did not ask is because deep down inside his heart he knew he was not a genuine apostle (1 Corinthians 9:4-7). Paul flatly rejected this innuendo in his letter to the Corinthians, giving a slightly different reason for his behavior among them than the reason now given

---

[24] When this denial was made, it simply meant that the missionaries did not go about begging for free meals. No doubt, from time to time, they accepted invitations to dine in the homes of some of the brethren, but they had not ministered with mercenary motives. They had paid their own way.

[25] This hard work in the city of Thessalonica was not an isolated instance. For example, we read elsewhere (e.g., Acts 18:3) that Paul regularly worked at his tent-making trade to support himself and the other missionaries.

[26] Geo. R. Berry, "New Testament Synonyms §53," in *A New Greek-English Lexicon of the New Testament* (Chicago: Wilcox & Follett, 1948), p.135.

for how the missionaries behaved at Thessalonica.   At Thessalonica it was to deliberately give the new Christians an example to follow.

But in order to offer ourselves as a model for you – "Model" translates *tupos,* the impression a signet ring would leave in wax, or the impression left by the blow of a chisel on metal or wood.   Paul and his co-workers were the kind of leaders who stayed ahead of the competition, doing more than they expected of others.   They had a God-given right to expect their disciples to take care of their financial needs, but they voluntarily chose not to press this right.   They were willing to go beyond what was required of them in order to persuade their Gentile converts to do the same in overcoming their aversion to manual labor.[27]

So that you would follow our example – The missionaries were followers of Christ (they imitated Him, 1 Corinthians 11:1), so they could rightfully ask their converts to imitate their example.

2.   An important principle.   10

3:10 – *For even when we were with you, we used to give you this order: if anyone is not willing to work, then he is not to eat, either.*

For even when we were with you – The preposition "for" which begins this verse indicates it is intended as a reason or an explanation of something already written.   If it is connected with verse 9 immediately preceding, it is giving a reason why Paul and his fellow missionaries worked: if they taught others to work, they could not very well remain idle themselves.   A better idea is that verse 10 is connected with the thought expressed back in verse 6.   'We do not hesitate in this letter again to command you to work rather than being undisciplined; after all, when we were first in your town, we used to emphasize this command.'

We used to give you this order – The imperfect tense Greek verb here translated "used to give this order" is the same military command verb used in verses 4 and 6.   It indicates the command was repeated on numerous occasions as the Christian leaders were trying to give their converts a thorough grounding in the Lord's expectations for them.   The instructions which were given then by word of mouth are here being repeated in writing.

---

[27] Hayden, *op. cit.*, p.260.

If anyone is not willing to work, then he is not to eat, either – The untranslated *hoti* with which this clause begins in the Greek indicates that the exact words the apostles used when they were in town are here repeated. "Anyone" can be either man or woman. "Not willing" says the person in view, though able-bodied, refuses to work. "He is not to eat" means at public expense.[28]   Christian brothers who refuse to work are not to be supported by church members who are willing to work.[29]   This precept which the preachers emphasized sums up the Christian work ethic: Christians recognize their obligation to care for widows, orphans, and the disabled.   While able-bodied men who cannot find work may expect limited assistance, Christian brothers who refuse to do honorable work, whether because of low wages or because the work is "out of his (or her) line," should not expect or even ask their more industrious brethren to support them.

3.   A command addressed to the idle brothers.   11,12

3:11 – *For we hear that some among you are leading an undisciplined life, doing no work at all, but acting like busybodies.*

For we hear that some among you are leading an undisciplined life – This verse explains why verses 6-10 have been written, in which the writers repeated a command given previously and often.   Some of the brethren were continuing to disregard the command from the Lord.   If we treat "we" as including Paul and Silas and Timothy, and if we note the verb "hear" is a present tense verb in the Greek (thus indicating they heard on more than just one occasion), then we must suppose several unnamed Christians, having come to Corinth, all brought it to the attention of the writers of this letter that the festering problem of the undisciplined lifestyle of some Christians in Thessalonica was a continuing issue.[30]

Doing no work at all – This explains exactly what is meant by the word translated "unruly" and "undisciplined."   Many Greeks held the general attitude "that work was to be done

---

[28] The Greek verb is a present tense imperative, which makes this prohibition a general rule, to which occasional exceptions may be made without disobeying the command.

[29] It appears most likely that this command specifically covered daily food supplies that might be sought by the undisciplined.   Whether or not the undisciplined also were to be excluded from the love feasts (basket dinners) that were served on the Lord's Day is difficult to determine.   Since the Lord's Supper was also observed at these basket dinners, the prohibition is not to be interpreted as meaning the undisciplined were excluded from the Lord's Table.

[30] The Greek verb translated "leading" in this clause, and the one translated "'doing" in the next, are both present tense verbs.   The idleness was a continuing idleness.

only by slaves.   Aristotle's ideal man wouldn't soil his hands with work."[31]   That Jesus was a carpenter (Mark 6:3) indicates He did not subscribe to a philosophy like Aristotle's.

But acting like busybodies – This is how the idlers were using the extra time that refusal to work gave them.   Idleness naturally disposes people to busy themselves with things that are less than spiritually beneficial, either for themselves or others.   What was indicated about "busybodies" in the author's commentary on 1 Timothy 5:13 deserves repeating here:

> A "busybody" (*periergos*) is usually defined as someone who meddles in what does not concern them.   People who have little or nothing to do of their own commonly fill their time by interesting themselves in the affairs of their neighbors.   There may be more here. This same Greek word is used at Acts 19:19 for "magic" (dabbling in the occult).   It is interesting, then, to compare what is said in 2 Timothy 3:13.   The "busybodies" at Ephesus (remember the religious emphases that abounded in that city!) could well be dabbling in the occult.[32]

The old idiom says it accurately: "Idle hands are the devil's workshop."

3:12 – *Now such persons we command and exhort in the Lord Jesus Christ to work in quiet fashion and eat their own bread.*

Now such persons – Following the command to the church members to keep away from unruly persons (2 Thessalonians 3:6-11), a second command is now addressed to the unruly offenders themselves, however many their numbers may have been.

We command and exhort in the Lord Jesus Christ – This is the fourth time in this context this military metaphor for passing along orders from a superior has been used by the writers.   The combination of the two verbs puts pressure on the unruly offenders to comply with the instructions.   When someone has been rebellious against authority for a good while (as the undisciplined folk at Thessalonica have been), a simple command may continue to be flouted.   The addition of "we exhort," an appeal to the will of the rebellious folk, asks them to make a deliberate decision to submit to the command to change their behavior.   "In the Lord Jesus Christ" may mean this command and exhortation are issued by the authority of Christ,   or it may mean that because the writers are united in the Lord

---

[31] Tesh, *op. cit.*, p.373.

[32] Gareth L. Reese, *New Testament Epistles: 1 and 2 Timothy and Titus* (Moberly, MO: Scripture Exposition Books, 2007), p. 237.

they could offer this command.[33]   Obedience to it will help you to remain in the Lord, and thus also with other Christians in that Body relationship.

To work in quiet fashion – The present tense participle translated "to work" carries the connotation that they were to work steadily, not just occasionally or sporadically. They were to abandon their past steady refusal to work at all. "Quiet fashion" is the polar opposite of "acting like busybodies" (verse 11).

And eat their own bread – "Eat bread" carries the same meaning which the same idiom had in verse 8. Christians are to provide for their own living expenses rather than depending on others to supply them with free food and lodging.

4. Continue doing what is right.   13-15

3:13 – But as for you, brethren, do not grow weary of doing good.

But as for you, brethren – Finished with their direct command and exhortation to the unruly brothers, the writers conclude by once again itemizing the Lord's expectations for to those Christians who have been working, and who have been taken advantage of by the unruly busybodies.

Do not grow weary of doing good – The prohibition (written with an aorist subjunctive verb) means "do not even begin to grow weary!" or "do not even begin to become discouraged!"   This is the only passage in the New Testament where the word *kalopoieō* ("doing good") appears. It is written as a present tense participle, which implies that before this they had been acting honorably and such behavior was to be continued.   The verb is a compound word, formed from *kalos* rather than *agathos*, suggesting their behavior had been such that everyone, even God, could see that it was beautiful, honorable, and excellent.   Whether they were supporting folk who truly were in need, or whether they were consistently refusing to enable the unruly to continue to refuse to work, their behavior had been right.   "Paul's exhortation seems to be, 'Although some among you are behaving incorrectly, don't you cease to do what you know is right according to God's standards.'"[34]

---

[33] There is a variation in the manuscripts at this place. The Textus Receptus reads *dia* followed by "Lord Jesus Christ" in the genitive case. The UBS[4] reads *en* with "Lord Jesus Christ" in the dative case. The former reading makes this command originate with the Lord. The latter may still be an appeal to His authority, but it also may be a dative of sphere. For the significance of the triple designation "Lord Jesus Christ," see comments at 1 Thessalonians 1:1.

[34] Tesh, *op. cit.*, p.373.

3:14 – *If anyone does not obey our instruction in this letter, take special note of that person and do not associate with him, so that he will be put to shame.*

If anyone does not obey our instruction in this letter – This verse identifies one action involved if the working brethren are to continue doing what is right. It is likely that the particular "instruction" chiefly in view is the one about able-bodied folk working and earning their own livelihood. "Obey" translates *hupakouō*, a compound word that means "to act upon what is heard." Because the Greek text allows "in this letter" to be taken either with what preceded, or with what follows, the thrust of the phrase is a bit uncertain.[35]

Take special note of that person – Just how the Christians were to take "special note" is also uncertain. Perhaps it means no more than mark or recognize in your own mind that such a person is to be avoided. Perhaps it means to point out those folk to the congregation by naming them during one of their public assemblies. If we connect "in this letter" with this phrase, then the verse means "read this letter to that person publicly."

And do not associate with him – This prohibition indicates the behavior that regularly and consistently is to follow taking special note of the offender. The meaning of this verb is similar to that translated "keep away from" in verse 6. In fact, the verb used here is the very same verb used in 1 Corinthians 5:9,11 where it is explained that the Christians are "not even to eat with" the offender concerned. What is called for is not formal excommunication, but social ostracism of the offender.

So that he will be put to shame – The refusal of the working brethren to associate with the unruly is intended for the good of the unruly person. One feels shame when the realization finally dawns that he has been doing wrong. Finding himself shunned by godly brethren, he may become ashamed of his idle behavior, repent, and then settle down to become a more useful and representative member of the Christian community. It is the goal of the working brethren, as they continue to do what is right, to turn the offender from his or her offensive course of behavior.

3:15 – *Yet do not regard him as an enemy, but admonish him as a brother.*

Yet do not regard him as an enemy – This verse identifies a second action involved if the working brethren are to continue doing what is right. The English conjunction "yet" is too strong. The Greek conjunction used here is "and" (*kai*), which beautifully pictures

---

[35] Where the NASB reads "in this letter," and the KJV and ASV have "by this epistle," Marshall's interlinear translates the Greek *dia tēs epistolēs* as "through the letter." If the Greek had the preposition *en* (followed by "the letter" in the dative case) rather than *dia* followed by the genitive, that grammatical construction might be decisive for connecting the phrase to the word "instruction" which precedes it.

the refusal to associate with the offender as being an act of brotherly kindness. No hostile feelings against the erring ones were to be part of this avoidance of association with them.

But admonish him as a brother – The unruly offender is still a "brother" – a member of the family of God – but he is in need of being instructed concerning the object and reason for the social ostracism. The Greek verb *noutheteite,* here translated "admonish," is the same verb translated "give instruction" at 1 Thessalonians 5:12. The verb tense here suggests repeated admonitions and instructions may be needed before the desired reformation is realized. "Disapproval, as a means of moral discipline, loses all its effect if the offender does not realize its object and reason (*noutheteite*), or if it is tainted with personal hostility."[36]

IV. TWO FINAL WISH-PRAYERS.   3:16

3:16 – Now may the Lord of peace Himself continually grant you peace in every circumstance.   The Lord be with you all!

Now may the Lord of peace Himself – The emphatic pronoun "Himself" stands first in the Greek sentence. Morris says it serves to draw the attention of the readers away from themselves and back to the Lord.[37] "Lord," in accordance with the writers' usual practice, is probably to be taken as referring to Jesus Christ. There may well be an allusion to Isaiah 9:6 where Messiah is foretold as being the Prince of Peace.

> Peace was disturbed by an irritating kind of disorder in the Church, by wild rumors and alarms respecting the Parousia (2 Thessalonians 2:1-2), as well as by the unrelenting persecution from without. St. Paul has done his best to tranquilize his readers' minds, and bring them all to a sober and orderly condition. But he looks to "the Lord of peace Himself" to shed on them His all-controlling and all-reconciling influence.[38]

Continually grant you peace in every circumstance – The optative mood verb makes this a wish-prayer.   "'Peace' does not mean the avoidance of difficult situations, such as

---

[36] Moffatt, *op. cit.*, p.53.

[37] Morris, *op. cit.*, p.150.

[38] Findlay, *op. cit.*, p.168.

the one just addressed by Paul.   Peace comes when such situations are handled in a manner pleasing to the Lord of peace."[39]   "Continually" is a good translation of *dia pantos* (literally, "through all," with the word for "times" being understood).   The better attested Greek text behind "in every circumstance" is *en panti tropō*, which has the idea of "at all times and in every way" or "in every shape and form."[40]   The writers have in mind more than just the topics covered in this epistle.   The writers could pray for no higher blessing for their converts and readers.

The Lord be with you all! – With the verb "may" being understood, this clause too becomes a wish-prayer.   This wish is likely founded upon Christ's own promise recorded in Matthew 28:20.   The thread of thought in these two wish-prayers is this: "May He bless you not only with His peace, but also with His presence."   "All" indicates that this prayer for blessing "is not limited to the mature and well-disciplined saints; it is asked for 'you all' – the ones commanded with rebuke as well as those commended with praise."[41] Indeed, the writers have written some strong words of correction and reproof in this letter, but this closing prayer is intended to communicate to the readers the truth that the writers bear no ill-will to any of the brethren.

PERSONALIZED, AUTHENTICATING GREETING & BENEDICTION.   3:17,18

3:17 – *I, Paul, write this greeting with my own hand, and this is a distinguishing mark in every letter; this is the way I write.*

I, Paul, write this greeting with my own hand – Since only a small portion of the populace was literate, getting a letter written in ancient times often required the employment of a professional scribe.   When the scribe had finished the body of the letter, the person who was actually sending it regularly took the pen in hand and added his mark. Sometimes the sender signed his name, and sometimes wrote only a word of benediction. Archaeology has produced examples of ancient letters in which the body was penned in neat uncial letters by a professional scribe while the signature and benediction were penned

---

[39] Hayden, *op. cit.*, p.262.

[40] A few not very old manuscripts read *en panti topō*, which would translate as "in every place."

[41] Hayden, *ibid.*

in rough script.[42]   With the writing of verse 16, the scribe had completed the main body of the letter.   At this point, Paul, taking up the pen on behalf of all three, personally penned these closing words to this second letter to the church at Thessalonica.   While the word "greeting" (*aspasmos*) means both to greet and to wish well to, it is not quite clear in what the "greeting" consists.   Does it look back at verse 16?   Is it just verse 17 that is the greeting?   Or, as seems most likely, are verses 17 and 18 both intended?

And this is a distinguishing mark in every letter – An examination of the epistolary close of Paul's epistles in the New Testament shows that in only three does he sign his name.[43] This fact leads to the conclusion that the "distinguishing mark" here alluded to is not his name, but rather some word of greeting written by Paul's own hand.[44]   Such a note in his own handwriting was the sign of authenticity by which a genuine letter from him could be distinguished from a counterfeit like those forged letters with which false teachers had troubled the Thessalonian church (2 Thessalonians 2:2).

The wording "every letter" has led some to theorize that other letters, now lost, had earlier been written by Paul.   This theory fails for at least two reasons: (1) It fails to pay attention to the fact it is Paul's handwritten greeting itself, and not a Pauline signature, that is the distinguishing mark.   (2) It fails to pay attention to the recent history in the church at Thessalonica, a history which calls for a need for the Thessalonians to have some criteria by which to guard against any new deceptive letters.

This is the way I write – 'This is a specimen of my handwriting.'   Paul calls on the Thessalonians to pay close attention to it.   "There was something peculiar and noticeable in Paul's penmanship which could not be mistaken.   Some infer from Galatians 6:11 that Paul's script was distinguished by its large and bold appearance."[45]

3:18 – *The grace of our Lord Jesus Christ be with you all.*

The grace of our Lord Jesus Christ be with you all – Paul closes every one of his letters by praying for a blessing on his readers.   "You all" in this benediction is as inclusive as

---

[42] An example of an ancient papyrus letter showing both styles of handwriting can be found in *The Good News: The New Testament of Our Lord and Savior Jesus Christ*, New York: American Bible Society, 1953, p.G24.

[43] 1 Corinthians 16:21; Colossians 4:18; Philemon 19.

[44] The Pauline signature at the opening of the letters identifies the writer, whether or not he actually signs his name at the conclusion of the letter.

[45] Findlay, *op. cit.*, p.169.

was "you all" in verse 16. "Grace" is lovingkindness. Thus, this benediction might be paraphrased, "I pray that our Lord Jesus Christ may be loving and kind to you all."

****

Readers familiar with the KJV find several more words at the close of this letter. However, the word "Amen" and the subscription included at the end of verse 18 in the KJV were not part of the original text; both were added later by scribes who were making copies of the Biblical letters.

The subscription reads "The second *epistle* to the Thessalonians was written from Athens." This is probably incorrect, as there is reason to think that this letter was written from Corinth. (See the Detailed Introduction to 2 Thessalonians and the notes at 2 Thessalonians 1:1.)

Detailed Introductions

to

1 & 2 Thessalonians

1 Thessalonians

A. HISTORICAL ALLUSIONS

The study of historical allusions in the letter is essential if we are to obtain an answer concerning authorship, date of writing, place of writing, to whom it was written, and why it was written. Once historical allusions have been studied, an effort is then made to compare the information learned in those allusions with the early history of the church found in the book of Acts.

1. Title – "1 Thessalonians"

Such titles were not found in the original, autograph copy of the letter. These titles were added by scribes who at some later date made copies of the original letter. The title found in the KJV is "The First Epistle of the Apostle Paul to the Thessalonians." However, in the oldest manuscripts still extant the title is simply *pros Thessalonikeis A* ("to Thessalonians 1"). Later scribes were not content with these brief designations. The more recent the manuscript copy, the longer the title tends to be. In the oldest manuscripts the word *epistolē* ("an epistle" or "a letter") was either affixed at the head of a collection of letters, or was simply added mentally by readers, so that the whole thought was "Epistle #1 to the Thessalonians."

D. Edmond Hiebert has given us a chapter on "the interpretation of the title."[2] He tells us the word *epistolē* simply means something sent to its destination by means of a messenger. It is a written communication sent to one person or to a group of people. The word occurs 24 times in the New Testament, and our English versions translate it as "letter" and "epistle" with almost equal frequency. Purists like Adolph Deissmann have insisted that "letter" is the proper term for an *ad hoc* communication intended for a particular individual, while "epistle" indicated a more polished literary production intended for the general public.[3] However, those who try to maintain these stricter definitions find it diffi-

---

[1] Paul's letters may be conveniently arranged in four groups:
- Group One (1 & 2 Thessalonians) has Eschatology as the overarching theme.
- Group Two (1 & 2 Corinthians, Galatians and Romans) all center around the theme of Soteriology.
- Group Three (Ephesians, Colossians, Philemon, and Philippians) deal with Christology.
- Group Four (1 & 2 Timothy and Titus) have Ecclesiology as their common topic.

[2] D. Edmond Hiebert, *The Thessalonian Epistles: A Call to Readiness* (Chicago: Moody Press, 1971), pp.27-29.

[3] Adolf Deissmann, *Bible Studies*, (Winona Lake, IN: Alpha Publications, 1979) p.3-12,42-49; *Light from the Ancient East*, (Grand Rapids, MI: Baker Book House, 1965) p.217-34.

cult to classify this or that particular New Testament work as an epistle or a letter. During the lifetime of this commentator, three English versions (KJV, ASV, NASB) have tended to influence his vocabulary, and as a result he finds himself using the terms "letter" and "epistle" interchangeably.

2. Historical allusions found in the beginning of the letter -- 1:1-10

1:1-4 – Ancient letters followed a common format. An epistolary opening usually included four things. First, the author signed his name. Next came the address or destination of the letter. Then came a word of personal greeting. Finally, the author would offer an expression of thanksgiving concerning the readers.

In this letter, we unexpectedly find three names in the author spot. This causes us to immediately begin to wonder how three men might have been involved in the composition of the letter.

The destination of this letter is indicated in the long phrase "To the church of the Thessalonians in God the Father and the Lord Jesus Christ." That long phrase causes us to pause and ask why all the words following "church of the Thessalonians" were added.

In many ancient letters, a simple word, "Greeting," served very well. (Compare James 1:1 where we find *charein*, a typical Hellenistic greeting.) The Jewish word of greeting was "Shalom" ("peace to you"). Could it be significant that the writers of this letter have used not only the Jewish word of greeting, but have also substituted *charis* ("grace") for their Greek word of greeting? We suppose the authors combined both Greek and Hebrew greetings for at least two reasons. First, the church at Thessalonica included Christians of both Jewish and Gentile ethnicity. Second, the terms "grace" and "peace" now have been given a new, Christian meaning, and that meaning is the most appropriate greeting for these readers. "Grace" seems to be a prayer that the readers may continue to experience God's loving-kindness; it may well be a wish-prayer for their salvation. "Peace" seems to be a wish-prayer for their spiritual well-being in the widest sense, including both peace with God and peace with man.

Ancient letter writers regularly included some words of thanksgiving after the greeting and before beginning the body of the letter. In some New Testament letters, thanks is given to God for something positive the readers are doing. Where the readers are not doing as well as they might, thanks is given to God for what He has done for the readers. Some thanksgivings even introduce some of the topics that are about to be covered in the body of the letter. There is good psychology in opening a letter with thanksgiving. Say a good word, complement the readers where you can, and the readers are likely to be more inclined to listen and heed what is about to be written as their mistakes and misunderstandings are brought out into the open.

The historical allusions in verses 1-4 have given us some information about the time and place when this letter was written. It was written at a time when the three men (Paul, Silvanus, [4] Timothy) named in the signature were together. Furthermore, the establishment of a church in Thessalonica occurred on what is known as Paul's second missionary Journey (Acts 15:31-18:22, especially 17:1-9). That journey can be dated from AD 51-54. 1 Thessalonians, of course, cannot have been written earlier than the mid-50's AD, the time (according to the history in Acts) when the church was planted.

1:5-9 – These verses contain several statements that summarize what happened in Thessalonica when the church was being planted. The newsworthy reception of the gospel by the Thessalonians is highlighted. So, also, is the fact that the new Christians soon were subjected to religious persecution. Verse 7 speaks of Christians in the areas of Macedonia and Achaia. That bit of information suggests 1 Thessalonians was not written immediately after the missionaries left Thessalonica. Acts indicates that after they departed from Thessalonica, new mission work was begun in Berea (a town in the province of Macedonia), and in Athens and Corinth (towns in the province of Achaia). These activities would have required multiple months. What was the "talk of the town" in Macedonia and Achaia is how thoroughly the Thessalonians had abandoned their old idolatry and began serving the living God. That bit of information tells us that many, perhaps a majority, of the Thessalonian Christians were ethnically Gentiles, rather than Israelites.

1:10 – Another newsworthy feature of the new faith of the Thessalonian Christians is that they were not only serving the living God, but they were awaiting the (second) coming of the risen Lord, who Himself is here called the "Son" of the living God. When He comes He will rescue both the missionaries and their faithful followers from the wrath to come. Verse 10 introduces what will become one of the major topics to be covered later in this letter.

3. Historical allusions found in the closing verses of the letter -- 5:12-28

Not much new information is gained from the ending in this letter to help us with the basic who, when, where, why, and to whom questions.

5:12ff – These verses give a brief picture of how the congregation functioned and some of the problems that were being faced. Church leaders are recognized, which raises a ques-

---

[4] It seems to be a correct deduction to say that "Silvanus" is another name for "Silas," since in other New Testament letters a man named "Silas" is a co-worker with Paul and Timothy.

tion about whether the congregational organization was rudimentary in contrast to church polity indicated in Pastorals?

5:27 – "Have this letter read to all the brethren." What is implied in this directive? Did small groups within the congregation meet consecutively in one location? Was the whole church large enough that several house churches were required to house them all? Were the leaders responsible to see to it that even those who were absent from the assembly when the letter was first read publicly were made familiar with it? Since this letter was addressed in the first instance to a particular church, by what course of reasoning may we determine that we, too, who are not part of that congregation, may read it as God's word to us, just as they did?

The Subscription – In the King James Bible, in smaller type face, a brief note follows the last verse of the letter. That subscription, as it is called, reads, "The first epistle unto the Thessalonians was written from Athens." This subscription, and similar subscriptions to other letters in the New Testament, are found in Uncials A, K, L. Where did these subscriptions, which first show up in 5th century manuscripts, come from? Is the information contained in the various subscriptions accurate, or is the information simply the studied judgment of the copyist who first appended such notes to the Biblical manuscripts? If indeed these subscriptions were composed by copyists, they should not be considered to be inspired.

4. Historical allusions found elsewhere in the letter.

2:1-6 – The missionaries are defending themselves, insisting that when they were in Thessalonica, they were not deceitful, nor had they used flattering speech, nor were they seeking the praise of men. It may be surmised that someone has been attempting to discredit the missionaries in the eyes of the Thessalonians. Who might these opponents have been?

2:9 – The Thessalonians are reminded that the missionaries, while in Thessalonica, supported themselves financially, earning their own living by manual labor – lest they behave like parasites. Why was this reminder given? Is it simply part of the missionaries' defense against accusations made by their opponents, or is some other lesson intended?

2:14 – Here we learn that the Christians at Thessalonica are being (or had been) persecuted for their faith. It was their "own countrymen" who were the persecutors. What is meant by that designation "own countrymen"?

2:17,18 – These verses tell us that Paul and Silas felt it necessary to explain their failure to return to Thessalonica after their hurried leave-taking. In fact, Paul tells the church members he personally has made several attempts to revisit Thessalonica. His attempts have been thwarted by the devil. How did the devil do that? Does this prolonged defense of the missionaries' continuing absence indicate someone in Thessalonica has blamed them for not coming back? The three writers proceed to give the Thessalonians necessary information to answer any criticisms (3:1ff).

3:1-3 – These verses contain a very helpful historical allusion. They tell us that after their departure from Thessalonica, the three missionaries were together in Athens. When Paul deemed it an opportune time to be left alone, Timothy was sent from Athens to Thessalonica to encourage and strengthen the brethren lest any of the new Christians should be disturbed by the persecutions they were enduring. Does this historical allusion harmonize with the account of the missionaries' travels as recorded in the book of Acts?

3:6 – According to this verse, Timothy has returned to Paul from his trip to Thessalonica before this letter to the Thessalonians was written. Later in this letter we shall discover that Timothy brought news about the faith and charity of the Thessalonian Christians, their steadfastness under persecution, and the failure of some to grasp the ethical implications of the gospel (4:1ff). As we read these verses, we are caused to pause and wonder why the writers felt the need to exhort the Thessalonians "to make it your ambition to lead a quiet life and attend to your own business and work with your hands" (4:11). We also may infer that Timothy brought information about some Christians' lack of hope concerning their fellow Christians who had already died physically (4:13). Does it appear the new Christians at Thessalonica thought those who had died were going to miss some future blessing? News of this mistaken belief leads the writers to include a long section in the letter about the second coming and the day of the Lord.

B. THESSALONICA AND THE ORIGIN OF THE CHURCH IN THAT CITY

1. The city of Thessalonica

The Aegean Sea is the large body of water that stands between the countries we call Greece and Turkey. At the northwest corner of the Aegean Sea stands the Thermaic Gulf, also called the Gulf of Salonika and the Macedonian Gulf. In New Testament times, Thessalonica, a city of about 200,000 people, was located on the natural harbor on the northeast shore of the Thermaic Gulf. The Via Egnatia, the great Roman highway that connected Rome with its eastern provinces, passed through the city. Major north-south trade routes also passed through Thessalonica, further enhancing its position as a wealthy commercial center. Ships from all parts of the Roman world might be seen in the comparatively sheltered harbor at Thessalonica. Located about one hundred miles west of

Philippi in the Roman province of Macedonia, Thessalonica served as the capital of the Roman province of Macedonia, and so enjoyed numerous civic and commercial privileges, including the right to mint its own coins. During the civil war fought after the death of Julius Caesar, the city sided with Antony and Octavian (the future "Caesar Augustus"). After their victory in 42 BC, Thessalonica was made a free city, governed by its own local rulers, a group of seven men known as "politarchs" (NASB "city authorities"; see Acts 17:6, 8).[5]

2. The beginning of Christ's church in Thessalonica

The sequence of events is derived from the book of Acts. In the course of what is known as Paul's second missionary journey, Paul and his fellow laborers, Silas and Timothy, arrived at Troas, where he was directed by vision to cross over the Aegean Sea into Macedonia (Acts 16:8). Before the missionaries left Troas, Luke joined the missionary team (see the transition from "they" to "we" as the verbs are written, Acts 16:8 v. 16:10). Sailing toward Macedonia, they would have landed at Neapolis, and then they would have traveled along the Via Egnatia for about 10 miles to the Roman colony of Philippi. Several noteworthy things happened while the missionaries were in Philippi (Acts 16:14-40). Lydia, the seller of purple, became a Christian. Others were converted, and Paul and Silas established a church in Philippi, but in the process, they had been arrested, beaten with lictor's rods, and imprisoned – all of this unlawfully – for healing a demon-possessed girl who had been following them around, crying out that they were presenting "a way" of salvation. An earthquake opened the prison doors, but the prisoners did not escape. Next, Acts records how the Philippian jailer became a Christian. The turmoil of those few hours led Roman city officials to ask Paul and Silas to leave. Timothy was apparently left behind in Philippi, as was Luke (the "we" passages in Acts stop here, and Luke is not mentioned between Acts 16:3 and 17:14). Paul and Silas traveled westward along the Via Egnatia for about 100 miles until they reached Thessalonica. As they traveled westward, Luke tells us the missionaries passed through Amphipolis and Apollonia. They apparently did not preach in either place. As Roland Allen has pointed out, it was Paul's missionary strategy to plant churches in large population centers with the confidence that from there the gospel would spread to the surrounding area.[6] Thessalonica would have been of crucial importance in carrying out this strategy.

Acts 17:1-11 is Luke's brief account of the beginning of the church in Thessalonica. On the Sabbath day, Paul entered into the synagogue, as was his custom, and preached the gospel (Acts 17:2).   When he came to an unevangelized town, Paul always started with

---

[5] A stone from the 1st century Vardar Gate at Thessalonica, which lists the names of seven politarchs, may be seen at the British Museum. Aerial views and satellite views of the harbor and modern city of Salonika may be seen on the Wikipedia web site.

[6] Roland Allen, *Missionary Methods: St. Paul's or Ours?* (Grand Rapids, MI: Wm. B. Eerdmans, 1962), p.12.

the synagogue, if there was one, because it gave him a ready-made audience. We do not read much about synagogues in the Old Testament Scriptures (perhaps one allusion to synagogues is found in Psalm 74:8). During the Babylonian Captivity, in order to keep the Law of Moses in peoples' minds, the role of synagogues in the life of the community grew. The exiled Jews must have felt the necessity of assemblies for united prayer and mutual exhortation, for the "singing of the songs of Zion" (Psalm 137:3), and for remembering the Word of the Lord (Deuteronomy 8:8-18). When the Jews returned from the Captivity in the time of Ezra, they wished to sustain the weekly reading of the Law. So everywhere the Jews went (e.g., to Thessalonica), they built synagogues. Any location that had ten family heads could have a synagogue. At the Jerusalem Conference, James could say, "For the law of Moses has been preached in every city from the earliest times and is read in the synagogues on every Sabbath" (Acts 15:21). Paul's opportunity to preach in a synagogue could come either as a result of his own request for an opportunity to speak, or at the invitation from the ruler of the synagogue. After all, here were men, lately come from the Holy Land, who could naturally be prevailed upon to speak. Luke informs us that Paul preached for three Sabbaths in the synagogue at Thessalonica (Acts 17:2), and that Paul emphasized the Old Testament prophecies, overlooked by most Jews of his time, that the Messiah, when He came, must suffer and rise again, and that he called attention to how Jesus fulfilled them, saying, "this Jesus, whom I preach unto you, is the Messiah" (Acts 17:3).

Considerable success attended the apostle's preaching (Acts 17:3,4). Some of the Jewish people became Christians. We could name Jason, whose hospitality the missionary team enjoyed in Thessalonica. Most likely another of the early converts was Aristarchus, who later was Paul's traveling companion and fellow-prisoner (Colossians 4:10; Philemon 24; Acts 19:29, 20:4, 27:2). A great number of God-fearing Greeks and many of the chief women ("upper class women") became converts. Those early converts formed the nucleus of the new church in Thessalonica. The church continued to grow rapidly as many Gentiles abandoned their idolatry and became servants of the living God (1 Thessalonians 1:9)

3. How long was Paul's stay in Thessalonica?

In Acts 17:2 we are told of a three-week ministry in the synagogue, but Acts does not say that three weeks is all that Paul spent in Thessalonica. Perhaps the specific mention of three weeks in the synagogue implies that ministry among the Gentiles began after that, just as happened at Pisidian Antioch (Acts 13:44,45).

There are Scriptural statements which lead us to infer that Paul's residence in Thessalonica was for a somewhat longer period. 1 Thessalonians 2:9 tells us that while he was there, he supported himself by manual labor. "You recall," the verse reads, "our labor and hardship, how working night and day so as not to be a burden to any of you, we proclaimed to you the gospel of God." It was his custom to so support himself and the missionary team members only when his stay in any city was prolonged. From the epistle to the Philippians we learn that the church there "more than once" sent a missionary offering to Paul while he was in working in Thessalonica (Philippians 4:15,16). The distance between the two cities was 100 miles; therefore, it seems that a Thessalonian ministry of longer than three weeks would be necessary for the Philippian church to supply of Paul's financial needs at least twice. Intimations concerning evangelism and teaching opportunities while the missionaries were in Thessalonica also suggest a longer than three-week stay. Assuming Paul worked at his trade of tent-making during the daytime, the workshop would have been a place for outreach to prospects. In the evening, the home of Jason, where Paul and Silas lodged, would have served as a suitable setting for the evangelism and instruction. 1 Thessalonians 2:8-12 indicates the missionaries spent much time encouraging and instructing the recent converts in the basics of their new faith, and becoming deeply attached to the new Christians in the process. A good case is thus made that Paul and Silas ministered in Thessalonica for 3-6 months, not just three weeks. Since it is important to treat both Acts and Thessalonians as being historically truthful accounts, we would suggest inserting the several-month ministry implied in Thessalonians between Acts 17:4 and 17:5.

The day came when the missionaries were forced to cut short their activities in Thessalonica. Acts 17:5 tells us that unconverted Jews stirred up a mob of wicked men from the marketplace to harass and mistreat the missionaries. Perhaps the unconverted synagogue leaders had formed the conclusion the message the missionaries preached was a perversion of the Jewish faith. Perhaps the rabble were disturbed by the number of their fellow Gentiles who were abandoning the worship of the pagan gods. The mob stormed the Jason's house, seeking Paul and Silas, who had been living with Jason. Not finding Paul and Silas, they took Jason and some of the other believers before the "politarchs." They charged the Christians with welcoming and sheltering revolutionaries who were acting in a treasonous way against the decrees of Caesar, especially distorting the preachers' gospel message about king Jesus into an accusation that He was a dangerous rival to Caesar. It was a charge the politarchs needed to be sensitive about, but in the face of the mob agitation, the politarchs were not panicked into violent action against the Christians who had been dragged into their presence. What they did was to require a pledge from Jason and the others that there would be no more trouble, or any more preaching by Paul and Silas, or Jason and the others would suffer the consequences. Ramsay characterized the action by the politarchs as "the mildest that was prudent in the circumstances."[7] By their action the politarchs guarded themselves against any charge of condoning treason, and the agitators were happy to have Paul and Silas silenced. Given this turn of events, Paul, and Silas had little choice but to leave Thessalonica. That Paul and Silas left unwillingly and sooner than they had intended is clear from 1 Thessalonians 2:17, in which they describe themselves has having been "torn away" from their new friends and fellow believers. The record in Acts is clear that Jewish folk were the instigators of the persecution, while the statement in 1 Thessalonians 2:14-16 indicates the persecution started by the Jews was continued against the Christians by their pagan neighbors, even after the missionaries were gone.

---

[7] Ramsay, *op. cit.*, p.230.

4. The continuing ministry of Paul and Silas

After leaving Thessalonica, Paul and Silas went to Berea (Acts 17:10). Here they were apparently rejoined by Timothy, who was last with them at Philippi. Paul and Silas went to the synagogue, taught the assembled worshipers about Messiah Jesus, and many Bereans believed. But after a while, the unbelieving Jews from Thessalonica followed them, and caused trouble for them there in Berea by agitating and stirring up the crowds. Some of the new converts helped Paul escape out of town, and accompanied him as far as Athens (Acts 17:15). Silas and Timothy stayed in Berea, after Paul left. The Christians who accompanied Paul were instructed to tell Silas and Timothy to join Paul in Athens as soon as possible. While waiting for them, on the Sabbath days Paul was reasoning in the synagogue with the Jews and the God-fearing Gentiles, and every day in the market place with those who happened to be present (Acts 17:17). It is not known whether Silas and Timothy both arrived while Paul was still in Athens. Timothy, we know, did come, for we learned from the historical allusions in 1 Thessalonians (3:1,2) that when Paul was at Athens, and deemed it an opportune time to be left alone, Timothy was sent to Thessalonica to strengthen and encourage the brethren there. The bits of information in both Acts and Thessalonians fit together. Apparently, Timothy had never before been to Thessalonica, and so his coming would not be a danger that Jason might have to forfeit his bond, as would have been the case if Paul or Silas had returned. This may be what Paul refers to in 1 Thessalonians 2:18 where he indicates that twice he had wanted to visit the Thessalonian Christians, but Satan had hindered him. That Timothy's name is included in the address of both Thessalonian letters does not require that Timothy had a part in the initial planting of the church there. Timothy had become acquainted with the church members when Paul sent him there from Athens.

Following his address on Mars Hill in Athens (Acts 17:22-33), Paul moved on to Corinth (Acts 18:1). There he met Aquila and Priscilla and with them took up his trade of tent-making in order to support himself. According to Acts 18:5 Silas and Timothy came to Corinth to meet with Paul. After they arrived, Luke tells us that Paul "began devoting himself completely to the word, solemnly testifying to the Jews that Jesus was the Christ." A note in 2 Corinthians 9:11 indicates that Silas and Timothy brought a missionary offering to Paul from Macedonia, and so Paul, at least for a while, did not need to work at his trade to support himself. The time came when Paul was no longer welcome in the synagogue, so he focused his efforts on winning Gentiles. He operated out of the house Titius Justus which was located next door to the synagogue. It was not long until the ruler of the synagogue, Crispus, along with his whole family became Christians (Acts 18:8), and so did many of the Corinthians, who, when they heard the gospel were believing and being baptized. About this time, the Lord said to Paul in the night by a vision, "Do not be afraid any longer, but go on speaking and do not be silent; for I am with you, and no man will attack you in order to harm you, for I have many people in this city." And so Paul settled there a year and six months, teaching the word of God among them (Acts 18:9-11).

We are given some help assigning a date to the events in Corinth for Luke tells us that when Gallio was proconsul at Corinth, the Jews rose up against Paul and dragged him into court before Gallio (Acts 18:12). An ancient inscription found at Delphi helps us date Gallio's proconsulship at about AD 51 or AD 52.[8]   When Silas and Timothy arrived in Corinth, Paul learned that the congregation in Thessalonica was growing, but problems were developing (1 Thessalonians 4:1-12).[9]

C. AUTHORSHIP AND ATTESTATION

1. Authorship

In 1 Thessalonians 1:1, *three names are found in the signature.* In the heart of both Thessalonian letters, the plural pronouns "we" and "us" constantly are employed.[10]   If Paul were the lone writer, might we not expect the singular "I" more times than it occurs?[11]

What do we observe in the signatures and the use of pronouns in the other letters in the Pauline corpus?

- Even though he lists Timothy's name in the signature of several letters (2 Corinthians 1:1; Colossians 1:1; Philippians 1:1; Philemon 1:1), in the body of those letters Paul regularly uses "I," not the plural "we."[12]

---

[8] Merrill F. Unger, Archaeology and the New Testament (Grand Rapids: Zondervan, 1962), p.245. J.H. Harrop, "Gallio," in *The New Bible Dictionary*, edited by J.D. Douglas (London: Inter-Varsity Fellowship, 1962), p.451, insisted that it is "virtually certain that he was proconsul in Achaia in AD 52-53."

[9] In this brief rehearsal of the early days of the church at Thessalonica, we have treated both Acts and Thessalonians as trustworthy historical records. Willie Marxsen (*Introduction to the New Testament*, [Oxford: Blackwell, 1968], p.32,33) and Ernest Best *(The First and Second Epistles to the Thessalonians* [New York: Harper, 1972], p.5-7) have cast doubt on the record in Acts, preferring instead to trust Paul's account in Thessalonians. Three reasons were advanced for doubting the record in Acts: it is alleged that Acts does not account for the presence of Gentile converts fresh from idolatry (1 Thessalonians 1:9); that Acts makes no reference to persecution of the church members (1 Thessalonians 3:4); and that Acts is in error when it limits the missionaries' stay in Thessalonica to three Sabbaths. None of these criticisms is valid.

[10] In 2 Thessalonians, the same three names are found in the signature, and the same plural pronouns are found throughout the letter.

[11] In 1 Thessalonians, one time (1 Thessalonians 2:18) the writer changes and says "I, Paul" to distinguish himself from the others. Only two other verses in the first epistle (3:5 and 5:27) read "I."

[12] When Paul uses "we" in 1 Corinthians 2:6-4:13, it is a true plural, referring to his fellow missionary leaders. When in 2 Corinthians 1:6-14 he uses the plural "we," Paul likely includes his fellow helpers and associates in the plurals. These plurals are not epistolary, for in 2 Corinthians 1:13 he uses the singular in distinction from the plural. In the first letter to the Thessalonians, twice we read "I" (3:5 and 5:27). In 2 Thessalonians 2:5 the writer uses "I" to distinguish himself from the others. One other time in the second letter (3:17) we read "I" when Paul picks up the pen to add his own personal handwritten authentication to show this is a genuine letter from him.

- Likewise, when he names Sosthenes in a signature (1 Corinthians 1:1), he uses "I" in the body of the letter.

It is probably a correct conjecture that in the writing of those letters Timothy and Sosthenes served as the penmen who put the letter on papyrus as Paul directed them to write. The letters were Paul's; Timothy and Sosthenes acted as Paul's secretary.

Thus, in the light of what we observe elsewhere, there is every reason to believe that we should treat the plurals ("we," "us") in the Thessalonian letters as literal plurals rather than epistolary plurals or the plural of majesty. Paul as well as his fellow workers are intended by the plural nouns.

How shall we view each man's involvement in the letters to Thessalonica? All three could speak by inspiration,[13] so the inspiration of the letters is not imperiled if all three somehow had a hand in their composition. Did the three talk over what was to be written before it was actually written down? Did Paul play the leading role in their composition with Timothy and Silas taking turns doing the secretarial work? Did Paul talk over the contents with the others before taking the lead in the composition of the letters? Could Paul have entrusted Silas to dictate a rough draft of the proposed letter, with Timothy acting as secretary?[14] Did all three then read the rough draft, with Paul adding a few emendations and additions of his own before a final copy was penned?[15] However it was that all three were involved in the letter writing, the name of Paul heads the list, and so the letters have traditionally been included in the Pauline corpus.[16]

2. Attestation

Attestation is a technical term which refers to external evidences concerning the existence, authorship, and recognition of the canonical authority attributed to the letter. Such attestation may fall under one of several categories. There are allusions, quotations,

---

[13] Paul was an apostle of Jesus. By the power of the Holy Spirit apostles could speak by inspiration. Silas was a prophet (Acts 15:32). Prophets spoke by inspiration. Timothy had a special gift by the laying on of an apostle's hands (2 Timothy 1:6).

[14] In 1 Peter 5:12, we read "Through Silvanus, our faithful brother (for so I regard him), I have written to you briefly." This may mean that Silas (a shortened form of "Silvanus") was the executive secretary in the composition of 1 Peter (given the excellent Greek within the letter), or that Silas was the one who carried the letter to its destination, or both. E.G. Selwyn (*The First Epistle of Peter* [London: Macmillan, 1961], p.9-17, 363-466) found considerable verbal similarity between 1 Peter and 1 & 2 Thessalonians. He concluded Silas had a major hand in the composition of all three letters.

[15] We reject Robert Scott's (*The Pauline Epistles*, Edinburgh: T&T Clark, 1909, p.215-33) conclusion that Silas and Timothy were responsible for producing 1 and 2 Thessalonians after Paul's death, and that they wrote in the period from AD 70-80 in order to continue the work of Paul. Scott's work, in which he tried to identify which paragraphs Silas wrote, and which Timothy wrote, is highly speculative.

[16] Theories have been advanced to explain the order of names. Perhaps the order represents a descending degree of ecclesiastical authority – apostle, prophet, evangelist.

annotated quotations, and canonical listings.   The external evidence for 1 Thessalonians is not as strong nor as early as might be wished, yet it is adequate.

a. Allusions[17]

1 Clement (AD 96) may allude to 1 Thessalonians 5:18 and 5:23 in chapter 38. Ignatius (AD 110) seems to refer to 5:17 in *Ad Polycarp* ch.1, and *Ad Romans* 2.1 depends on 1 Thessalonians 2:4.   Polycarp (AD 115) also seems to refer to 1 Thessalonians 5:17, and 5:22 in *Ad Philippians* 4.6 and 11.2.   The *Didache* (AD 140) may have used 1 Thessalonians 4:16,17 in chapter 16.   The *Shepherd of Hermas* (AD 140) at 3.9.10 repeats the phrase "Live at peace among yourselves" found at 1 Thessalonians 5:13.

b. Annotated quotations[18]

Irenaeus (AD 130) is the first early Christian writer to refer to 1 Thessalonians by name.   In *Adv. Haers* v.6.1 he wrote, "And on account of this the apostle, explaining himself, has set forth the perfect plan of salvation, saying thus in the First Epistle to the Thessalonians: 'And may the God of peace sanctify you wholly, and may your whole spirit and soul and body be preserved without complaint until the advent of the Lord, Jesus Christ'." (Compare 1 Thessalonians 5:23)

Clement of Alexandria (AD 190) is the first to specifically ascribe 1 Thessalonians to Paul.   Quoting 1 Thessalonians 2:7, he wrote, "This the blessed Paul plainly signified, saying: 'When we might have been burdensome as apostles of Christ, we were gentle among you even as a nurse cherisheth her children." (*Pedagogue* i.88; *Instructor* I.5)

Tertullian (AD 200) quotes 1 Thessalonians 5:1,2 on this fashion: "And therefore the majesty of the Holy Spirit which discerns such senses, suggests in the epistle to the Thessalonians itself: 'But of the times and seasons, brethren, ye have no need that we write unto you.   For yourselves know perfectly, that the day of the Lord will come as a thief in the night'." (*De Resurrect. Carnis*. ch.24)

c. Canonical authority

Marcion (AD 140) accepted both 1 and 2 Thessalonians into his canon.   The Muratorian Canon (AD 170) places it sixth in its listing of Paul's Epistles.   Its recognition as canonical came quite early throughout Christendom, as attested by its inclusion in the Old Latin and Old Syriac versions, both of which were made before AD 200.

---

[17] An allusion is a reference that shows the passage or book being quoted exists.   Ideas from the book are quoted, or paraphrased, without citing the author or the source.

[18] Annotated quotations name either the title of the work, or the author of the work being quoted.

3. Higher critical conclusions

A full discussion of critical conclusions before the turn of the 20th century can be found in Theodore Zahn, *Introduction to the New Testament* (Grand Rapids: Kregel, 1953 reprint), Vol. I, p.248ff. Zahn tells us that 19th century doubts about the Pauline authorship of Thessalonians stem from the scholarly articles published by F.C. Baur and the Tubingen School. Baur accepted only four letters (Romans, 1 and 2 Corinthians, and Galatians) as being Pauline.[19] He called these four *hauptbriefe*. Evidences claimed to show that 1 Thessalonians was not Pauline were: (1) an alleged non-Pauline vocabulary; (2) resemblances to 1 and 2 Corinthians, which were said to suggest those letters were used in the composition of 1 Thessalonians; (3) the absence of Old Testament citations; and (4) the absence of characteristic Pauline doctrines (law, justification, etc.). Each of the alleged evidences has been credibly answered. For example, the alleged non-Pauline words are found in clusters when topics not treated extensively elsewhere in Paul's writings are covered in the Thessalonian epistles. Also, Paul did not use many Old Testament citations when his audience is Gentile. In Thessalonians, Paul is not dealing with an audience where the Law of Moses and justification were the topics needing emphasis.

With the advent of computer technology, new tools have been employed in an attempt to determine possible authorship of this epistle, but with conflicting results. A.Q. Morton and James McLeman, using statistical analysis of sentence length and the frequency of commonly occurring words, argued that only Romans, 1 and 2 Corinthians, Galatians, and possibly Philemon are Pauline. They also concluded that although 1 and 2 Thessalonians were not written by Paul, they were very probably written by the same person.[20] Other writers, using different forms of statistical analysis, arrived at the conclusion that both Thessalonian letters are genuine Pauline writings. Using *hapax legomena* for their statistical analysis, Kenneth Grayston and G. Herdan have argued that 1 and 2 Thessalonians are Pauline.[21] H.H. Somers, using still other methods of statistical

---

[19] One of Baur's disciples, R.A. Lipsius, disagreed with his teacher's conclusions. By detecting an anti-Judaizing tendency in the letter, he was able to fit 1 Thessalonians into Baur's historical reconstruction of primitive Christianity (i.e., some books are Petrine, i.e., pro-Jewish, and some books are Pauline, i.e., anti-Jewish). If it has an anti-Judaizing tendency, he argued ("*Uber und Veranlassung des ersten Thessalonicer-briefs*"), 1 Thessalonians could be a Pauline letter.

[20] A.Q. Morton and James McLeman, *Christianity and the Computer* (London: Hodder and Stoughton, 1964), p.33. Instead of making the structure of the Thessalonian letters (i.e., the outline of these letters is not the usual two-point emphasis on doctrine and then practice) an argument against Pauline involvement in the composition of the letters, perhaps it is a defendable hypothesis to say that the lack of structural similarity to others of Paul's letters does argue for a stronger hand by Silas and/or Timothy in the composition of the Thessalonian correspondence.

[21] Kenneth Grayston and G. Herdan, "The Authorship of the Pastorals in the Light of Statistical Linguistics," *NTS* 6 (1959), p.1-15.

analysis, reached the conclusion that all fourteen letters of the Pauline corpus are genuine.[22] At least to some degree, given the widely divergent results of these statistical analyses, it appears the results reflect the logic and structure of the analysis defined by the analyst.

Another commentator has rightly written about 1 Thessalonians, "No convincing explanation for its appearance has yet been produced if the letter is a forgery."[23] Pauline involvement in the authorship of 1 Thessalonians should no longer be seriously challenged.

D. TIME AND PLACE OF WRITING

The most effective way to determine the time and place of writing for most of Paul's letters is to compare the historical allusions in the letter with the historical information we find in the book of Acts. The events in Acts can be dated with some accuracy.[24] As far as the pertinent historical allusions are concerned: (1) The letter is written after the church had been planted in Thessalonica.   (2) The signature on the letter indicates that both Silas and Timothy are with Paul.   (3) The ministry of Paul and Silas in Thessalonica was still fresh in their minds (1:9; 2:1).   (4) Timothy had been sent to Thessalonica from Athens, but has now rejoined Paul and Silas (3:1-6).   (5) 3:6 implies that 1 Thessalonians was written after Timothy returned.   When these allusions are compared with the history in Acts, as indicated above (see "The continuing ministry of Paul and Silas" on page 173), the place where all these allusions match is the year and a half when Paul was ministering in Corinth. According to Acts 18:5, Corinth is where Silas and Timothy joined Paul. As indicated earlier, the reference to Gallio (Acts 18:12-17) gives us a date in the early AD 50's. Thus, there is little doubt that this letter was written from Corinth, just after these two workers joined Paul,[25] and the year of writing would be c. AD 52 or 53.[26]

---

[22] H.H. Somers, "Statistical Methods in Literary Analysis," in *The Computer and Literary Style*, ed. by Jacob Leed (Kent, Ohio: Kent State University Press, 1966).

[23] D. Edmond Hiebert, *The Thessalonian Epistles* (Chicago: Moody Press, 1971), p.26.

[24] Gareth L. Reese, *New Testament History: Acts* (Moberly, MO: Scripture Exposition Books, 2002), p.x-xxi.   In strong opposition to much current scholarship which rejects the validity of the account in Acts, this commentator treats both Acts and Thessalonians as being true records of the events that occurred. See notes below under "Interests of Recent Scholarly Examinations."

[25] We do not know whether 1 Thessalonians was written before or after the hearing before Gallio.

[26] The subscription found in the KJV, which has the letter being written from Athens, is apparently a mistake, a mistake resulting from a careless inference drawn from 1 Thessalonians 3:1. The Epistle could not have been written from Athens, for Silas and Timothy apparently were not both there with Paul. Further, it was not written until the return of Timothy from Thessalonica, which occurred when Paul was at Corinth. Nor is there any ground for the supposition that Paul and his companions, during his residence at Corinth, made a short excursion back to Athens.

Possible dates of writing, both earlier and later than AD 52 or 53, have been proposed. For example, John Knox, having rejected the historical accuracy of Acts, challenges any attempt to base a chronology of Paul's life and letters on evidence supplied by Acts. He speculates that Paul made a trip to Macedonia and Corinth as early as AD 45, and then dates the Thessalonian letters this early. He then has Paul, at a later time, making another trip to Corinth, during which visit he was dragged before Gallio for trial.[27] At the other extreme are proponents for a later date for the writing of Thessalonians. For example, after having made an attempt to show that the opponents being critiqued in Thessalonians were Gnostics, Walter Schmithals argued that the historical allusions in 1 Thessalonians 3:1-10 should not be correlated with Acts 17:15-34. Instead, he proposed that Paul must have made an unrecorded stop in Athens at the time he made his intermediate trip from Ephesus to Corinth (2 Corinthians 2:1).[28] In reply to this, it must be said that there is little in Thessalonians that can be pointed to as requiring that we posit a gnosticizing tendency in order to understand what was written, nor can it be shown that Silas and Timothy were with Paul when he made his intermediate trip to Corinth.

None of the efforts to arrive at an earlier or later date than AD 52 or 53 are convincing. There is no reason to abandon the view that this epistle was written in Corinth, the time in Paul's missionary journeys when all the historical details converge (Acts 18:5, 1 Thessalonians 1:1).

E. OCCASION AND PURPOSE OF WRITING

In a strict sense, the immediate occasion for the writing of 1 Thessalonians was the news Timothy brought back to Paul from Thessalonica (1 Thessalonians 3:6-10). According to Luke's account in Acts 17:15,16, after Paul and Silas had been forced to leave Thessalonica, and then in turn Paul had to flee from Berea, Paul was taken to Athens, from whence he sent instructions for his companions Silas and Timothy to rejoin him. When Timothy did arrive in Athens, Paul sent him to Thessalonica to see how the new converts there were faring (1 Thessalonians 3:1-5). Those new converts had been warned that they could expect persecution, and because of that they would need strengthening and en- couraging. Timothy could go to help the church there without endangering the bond taken from Jason, and after doing so, could report back to Paul.

We can judge the purpose behind the writing of 1 Thessalonians by studying the content of this letter. The letter records the reactions of the writers to the news Timothy reported, and addresses some needs of the readers, as was indicated by Timothy's report.

---

[27] John Knox, *Chapters in A Life of Paul* (London: A & C Black, 1954), p.85f.   George Ogg, *The Chronology of the Life of Paul* (London: Epworth Press, 1968), p.104-111, criticizes Knox's approach.

[28] Walter Schmithals, *Paul and the Gnostics* (Nashville: Abingdon Press, 1972), p.123-218.

The significant items in Timothy's report included: (1) attempts had been made by some enemies of the gospel to damage the reputation and sincerity of the missionaries, thus creating doubt about their message;   (2) the Thessalonians were staying faithful to Jesus even in the face of fierce opposition;   (3) some of the Thessalonians had developed mistaken ideas about what happens to folk who have died before the second coming of Christ occurs;[29]   and (4) there were certain areas of Christian living where many of the Thessalonians were missing the mark.   Beginning in chapter 2, each of these items of need is given special attention.   "The new Christians, coming out of paganism, had in their traditions nothing that set any standards or demands for purity of life, especially in sex relationships.   The writers remind them that they had given explicit instructions on this point when they had been among them."[30]

F. HELPFUL CONTENTS FOR CONTEMPORARY READERS

1 Thessalonians presents *a high view of the Lord Jesus Christ.*   This very early letter indicates that such a high view is not something that had to grow and develop over several decades before it became Christian doctrine.   It was a valuable truth taught from the very beginning.

- We read "Lord Jesus Christ" twice in the first 3 verses of 1 Thessalonians, and we find "the Lord" and "our Lord" some two dozen times in the letter.   Modern readers may miss what is being claimed for Jesus by the use of this title.   In Old Testament times, a believing Jew was extremely cautious lest he take the four-letter sacred name of God (YHWH) in vain.   So, when he was reading Scripture, he would substitute a different word (*adonai*, "Lord") for the YHWH, the name which emphasizes the eternal, changeless existence which is true of the living God.   When the Septuagint translation of the Bible was made, the Greek word used every time YHWH occurs in the Hebrew was *kurios*, "Lord."   When Jesus was here on earth, He affirmed it was proper to call Him "Lord" ("you call Me ... Lord, and that is what I am," John 13:13) and so His followers, from the first, took up the title and gave it to Jesus.   That practice is tantamount to saying that Jesus is eternal and changeless just like God the Father is. The verses where God the Father and the Lord Jesus are conjoined certainly reflect Jesus' affirmation that "The Son can do nothing of himself" (John 5:19).   There is an identity of working without any resulting confusion of persons.
- Prayer is addressed to both God the Father and the Lord Jesus (1 Thessalonians 3:11), and a specific request is addressed to the Lord (1 Thessalonians 3:12).
- 1 Thessalonians has Jesus now in heaven, from which He one day will descend (1 Thessalonians 4:16).

---

[29] "An analysis of 1 Thessalonians indicates that eschatology was not the focus of Paul's concern when writing and does not represent the main purpose of the letter."   Richard Longenecker, "The Nature of Paul's Early Eschatology," *NTS* 31 (1985), p.88.

[30] John W. Bailey, *The First and Second Epistles to the Thessalonians*, in The Interpreter's Bible (New York: Abingdon Press, 1951), vol.11, p.249.

- He is coming again, and is the cause of the resurrection and life (1 Thessalonians 4:14-18).
- He is our Redeemer, delivering us from wrath (1 Thessalonians 1:11).
- He has made our salvation possible (1 Thessalonians 5:9).

Paul's theology did not change as different crises and problems arose during His ministry. Early Pauline theology did not differ from his theology found in his later letters. Paul's first recorded sermon was preached at Antioch of Pisidia (Acts 13:16-41), and in that sermon we are introduced to many of the doctrines that were emphasized all during Paul's life and ministry. In that first sermon, Paul demonstrated that Jesus was the long-promised "Messiah" (Acts 13:23-27). Ten times in 1 Thessalonians we read the word "Christ," which is the Greek equivalent of the Hebrew word "Messiah." At Antioch, Paul proclaimed that "through Him forgiveness of sins is proclaimed" (Acts 13:38), while he worded it that "Christ died for us" in 1 Thessalonians 5:10. In both Acts 13:30 and 1 Thessalonians 1:10 we have the emphasis that Christ was "raised from the dead." In both records we read that the message proclaimed was "the gospel of God" (1 Thessalonians 2:2) or "the good news" (Acts 13:32). Physical death is treated under the same figure of speech, "asleep in Christ" (1 Thessalonians 4:13,14) or "fell asleep" (Acts 13:36). As we read all the calls to faithfulness in 1 Thessalonians 3:2,5,8, we cannot help but compare that with "everyone who believes is justified" (Acts 13:39). It is not proper to say that the idea of justification on the condition of faith (faithfulness) is absent from Thessalonians. 1 Thessalonians 5:9 speaks of "salvation through Jesus Christ" and 2:16 reads "so they may be saved," both of which match "forgiveness of sins" in Acts 13:38. At Antioch, when the Jews repudiated the gospel, the missionary turned to the Gentiles (Acts 13:46), something that was done also at Thessalonica (1 Thessalonians 2:16). Romans and Colossians continue to underscore many of the same truths stated at the beginning of Paul's ministry. It is not at all proper to affirm that Paul's theology grew by bits and pieces as the years of his ministry passed. He learned his gospel by revelation from Christ (Galatians 1:11.12) and that is what he preached from day one. It must be remembered that Paul has been preaching the gospel message for 15 years before he and his fellow missionaries preached in Thessalonica, and before this letter was written to Thessalonica.

Paul's doctrine concerning Christ's second coming matches what Jesus taught.[31] Jesus used *parousia* ("coming" NASB) when he spoke of His return (Matthew 24:27,37,39); so did Paul (1 Thessalonians 3:12; 4:15). Both used "like a thief in the night" as they spoke about when the day of the Lord would come (Luke 21:34; 1 Thessalonians 5:1-3), and both indicated that no one knows the day nor the hour (Mark 13:32; 1

---

[31] What is being affirmed in this paragraph is that Jesus' eschatological teaching did not have its source in uninspired Jewish apocalyptic thought (which is a hypothesis set forth by Albert Schweitzer, Rudolph Bultmann, Ernst Käsemann, and C.H. Dodd). Rather, Jesus (who spoke nothing on His own initiative, but rather spoke what God commanded Him to say and speak, John 12:48) was speaking God's pure holy truth. This paragraph also is intended as a flat rejection of more than a century of critical views concerning the alleged sources and development of Paul's eschatology, such as summarized by Charles Buck and Greer Taylor, who have Paul beginning with an "extremely simple" eschatology that was "completely consistent with current Jewish apocalyptic," but who then went on to depart "further and further from this position as years passed." (*St. Paul. A Study of the Development of His Thought* [New York: Scribner's Sons, 1969], p.12,13.)

Thessalonians 5:1).   Jesus taught there would be a resurrection (John 5:28,29) and a final judgment (Matthew 11:22-24; 12:41,42) when He came again.   1 Thessalonians likewise makes reference to the resurrection (4:16) and the final judgment (1:10; 3:13; 5:23).   The doctrine in Thessalonians is no different than Enoch's prophecy made thousands of years before Christ came the first time.   Enoch, the seventh from Adam, prophesied that the Lord would come "with many thousands of His holy ones to execute judgment on all the ungodly" (Jude 1:14,15).   Jesus likewise spoke of angels being involved in gathering folk before the judgment (Matthew 13:41; 24:31).   1 Thessalonians 3:13 has Jesus coming "with all His holy ones."   In light of what is written about the second coming in 1 Thessalonians 5:10 ("that whether we are awake or asleep, we will live together with Him"), 1 Thessalonians 4:17 should not be interpreted as a proof text that Paul mistakenly expected the second advent in his own lifetime.   Even this anticipation matches how Jesus emphasized His expectations for His followers to always be ready for His reappearance. Was it not "Jesus' intention to place His generation, and each successive generation, in the position of those who *might* be alive at His coming, at the same time so adjusting the perspective of His teaching that those who lived far away should be able to apprehend the precise point of view better than His own contemporaries,"[32] as W. Alexander has written? In harmony with Jesus' intentions, the closing emphasis in 1 Thessalonians is on the kind of Christian life His followers should be leading, if they would be prepared for that great day (1 Thessalonians 5:12-23).

G. INTERESTS OF RECENT SCHOLARLY EXAMINATIONS

1. The Integrity of the Letter

Integrity is a technical term referring to the wholesome preservation of the text in substantially the same form as it proceeded from the pen of the author.   Textual critics have debated questions about individual words in 2:7,8,12;   3:3;   4:1,8;   and 5:3.   In two places, suspicions about the integrity of whole verses have been raised.

(a) At the close of the 19th century, some German scholars hypothesized that the strong language of 5:27 (which emphasizes the importance of this letter) might be an interpolation added by a reader in the 2nd century when the apostolic letters came to be circulated and specially authoritative.[33]   A serious flaw in this hypothesis is the idea the letters were not circulated and accepted as authoritative until the 2nd century.   Evidence for their early circulation is found in Paul's encouragement of congregations to exchange letters (Colossians 4:16), and 2 Peter 3:16 indicates Paul's letters were already circulating among the churches before 2 Peter was written (about AD 67 or 68).   As is true with us, apostolic letters were accepted as authoritative when they were first received.

---

[32] William Alexander, "1 Thessalonians" in *The Bible Commentary*, edited by F.C. Cook (New York: Charles Scribner's Sons, 1886), New Testament Vol.3, p.694.

[33] Walter Lock, "1 Thessalonians" in *Hastings Dictionary of the Bible* (New York: Charles Scribner's Sons, 1909), vol.4, p. 746.

(b) More recently, a number of scholars have insisted that 2:13-16 is a later non-Pauline interpolation into the letter.[34]   These critical scholars point to three features found in these verses as evidence for their conclusion.   (1) They allege there is a contrast between the condemnation of the Jews expressed in these verses as compared with what Paul writes in Romans 9-11 where he expresses a high regard for and a hope for the salvation of non-Christian Jews.   (2) They propose that the phrase in verse 16, "wrath has come upon them to the utmost," interpreted as being a reference to the AD 70 destruction of Jerusalem, is too late for the traditional date for the writing of 1 Thessalonians.   (3) Whereas all other Pauline letters have one thanksgiving and one prayer, the fact that Thessalonians has two thanksgivings (1:2ff; 2:13ff) and two prayers (3:11-13; 5:23) has led some form critics to infer that parts of two original letters have been conflated into our one letter.   For example, Walter Schmithals proposed that both the Thessalonian letters we now have are the product of editing together of what was once four letters.   For example:

- 2 Thessalonians 1:12 and 3:6-16 were letter A;
- 1 Thessalonians 1:1-2:12 and 4:2(3)-5:28 were letter B;
- 2 Thessalonians 2:13-14, 2:1-12, 2:15-3:5 and 3:17-18 were letter C;
- 1 Thessalonians 2:13-4:1(2) were letter D.[35]

None of these alleged evidences is convincing.   (i) A careful reading of the text[36] will show that not *all* Jews are condemned in Thessalonians; rather, the condemnation is limited specifically to a particular subset: those who are described as having persecuted Christians in Judea, as those having killed the Messiah and the prophets,   as those driving

---

[34] See B.A. Pearson, "1 Thessalonians 2:13-16: A Deutero-Pauline Interpolation," *HTR* 64 (1971), 79-94, and Bo Riecke, *Re-Examining Paul's Letters: The History of the Pauline Correspondence*, ed. David P. Moessner (Harrisburg: Trinity Press International, 2001), p.30-34.

[35] Walter Schmithals, "DieThessalonicherbriefe als Briefkompositionen" in *Zeit und Geschichte* (Festschrift für R. Bultmann), Tubingen: Mohr, 1964, p.295-313. Cited by E. Best, *A Commentary on the First and Second Epistle to the Thessalonians* (New York: Harper, 1972), p.31.

[36] Frank D. Gilliard ("The Problem of the Anti-semitic Comma Between 1 Thessalonians 2:14 and 2:15," *NTS* 35 [1989], p.481-502) gives us help to arrive at this careful reading. He builds a strong case that no punctuation mark (whether it be a period, a colon, or a comma) should be placed in the text after the word "Jews" in verse 14, since the addition of a period or comma tends to suggest to readers that "Jews" is a generalizing term referring to all Jews. He documents that articular participial phrases are restrictive and are not customarily separated from the noun they modify by any punctuation marks in 32 other examples where the construction appears in Paul's writings. He then argues persuasively that the following clause (an articular participial phrase, parallel in form to part of the phrase that defines the churches in v.14a) is restrictive, referring just to the kind of Jews described by the four participles in these verses. Once this is observed, no longer is 1 Thessalonians supposedly in contrast to the writer's positive attitude toward Jewish folk in general, as seen in Romans and Galatians. Furthermore, from a logical perspective, it is unlikely that Paul could have meant literally "all Jews," since a substantial portion of those who acknowledged Jesus as Messiah, including Paul himself, were in fact Jews (cf. Romans 11:1). In addition, W.D. Davies, ("Paul and the People of Israel," *NTS* 24 [1977-78], p.4-39) documents that when Paul speaks of the Jewish people as a collective, he calls them "Hebrews" or "Israel/Israelites."

the missionaries out of Thessalonica, as those ones who are not being pleasing to God, and as those who are continuing to hinder the missionary efforts of Paul and his co-workers. (ii) In 2:16, the "them" upon whom wrath has come refers back to the Jewish opponents just described in verses 14 and 15. They are contemporaries to Paul and Silas; they are not Jews living nearly two decades later. There is nothing in the context of verse 16 that would suggest "wrath" is intended to allude to the destruction that befell Jerusalem in AD 70. In the commentary section on verse 16, it is suggested that "wrath" here may be similar to the "wrath" described in Romans 1:18ff, where God withdraws his gracious aid, and allows a person to go on in sin, and then to suffer the temporal and eternal consequences of unforgiven sin. (iii) D. Michael Martin has written about the unconvincing hypothesis of multiple letters being combined:

> There is no manuscript evidence supporting the independent existence of four letters. And if 1 Thessalonians 2:13 to 4:1 was originally an independent letter it would have included introductory and conclusion remarks and a Pauline benediction. For these (especially the latter) to disappear entirely from the textual tradition is highly unlikely.[37]

2. The Sequence of the Thessalonian Letters.

It is well known that the arrangement of the letters in the Western canon places Paul's letters to churches first, sequenced from longest to shortest; then Paul's letters to individuals, also sequenced from longest to shortest; then the letters of other writers, also sequenced from longest to shortest. This is an arrangement based on the length of the letters, not on the date of writing. This has left some room to argue that 2 Thessalonians, which is shorter than 1 Thessalonians, could have been the first letter Paul wrote to the church in Thessalonica.

A few writers in the 20th century have chosen to champion the priority of 2 Thessalonians as being the simplest solution to the alleged problems in the Thessalonian letters.[38] (1) For most of these writers the chief stumbling-block to the traditional sequence for these letters is the prophecy about the rebellion and the man of lawlessness in 2 Thessalonians 2:1-12. It is proposed that if the readers addressed had already received the teaching about the day of the Lord of found in 2 Thessalonians 2:1-12, then the statement in 1 Thessalonians 5:1 that they had no need of instruction about "times and seasons" is easily explained. (2) Some of these writers have advocated that 2 Thessalonians 1:4,5 pictures the readers as presently being persecuted, while 1 Thessaloni-

---

[37] D. Michael Martin, "1,2 Thessalonians" in *The New American Commentary* (Nashville: Broadman and Holman, 1995), p.30.

[38] Authors who have argued that 2 Thessalonians was written first include J.S. West, "The Order of 1 and 2 Thessalonians," *Journal of Theological Studies*, XV (1913), p.66-74; T.W. Manson, "St Paul in Greece: The Letters to the Thessalonians," *BJRL* 35 (1952-53), p.428-47; R. Gregson, "A Solution to the Problems of the Thessalonian Epistles," *Evangelical Quarterly* 38 (1966), p.76-80; Charles Buck and Greer Taylor, *St. Paul: A Study in the Development of His Thought* (New York: Charles Scribner's Sons, 1969); and C.A. Wanamaker, *1 and 2 Thessalonians* in NIGTC (Grand Rapids: Wm. B. Eerdmans, 1990), p.37-45.

ans 2:14 pictures the persecution as a thing of the past.   (3) Others appeal to the verses in 1 Thessalonians that begin with the words "now concerning" to propose that (just as is true in 1 Corinthians 7:1ff) such language is the answer to questions asked by the readers.   For example, since 1 Thessalonians 4:9 begins with "now concerning" (*peri de* in the Greek), it is alleged to be evidence that a question about brotherly love touched upon in 2 Thessalonians 3:6-15 is now being answered.   Or again, the *peri de* at 1 Thessalonians 5:1 is imagined to be an answer to a question about times and seasons touched upon in 2 Thessalonians 2:1-12.   (4) The references to the shameful idleness of some church members is also made an argument for the priority of 2 Thessalonians.   This is done by interpreting 2 Thessalonians as being something that has just come to the writer's attention, while the references in 1 Thessalonians 4:10-12 and 5:14 are treated as something well known to the writers.

Advocates of the traditional sequence of letters affirm (1) that Paul and Silas, during the time they were in Thessalonica, had already taught about the day of the Lord.   That is why 1 Thessalonians 5:1 indicates they need no further teaching on the topic.   (2) Rather than interpreting 1 Thessalonians 2:14 to mean that all persecution was a thing of the past, the same letter that referred to persecution as having been experienced when the readers became Christians also indicates at 3:4,7 that the persecution was a regular and recurring event in the life of believers.   (3) If "now concerning" is evidence that questions being asked by the Thessalonians are being answered, all that must be assumed is that Timothy relayed these questions to Paul and Silas when he returned from his mission to Thessalonica (1 Thessalonians 3:1-6).   The "now concerning" phrase in 1 Thessalonians does not require that the letter we know as 2 Thessalonians be written first.   (4) Since 1 Thessalonians 4:11 indicates the problem of idleness had been addressed while the missionaries were still in Thessalonica, it can be said that the problem was well known when 1 Thessalonians was written.   What 2 Thessalonians says is not correctly interpreted as first-time information.   Rather, it indicates the problem has not gotten better since 1 Thessalonians was written.

The effort to reverse the sequence of the letters raises further difficulties.   (1) If the letter we know as 2 Thessalonians was written and sent prior to the one we call 1 Thessalonians, then 2 Thessalonians 2:15 ("Hold fast the traditions which you were taught, whether by word of mouth or by a letter from us") would require us to postulate a lost letter.   That a letter from an apostle of Jesus to a church may have been allowed to become lost is an idea that is not easily defended.   If 1 Thessalonians was the first letter, then it is the letter alluded to 2 Thessalonians 2:15.   What the missionaries taught in person while they were in Thessalonica and what they wrote in 1 Thessalonians were consistent and harmonious.   (2) Had a letter already been sent to the church at Thessalonica, in 1 Thessalonians 2 and 3, when the writers are assuring the readers of their continuing heartfelt interest in their welfare, it certainly would have been appropriate and germane to mention that previous letter.   However, no such reference is made, and that is difficult to harmonize with the hypothesis that 2 Thessalonians was written first.   (3) Whoever added the titles to these letters identified them as "To the Thessalonians A" and "To the Thessalonians B" – and this was before the arrangement into the canon by length. It cannot be defended that the reason we call the letters "first" and "second" is because of length. Early Christian literature already identifies what we call 2 Thessalonians as "2 Thessalonians" – and this before the books were arranged by length as the Western canon now has them.[39]

There is no compelling reason to abandon the traditional view that the letters to Thessalonica were written in the sequence we have them in our New Testaments. Indeed, any attempt to reconstruct Paul's early theology and eschatology on the basis of 2 Thessalonians being his first letter should be approached with caution.

3.   Reconstruct the history of the Thessalonian mission (after Acts is rejected)

Since early in the last century, critical scholars have denied Luke's authorship of Acts, and have rather consistently set forth their belief that the book of Acts is not historically accurate.[40] These critics have also rejected the idea that any supernatural help was given to whomever the author/redactor was. They speculate that Acts was not written until AD 80 to 90, in order to affirm the hypothesis that Acts does no more than reflect the opinions of some second or third generation church members.[41]

This denial of the historicity of Acts is then applied when it comes to the study of the Thessalonian letters. For example, Ernest Best opens his commentary on 1 and 2 Thessalonians with a denial of the historicity of Acts 17. He says, "Luke envisioned" what Paul's preaching was like.[42] That is certainly a prejudicial way of introducing the subject. Then he wrote, "It is when we compare this [Acts 17] account with what we learn from Paul's [Thessalonian] letters (in particular the first) that we begin to doubt Luke's accuracy."[43]

---

[39] Irenaeus, *Adv. Haers.* iii.7.2 and v.25.1, and Tertullian, *On the Resurrection of the Flesh*, 24.

[40] Claudia J. Stetzer has summarized in these words: "British scholarship has been relatively positive about Acts' historicity, from Lightfoot and Ramsay to W.L. Knox and Bruce. German scholarship has, for the most part, evaluated negatively the historical worth of Acts, from Baur and his school to Dibelius, Conzelmann, and Haenchen. North American scholars show a range of opinion." *(Jewish Responses to Early Christians: History and Polemics, 30-150 C.E.* [Minneapolis: Fortress Press, 1994], p.94.)

[41] Richard L. Pervo worded it this way: "Luke's Paul is ... a 'revisionist' Paul, a figure shaped to meet the needs of a later era." *(Dating Acts: Between the Evangelists and the Apologists* [Santa Rosa: Ca.; Polebridge, 2006], p.55.)

[42] Ernest Best, *The First and Second Epistles to the Thessalonians* (Peabody, MA: Hendrikson Publishers, 1972), p.3.

[43] *Op. cit.*, p.5

Writers who have pitted Thessalonians against Acts tend to parrot the same alleged evidences of discrepancy. They include (a) the length of Paul's and Silas' stay in Thessalonica;[44] (b) the ethnic background of the newly planted congregation's members;[45] (c) the place and emphasis of Paul's preaching in Thessalonica;[46] (d) a question concerning Timothy's whereabouts during the Thessalonian mission;[47] and (e) what the "pledge" elicited from Jason involved.[48]

Having rejected the historical accuracy of Luke's history, redaction critics next attempt to reconstruct the "life situation" from which the Thessalonian letters were written. From 1 Thessalonians 2:2 it is learned that Paul had been to Philippi before coming to Thessalonica. Since 1 Corinthians 16:15 says the household of Stephanas were Paul's first converts in Achaia, that verse is theorized to indicate a trip to Corinth before the visit to Philippi and Athens. To complete this imaginary reconstruction of Paul's early travels, the critics turn to the epistle of the Galatians. The 14-year period of time, indicated in Galatians 1:21 thru 2:1, is enlisted as the possible time frame for Paul's journey to Corinth, Philippi, and Thessalonica. Paul's visit to Jerusalem, alluded to in Galatians 1:18, is dated about AD 37. His next trip to Jerusalem, 14 years later, would be dated AD 51. By staying within these parameters, the letters to Thessalonica are then assigned a supposed date in the early and mid-40s AD.

---

[44] This charge is worded to say that the three or four weeks that Luke has Paul reasoning in the synagogue is contradicted by Paul's statements that he worked night and day to support himself while in Thessalonica (1 Thessalonians 2:9) and that he received help "more than once" from Philippi (Philippians 4:16).

[45] It is alleged that Luke has the congregation made up of some Jews and a greater number of God-fearers (Acts 17:4), while Paul characterizes the members of the congregation as being Gentile since he says they have turned from idols to serve the living God (1 Thessalonians 1:9). "Such a difference is crucial for analyzing 1 Thessalonians and calls into question Luke's knowledge of the facts ..." says Earl J. Richard, *First and Second Thessalonians*, volume 11 in the Sacra Pagina series (Collegeville, MN.: The Liturgical Press, 1995), p.6.

[46] Concerning the place of Paul's preaching, Luke has Paul preaching in the synagogue (Acts 17:1,2), whereas Paul's mention of working night and day to support himself (1 Thessalonians 2:9) implies the workshop must have been the place where Paul did his preaching. Concerning the emphasis in Paul's preaching, 1 Thessalonians 4 and 5 indicate the content of his preaching had an eschatological emphasis. This alleged emphasis is different from what Luke mentions in Acts 17.

[47] Luke does not mention Timothy as being a member of the missionary team that evangelized in Thessalonica, whereas the inclusion in 1 Thessalonians 1:1 of Timothy's name as one of the senders of the first letter to Thessalonica is questionably interpreted to mean he was involved in the planting of the congregation in Thessalonica.

[48] For some reason that is difficult to elicit from 1 Thessalonians, it is hypothesized that the Thessalonians were anxious for Paul's return, so they must have understood that the "pledge" or "bond" taken from Jason (Acts 17:9) did not require that Paul and Silas not to return to Thessalonica. What Paul actually says in 1 Thessalonians 2:17,18 does not refer to their wish for Paul to return, but rather speaks of Paul's wish to return (a wish that he could not fulfill because of Satan's hindrance).

In reply to this reconstruction, Galatians 4:13 indicates that Paul came to Galatia the first time because he was sick. To speak of "the first time" indicates Paul has been to Galatia twice prior to writing his letter to the Galatians. This reference from Paul's Galatians letter corroborates the historical accuracy of Luke's record at this place. Luke has Paul accompanied by Barnabas visiting Galatia during his first missionary journey (i.e., Pisidian Antioch named in Acts 13:14 is in province of Galatia). Luke then has Paul accompanied by Silas coming to Galatia a second time during the second missionary journey (Acts 16:6), and then moving on to Philippi and Thessalonica. If Luke is historically accurate when he wrote Acts 13:14 and 16:6, what justification can critics give for their hypothesis of a westward path for Paul's first missionary journey when he left Antioch? It is more credible to affirm what Luke wrote at Acts 14:1, 14:8, and 14:20 that has Paul and Barnabas going south and east to Iconium, Lystra, and Derbe, before retracing his steps and going to Jerusalem. Furthermore, even the critics treat 1 Thessalonians 1:1 as evidence Paul and Silas were together when they came to Thessalonica. Luke has Paul and *Barnabas* (not Paul and *Silas*) together on the first visit to Galatia and their subsequent trip to Jerusalem. If Luke is historically correct about the *itinerary* of the first visit, should he not also be treated as historically accurate when he lists the *participants* on that journey as Paul and Barnabas? More and more it appears the critic's hypothetical reconstruction of Paul's early journey concluding with a mission to the West is somewhat fanciful and highly difficult to support, fueled by the obviously mistaken notion that Luke is not historically accurate.

Numerous books and journal articles substantiate Luke's historical accuracy. Among the authors defending Luke as a historian are J.B. Lightfoot,[49] William Ramsay,[50] W.L. Knox,[51] and F.F. Bruce.[52] More recent magisterial defenses of Luke's historical ac-

---

[49] In J.B. Lightfoot's work defending the supernatural character of the New Testament, he said of the book of Acts, "... [N]o ancient work affords so many tests of veracity; for no other has such numerous points of contact in all directions with contemporary history, politics, and topography, whether Jewish, Greek, or Roman." *(Essays of the Work Entitled Supernatural Religion,* [London: Macmillan, 1893], p.19-20.)

[50] Sir William Ramsay was trained in and accepted the German higher critical theories. When he actually began archaeological work in Asia Minor, he was forced to abandon the attitude he had learned toward Acts and eventually became one of the most ardent defenders of Luke's reliability. Cf. Ramsay's *The Bearing of Recent Discovery on the Trustworthiness of the New Testament* (London: Hodder and Stoughton,1915).

[51] Wilford L. Knox, *The Acts of the Apostles* (Cambridge: At the University Press, 1948).

[52] F.F. Bruce, *Commentary on the Book of Acts*, in the New International Commentary on the New Testament series (Grand Rapids: Wm. B. Eerdmans, 1954).

curacy include Colin Hemer,[53] B.W. Winter,[54] W. Ward Gasque,[55] Charles H. Talbert,[56] and Tim McGrew.[57]   Research by these scholars in geography, archaeology, and history has thoroughly vindicated both the historical trustworthiness of Acts and established that it is a 1st century document.   What is needful is to treat both Acts and Thessalonians as providing reliable historical testimony and then to use information from both to reconstruct the historical situation out of which the Thessalonian letters arose.

4.   The search for a method by which to interpret the letter.

It must be kept in mind that the search, begun in the 18th century and continuing to the present, to find a method by which to interpret the letters of the New Testament is rooted in a denial of Holy Spirit inspiration or any supernatural hand in their original composition.   Most of the proposed methods were an attempt to make the Bible match whatever was the current popular philosophy, with the result that when philosophy changed a new and corresponding method of interpretation had to be developed and then applied to books of the Bible.

---

[53] Colin Hemer & Conrad J. Gempf, "*The Book of Acts in the Setting of Hellenistic History*" (Warsaw, IN: Eisenbrauns; Reprint edition 1990) covers the historical accuracy of the first 9 chapters of Acts.

[54] Bruce W. Winter and Andrew D. Clark, eds., *The Book of Acts in Its First Century Setting, Vol. 1: The Book of Acts in Its Ancient Literary Setting* (Grand Rapids: Wm. B. Eerdmans, 1993).   This volume describes the Jewish and Hellenistic background of Acts.   Again and again it can be shown that Acts coheres accurately with this background.

[55] W. Ward Gasque, "The Historical Value of the Book of Acts," *The Evangelical Quarterly* 41 (1969): p.68-88, is "an essay in the history of New Testament criticism."   _____, "The Historical Value of the Book of Acts," *Theoligische Zeitschrift* 2 (1972), p.177-196, deals with "the perspective of British Scholarship on the historical accuracy of Acts."   British theologians have been regularly positive about the historicity of Acts.

[56] Charles H. Talbert, *Reading Luke-Acts in its Mediterranean Milieu* (Leiden: Brill, 2003), p.198-200, lists nine places in Acts 13-19 where Luke is historically accurate.   His first item concerns the term "politarchs" for the government officials in Thessalonica (Acts 17:6-8).   There was a time when this term was used by higher critics as an argument against Luke's accuracy.   The claim had been made in 1898 by Ernest DeWitt Burton ("The Politarchs" in *The American Journal of Theology*, Vol.2, No.3 [July 1898], p.598-632) that the term occurred nowhere else in Greek literature.   But in fact, in a footnote on pages 588,89, Burton cites a passage from Tacitus (who predated Paul) where the masculine Greek form of "politarch" occurs.   John McRay (*Archaeology and the New Testament* [Grand Rapids, MI: Baker, 1991], p.295) has shown that this technical name for city officials has been documented in more than 40 inscriptions from all over Macedonia, including one from the Vardar Gate into the city of Thessalonica.   Earlier, in 1960, Carl Schuler had published a list of thirty-two inscriptions which contain the name, nineteen of which come from Thessalonica, and three of which date from the 1st century ("The Macedonian Politarchs," *Classical Philology* 55 [1960], p.90-11).   The fact that politarchs was the proper title for city officials who ruled Thessalonica during the travels of Paul now stands as indisputable.

[57]   Tim McGrew, "On the Historical Accuracy of the Book of Acts," accessed at https://crossxamined.org/historical-accuracy-book-Acts.   McGrew lists 41 places in Acts 13-20 where Luke is historically accurate.   Three of these are from Acts 17:1-6.   They are: "The proper location (Amphipolis and Apollonia, cities about 30 miles apart) where travelers would spend successive nights on this journey to Thessalonica (17:1)";   the presence of a synagogue in Thessalonica (17:1), which is attested by a late 2nd century inscription (CIJ 693)"; and "the proper term ('politarchs') used of the magistrates in Thessalonica (17:6)."

When German rationalism was the prevailing philosophy, **historical criticism** (i.e., looking for places where there are alleged historical mistakes in the Bible) was the method. Some of the assured conclusions reached by this method of interpretation include: Moses did not write the Pentateuch, Isaiah is a composite of two or three works, Daniel was written late and made to look like prophecy, John's Gospel is rejected because it is so different from the other three, Mark was said to have been written first and copied by Matthew and Luke, and several letters which have Paul's signature on them were judged to be non-Pauline (only Romans, 1 and 2 Corinthians, Galatians, Philippians, 1 Thessalonians, and Philemon are judged to be genuine).

When Hegel's dialectic (with its thesis, antithesis, and synthesis) became the popular philosophy of history, scholars in **the Tubingen school** supposed they found some New Testament books to be Petrine (Jewish Christianity), some to be Pauline (Gentile Christianity), and some to be peacemakers between the two alleged factions.   Only four of the letters with Paul's name on them were considered to be genuine – 1 and 2 Corinthians, Galatians, and Romans – and were given the designation *hauptbriefe*.   A mid-2nd century date was assigned to those books (including Acts) thought to be peacemakers.

Next came the **Religionsgeschichtliche Schule** (i.e., history of religions school) when evolution became the popular philosophy of history.   The interpretive method used was **source criticism**, which was concerned with trying to identify the alleged sources underlying the text and so emphasized the degree to which the Bible and the ideas contained within it were the products of their cultural milieu.   What were the sources of the ideas in the Bible?   From whence were those ideas borrowed?   Once ideas were found which were considered to be similar emphases in the world's great religions, Christianity was deprived of any special significance.

Kierkegaard's existentialism gave rise to the neo-orthodoxy movement.   In the background, Kant's *noumenon* versus *phenomenon* gave rise to an emphasis between *historie* (what actually happened) and *geschichte* (men's interpretations of what happened). With Kierkegaard's and Kant's ideas guiding them, German scholars shortly after World War I developed a new method of Biblical interpretation now called "**form criticism**" (*formgeschichte*) and they applied it with fervor to the Old Testament and the synoptic Gospels.   They attempted to determine how the various units or forms now strung together in our Bible books developed during the period of oral tradition before the "forms" were committed to writing.   The assumption was that, as the stories were told and retold, details were added and omitted until the stories arrived at the form we now have.

Heidegger's existentialism replaced Kierkegaard's, and about the time of World War II, neo-liberalism developed.   Now the preferred method of interpretation became "**redaction criticism**" (*redaktionsgeschichte*, from the German word for editor, *redaktor*). A serious weakness in form criticism had been its lack of interest in how the individual items came to be strung together to form our Bible books.   Redaction criticism stepped in to concentrate on the final product.   Redaction critics attempt to determine why the final authors or editors of the material arranged and modified the pieces of material they received in the way they did, and determine the special purpose each author or editor might have had for including or omitting items that had come to them. Originally used to study the synoptic Gospels, this method of interpretation is now applied to the study of the epistles.

Briefly, in the 1970's, structuralism was the prevailing philosophy, which gave more attention to the present form of the books of the Bible. **Literary criticism** became the tool by which to study the literature of the Bible. The narrative shape of much of the Bible received fresh attention, and questions such as the role of the narrator, the shape of the plot, and the portrayal and development of characters were explored. In the years since, the many different schools of criticism used to study secular literature began to be applied to the study of Scripture. As postmodernism (with its mantra that there is no such thing as absolute truth) became the prevailing philosophy, the number of interpretive methods soon became mind-boggling. Social-science critics use the tools of psychology, anthropology, sociology, and linguistic analysis. Other critics champion rhetorical criticism, or reader-response criticism, or post-colonial criticism, or gender criticism, or feminist criticism, or numerous other methods of reading the text. Each critic has a personal preference concerning the interpretive approach to be used, and each critic is confident his or her method is best. But the fact is that the sad and disconcerting result of such a smorgasbord of methods is that we are left with no clear message to be found in the Scriptures.

If the purpose of Biblical interpretation is to make the meaning and message of the biblical writings plain to their readers, it is evident that all the newer methods tried since the 1800's have been failures. What method, then, shall we choose when we want to interpret Scripture?

In everyday life, most of us use what is known as **the historical-grammatical method** of interpretation, whether we are reading a letter from a friend, or a newspaper, or ordering from a menu, or paying our taxes on time. For example, when reading a newspaper, we keep in mind that the paper has news, comics, sports, editorials, advertisements, and feature articles. We keep these categories, as well as the date of the newspaper, in mind as we try to decipher what the pages are telling us. When individual readers each apply the same rules, we all come out at the same place. We have an accurate picture of what the news is telling us, and as well who won and lost as we read the sports pages. We arrive at an understanding of the author's intent behind what has been written. We can adopt the same method in the interpretation of Scripture.

The historical-grammatical method is a time-honored method.

- It is the method used by David. He was meditating on Genesis 1:26,27 as he wrote Psalm 8. David took the words in Genesis about man having dominion over the fish of the sea, the birds of the sky, and the cattle over the earth, at face value, and found in those words evidence that man was something special in all of God's creation.

- It is the method of interpretation used by Jesus. On the day of great questions, Jesus had a discussion with the Sadducees (Matthew 22:29-32) concerning the resurrection of the dead. Sadducees did not believe there would be a resurrection of dead bodies, and also did not believe a person's inner man continued to exist after physical death had occurred. In each account of the dispute (Mark 12:18-28, Luke 20:27-40), Jesus used Exodus 3:6 to show that the physical dead are still living. That verse has God saying "I am the God of Abraham, Isaac, and Jacob." Jesus' argument that those patriarchs were still living rested on the verb tense used in that passage. God said "I *am*," not "I *was*." From this little bit of grammar Jesus could affirm "God is not the God of the dead but of the living."

- It is the method of interpretation used by the apostle Paul. In Galatians 3:16, Paul is driving home the meaning of the prophecy in Genesis 22:18, where God promised Abraham, "In your seed all the nations of the earth will be blessed." This is how Paul words his argument: "The promises were spoken to Abraham and to his seed. The Scripture does not say 'and to seeds,' meaning many people, but 'and to your seed,' meaning one person, who is Christ." Paul's whole argument is based on the grammar where "seed" is singular, not plural.

- It is the method of interpretation used by such early church fathers as Ignatius of Antioch, Irenaeus, and Justin Martyr.

- In the Middle Ages the method was reactivated by Luther and Calvin. Rejecting an elaborate, man-made method of interpretation then popular in the Catholic church, Luther insisted that each Bible passage had one basic meaning. That meaning was firmly rooted in historical truth, and could be ascertained accurately by following the common principles of understanding human language.

The time honored historical-grammatical method is not tied to the currently popular prevailing philosophy, for men's philosophy has changed numerous time since the days of David. The historical-grammatical method all these years has unfailingly provided readers with the Author's intended meaning of the Biblical text. The *historical* emphasis in this historical-grammatical method takes into account historical context, setting, and circumstances in which the words of Scripture were written. The *grammatical* emphasis studies the impact that grammar plays in any given text. Wycliffe's rules of interpretation are practical applications of the historical-grammatical method of interpretation. He taught readers of any text to pay attention to who is speaking, to whom, for what age, and for what purpose, if they wish to understand the passage as the original readers would have understood it. Once the Author's intended meaning has been ascertained, then application of the truth to theology and lifestyle behavior becomes the next step.

5. The Delay of the *Parousia*

Quite commonly, modern writers affirm the idea that initially Jesus and the apostles mistakenly believed His second coming would occur within the generation then living. These same writers will then affirm that, as the early decades of church history passed, the doctrine about the time of the *parousia* evolved so that His second coming was no longer expected within the lifetime of the apostles. Because the Thessalonian letters are the earliest of the New Testament letters included in our Bibles, they have been mined in search of evidence that might justify the claim of an early belief in an imminent second coming (*parousia*). Later New Testament writings are then carefully studied for possible evidence of an alleged change of tone, one that introduces the idea of a delay in the time of the *parousia* (second coming). This suggestion that the apostolic eschatology changed and evolved results in a subtle attack on the truthfulness of the Biblical records; this topic, therefore, merits some careful evaluation.

We treat the Gospel accounts as being independent and correct representations of what was said and done by Jesus. We reject using methods of source, form, and redaction criticism as interpretive tools. When this is done, as the following paragraphs will show, it is not that easy to build the case that a change from imminent coming to delayed coming actually and gradually occurred.

Four times in 1 Thessalonians, the word *parousia* is used to refer to Christ's second coming (2:19; 3:13; 4:15; and 5:23). The first time it occurs, the explanation given in this commentary reads:

> The Greek word translated "coming" is *parousia*, and it is the first time this word occurs in the Thessalonian letters, but it evidently was familiar to the readers. It was the word used to describe a royal visit, such as when a visiting dignitary arrived in town and games were held in his honor.[58] Jesus Himself had used the word when He talked about His second coming (Matthew 24:37-39). Following Jesus' example, the New Testament writers picked up the term and continued to use it often when writing about His second advent.

Jesus often spoke about things that would happen in the future, and on most occasions He used terms other than *parousia* to describe them. He spoke about the "Kingdom of God" (or Kingdom of heaven) as being "at hand" (Matthew 4:17; John the Baptist had preached a similar message, Mark 1:15) and He told one audience that some of them listening to His sermon would live to see the Kingdom (Matthew 16:28, and parallel at Mark 9:1). Speaking about Himself, Jesus often used the verb *erchomai* as He spoke about the Son of Man "coming" in the future (e.g., Matthew 24:42-44; Mark 8:38). He also used the verb *hēkō*, which means to come or to arrive (Matthew 24:50; Revelation 2:25). It is impressive how many times *erchomai* is written as a present tense verb (meaning "I am coming"). It is so sure to happen that Jesus worded it as though it were already happening.

As we attempt to build a full picture of what was predicted for the future, great care must be exercised when we start weaving these passages together. For example, the coming of the kingdom of God should not be equated with *parousia*, as though the two were interchangeable. Yet that is what some have done as they try to marshal evidence that Jesus and the apostles were, early on, mistaken in their belief that the second coming was near. There are a number of the *erchomai* ("coming") passages which speak of the same end of the age events as do those passages that use *parousia* in regard to end-time events. But there are also a few *erchomai* and *parousia* verses which may not refer to the same end of the age events. It is this latter group of verses that are commonly singled out

---

[58] A. Deissmann, *Light from the Ancient East* (London: Hodder and Stoughton, 1927), p.372.

to make it look like Jesus spoke of His "coming" as being imminent. When these passages are treated as being synonymous with other passages which speak of the end of the age, then Jesus is accused of being mistaken about the time of His coming (*parousia*). So, we must carefully evaluate the verses and the words used in these verses in order to rightly assess claims that the early Christians' beliefs about the time of Christ's *parousia* gradually shifted from being within their present generation's lifetime to a time way off in the future.

To fully make this evaluation, we must do three things. We must study the passages that are alleged to teach an imminent return. Then we must examine the passages that are alleged to introduce the idea of a long delay. Finally, it is imperative that we study the passages which do refer to the second advent and to the day of the Lord.

Passages Portrayed as Teaching an Imminent Return

Five passages are commonly singled out as teaching Christ's imminent return.

(1) Matthew 10:23 – "But whenever they persecute you in one city, flee to the next; for truly I say to you, you will not finish *going through* the cities of Israel until the Son of Man comes."[59] Those who accuse Jesus of being mistaken about the time of His second coming interpret these words to refer to the apostles' post-Pentecost ministry. That likely is a mistake. According to Matthew 10:5,6, Jesus spoke these words to the twelve as they were being sent on a short evangelistic tour of the cities of Galilee late in Jesus' earthly ministry. Jesus is saying that He Himself planned to follow them. He is talking about visiting the cities of Galilee, rather than about His second coming.

(2) Mark 14:62 records that when Jesus was on trial before the Sanhedrin, He boldly said to the high priest, "You will see the Son of Man seated at the right hand of power and coming (*erchomenon*) with the clouds of heaven." The argument is then made that, because Jesus obviously did not return on the clouds of heaven before the high priest died, He was mistaken. However, before one agrees with the argument that Jesus was mistaken, several things must be taken into account. First, according to the parallel account in Matthew 26:64, Jesus said "Hereafter you will see the Son of Man sitting at the right hand of Power, and Coming on the clouds of heaven." Jesus began sitting at the right hand of Power after His ascension back to heaven. Did the high priest see that with his own eyes? Second, before one accepts this argument that Jesus was mistaken, it must be recognized that the argument is based on a literal interpretation of "you will see." Are there any options (besides one that assumes Jesus is talking about the high priest living on earth when he sees Jesus "coming on the clouds") that might explain this future tense verb? Might it not just as well be assumed that Jesus is making reference to what all people (whether living on earth or in the intermediate state) will see when the second coming takes place?[60]

---

[59] The word translated "comes" is an aorist subjunctive form of the verb *erchomai*.

[60] Another way of understanding the verb "you will see" is given in notes below.

(3) James 5:7,8 is the lone passage where *parousia* occurs and which, on first reading, can be affirmed to show that early on, the *parousia* was thought to be imminent.[61] It reads, "Therefore be patient, brethren, until the coming (*parousias*) of the Lord. The farmer waits for the precious produce of the soil, being patient about it, until it gets the early and late rains. You too be patient; strengthen your hearts, for the coming (*parousia*) of the Lord is near." Is James making reference to what is known as Christ's second coming? Or is he using *parousia* in a different sense? We treat James (who is called an apostle in Galatians 1:19) as Spirit-inspired when he writes this passage,[62] so we are not justified in simply discrediting this passage as being mistaken or inaccurate. The context (James 5:1ff) relates to how Christians are to respond when rich oppressors take advantage of them. Christians are to be longsuffering and let the Lord settle accounts with those oppressors. How soon He will settle accounts is the point at issue. In this writer's commentary on James it is suggested these verses refer to the AD 70 destruction of Jerusalem as the time when the Lord made His presence known to those who were oppressing the Christians.[63] If this understanding is correct, then it is also possible to affirm that the word *parousia* is not limited to Christ's second coming. In fact, the word is used of His first coming into the world at 2 Peter 1:16. The immediate allusion to His transfiguration (2 Peter 1:17) indicates that the "powerful coming" about which verse 16 speaks is His first coming. Thus, it is clear that we should not operate from the assumption that whenever *parousia* occurs, it is a reference to what is to occur at the end of the present age.

(4) In His message to the church at Thyatira (Revelation 2:25), the risen and exalted Lord Jesus says to them, "Hold fast what you have until I come."[64] It may well be an erroneous assumption to affirm that *hēkō* ("I come") is a reference to the second coming. Certainly, some of the passages in Revelation (e.g., Revelation 22;7,29, "Behold, I am coming quickly") where *erchomai* is used do refer to the second coming. But Revelation is not an early writing.   It was written long after the supposed shift of

---

[61] Later in this study we shall look at the other New Testament passages where *parousia* is used.

[62] In a number of passages (e.g., Jeremiah 26:5, Ezekiel 38:17, and Zechariah 1:6), God calls the Old Testament prophets who spoke His message by inspiration "My servants, the prophets." James uses the same term as he identifies himself as a "*bondservant* of God and the Lord Jesus Christ" in James 1:1.

[63] The comments in the James commentary are as follows: "The Greek word translated 'coming' is *parousia*, a word the Greek used to describe the official visit of a monarch to some city within his realm. On such state occasions the royal 'presence' (for that is the literal meaning of the word) was such that none could fail to recognize the sovereign for what in fact he was. *Parousia* was also used of the invasion of a country by an army. When Jesus arrives (in this case to deal with unbelieving Jerusalem), it is heaven invading earth. When Jesus 'came' (in the sense the 'king sent his armies to destroy those murderers,' Matthew 22:7) and Jerusalem was destroyed leaving the Jewish economy in shambles, the exploitation of poor Jewish Christians by rich unbelieving Jewish people would be over. Until then, James urges his brethren to be patient in their waiting and valiant in their endurance. It was only a short time – less than 20 years if our date for the writing of this letter by James is correct. When Jerusalem has fallen, Jesus will be seen to be Lord, and everyone also will know the Judaizers are wrong!" (Gareth L. Reese, *New Testament Epistles: James and 1,2,3 John*, [Moberly, MO: Scripture Exposition Books], p.171.)

[64] The verb here is *hēxō*, the aorist subjunctive form of the verb *hēkō*, and it would be better translated "have come, have arrived."

emphasis to a delayed coming. How can it logically be pressed into service to support the idea that some believed in an imminent return? Long after others on earth were supposedly speaking of a delay, can we affirm that the glorified Lord was still mistaken about the time of His return?

(5) 1 Thessalonians 4:15, "We who are alive and remain unto the coming (*parousian*) of the Lord," is interpreted to mean that when Paul wrote this letter to the Thessalonians, he expected to be among those still living on earth when the Lord returns. But this passage must be balanced against what he writes elsewhere. Our comments at 4:15 read:

> What is implied in what is being written in 4:15 would hardly be contradictory to what is about to be written just a few verses later. In this same letter (5:10), where we have the phrase "whether we wake or sleep," that language indicates Paul did not know whether the second coming would be in his lifetime or not. Indeed, in Paul's other writings, there is evidence he did not know the time of the second coming, for he sometimes writes as though he might be among the living (1 Corinthians 15:51), and sometimes among those who have died before the Lord returns (1 Corinthians 6:14; 2 Corinthians 4:14; 2 Timothy 4:6). 2 Thessalonians 2 does not leave the impression the return of the Lord is going to be soon after these letters were written. The likely explanation to be advocated is that "we" in this passage refers in general to folk like "us Christians."

It will not do to affirm that, because the letters to the Corinthians and Timothy were written later than 1 Thessalonians, they reflect a changed view of the time of the second advent. 2 Thessalonians was written before those letters were, and it already reflects the view that, though we know not when, there are things that have to transpire before the *parousia* occurs and the day of the Lord dawns.

Having studied these five passages, it is not easy to justify the theory that to begin with Jesus and the apostles were mistaken about the time of the second coming. Instead, there are alternate explanations for these verses that nullify the allegation that Jesus and the apostles were mistaken in their belief that Jesus' second coming would occur within the generation in which they were living.

Passages Portrayed as Introducing the Idea of a Long Delay for Christ's Return

What, then, do we find when we look at the passages alleged to be evidence of a slowly developing belief that the second coming was going to be delayed? Several passages in the writings of Luke, Paul, and Peter are heavily relied upon by proponents of the view that the idea of a possible delay was slowly introduced into apostolic teaching.

(1) Redaction critics, whose hypothesis is that Luke wrote years later than Mark and was deliberately altering and editing some of what Mark wrote, say that Luke contributed to the growing popularity of the delay motif. For example, this seriously flawed method of interpreting Scripture affirms that Luke deliberately changed Jesus' words

to the high priest (as recorded at Mark 14:62) so that they read "from now on the Son of Man will be seated at the right hand of the power of God" (Luke 22:69). As a result, now in Luke's version, no longer does Jesus predict that the high priest himself will be alive when the end comes. Thus, it becomes acceptable to begin to believe there may be a delay in His return. But instead of this flawed interpretation, may we not instead harmonize the various accounts by saying Luke gives the meaning of what Jesus was saying to the high priest. Such a harmonization causes us to treat Mark's "you will see" as being a forceful way of saying "this is what is going to happen."

(2) To make an argument that Paul's eschatology gradually evolved requires that we give radical higher critical conclusions preference over long-established conservative views. These critical conclusions operate either from the view that 2 Thessalonians was written before 1 Thessalonians, or from the view that our Thessalonians letters are a composite of fragments of four different letters. The critical scholars then cherry pick passages, giving some a peculiar interpretation, and so arrive at the "assured" conclusion that Paul's early evolving eschatology went through several stages.[65] Stage 1 was Paul's preaching at the founding mission to Thessalonica. It is supposed that, to begin with, Paul did not teach a futurist eschatology but that his eschatology was simple and completely consistent with the current Jewish apocalyptic. The long-promised Messiah had come and inaugurated a new order of things. The new birth was resurrection, and Jesus' *parousia* had already occurred and folk were living in the kingdom of God. Paul's Stage 2 modifications of doctrine began to occur because some new Christians mistakenly thought there would be no more physical death, since "resurrection" and "kingdom" had already occurred. When Christians started dying, questions about Paul's teaching were sent to Paul by letter and/or messenger. Events were making it obvious that Paul's doctrine had to change. In response to their questions, Paul began to develop the idea that *parousia* had reference to a "second coming" of Jesus.[66] Now in Stage 3, 1 Thessalonians was composed and sent. In this letter Paul began to publicly teach his changed eschatology. He now affirms that the *parousia* refers to a second coming, rather than to Christ's first coming. Stage 4 came later, when it became obvious that Paul was not likely to be alive when the *parousia* occurred. He then wrote 2 Thessalonians, in which he indicates another slight shift. The *parousia* would not occur as soon as had been expected. The idea was introduced that certain momentous events (rebellion, man of lawlessness) had to occur before the *parousia*.

In diametric opposition to this alleged development in Paul's eschatology, conservative Bible scholars do not accept the view that Paul's doctrine was but personal concepts which grew incrementally because of changes in audience and historical events. Paul

---

[65] C.L. Mearns, "Early Eschatological Development in Paul: The Evidence from I and II Thessalonians," *NTS* 27 (1981), p.137-157.

[66] The Thessalonian epistles were written some 20 years after Pentecost (Acts 2). Had no Christians died in that period of time, so that the first time Paul had to confront this fact was when some Christians at Thessalonica died? Was he not present at the stoning of Stephen? Surely Paul never taught that since the resurrection (new birth) was already past, so was Christ's *parousia*.

got his teaching by revelation from the Lord (Galatians 1:11,12 and 1 Thessalonians 4:15, "this we say to you by the word of the Lord").[67] Conservative scholars do not treat 2 Thessalonians as pseudonymous and so written many years after 1 Thessalonians. Conservative scholars do not treat 2 Thessalonians as fundamentally teaching a different time schedule for the *parousia* than what Paul wrote in 1 Thessalonians. "Do you not remember I used to tell you these things?" (2 Thessalonians 2:5) indicates that 2 Thessalonians is not a different eschatology than what Paul taught when he was preaching in Thessalonica.

(3) Proponents of the theory that a delay motif slowly developed in the early church appeal to 2 Peter 3 and claim that the second epistle of Peter is a late attempt (possibly as late as the late 2nd century) to explain away the obvious fact that the second coming had not arrived at its appointed time.[68] Conservative Bible scholars have traditionally dated 2 Peter about AD 67 and accept Peter's signature at 2 Peter 1:1 as being historically accurate. Chapter 3 is Peter's answer to unbelieving scoffers who, in the middle of the 1st century AD, denied there would be a future *parousia* of Christ. It is misinterpreting the chapter to use it to say that it is evidence that Christians in the churches to whom Peter wrote were troubled by an alleged delay of the *parousia*. The scoffers were not church members; they were Gnostics who were flatly denying Christian eschatology. Peter does indeed affirm that the *parousia* and the day of the Lord will occur (verse 10). In 2 Peter 3:8, Peter appeals to Psalm 90:4 to suggest that some time may elapse before the *parousia* occurs.[69] As Woollard says, the appeal to Scripture to substantiate his point is certainly not to be characterized as "a novel idea produced in an ad hoc kind of way to meet the urgent issue raised by the false teachers."[70] It is simply an appeal to God's eternality. After all, to God who is eternal, what seems like a thousand years to mortal men is comparable to one day. In verse 9, Peter indicates that God is being patient in order to give as many people as possible an opportunity to repent. 2 Peter 3:8 is not a new argument, invented late in Peter's life. It is the same eschatology Peter presented in his second recorded sermon following the birthday of the church on Pentecost AD 30. In that sermon (Acts 3:19-21 NIV) Peter preached, "Repent, then, and turn to God, so that your sins may be wiped

---

[67] Stephen Smalley ("The Delay of the Parousia," *JBL* 83 [1984], p.47) has succinctly asked, "What justification is there for insisting ... that 'Paul grew in eschatological insight ...?' And what does that imply? Are we to suppose a steadily evolving and developing line of eschatology, in the course of which (within about 15 years) an unmistakably Pauline view of the end emerges, jerkily freeing itself, like a hatching moth, from the cocoon of a pre-Christian apocalyptic apparatus? And does this in turn mean that to cut across the Pauline *corpus* at one point, say, Ephesians, is to discover doctrine of a sort different from that an earlier point, say 1 Thessalonians?" Later (p.50), he wrote "[W]e are confronted in the Pauline epistles with a homogeneous eschatological outlook ...."

[68] See Ernst Käsemann, "An Apologia for Primitive Christian Eschatology" in *Essays on New Testament Themes,* tr. by W.J. Montague (London: SCM Press, 1964).

[69] To interpret verse 8 to mean the judgment will last a thousand years contributes nothing to the argument against the scoffers.

[70] Whitney Woollard, *2 Peter: The Delay of Jesus' Return & the Crisis of Patience*, The Bible Project, December 10, 2017. (https://bibleproject.com/blog/2-peter-delay-jesus-return-crisis-of-patience/)

out, that times of refreshing may come from the Lord, and that He may send the Christ, who has been appointed for you – even Jesus. He must remain in heaven until the time comes for God to restore everything, as He promised long ago through His holy prophets."[71]   The presentation in 2 Peter of the *parousia* and day of the Lord as being "the day of judgment and destruction of ungodly men" (verse 7), the time when the renovation of the universe occurs, and "the new heavens and a new earth, in which righteousness dwells" (verse 13), will be introduced, matches exactly what Jesus Himself preached about the future.   Peter's statement that "the day of the Lord will come like a thief" (verse 10) repeats the very words of Jesus (Matthew 24:37-39).

A Study of the Passages Which Refer to the Second Advent and to the Day of the Lord

An examination of the passages that do speak of the second advent will further refute the idea that, to begin with, Jesus and apostles taught the *parousia* would be within a few years after His resurrection and ascension.   Of the twenty-four times the word *parousia* occurs in the New Testament, fourteen times the word *parousia* refers to Christ's second coming.[72]   A question to Jesus about the time of His future *parousia* (Mathew 24:3) led to Jesus' famous Olivet Discourse (Matthew 24:4-25:46).   In it, Jesus used the word *parousia* three times (Matthew 24:27,37,39) and *erchomai* several times to refer to His second coming at the end of the age.[73]   In none of these verses does Jesus give a possible time when His return would occur.   In addition to the four times the word *parousia* is used of the second coming in 1 Thessalonians, *parousia* is the word used of the second coming in 1 Corinthians 15:23; 2 Thessalonians 2:1,8; 2 Peter 3:4,12; and 1 John 2:28.   In each of these fourteen times *parousia* occurs, it is in a context which speaks of events at the end of the church age, but in none of them is anything said about the timing of the *parousia*.   So, with no definite date given for the *parousia* in any passage, it becomes impossible to speak of a delay, for the word delay implies a knowledge of the date and time when the Lord's second coming was predicted to occur.   Neither can we look to Jesus' words for such an

---

[71] How the motif of delay as being a late invention by Jesus' followers can be defended is hard to understand in light of what both Paul (in 2 Thessalonians 2, written about AD 51 or 51) and Peter (in 2 Peter 3) have affirmed will transpire before the *parousia* occurs.

[72] Three verses using *parousia* (2 Peter 1:16, James 5:7,8) for an event other than the second coming have already been commented upon. Paul used *parousia* to refer to the coming of "the lawless one" who is Christ's opponent at the end of history (2 Thessalonians 2:9). Elsewhere, *parousia* is used six times – of the coming of Stephanas, Fortunatus, and Achaicus (1Corinthians16:17) and Titus (2 Corinthians 7:6,7), and of the physical "presence" of Paul himself (2 Corinthians10:10; Philippians 1:26; 2:12).

[73]In His Olivet Discourse, Jesus spoke both about the coming AD 70 destruction of Jerusalem (Matthew 24:4-28), as well as about His second coming at the end of the age (Matthew 24:29-25:46). In 24:4-28, He gave signs that would help His followers know when the Jerusalem destruction was about to occur so that they would know when to flee in order to avoid the distress and tribulation that those who did not flee would experience. In contrast to the signs of the times leading to AD 70, over and over again in the rest of the discourse (24:29ff), Jesus indicates there are no signs to ascertain when the *parousia* is about to occur. If Matthew's account were all we had, since in verse 29 we read about the cosmological changes that accompany the second coming, we might be led to think His second coming would follow the destruction of Jerusalem immediately. But Luke 21:20-24 tells us the "times of the Gentiles" will be fulfilled between the time armies destroyed the city and the time the cosmological changes begin (Luke 21:25).

exact date, for He categorically indicated that no one, not even one, other than God the Father knew the time when the *parousia* would occur (Matthew 24:36). His apostles likewise never set a date as they used the word *parousia* with reference to Jesus' second coming. In fact, it would likely be presumptuous to affirm inspired apostles had messages about the time of the second coming that were different and sometimes contradictory to what King Jesus who sent them on their mission had taught.

While 1 Thessalonians 1:10 does not use word *parousia,* it does talk about "wait[ing] for His Son from heaven." This is obviously a reference to the second coming since the verse also refers the time of God's final judgment upon all people. For this reason, New Testament authors also made use of the term "the day of the Lord" in reference to the final judgment (e.g., 2 Peter 3:10-14). "Day of the Lord" was also a phrase commonly used in the Old Testament. In these Old Testament passages that allude to the future day of the LORD, recall that this "day" is always said to be "at hand," yet years passed before the threatened event occurred. Should not this perspective give us some help with New Testament prophecies about the coming *parousia* and the "day of the Lord"?

After giving a brief overview of the history (which began in the 20th century) of the dogma that the eschatology of Jesus and the apostles underwent a gradual evolution, N.T. Wright wrote these words in a closing paragraph of his study of the matter:

> The [dogma of the] delay of the *parousia* is, in fact, a modern myth (that is, an invented story about the past designed to explain or legitimate certain features of the present). It has become a modern dogma, held in place by firm, sometimes shrill, reassertion and the angry scorn used by emperors to silence those who point out their nakedness. But the theory underneath the dogma is indeed naked. It is time to reject it outright.[74]

6.   Conclusion of our review of the interests of recent scholarly examinations.

It appears that the common denominator linking each of the topics reviewed in this section on "Interests of Recent Scholarly Examinations" is an *a priori* denial of the supernatural. While the negative conclusions reached in each study give little or no help when it comes to understanding 1 Thessalonians, our investigation of the issues has caused us to come to grips with a number of topics to which we might not have given sufficient thought had it not been for the study. Such careful thought has helped us to appreciate what can be learned from a mindful study of the word of God.

H. OUTLINE

An outline of the material in 1 Thessalonians is included in the concise introduction to the letter found at the beginning of this volume.

---

[74] N.T. Wright, "Hope Deferred: Against the Dogma of Delay," *Early Christianity* 9 (2018), p.81. Further information on this alleged change of eschatology will be found in the Detailed Introduction to 2 Thessalonians.

THE PAULINE EPISTLES: GROUP ONE [1]

2 Thessalonians

A. HISTORICAL ALLUSIONS

The study of historical allusions in the letter is essential if we are to obtain an answer concerning authorship, date of writing, place of writing, to whom it was written, and why it was written. Once historical allusions have been studied, an effort is then made to compare the information learned in those allusions with the early history of the church found in the book of Acts.

1. Title

The title found in the KJV is "The Second Epistle of Paul the Apostle to the Thessalonians." The title found in the oldest manuscripts is simply *pros Thessalonikeis B* ("to Thessalonians 2").[2]

2. Historical allusions in the beginning of the letter -- 1:1-8

1:1,2 – Ancient letter writers typically began their letters with a signature, address, and greeting. The signature and address of 2 Thessalonians are nearly identical with the opening of 1 Thessalonians: the same three names ("Paul, Silas, and Timothy") and the same destination ("to the church of the Thessalonians in God our Father and the Lord Jesus Christ"). The only difference is that 1 Thessalonians reads "God *the* Father" whereas 2 Thessalonians has "God *our* Father." The beginning of the greeting in 2 Thessalonians ("grace to you and peace") also is identical with the greeting of 1 Thessalonians; however, in 2 Thessalonians we find the added words "from God the Father and the Lord Jesus Christ." It certainly may be affirmed that, on the basis of the nearly identical epistolary openings, we might expect the second letter to have been written at about the same time and place as was 1 Thessalonians, and that both are addressed to the same audience. We must look for other indications of time and place as we search the remaining historical allusions found in this letter.

---

[1] Paul's letters may be conveniently arranged in four groups:
- Group One (1 & 2 Thessalonians) has Eschatology as the overarching theme.
- Group Two (1 & 2 Corinthians, Galatians and Romans) all center around the theme of Soteriology.
- Group Three (Ephesians, Colossians, Philemon, and Philippians) deal with Christology.
- Group Four (1 & 2 Timothy and Titus) have Ecclesiology as their common topic.

[2] For more details concerning the titles affixed to New Testament Scriptures, and how the titles tended to get longer as copies were made after some time had passed, see the paragraph concerning Title in the Detailed Introduction to 1 Thessalonians.

1:3-6 – Following the usual format for ancient letters, which regularly included some words of thanksgiving after the greeting and before beginning the body of the letter, here in 2 Thessalonians we find both words of thanksgiving and commendation (verse 4) for how the readers were remaining faithful even while facing continuing persecution for their faith.

1:7,8 – The second coming of Christ is introduced. Details about that event are given. Jesus is revealed from heaven. Angels accompany Him. A judgment occurs after which unbelievers and persecutors of Christians are sent away from the presence of God. In contrast to what happens to the unbelievers, saints (among whom the faithful Thessalonian Christians are numbered) will bring glory to Christ on that day.

3. Historical allusions in the closing verses of the letter -- 3:1-17

3:1,2 – The Thessalonian Christians are asked to pray that the writers of this letter may be delivered or rescued from perverse and evil men. If we search the record in Acts, can we match this allusion to any event that happened after Paul and Silas left Thessalonica?

3:6-13 – Verse 11 indicates someone has brought news to the writers of this letter that a problem addressed in 1 Thessalonians 5:14 had apparently gotten worse. We wonder who brought the news to the writers concerning those Christians who are characterized as being "unruly." As a result of this report, the faithful Christians are now directed to "keep away" from every Christian brother who persists in living an "unruly" life (i.e., able-bodied persons who were not willing to work to provide their own living expenses). The unruly brethren are directed to abandon their idle lifestyles and so be able to support themselves. At the same time the faithful Christians are encouraged to not grow weary when it comes to helping any brethren who are truly in need of help. It is reasonable to suppose that the reason for refusing to work alluded to in comments at 1 Thessalonians 5:14 still holds true.

3:14,15 – Further instructions are given to the faithful Christians concerning how to help the unruly brethren to come to repentance.

3:16 – The closing greeting in this letter is a prayer that the Lord would continue to be with the readers and would grant them peace in every circumstance. This certainly is a prayer that the Lord would providentially intervene to end the persecutions the readers were experiencing.

3:17 – The language of this verse indicates the letter has been inscribed by a secretary (amanuensis) as its contents were dictated or directed. Now that the body of the letter is complete, Paul took the pen in hand and added a few words of greeting in his own handwriting. He indicates that it is his habit to personally pen a closing greeting "in every letter" over which he has authorial responsibility.[3] The words "every letter" has caused

---

[3] Care must be exercised here. It does not say he actually signed his name in the closing greetings he wrote, but it does say that he affixed a note in his own handwriting as part of the evidence of authenticity/genuineness for his letters.

questions to be asked.   What letters authored by Paul would the Thessalonians know about?   As far as we know, the only genuine letter they have from Paul is 1 Thessalonians. It looks like the letter purporting to be from Paul (alluded to in 2 Thessalonians 2:2) did not have such a personally-written greeting at its close.   That should have been a clue to the readers that it was a fake and its contents should be disregarded.

The Subscription – In King James Bibles, in smaller type face, a brief note follows the last verse of the letter.   This subscription, as printed in the KJV, reads "The second epistle to the Thessalonians was written from Athens."   While some manuscripts which carry a subscription read "from Athens," other manuscripts read "from Rome" and still others "from Laodicea."[4]

4.   Historical Allusions found in chapter 2.

2:1,2 – The first sentence in chapter 2 reads, "Now we request you, brethren, with regard to the coming of our Lord Jesus Christ and our gathering together to Him, that you not be quickly shaken from your composure or be disturbed either by a spirit or a message or a letter as if from us, to the effect that the day of the Lord has come."   The phrase "by a spirit or a message or a letter as if from us" has proven to be difficult to interpret.   The content of the misleading message being delivered by these sources was to the effect that the day of the Lord had already come.   It is clear that correcting this false impression was one of the leading reasons for writing this letter.   However, there are details (which would have been obvious to the Thessalonian Christians, but are not to us) that require us readers to make an educated judgment.   For example, questions long-raised by interpreters of 2 Thessalonians include "By whom was this false report being circulated?" and "What evidence did they cite to verify their claim?"   Did some of those teaching the misleading message claim to have received their message from an angel ("a spirit")?   Did some claim they received their message by inspiration from the Lord ("a message")?   Did still others claim to have in their possession a letter sent by Paul and Silas ("a letter as if from us"[5])?   Another debated question is, "Do the words 'as if from us' modify only 'a letter,' or do they modify all three named sources?"[6]   It is this commentator's studied conclusion that

---

[4] What was written about such subscriptions in the commentary section of this book at 1 Thessalonians 5:28 and 2 Thessalonians 3:18 may also be referenced.   This subscription was evidently not part of the original letter.   It is found only in some manuscripts, and did not begin appearing until the 5th century.   Such subscriptions were added by men and often include mistaken information.

[5] It should be noted that "from us" indicates it is not just Paul alone who is referenced as being involved in the composition of the misleading information.

[6] Even modern critics, who affirm that pseudonymous letters were accepted by later generations, have resisted the possibility that Paul and Silas ["us"] could have conceived of letters being forged in their names at a date as early as the AD 50's, nor are they ready to accept the idea that early Christians would have been fooled by such forgeries.   As a result, some have expended much effort trying to explain the enigmatic "as though from us," while others have tried to limit the words to the letter we know as 1 Thessalonians, with the explanation that "as if from us" means that a genuine letter was being misinterpreted.   Such views have been rejected as we commented on the passage earlier in the commentary section of this volume.

2:2 refers to a spurious letter, and because such was being claimed to exist and even possibly being brandished by the folk teaching the misleading message, the statement in 3:17, about looking for a note in Paul's own handwriting, is given to guard against any such spurious letter being accepted in the future.

2:3-12 – These verses are a reminder to the Thessalonians concerning what had already been taught to them by Paul himself, while he was still in Thessalonica, concerning the time of the second coming (2 Thessalonians 2:5). As Christians are thinking about when the *parousia* and the day of the Lord will come, they must keep in mind that before that event occurs several things must happen – namely, an apostasy/rebellion, the appearance of the man of lawlessness on the scene of history, and the restraints which presently limit the activities of lawlessness will be removed. Obviously those events had not happened when 2 Thessalonians was being written, so it was not possible that the day of the Lord was already present.[7] Verse 5 ("Do you not remember that while I was still with you, I was telling you these things?") is a very important verse. It guards us against any suggestion that Paul's eschatology had undergone a significant change since he wrote 1 Thessalonians.[8] When 1 Thessalonians was read publicly to the congregation in Thessalonica, Paul and Silas certainly could have assumed the listeners would remember that all these things had been taught to them before the missionaries were ever forced to leave town.

2:13-15 – Paul, Silas, and Timothy, who have preached the gospel in Thessalonica, now call on the readers to stand firm in the traditions taught by word of mouth by Paul, Silas and Timothy and that had been taught in a "letter from us." The "letter from us" (verse 15) is (most likely) a reference to the letter known as 1 Thessalonians.[9]

B. A COMPARISON WITH THE HISTORY IN THE BOOK OF ACTS

In the Detailed Introduction to 1 Thessalonians, we ended our examination of the Acts record in the 18th chapter. Following the missionaries' ministry in Thessalonica, Paul and Silas moved on to Berea. When Jewish opponents to the gospel stirred up trouble there, Paul was spirited out of town and moved on to Athens. Let's begin our study of Acts at this point.[10] Acts 18:1 indicates that after a short time in Athens, Paul left Athens

---

[7] See also the Special Studies concerning the rebellion, the man of lawlessness, and the restrainer.

[8] The popular explanation that Jesus and the apostles (including Paul) were mistaken about the time of the second coming, and that Paul, in particular, was responsible for introducing the idea that there would be a delay before the Lord returns, will be studied in detail in a later section of this Detailed Introduction to 2 Thessalonians.

[9] See in the Detailed Introduction to 1 Thessalonians concerning the sequence of the letters.

[10] Recall, we unhesitatingly advocate the historical trustworthiness of Acts.

and moved on to Corinth. We saw (according to 1 Thessalonians 3:1-6) that while Paul was at Athens, he sent Timothy to Thessalonica, and that, before 1 Thessalonians was written, Timothy had returned from his trip to Thessalonica and reported to Paul concerning the welfare of the new church. In the meantime, before Timothy's return, Acts 18:3 tells us that after Paul came to Corinth, he found a job with Aquila and Priscilla in the tent-making trade. He labored at this job to support himself just as he had also done before in Thessalonica (2 Thessalonians 3:8). Each Sabbath he attended the synagogue services and tried to persuade the worshipers to commit their lives to Jesus, their long-promised Messiah. During the time Paul was in Corinth, Acts 18:5 tells us that Silas and Timothy came from Macedonia, and it was after their arrival that 1 Thessalonians was written. Acts 18:5 indicates that Paul now devoted himself "completely to the word, solemnly testifying to the Jews that Jesus was the Christ." We may understand that Silas and Timothy brought a missionary offering from Macedonia, and this financial support allowed him to temporarily cease his work at tent-making and give himself full time to evangelizing. It was not long until many of the Jews resisted and blasphemed as they rejected Christ, so Paul ceased visiting the synagogue. He turned his attention to evangelizing the Gentiles. A new Christian named Titius Justus, whose home was next door to the synagogue, made his home available to Paul as a place to meet with interested prospects. Crispus, the synagogue ruler, became a convert and so did many Corinthians (Acts 18:8). One night, Paul received a vision. The Lord appeared to him and said, "Do not be afraid any longer, but go on speaking and do not be silent; for I am with you, and no man will attack you in order to harm you, for I have many people in this city." Luke tells us that Paul stayed in Corinth for a year and 6 months. During this period of time, Gallio became the new proconsul in the province (Acts 18:12). The unconverted Jews rose up against Paul, and dragged him to the judgment seat where Gallio adjudicated cases. They accused Paul of persuading men to worship God contrary to the law. The Romans allowed conquered peoples to keep all their old religions, but did not permit them to introduce any new religions. Perhaps the Jews were accusing Paul of introducing a new and therefore illegal religion. But because Gallio understood them to be talking about the Law of Moses, he threw the case out of court. Acts 18:18 tells us that Paul remained in Corinth many days longer, and then finally took leave of the Christians, and sailed away toward the Holy Land.

Because there is no mention of Silas or Timothy in Acts 18, several questions arise as we attempt to integrate what we read in 2 Thessalonians with what we read in Acts. One question involves a possible date for the writing of 2 Thessalonians. 2 Thessalonians 1:1 has Paul and Silas and Timothy together when that letter was written. Acts 19:22 tells us that Timothy later joined Paul when Paul was at Ephesus, but there is no record that both Silas and Timothy were ever with Paul again after Paul left Corinth.[11] As we attempt

---

[11] After Silas and Timothy join Paul in Corinth (Acts 18:5), as far as Luke's record in Acts is concerned, Silas drops out of the picture completely. 2 Corinthians 1:19 makes reference to a time when Paul and Silas and Timothy preached the gospel in Corinth, a reference which can be harmonized with Acts 18. Silas is also named in 1 Peter 5:12, a reference which would have occurred about AD 66-67 when Silas and Peter would have been together in Rome. According to early Christian literature, at the same time that Peter was in Rome, Paul was also there, being held prisoner in his second Roman imprisonment. From Rome Paul wrote a letter (2 Timothy) to Timothy who was at the time preaching in Ephesus. 2 Timothy 4:9 has instructions for Timothy to join Paul in Rome.

to date 2 Thessalonians, are we limited to the years Paul ministered in Corinth (roughly AD 52 to 54)?

Another question concerns 2 Thessalonians 3:2, in which the writers of the letter ask for the readers to pray to God "that we will be rescued from perverse and evil men." Was the vision Paul received from the Lord an answer to that prayer? Was the abrupt ending to the trial before Gallio an answer to that prayer? Or was there a time (unrecorded in Acts) when all three men named in the epistolary opening of 2 Thessalonians were in serious trouble at the hands of evil men?

C. AUTHORSHIP AND ATTESTATION

1. Authorship

Paul's name appears twice in this epistle, at 1:1 and 3:17, but the signatures of 1 and 2 Thessalonians indicate that both were sent out under the name of not one but three people, Paul, Silas, and Timothy. The consistent use of plural pronouns ("we" and "us") in the letters indicates that all three missionaries are together giving the words of command, encouragement, and instruction found in the letters to the Christians at Thessalonica.[12] The conclusion from internal evidence concerning the authorship of 1 Thessalonians may be repeated here. However, in whatever way it was that all three were involved in the letter writing, the name of Paul heads the list, and so the letters have traditionally been included in the Pauline corpus.

2. Attestation

As explained in the Detailed Introduction to 1 Thessalonians, "attestation" is a technical term which refers to external evidences concerning the existence, authorship, and recognition of the canonical authority attributed to the letter. Such attestation may fall under one of several categories. There are allusions, quotations, annotated quotations, and canonical listings. The external evidence in favor of the genuineness/authenticity of 2 Thessalonians is even stronger than that in favor of 1 Thessalonians.[13]

---

[12] The comments made in the section about Authorship in the Detailed Introduction to 1 Thessalonians hold true for 2 Thessalonians, also. S.R. Llewelyn, in "Letters in the Early Church" (*New Docs* 7, p.53-54) gives a comparison of the uses of plural and singular pronouns in several New Testament letters. To corroborate the conclusion that all three men named in Thessalonians were involved in the authorship of these letters, Llewelyn tells us that the frequency of "we" as opposed to "I" is 96.7% in 1 Thessalonians, and in 2 Thessalonians it is 93.9%. He then compares this to Philippians (where both Paul's and Timothy's names are included in the signature) but the frequency of "we" compared to "I" is only 8.7%. Philippians is Paul's letter, and the likely explanation of Philippians 1:1 is that Timothy served as Paul's amanuensis, inscribing the letter as Paul dictated.

[13] P.J. Gloag, "2 Thessalonians" in vol.21 of *The Pulpit Commentary* (Grand Rapids: Wm. B. Eerdmans, 1950), p.i.

a. Allusions

Ignatius (AD 110) likely alludes to 2 Thessalonians 3:5 ("into the steadfastness of Jesus Christ") in his *Epistle to the Romans* 10.3. Polycarp (AD 115) has allusions to 2 Thessalonians 1:4 ("for he boasts about you in all the communities") and to 3:15 ("do not treat such men as enemies") in his *Epistle to the Philippians* 11.3-4. Since Polycarp also had allusions to 1 Thessalonians in his *Epistle to the Philippians* 4.6 and 11.2, both letters to the Thessalonians had to have been written early enough in the second half of the 1st century that they could be included in the collection of Pauline letters cited as Pauline by Polycarp.[14] The *Didache* (AD 140) in chapter 12 alludes to 2 Thessalonians 2:3,4,8 and in chapter 16 to 2 Thessalonians 3:8,10. Justin Martyr (AD 150) in his *Dialogue with Trypho* (ch. 110.2) alludes to 2 Thessalonians 2:3 ("man of lawlessness").

b. Annotated Quotations

Annotated quotations found in the writings of several early church fathers indicate that 2 Thessalonians was known and used by the early church as a genuine Pauline letter. Two quotations are found in the writings of Irenaeus (AD 180). His *Adv. Haeres.* iii.7.2, quoting 2 Thessalonians 2:8, reads:

> And again in the Second Epistle to the Thessalonians, speaking of Antichrist, Paul says, "And then shall that wicked one be revealed whom the Lord Jesus shall slay with the spirit of his mouth, and destroy with the presence of his coming."

His *Adv. Haeres.* v.25.1, quoting 2 Thessalonians 2:3,4, reads:

> Concerning whom the apostle in the Epistle which is the Second to the Thessalonians thus speaks: "Except a falling away come first, and the man of sin be revealed, the son of perdition: Who opposeth and exalteth himself above all that is called God or that is worshiped."

Clement of Alexandria (AD 190) quotes 2 Thessalonians 3:2 in his *Stromata* v.3,1.

> And the apostle says, "There is not in every man that knowledge, but pray ye that we may be delivered from unreasonable and wicked men, for all men have not faith."

---

[14] The date assigned to the writings of Polycarp and Ignatius is determined by the date of Ignatius' martyrdom in Rome. Eusebius (*Chronicle,* from the Latin translation by Jerome, p.275) tells us the martyrdom happened while Trajan was emperor (AD 98-117). While he was being conveyed as a prisoner from Antioch of Syria to Rome, Polycarp wrote a series of letters, some (Ephesians, Magnesians, Trallians, and Romans) while he was in Smyrna, and some (to Philadelphia, Smyrna, and to Polycarp) when he was in Troas. His guards next took him to Philippi where he was permitted to meet with the church's leaders. After that visit, when the church at Philippi heard of the existence of Ignatius' letters, they contacted Polycarp asking him to send them copies of any of Ignatius' letters he might have. Polycarp complied with their request and sent a covering letter (the *Epistle to the Philippians*). In chapter 9 of that cover letter, Polycarp seems to be aware of Ignatius' death, but in chapter 13 he asks them to send him the latest news about Ignatius and his companions. A footnote in ANF (on chapter 13) tells us tells us, "Polycarp was aware of the death of Ignatius (ch.ix), but was as yet apparently ignorant of the circumstances attending it." If that interpretation is correct it implies that Polycarp was writing very early in the 2nd century, shortly after Ignatius' martyrdom which occurred c. AD 110.

Another early church father, Tertullian (AD 200), wrote a work known as *On the Resurrection of the Flesh*. In chapter 24 he quotes 2 Thessalonians 2:1,2. It reads:

> And in the second epistle to the same persons [the Thessalonians], he [Paul] writes with greater solicitude: "But I beseech you, brethren, by the coming of our Lord Jesus Christ, that ye be not soon shaken mind, nor be troubled ...."

c. Canonical Listings

Though not technically in what might be called a canonical listing, 2 Thessalonians is included as Pauline in P[46], a codex manuscript containing a collection of Paul's letters. According to Y.K. Kim (*Biblia* 69:2 [1988], p.248-257) this codex manuscript may be dated as early as the mid AD 80's.[15]

2 Thessalonians was included in Marcion's canon (AD 140), and in the Muratorian Canon (AD 170). 2 Thessalonians also is present in the Old Syriac and Old Latin versions, both of which antedate AD 200.[16]

3. Higher Critical Arguments Concerning Authorship

Discussions concerning the Pauline involvement in the authorship of 2 Thessalonians are sometimes titled "genuineness" and sometimes "authenticity." "Genuineness" is a technical term meaning the work was written by the person whose name appears in the signature. The names of Silas and Timothy, though also included in the signature of 2 Thessalonians, seldom rate a comment in the critical discussions.

While Pauline involvement in the writing of 1 Thessalonians is almost universally accepted, the same cannot be said with regard to 2 Thessalonians. Before the 1970's, the scholars who questioned Paul's involvement in 2 Thessalonians found they had the burden of proof.[17]   Since the 1970's, scholars who champion Paul's involvement find they have

---

[15] 2 Peter 3:16 indicates that a collection of Paul's letters was already in existence (2 Peter was written before Peter's death which occurred in AD 68), and were called "Scripture." It is not beyond belief that 2 Thessalonians was one of the letters in that collection, in which, Peter tells us, were "some things hard to understand."

[16] Merrill F. Unger, *The New Unger's Bible Dictionary* (Chicago: Moody, 1988), p.1275.

[17] The Pauline involvement in the authorship of 2 Thessalonians seems never to have been questioned in the early church. Attacks by Schmidt, Baur, Wrede upon the Pauline involvement began at the opening of the 19th century. The main arguments (all from internal evidence) against Pauline involvement include: (1) a perceived difference in eschatology between 1 and 2 Thessalonians; (2) an assertion that the tone of 2 Thessalonians is less warm and affectionate than 1 Thessalonians; (3) a side-by-side comparison of the two letters that seemed to indicate that 2 Thessalonians was produced by someone copying much of 1 Thessalonians; and (4) a conviction that the self-referencing signature at the end of 2 Thessalonians was likely deliberately added by the hypothetical forger of the epistle to authenticate what he had written.

the burden of proof.[18]   This change has not come because of any discovery of impressive new evidence.[19]   Nevertheless, champions of Paul's involvement now find they must defend Paul's authorship against the questions raised by higher criticism.   The following points may be presented as strong evidence the scholarly consensus has it wrong:

(1) The claim that Paul's eschatology underwent a gradual change is seriously flawed. It cannot be shown that 1 Thessalonians teaches an imminent or almost immediate second coming.   1 Thessalonians 5:2 does say "suddenly," but it is not the advent that will occur suddenly; it is the destruction of the wicked that will occur suddenly when the Lord does return.   Furthermore, when the missionaries were still in Thessalonica, the Thessalonians had been taught about the restrainer, the man of lawlessness, and the rebellion (2 Thessalonians 2:5).   When, later, 1 Thessalonians was written, the writers were aware of what had already been taught by word of mouth.   How can it be said they must have been mistaken about the time of the *parousia* when they wrote 1 Thessalonians?   It is far more credible to assert that the writers of 1 and 2 Thessalonians held a view of the end-times similar to that of Jesus, who did not know when the second coming would occur, but did counsel His followers to be ready constantly for it whether it be today or tomorrow or many days hence.

(2) It is claimed that 2 Thessalonians is less warm and affectionate than 1 Thessalonians.   But a careful study the verses on which the claim is based actually results in a conclusion which is the exact opposite of the claim that Paul could not have been involved in the authorship of both letters.   (a) Critics point to the change of wording in the thanksgivings of the two letters.   In 1 Thessalonians Paul gave thanks for the Thessalonians (1:2; 2:13; 3:9).   In 2 Thessalonians he was "bound" (RSV) or "obligated" to give thanks (1:3)."   However, the "obligated" thanksgivings in 2 Thessalonians do not have to be the result of cold feelings.   It is the readers' faithfulness to Christ that led to the thanksgivings.   It is altogether possible that warm feelings for the readers and gratitude for their faithfulness impelled the writers to give thanks to God for the Thessalonians. (b) Critics also say that in the first letter the writers coax (1 Thessalonians 4:1,2,9-12; 5:1-11), but in the second letter they command (2 Thessalonians 2:1-4; 3:6,12-14).   However, remember that 2 Thessalonians 3 was written because 1 Thessalonians 5 had been ignored. Both passages were written by missionaries who cared greatly for their new converts.   If the readers did not respond in a positive way to the "coaxing" might we not expect that the writers, who were concerned about the eternal destiny of the readers, would speak in a more forceful manner?   Those who rebuke unrepented sin in others must have a great deal of love to even get involved in making a rebuke.   Yet, all the time knowing they may be

---

[18] Two books, one by Charles Masson (*Les deux epitres de Saint Paul aux Thessalonians*, CNT [Neuchatel: Delachaux & Niestle, 1957]), and the other by Wolfgang Trilling (*Untersuchungen zum zweiten Thessalonicherbrief* [Leipzig: St. Benno, 1972]), have been influential in turning the tide of many scholars against any Pauline involvement in 2 Thessalonians.

[19] Higher critics tend to try to make Scripture match the current prevailing popular philosophy. Since no genuinely new evidence has been offered to justify the now-fashionable rejection of Paul's involvement in the authorship of 2 Thessalonians, the shift of consensus cannot be a matter of arguments or evidence, but rather reflects a shift in the prevailing philosophy from which the critics are operating.

rejected, they make the rebuke because they care deeply for their sinning brethren and desperately want the sinners to repent.

(3) Since the 1970's, the purported evidence of literary dependence (i.e., 2 Thessalonians is alleged to be but a clumsy copy of 1 Thessalonians) has become the chief argument against any Pauline involvement in the authorship of 2 Thessalonians. What is the purported evidence? Critics call attention to similar features found in both letters which are apparent even to the casual reader.

- Both Thessalonian letters, unlike the seven critically accepted Pauline letters, have two thanksgivings.
- The epistolary openings of both letters are nearly verbatim, a phenomenon which occurs nowhere else in Paul, not even in the two letters addressed to Corinth.
- Both Thessalonian letters contain parallel, double prayers and double conclusions.
- When the two letters are arranged in parallel columns, the result soon becomes evident there is a similarity of topics, structure and language.[20]

As long ago as Wrede,[21] this similarity was attributed to someone who, long after Paul was dead, used 1 Thessalonians as an exemplar, and who did so because the copyist was deliberately modifying the eschatology found in 1 Thessalonians. The copyist intentionally put Paul's name in the signature to give his ersatz document some believability.

While recognizing and acknowledging all the similarities that have been highlighted, there is no convincing reason to choose unconscionable copying as the likeliest explanation, and certainly there is no reason to appeal to the similarities to deny the Pauline involvement in the authorship of 2 Thessalonians. After all, 2 Thessalonians has no greater resemblance to 1 Thessalonians than do the epistles to the Romans and Galatians, two letters which the critics agree were both authored by Paul. Is it improbable that an author, writing a second letter within a short period of time to the same audience concerning the same continuing issues, would appeal to what was stated in the first letter? Theodore Zahn was on solid ground when he suggested that Paul would have in his possession a copy of 1 Thessalonians, which he could read again before joining in the authorship of the second letter.[22] After all, it was the practice (if a patron was involved who covered the expenses involved in the production of the letter) to make three copies of a letter: one stayed with the author, one was given to the patron, and one was sent to the addressee. It requires a great stretch of the imagination to invent an unknown copyist to explain the similarities found in 1 and 2 Thessalonians.

---

[20] Edgar M. Krentz, "2 Thessalonians," Vol.4 in *Anchor Bible Dictionary*, edited by David N. Freedman [New York: Doubleday, 1992], p.518) offers a convenient table to show the places where the two letters are similar.

[21] W. Wrede, *Die Echtheit des zweiten Thessalonicherbriefs* (Leipzig: Hinrichs, 1903), p.95.96.

[22] Theodore Zahn, *Introduction to the New Testament* (Grand Rapids: Kregel Publications, 1953 reprint), vol. I, p.250.

(4) The signature in 2 Thessalonians 3:17 is an important element as we consider the Pauline involvement in the authorship of 2 Thessalonians. If Paul had a hand in writing this letter, the fact that some of the Thessalonians had been fooled by a letter purporting to be from Paul (2 Thessalonians 2:2) makes this note precisely what was needed to guard the readers from being deceived by a forgery in the future. Proponents of inauthenticity are hard pressed to explain a reason for a forger adding this verse. About all they can say is that the forger hoped by this means to make his spurious letter and its doctrine more acceptable to the readers.[23] But left unanswered are such questions as these: Why did the forger pose as Paul? Why add the names of Silas and Timothy? When, where, to whom, and why was the forged letter written? And especially troubling is what results when an attempt to explain the meaning of the whole letter is attempted in the light of the answers to those questions.

(5) The signature at 2 Thessalonians 1:1 carries three names, Paul, Silas, and Timothy. When critics deny Pauline involvement in the authorship of 2 Thessalonians, they find it necessary to explain how Paul's name got there. The only option open to these critics is to defend the idea that an unknown person wrote this fake letter, sometime between five and 50 years after Paul's death, and forged Paul's name to the document.[24] Instead of using the terms forged or fake, the critics prefer to use the term pseudonymous.[25] In light of the fact that there is a growing consensus among critics to treat 2 Thessalonians as a forgery, it is crucial to call attention to the fact that any theory of pseudonymy is fraught with serious problems. (a) While there were pseudonymous works in the ancient world (such as Jewish apocalyptic writings and the pseudepigraphic works produced by 2nd century Gnostics), a proper question to ask is where is the evidence that pseudonymy was acceptable to the early Christian community? [26]   (b) Evidence exists that shows pseudonymy was not acceptable to the early Christians. When it became known that the work known as *The Acts of Paul and Thecla* was a forgery, the church leader responsible for its composition was excommunicated.[27] Christianity has high moral standards taught

---

[23] Bart Ehrman, *Forged: Why the Bible's Authors Are Not Who We Think They Are* (New York: HarperCollins, 2012), p.121-123.

[24] For example, see J.A. Bailey, "Who Wrote II Thessalonians," *NTS* 25 (1979), p.131-145.

[25] One wonders why critics prefer the use of words like pseudonymy and pseudepigraphic instead of the word "forgery." Is it deliberately done in an attempt to hide from unsuspecting listeners and readers the monstrous nature of the theory they are espousing?

[26] It is sheer bluster (and assuming the point to be proved) to appeal to the Pastoral Epistles, or to 2 Peter, or to the sermons of Jesus in John's Gospel (which critics now affirm are the product of the redactor's pen and falsely attributed to Jesus) as being examples of Christian acceptance of pseudepigraphy. In the 2nd century there were letters written by Gnostics and sent forth as having been written by famous church leaders before they died. But also in the 2nd century and afterwards, Christians went to great lengths to identify what was genuine and what was fake. Three groupings of ancient writings were established: canonical, New Testament apocryphal, and Pseudepigraphical. Far from being accepted, the pseudonymous Gnostic letters were all relegated to the pseudepigraphic category.

[27] Tertullian, *De baptismo* 17:5.

by Jesus. Is it not a lie to forge someone else's name to a document? Who is ready to defend the idea that to a Christian lying is morally unobjectionable?[28]   (c) Since advocates of pseudonymity must opt for a late date for the writing of 2 Thessalonians, it certainly is correct to call into question their reasons for assigning a late date. In the past, the attempt to establish a late date often was based on an alleged use in 2 Thessalonians 2 of the Nero Redivivus Myth. [29]   More recently, 2 Thessalonians 2:2-12 has been proposed as post-Pauline, reflecting on the conjecture that the writer of that chapter was dependent on the book of Revelation (written AD 96) for his information.[30]   When such arguments and speculations are rejected due to a lack of credible evidence, there no longer remains any need to advocate a late date for 2 Thessalonians. Likewise, if there is no need to attempt to defend a late date for the writing, what reason is there to still advocate that Paul was not personally involved in the authorship of 2 Thessalonians?   (d) Why did the forger also add Silas' and Timothy's names? Why do we not read that those two names are pseudony-mous just as it is claimed for Paul's name? Why do we not find plausible suggestions set forth to explain the presence of the names of Silas and Timothy? If Paul's name is fake, are not the others? If it be suggested that the two names were deliberately added in an attempt to deceive the readers about the authority behind this fake letter, how can it be said that this is innocent pseudonymous impersonation?   (e) The annotated quotations cited above show strong external evidence of early Christian acceptance of Pauline involvement in the authorship of 2 Thessalonians. Those who deny the genuineness of 2 Thessalonians have yet to offer satisfactory explanations for how this epistle came to be unhesitatingly accepted as genuine.   (f) If 2 Thessalonians is pseudonymous, why should we study it, for if neither Paul, nor Silas, nor Timothy was involved in the authorship of 2 Thessalonians, it is no longer the Word of God. Holy Spirit inspiration (as presented in 1 Corinthians 2:6-16, especially verse 13) resulted in the speaker or writer using God-chosen words to deliver the God-directed message. We would affirm that inspiration and pseudonymy are mutually exclusive categories. All these serious problems and questions are avoided by ready acceptance of what 2 Thessalonians 1:1 and 3:17 say – Paul, Silas, and Timothy were involved in the authorship of 2 Thessalonians.

---

[28] Readers who require more detailed information to critique the critic's assertion that the Biblical letters identified as being pseudonymous were innocent impersonations (as distinguished from a deliberate attempt to deceive) will find help in these sources: Donald Guthrie, "Epistolary Pseudepigraphy," *New Testament Introduction* (3rd ed. London: Tyndale, 1970), p.680; Bruce Metzger, "Literary Forgeries and Canonical Pseudepigrapha," *JBL* 91 (1972), p.1-24; and T.L. Wilder, *Pseudonymity, the New Testament, and Deception* (Lenham: University Press of America, 2004), who shows that (contrary to some of Metzger's conclusions) the early church did not see pseudepigraphy as a harmless literary technique (p.246).

[29] Nero was emperor from AD 54-68. It was not until after Nero was dead that a rumor was spread that he was still alive and would return to power shortly. Since Paul was executed in AD 68, if the man of lawlessness is a reworking of the Nero Redivivus myth (an interpretation of 2 Thessalonians 2 that has no credible basis), that chapter cannot have been written by Paul.

[30] What indisputable evidence is there to say that the writer of 2 Thessalonians had to be acquainted with Revelation? This commentator has reached the studied conclusion that the man of lawlessness (2 Thessalonians) and the eighth beast of Revelation (17:11) refer to the same future historical event, but this conclusion is not dependent upon any supposition that one writer was copying the other. It is based on the conviction that both the apostles Paul and John were dependent on Jesus for their teaching.

Pseudonymy (the forging someone else's name to a document that came to be accepted into the New Testament canon) was not an accepted practice in the early church, nor should it be proposed or defended by 21st century Christians. The letter itself claims Paul had involvement with the writing of 2 Thessalonians, and early Christians accepted the signature as being authentic. There is no reason to exhibit skepticism about the authorship of this letter.

D. DESTINATION

According to Acts 17, Paul and Silas planted a church in Thessalonica. The address of 2 Thessalonians, like that of 1 Thessalonians, has the letter being addressed to that congregation. However, once Pauline involvement in the authorship of this letter has been questioned, critics also begin to speculate concerning the destination. In an attempt to rescue the Pauline authorship (while also offering a suggestion how the alleged change of tone could be explained), Adolph Harnack and Kirsopp Lake proposed that 1 Thessalonians was addressed to the Gentile Christians who comprised the majority of the congregation at Thessalonica, while 2 Thessalonians was addressed to a different audience, namely, the Jewish Christians in the same congregation.[31] Since the address in both letters is the same, Harnack had to conjecture that the original address of 2 Thessalonians was changed when the letters were collected. This conjecture did not receive widespread acceptance since there is no evidence of any such cliquish division in the congregation, nor is there any manuscript evidence the address once contained specific reference to "those of the circumcision." E. Earle Ellis believed the way to rescue Pauline involvement in the authorship of 2 Thessalonians is to maintain that the first letter was written to the entire church but that "brethren" in 2 Thessalonians 1:3 is an indication that the second letter was addressed especially to Paul's co-workers rather than to the whole congregation.[32] That is an unusual limitation being imposed on the word "brethren," especially in light of the fact that the word is used for the whole congregation at least 18 times in 1 Thessalonians.

Another expedient was adopted by some critics who were trying to explain differences they believed they had identified between 1 and 2 Thessalonians. Rather than a different audience in the church at Thessalonica, they proposed a different destination for 2 Thessalonians than the one found in 2 Thessalonians 1:1. (a) Based on the greater use of the Old Testament in 2 Thessalonians than in 1 Thessalonians, and on the passage in Acts 17:10ff which tells how the Jews in Berea welcomed Paul and carefully examined the Old Testament Scriptures, Maurice Goguel advanced the hypothesis that Berea was originally the destination of the letter we know as 2 Thessalonians.[33] To sustain this hypo-

---

[31] Adolf Harnack, 'Das Problem des zweiten Thessalonicherbriefs,' *Sitzungsberichten der Königlichen Preussischen Akadamie der Wissenschaften*, *Phil-Hist. Kl.* (Berlin: Deutsche Akademie der Wissenschaften zu Berlin, 1910), p.560-78; Kirsopp Lake, *The Earlier Epistles of Paul* (London: Rivingtons, 1911), p.83-86.

[32] E. Earle Ellis, "Paul and his Coworkers," *NTS* 17 (1970-71), p.449-51.

[33] Maurice Goguel, *Introduction au Nouveau Testament*, (Paris: Leroux, 1925), vol. IV, part 1, p.335-37.

thesis, Goguel had to propose that when the Pauline letters were collected, a copy of 2 Thessalonians was found at Thessalonica with the initial address missing. Since it was found at Thessalonica, the collector assumed a Thessalonian destination, and inserted the missing address. (b) Eduard Schweizer proposed the original destination was the church at Philippi. Appealing to a passage in Polycarp's *Epistle to the Philippians*, he suggested that he had found evidence that what we call 2 Thessalonians was actually a letter addressed to Philippi.[34] In that epistle (3.2), Polycarp spoke of Paul's "letters" to Philippi. Polycarp's letter has allusions to Philippians (as well as allusions from nearly all the books in the New Testament), so Schweizer postulated that, since he spoke of "letters" (plural) to the Philippians, Polycarp must have known that the original address of the letter we call 2 Thessalonians was "to the Philippians." He imagined that a copy was sent to Thessalonica, from which it entered the collection of Pauline letters as a letter to the Thessalonians. By way of rebuttal, let it be affirmed that we know of no other New Testament letter that had its address changed by those who later made copies. Why should it be supposed that the destination of 2 Thessalonians was deliberately altered?

How refreshing to take at face value the destination found at 2 Thessalonians 1:1, rather than attempting to invent numerous possible and hard-to-believe scenarios which might (in the critic's mind) point to mistake in the text that has come down to us.

E. PLACE AND DATE OF WRITING

1. Place of writing

Our study of the historical allusions in this letter has resulted in this finding, that the only verse that offers any precise help concerning the place of writing is 2 Thessalonians 1:1. If we reject what that verse says about Paul, Silas, and Timothy together being involved in the authorship this letter, we also have destroyed any information we might have as to either the place or time of writing. Since we have found no credible reason to deny what verse 1 affirms, the proper thing to do is to look for any record that might inform us when Paul, Silas, and Timothy were known to be together in order to determine he place and time of writing. Such a search has already been conducted in the Detailed Introduction to 1 Thessalonians. The historical account in Acts 18 has the three together in Corinth in the early AD 50's, at which time the first letter to the Thessalonians originated at their hands.

A search of the chapters in Acts following 18:11-18, as well as a search of Paul's epistles, shows there is no record the three were ever together again after Paul concluded his eighteen-month or so ministry in Corinth. In fact, what is observable is, that after Acts 18, Timothy is named several more times in Acts and in Paul's letters, but Silas is not named again in Acts, nor is he named in any of Paul's letters. While there are gaps in the history recorded in Acts, based on the information available to us the only known time the

---

[34] Eduard Schweizer, 'Der zweite Thessalonicherbriefe ein Philipperbriefe?' *TZ* 1 (1945), p.90-105.

three were together was during the eighteen or so months that Paul was in Corinth during his second missionary journey.

Based on the information available to us, it is affirmed that 2 Thessalonians was written from Corinth, just like 1 Thessalonians was.

2. Time of writing

Two passages in 2 Thessalonians have indications as to the time of writing. 2 Thessalonians 1:1 is one of these. It was during Paul's second missionary journey, about AD 52 or 53, that 1 Thessalonians was written. In our New Testament chronology, we have dated Paul's second missionary journey from AD 51 to AD 54.[35] If 2 Thessalonians was written while the three were still together in Corinth, the time of writing would be dated c. AD 53 or 54. 2 Thessalonians 3:2 is the other passage. In that passage the Thessalonians are encouraged to pray that "we will be rescued from perverse and evil men." Can that request be matched to anything that happened in Corinth in the AD 52-54 timeframe? If Paul used an editorial "we," then Paul was asking for deliverance for himself. Under this scenario, the incident when Paul was brought before Gallio (Acts 18:12-17) may have been the situation for which petitions to God for His protection were being requested, and the outcome of that trial could be seen as the speedy answer to their prayers. If the "we" is a true plural, then while we have no information in Acts about a particular dangerous crisis that involved all three missionaries when they were together in Corinth, we can surely sympathize with a request for providential protection, so that the missionaries might be relieved from anxiety rather than having to constantly look over their shoulders to see if more trouble is about to engulf them.

Questionable dates of writing, both earlier and later than AD 53 or 54, have been proposed. (a) Commentators who believe 2 Thessalonians was written before 1 Thessalonians must find a date before AD 52.[36] (b) One example of an attempted later dating is A. H. McNeile's, who speculated that since Paul and Timothy were known to have been together later at Ephesus (Acts 19:1-22), might it not also be supposed that all three may have actually worked together at Ephesus and that 2 Thessalonians might have been written from that city about AD 57.[37] (c) Another example of an attempted later dating is John Calvin's, who has 2 Thessalonians written from Corinth about AD 58, just before Paul's trip to Jerusalem at the close of this third missionary journey. Calvin supposed the "perverse and evil men" (2 Thessalonians 3:2) were the Judaizers who dogged

---

[35] See Gareth L. Reese, *New Testament History: Acts* (Moberly, MO: Scripture Exposition Books, 2002), p.xx.

[36] See this conjecture examined and rejected in the paragraph titled "The Sequence of the Thessalonian Letters" in the Detailed Introduction to 1 Thessalonians.

[37] A. H. McNeile, *An Introduction to the Study of the New Testament* (Oxford: At the Clarendon Press, 1953), p.128.

his steps (Acts 20:3).[38]   Since Jewish folk were involved in the opposition faced at Corinth (Acts 18:12), Calvin may well have been right about the identity of the perverse men. However, Calvin is likely mistaken about the time.   Paul's information prior to the writing of 2 Thessalonians is based on reports he received (2 Thessalonians 3:11), not from first-hand knowledge.   By the time Paul is closing his third missionary journey, he has again visited Macedonia, and so would have had first-hand knowledge of the situation in Thessalonica.   The writing of 2 Thessalonians must have preceded any second visit Paul may have paid to Thessalonica.   (d) As discussed above in the section on Authorship, proponents of the idea that 2 Thessalonians is a pseudonymous work are another example of attempted later dating.   Identifying the letter as being post-Pauline requires a much later date of writing being assigned to the letter.

This brief overview of the available evidence shows there is no compelling reason to look for different place or time for the writing of 2 Thessalonians than Corinth in the early AD 50's.[39]   The time between the writing of 1 Thessalonians and 2 Thessalonians could have been anywhere from several months to a year.

F. OCCASION AND PURPOSE OF WRITING

Paul, Silas, and Timothy were together when 1 Thessalonians was written, and they are together when 2 Thessalonians was written.   We do not know who carried 1 Thessalonians to Thessalonica.   Did Timothy stay in Corinth, and someone else carried the first letter to Thessalonica?   Or was Timothy given responsibility to deliver the first letter?   If he was, we might conjecture that, after delivering that letter, he then returned to Corinth where Paul and Silas had stayed.   Either of these two scenarios would account for how all three men were together when this second letter was composed.

2 Thessalonians 3:11 reads "we hear that some among you ...."   If we treat "we" at face value it includes all three men named in 2 Thessalonians 1:1, and it also would indicate that Timothy was not the bearer of the report.   Note that the verb "we are hearing" is present tense, indicating continuing action – i.e., they heard on more than one occasion. We do not know who brought the reports about the church in Thessalonica to Corinth.   If we connect the financial gifts mentioned in 2 Corinthians 11:9 with those referred to in Philippians 4:15,16, perhaps several unnamed Christians who came to Corinth from Macedonia brought to the attention of the writers the current conditions in the congregation at Thessalonica.   However the information arrived, the immediate occasion for the writing of 2 Thessalonians was the nature of the information recently received by Paul and the others concerning the situation in the church at Thessalonica.

---

[38] John Calvin, *The Epistles to the Romans and the Thessalonians,* Ross Mackenzie translator, (Grand Rapids: Wm. B. Eerdmans, 1961), p.386, 414.

[39] The two key reasons necessitating the postulation of a late date are alleged pseudonymy of authorship and the alleged slow change in of Paul's changing eschatology, both of which have been shown to be mistaken notions.

We can judge the purpose behind the writing of 2 Thessalonians by studying the content of this letter.   The reports that the writers kept receiving about the Thessalonians contained both favorable and unfavorable elements.

- It looks as if the purpose of chapter 1 is to commend the new Christians for their remarkable growth in faith and love (1:3), and to encourage them to persevere in the faith in spite of the persecutions they were continuing to endure (1:4).   The Christians are assured their persecutors would be justly dealt with when the Lord returns and the final judgment occurs (1:5-12).

- The purpose of chapter 2 is to counteract a false idea beginning to circulate among the Christians that the day of the Lord had already begun.   The source of that wrong idea was not a misunderstanding of what had been written in chapters 4 and 5 of 1 Thessalonians, but a pseudo-Pauline letter and other false representations that were being circulated among the brethren.   The writers remind the readers of what had been taught about the *parousia* and the day of the Lord while the missionaries were present and preaching and teaching in Thessalonica.

- Chapter 3 opens with a request that the Thessalonian Christians will pray that the Lord will rescue the writers from the dangerous opposition they are facing from perverse and evil men.

- The rest of chapter 3 contains a strong rebuke of the unruly loafers who have disregarded the instructions in 1 Thessalonians that they should work to support themselves rather than depend on the philanthropy of the members who were working and earning a living wage.   It also gives the congregation specific instructions how to deal with the unruly, with the intent of leading the unruly ones to repentance.

G. DIFFERENT ESCHATOLOGY IN 2 THESSALONIANS?

During the last two centuries, certain Bible critics have been repeating a claim that the teaching about the second coming of Christ in 2 Thessalonians differs from the teaching found in 1 Thessalonians.[40]   Such critics affirm the view that in 1 Thessalonians Paul believed the second coming was imminent and would occur within just a few years.   The claim is that 2 Thessalonians introduces a new idea, that certain recognizable preliminary signs had to occur before the second coming would come to pass.   This claimed change in eschatology is a manufactured, false characterization of what is actually written in the two letters.

The Detailed Introduction to 1 Thessalonians includes a lengthy rebuttal of the modern dogma that Jesus and the apostles all were mistaken about the time of the second

---

[40] Paul Foster ("Who Wrote 2 Thessalonians: A Fresh Look at an Old Problem," *JSNT* 35:2 [2012], p.154) tells us that "In 1801 J.E.C. Schmidt published a work that introduced one of the classic arguments against Pauline authorship of 2 Thessalonians.   The argument was based upon the perceived change in theological perspective concerning the parousia."

advent.[41]   Here in this Detailed Introduction to 2 Thessalonians, the intent is to show that what is actually written in 1 and 2 Thessalonians cannot be used to accuse Paul in particular of contributing to such a deliberate change in eschatology.

The claim that there is a gradual change in Paul's eschatological viewpoint is problematic. For several reasons, it is wholly misleading to affirm there is a difference between the eschatological ideas of 1 Thessalonians and those of 2 Thessalonians.

(1) Even if 1 Thessalonians 4:14-18 were the only passage that recorded Paul's beliefs, it would still be an overstatement to affirm he advocated an imminent second coming, perhaps within his own lifetime. In that passage, Paul no more indicates the time when the *parousia* would take place than did Enoch, the seventh from Adam, when he announced the Lord's coming at the end of earth's history. Enoch prophesied, "Behold, the Lord is coming with many thousands of his holy ones to execute judgment on all, and to convict all the ungodly of all their ungodly deeds which they have done in an ungodly way, and of all the harsh things which ungodly sinners have spoken against Him" (Jude 14,15). It may have sounded as if the Lord's coming was imminent, but we have been waiting many millennia for Enoch's prophecy to come true.

(2) It cannot be shown that 1 Thessalonians teaches an imminent or almost immediate second coming. While 1 Thessalonians 5:3 does say "suddenly," it is not the advent itself that is about to occur suddenly; it is the destruction of the wicked that will occur suddenly when the Lord returns.

(3) Redaction criticism's hypothesis that the alleged change in eschatology represents a new perspective that arose only after the destruction of Jerusalem in AD 70 is not demonstrable. Paul's presentation is consistent with Old Testament prophecy. Paul plainly asserts in 2 Thessalonians 2:7 that the doctrine about a coming man of lawlessness was a "mystery" (that is, something that was not as clearly revealed in Old Testament times as it now is in apostolic times). Paul is not teaching something brand new; it was already known (however dimly) in Old Testament times. Paul cannot be accused of initially inventing the idea as his eschatology allegedly slowly evolved. Rather, he is simply doing what (according to Ephesians 3:4,5) apostles of Christ were entrusted with doing – making known the mystery in greater detail.

(4) Paul did not concoct his theology unchecked and single-handedly. In the Detailed Introduction to 1 Thessalonians, it was documented how Paul's eschatology agreed with the eschatology taught by Jesus. Both Thessalonian letters are signed by Paul, Silas, and Timothy, indicating all three men agreed upon the contents of both letters. Given both of these facts, it is misleading to accuse Paul of acting alone to introduced a subtle change in eschatology.

---

[41] *Supra*, p.192-200.

The joint authorship of the Thessalonian letters is an important element in this discussion. Recall that all three men were able to speak by Holy Spirit inspiration; Paul was an apostle, Silas was a prophet, and Timothy had received a spiritual gift by the laying on of Paul's hands. If one of them began introducing a novel eschatology, would not the others have objected to such a deviation from what had been learned from Christ? And if a change in eschatology was being introduced, would not the fact that all three signed these letters indicate that such a change was something all three had agreed upon? Is it actually believable to accuse all three of being less than straightforward and honest as they gradually and surreptitiously departed from what Christ taught?

(5) Also, keep in mind that according to 2 Thessalonians 2:5, when the missionaries were still in Thessalonica, Paul had taught the Thessalonians about the momentous events – the restrainer, the man of lawlessness, and the rebellion – that precede the *parousia* and the day of the Lord. Since 1 Thessalonians was likewise written after the missionaries had left Thessalonica, we can rightly presume Paul and the other two writers were aware of what the new Christians had already been taught by word of mouth. If so, how can it be said that what is written in 2 Thessalonians regarding these preliminary signs was the introduction of a new eschatology, unknown when 1 Thessalonians was written? Given the writers' clear statement in 2 Thessalonians 2:5, the emphasis in the second letter on the preliminary signs of the second coming cannot rightly be interpreted as indicating a change in eschatology.

At the risk of restating the point already made, the claim that there is a gradual change in Paul's eschatological viewpoint is problematic. The eschatological ideas of 1 Thessalonians and those of 2 Thessalonians are not different and they are not novel. In both letters, at 1 Thessalonians 5:1 and again at 2 Thessalonians 2:5, the writers themselves indicate that what is now being written about the Lord's second coming is not new teaching. Rather, it is a reminder and reaffirmation of what the missionaries had already shared with the Thessalonian Christians face to face.

H. OUTLINE

An outline of the material in 1 Thessalonians is included in the concise introduction to the letter found at the beginning of this volume.

Special Studies

on

1 & 2 Thessalonians

Special Study #1

THE DAY OF THE LORD

The exact meaning of the key eschatological topics which form the core of 2 Thessalonians 2 has been the subject of scholarly debate for centuries. As a result, readers who pick up commentaries on 2 Thessalonians will encounter an almost bewildering number of conflicting explanations offered for these key topics. Soon, many readers will begin to despair of ever understanding Biblical eschatology, and as a consequence decide to just dismiss any study of the whole matter.

It is vital to read Bible books like 1 and 2 Thessalonians, and to attempt to grasp the essence of what God is telling us in these books. To encourage further study it seems appropriate to conduct a special study of each of the key eschatological topics in the order they are introduced in 2 Thessalonians 2, namely, (1) the day of the Lord, (2) the rebellion (or apostasy), (3) the man of lawlessness, and (4) the restrainer.

The expression "day of the LORD" (Hebrew, *yom YHWH*) occurs as far back as the 8th century BC in the writings of the prophet Amos (Amos 5:18,20), and then as later prophets appeared, we find the expression used more and more.[1] What is being pictured when this expression is used is a dramatic intervention of God in history. Some prophetic passages are a warning of coming judgment against peoples or nations who are Israel's enemies. Some passages are a warning of coming judgment against unfaithful Israelites. Some passages picture God's intervention to save and bless His faithful people. As the prophets issued their warnings of God's intervention, they spoke of the stars and constellations going dark (Isaiah 13:9,10), or of the sun and moon not giving their light (Joel 3:14). To avoid taking God's sacred name (YHWH) in vain (a behavior one of the Ten Commandments prohibited, Exodus 20:7; Deuteronomy 5:11), the Old Testament folk would substitute the Hebrew word "Lord" (*adonai*) for the sacred name when reading the Scriptures. When the LXX was produced, the "day of the LORD" (*yom YHWH*) in the Old Testament became *hēmera kuriou*, which is the same spelling for "day of the Lord" we find in the Greek New Testament.

In the Old Testament

In the years between the time of Amos and the coming of Jesus into the world, both near-term historical events and future eschatological events were described as a "day of the Lord."

---

[1] For example, see Isaiah 13:6-9; 34;8-12; Jeremiah 46:9-12; Ezekiel 30:1-9; Obadiah 15-18; Zephaniah 2:1-15; 14:1-21; Joel 1:1-2:27; Malachi 3:13-4:6.

- The "day of the LORD" prophecy in Amos 5:18,20 found fulfillment in the Assyrian captivity (722 BC).

- Isaiah 13:6 was fulfilled in the Babylonian exile (605-586 BC).

- Ezekiel 30:3 was a prediction of the Babylonian defeat of Egypt (568 BC).

- Obadiah, using the language "day of the LORD," predicted doom on Edom because the Edomites participated in the plunder of the city of Jerusalem (586 BC). They would be "cut off forever" (verse 10) and "become as though they had not existed" (verse 16), the prophet predicted. That prophecy began to be fulfilled in 582 BC when the Babylonians destroyed Edom. The Edomites who were left continued to be active enemies of the Jews. In 126 BC they were subdued by John Hyrcanus, one of the Maccabean rulers. Soon after the Holy Land was conquered by the Romans in 63 BC, they placed an Edomite named Antipater (the father of Herod the Great) in control of Judah. That began the last phase of the Edomites. With the destruction of Jerusalem in AD 70, they disappeared from history, just as Obadiah said they would.

- Joel, another Old Testament prophet, used "day of the LORD" language to designate a divinely-sent locust plague (Joel 1:15), and he anticipated an event far into the future when he spoke of "the great and awesome day of the LORD" (Joel 2:31). He described how before that day came, God would "grant wonders in the sky above and signs on the earth below, blood, and fire, and vapor of smoke. The sun will be turned into darkness and the moon into blood."

- Malachi (4:5,6) predicted that God would "send you Elijah the prophet before the coming of the great and terrible day of the LORD. 'He will restore the hearts of the fathers to their children and the hearts of the children to their fathers, so that I will not come and smite the land with a curse'."[2]

In the New Testament

Jesus spoke about a future "day" when men would be judged. At the close of His Sermon on the Mount, He described how many would say to Him on that day, "Lord, Lord, did we not prophesy in Your name, and in Your name cast out demons, and in Your name perform many miracles?" In response, Jesus says He "will declare to them, 'I never knew you; depart from me, you who practice lawlessness'" (Matthew 7:22,23). During His ministry, when certain cities rejected Him and His message, he warned them, "It will be more tolerable for the land of Sodom and Gomorrah in the day of judgment than for that city" (Matthew 10:15). Likewise, He warned Capernaum that "it will be more tolerable for the land of Sodom in the day of judgment than for you" (Matthew 11:24).

In his first recorded sermon on the day of Pentecost, Peter (Acts 2:16-21) made reference to the prediction in Joel 2:28-32. He said that what was happening on that day

---

[2] Jesus explained that this prophecy about Elijah was fulfilled in John the Baptist and his ministry (Matthew 11:14).

was a partial fulfillment of Joel's prophecy. When Joel spoke of God pouring out His Spirit on all flesh, it was a prediction of the beginning of the church age ("the last days"), and when he spoke of blood and fire and vapor of smoke, he had reference to the great and terrible day of the LORD that would bring the church age to a close.

In Jesus' eschatological discourse (Matthew 24,25), He spoke both about the coming destruction of Jerusalem by armies[3] (Matthew 24:4-35, Luke 21:20) and about His own second coming (Matthew 24:29-25:41). While the destruction of Jerusalem would occur within "this generation" of those who were then listening to Jesus (Matthew 24:34), the day and hour of His second coming was known only to His Father in heaven (Matthew 24:36). He used the word *parousia* to describe His future second coming (Matthew 24:37,39). As He spoke about this future second coming, Jesus described the cosmological changes (Matthew 24:29) that would occur when He becomes visible in the sky, and how he would come on the clouds of heaven with power and great glory (Matthew 24:30). He tells how with a great trumpet blast He will send His angels to gather the elect together (Matthew 24:31). The sermon includes glimpses of the final judgment that will occur when He comes again (Matthew 24:50,51; 25:31-46).

After Jesus' earthly ministry was completed, prophecies of a future day of the Lord are found in the New Testament Scriptures. In his sermon on Mars Hill, Paul declared that "having overlooked the times of ignorance, God is now declaring to men that all people everywhere should repent, because He has fixed a day in which He will judge the world in righteousness through a Man whom He has appointed, having furnished proof to all men by raising Him from the dead" (Acts 17:30-31).

In 1 Thessalonians 5, "day of the Lord" encompasses several significant events. Verse 1 ties chapter 5 together with 4:13-18. Those verses have pictured the coming (*parousia*) of Christ, the resurrection of the dead in Christ, the rapture of all the redeemed to meet the Lord as He comes on the clouds of heaven, and the promise that the redeemed would from then on always be with the Lord. Verses 3 and 9 of chapter 5 indicate that the day of the Lord will be a day of destruction and wrath upon those who have been living in (spiritual) darkness.[4] For them, the coming of the "day of the Lord" will be as unexpected "as a thief in the night." But "the day of the Lord" will not take by surprise those who "are sons of light and of the day." After all, sons of light have been living in the light of

---

[3] History tells us it was Roman armies that destroyed Jerusalem in AD 70.

[4] The Thessalonians are not among those living in darkness. The Christians at Thessalonica are addressed by the second person plural pronoun "you, brethren," whereas those living in darkness who are thinking to themselves that all is peace and safety are referred to by the third person plural pronoun "they" and "them".

Proponents of a pre-, mid-, or post-tribulation rapture struggle to match their systems to what is written in Thessalonians. Some attempt to make the "day of the Lord" include the great tribulation by finding reference to the tribulation in the words "destruction" and "wrath." However, the fact that destruction and wrath are said to come on those who live in spiritual darkness makes it difficult to see in these two words any reference to the great tribulation (Revelation 7:14) which precedes the final judgment. Rather, it is better to take "destruction" and "wrath" as references to the eternal punishment which follows the judgment.

God's revelation which guides them not only in how to live in this world, but also to expect that the Lord will return just as He said He would.[5]   For the sons of light, whether they be awake or sleeping (i.e., living on earth or are among the dead in Christ), the day of the Lord will be a day of salvation.   They will live together with Christ (verse 10).

2 Thessalonians 2 adds more details about the coming of the "day of the Lord." Verse 1 indicates that the *parousia* of Christ and the rapture of the saints are events that occur when that day comes.   Verse 3 indicates some momentous things that are to happen before the day of the Lord comes.   There will be a rebellion (or apostasy),[6] the removal of a restraint[7] that hitherto kept the man of lawlessness from appearing, and with the restraint gone there will be the coming of the man of lawlessness onto the scene of history.[8] Once the man of lawlessness has his *parousia*, then Jesus also has His *parousia*, at which time He will destroy man of lawlessness.   This occurs at the beginning of the day of the Lord (verse 8).   Verse 12 indicates that when the day of the Lord occurs, those who have been deceived by the man of lawlessness will be judged.

By the time Peter wrote his letters in the mid-60s AD, scoffers were derisively asking "where is the promised coming (*parousia*) of the Lord?" (2 Peter 3:4).   Peter responds that what may seem a long time to men is not a long time to God.   To a Being who is eternal, what is a thousand years to men is like a day.   Peter then confidently affirms the day of the Lord will come.   Peter thus makes the same connection between the *parousia* and the day of the Lord that was made in the Thessalonian letters.   In verse 10, in language already familiar from 1 Thessalonians 5:4, Peter says "the day of the Lord will come like a thief." In 2 Peter 3:7 Peter writes that by the word of God "the present heavens and earth are reserved for fire, being kept for the day of judgment and destruction of ungodly men."   In verse 13 (NIV), Peter adds that "in keeping with His promise we are looking forward to a new heaven and a new earth, the home of righteousness."   The renovation of the universe is thus declared to be something that occurs on the day of the Lord.   Peter also connects the judgment and the sending of ungodly men to their destruction following the judgment to this same day.   Verse 14 alludes to the final judgment when Peter urges his Christian readers to "be diligent to be found by Him in peace, spotless and blameless."   Peter's language about what happens to those who are found to be spotless and blameless ("salvation") and what happens to the ungodly ("destruction") indicates that what follows the judgment on the day of the Lord is heaven for the godly and hell for the ungodly.

---

[5] When verse 4 says the day of the Lord will not overtake the Thessalonians like a thief in the night, it would be reading into the text more than is permissible to affirm that this statement means the Thessalonians will not be involved in the day of the Lord because they have already been raptured before the day of the Lord begins.   Verse 9 indicates they *are* involved in what happens on the day of the Lord. Eschatological schemes that treat the *parousia* and rapture as preceding the day of the Lord cannot be harmonized with what is written in 1 Thessalonians 5.

[6] For more details, see Special Study #2 concerning this *apostasia* (an apostasy or a rebellion).

[7] For more details, see Special Study #4 concerning the restrainer.

[8] For more details, see Special Study #3 concerning the man of lawlessness.

There are no other passages in the New Testament which use the precise language "day of the Lord," but there are passages that have similar and evidently synonymous expressions. Since Jesus is both Lord and Christ, we may conclude that "day of Christ" (Philippians 1:10; 2:16), "day of Jesus Christ" (Philippians 1:6), "day of our Lord Jesus Christ" (1 Corinthians 1:8), and "day of the Lord Jesus" (1 Corinthians 5:5; 2:14) all have reference to the same end-of-time event as does "day of the Lord."[9] Perhaps the wording of these verses is intended to signify that Christ Himself will be the prominent actor when that day dawns.

Based on the passages above, a summary of events connected with the great and terrible "day of the Lord" includes the following: just before the day of the Lord arrives there will occur a rebellion, a restraint being withdrawn, and the coming of the man of lawlessness. The man of lawlessness and his activities will be brought to an abrupt end at the moment Jesus first becomes visible at the time of His coming (*parousia*). Great cosmological changes occur when the Lord returns, including the renovation of the earth by fire. The resurrection of the dead in Christ and the rapture happen at the *parousia*. Angels gather the elect. The final judgment occurs at the *parousia*, with the wicked being sentenced to Hell while the righteous are welcomed into heaven. With all these events happening on the day of the Lord, it becomes obvious we should think of a period of time (maybe as long as weeks or months as man reckons time) rather than a twenty-four-hour day.

---

[9] Proponents of premillennial views tend to give these verses a slightly different interpretation. It is common among these proponents to find the word *parousia* used to refer to a coming of Jesus before the great tribulation begins, and to use the word "revelation" to refer to a coming after the tribulation. This "revelation" coming of Jesus is then presented as being followed by the millennium, which closes with the final judgment. Early in the 20th century, this common premillennial view on the day of the Lord was made popular by a footnote in *The Scofield Reference Bible*. "The day of Jehovah (called, also, 'that day' and the 'great day') is that lengthened period of time beginning with the return of the Lord in glory [revelation coming], and ending [1000 years later] with the purgation of the heavens and the earth by fire preparatory to the new heavens and the new earth (Isaiah 65:17-19; 66:22; 2 Peter 3:18; Revelation 21:1)." (C.I. Scofield, ed., *The Scofield Reference Bible* [New York: Oxford University Press, 1917], 1349 n.1.) In harmony with this eschatological scenario, the expression "day of Christ" came to be attached to the *parousia* and rapture, while the expression "day of the LORD" (*yom YHWH*) came to be attached to the long period of time from the "revelation" of Christ to the final judgment.

If we have grasped correctly what is written in the Thessalonian letters, this premillennial scenario is flawed, since both letters associate the rapture with the 'day of the Lord" (1 Thessalonians 4:15-5:2, and 2 Thessalonians 2:1-2), and also seem to connect the "revelation" of Christ with His *parousia*. (Compare 2 Thessalonians 1:7 ["when the Lord will be revealed from heaven with His mighty angels"] with 2 Thessalonians 2:1,2 ["Now we request you, brethren, with regard to the coming of our Lord Jesus Christ and our gathering together to Him, that you not be quickly shaken from your composure or be disturbed either by a spirit or a message or a letter as if from us, to the effect that the day of the Lord has come."]). Furthermore, the Thessalonian letters connect the final judgment with the *parousia*.

Special Study #2

THE *APOSTASIA*

Concerning the events that precede the day of the Lord, 2 Thessalonians 2:3 does not read alike in the various Bible translations:

- The NASB reads, "Let no one in any way deceive you, for *it will not come* unless the apostasy comes first."
- The NIV reads, "for that day will not come until the rebellion occurs."

The Greek word that is the subject of this special study – *apostasia* – is crucial to how 2 Thessalonians affects the entire subject of eschatology. "Apostasy" and "rebellion" represent the two possible English equivalents for *apostasia*, and the thrust of the whole passage differs significantly based upon which of these two English renderings is chosen. In fact, whatever conclusions are reached about the meaning of this single Greek word exert considerable influence on how a great portion of the rest of 2 Thessalonians 2 is interpreted. How are we to decide which of the two possibilities is the better translation?

The English word "apostasy" now carries the connotation of abandoning or renouncing one's religious faith. "Rebellion" has the connotation of open resistance to, or defiance of, governmental authority, its officers and laws. "In the papyri *apostasia* is used in the general sense of rebellion."[1] In the LXX, *apostasis*, the older substantive from which *apostasia* is derived, is always used "with the meaning of revolt (usually religious rebellion)."[2] Even in Acts 21:21, the only other place *apostasia* appears in the New Testament, it could well be translated "rebellion."

Several expressions in 2 Thessalonians 2 are given to describe and characterize the man of lawlessness. These expressions include "lawlessness," "opposes every so-called god or object of worship," "displaying himself as being God," and "deception of wickedness." These expressions nicely match the idea that the man of lawlessness will lead a rebellion against God; they do not as easily support the idea that the man of lawlessness will cause the apostasy of the faithful. The phrase "they did not receive the love of the truth" is not easily harmonized with the idea that the topic here is apostasy from Christ, for the people described by that phrase had never become Christians.

---

[1] Moulton and Milligan, *The Vocabulary of the Greek New Testament* (Grand Rapids: Wm. B. Eerdmans, nd) p.68,69). This volume gives meanings of Greek words as found in koine Greek.

[2] Charles Ryrie, "Apostasy in the Church," *BibSac* 121 (Jan 1964), p.44. Typical passages are Joshua 22:22, 2 Chronicles 28:19, and Jeremiah 2:19.

Do Not Confuse 2 Thessalonians 2 With Other New Testament Predictions of Apostasy

Many of the Bible verses often appealed to as corroboration of the idea of an end-times "apostasy" in fact do not deal with the time just before Christ's *parousia*.

(1) At the time they were written or spoken, many of these warnings of coming temptations to abandon Christianity were references to the heresy now known as Gnosticism, a heresy which began to infiltrate the churches in the early AD 60s. Among these are passages in Colossians, like 2:8-15; 1 Timothy 4:1, which says, "But the Spirit explicitly says that in later times some will fall away from the faith, paying attention to deceitful spirits and doctrines of demons"; 1 John 2:18, which speaks of "many antichrists" who had already appeared on the scene of history; and Jude 4, which indicates that already "certain persons have crept in unnoticed," these very persons being identified in Jude 18 as the fulfillment of the prophecy made in 2 Peter 3:3 about "mockers [i.e., the Gnostics] … who follow their own lusts."[3]

(2) There are passages in Jesus' eschatological discourse (Matthew 24-25) which speak of a coming apostasy from the Christian faith, and which have been appealed to by some writers as being a reference to an apostasy just before Christ's second coming. However, those prophecies actually refer to an apostasy which would occur before the coming destruction of Jerusalem by the Romans in AD 70. To see this, observe that Matthew 24:4-28 has reference to the coming destruction of Jerusalem, while 24:29-25:46 refer to Christ's second coming (*parousia*).[4] Luke's account of Jesus' discourse makes it plain that in the first part of His discourse, Jesus had in view the AD 70 destruction of Jerusalem. As He spoke, He indicated that the passage in Daniel which has the expression "abomination of desolation" (Daniel 9:24-27) was a prediction of the AD 70 destruction of Jerusalem.[5] Jesus instructed the Christians who lived in Judea to flee to the mountains when they saw the abomination of desolation approaching. Luke in his parallel account (Luke 20:21,22) wrote "when you see Jerusalem surrounded by armies, know that its destruction is at hand, then recognize that her desolation is near. Then those who are in Judea must flee to the mountains, and those who are in the midst of the city must leave."[6]

---

[3] "Last days" in 2 Peter 3:3 is an expression that covers the whole church age, not just the end of that age.

[4] Some have questioned this broad outline of the eschatological discourse because Matthew 24:14 reads, "This gospel of the kingdom shall be preached in the whole world as a testimony to all the nations, and then the end will come." Mark's Gospel was written before AD 70, and so were Paul's letters. Mark 16:20 indicates the gospel had been preached "everywhere" while Paul indicates this was done before AD 70 in Romans 10:17,18; Romans 16:26; and Colossians 1:6,23. Of course, the language of both Jesus and Mark and Paul is to be understood to have reference to the Roman world of their day.

[5] Daniel 11:31 and 12:11 in the LXX also has "abomination of desolation" (the same construction as here), but those chapters refer to Antiochus Epiphanes (160 BC), not to the destruction of Jerusalem in AD 70. 1 Maccabees 1:54 applied these two passages from Daniel to the time of Antiochus Epiphanes.

[6] When time arrived and the Roman armies came upon Jerusalem, Christians, heeding Jesus' instructions, fled from Jerusalem and Judea and settled in the city of Pella in Perea.

Since Matthew 24:4-28 refers to AD 70, the verses which speak of a falling away from the faith do not deal with the second advent, but with the 1st century AD. Matthew 24:4-28 gives signs of the coming destruction of Jerusalem, among which are one that predicts false Christs would "lead many astray" (Matthew 24:5), and another that warns "there shall arise false Christs, and false prophets, and shall show great signs and wonders; so as to lead astray, if possible, even the elect" (Matthew 24:24).

(3) Two other passages have been misapplied. Luke 18:1ff speaks not of Christianity, as such, but of the "faith" to continue persistent in prayer. In Acts 20:29, as he is speaking to the Ephesian elders, Paul warns that "savage wolves will come in among you, not sparing the flock," and that "from among your own selves men will arise, speaking perverse things, to draw away the disciples after them." "Among you" shows that Paul is not speaking about a falling away at the end of the church age; instead, Paul was warning the elders about the Gnostic heresy that was just beginning to show up on the horizon.

These New Testament passages, which do predict an apostasy from the Christian faith, apparently refer to a falling away from the faith sometime earlier in church history, rather than an apostasy just before Christ's second advent. 2 Thessalonians 2 is concerned with the timeframe surrounding Christ's second advent. As we translate *apostasia*, passages which are *not* about the second advent should not unduly influence or miscolor our translation of a word or verse whose focus is Christ's second advent.

The Use of "Apostasy" Within Our English Translations

When the Greek word *apostasia* signifies "rebellion," how did English versions in both Catholic and Protestant Bibles come to read "apostasy" at 2 Thessalonians 2:3? Both the Douay-Rheims (1609) version and the KJV (1611) transliterated *apostasia* instead of translating the word. At that time in history there was a fierce struggle between Catholics and Protestants. Catholics accused Protestants of apostasy, and Protestants accused Catholics of apostasy from the faith. "The preface of the Rheims New Testament asserts that this work has been rendered necessary by the circulation of many 'false translations' by Protestants, who have corrupted the truth of Holy Writ, 'adding, detracting, altering, transposing, pointing, and all other guileful means: specially where it serveth for the advantage of their private opinions'."[7] Toward the end of the third paragraph of the Dedicatory Epistle printed in the older editions of the KJV is a parenthetical note, declaring that this version was one "(which hath given such a blow unto that man of sin, as will not be healed)." This note appears to indicate that the KJV translators were reflecting the Reformation idea that the Roman Catholic church had departed from the apostolic order for the church (i.e., apostasy), and that the pope is the "man of sin" whom 2 Thessalonians predicts will take advantage of the apostasy and lawlessness to gain his ascendancy onto the scene of history.

---

[7] F.F. Bruce, *The English Bible: A History of Translations* (New York: Oxford University Press, 1961), p.114.

In other words, it appears both groups of translators – Protestant and Catholic – transliterated the word "apostasy" at 2 Thessalonians 2:3 in order to give more ammunition to their arguments in the midst of the monumental upheaval created by the Reformation.

Apostasia Within the Different Eschatological Systems

A word of encouragement is needed as we continue these special studies, so that we do not become discouraged thinking the material is too hard to comprehend. When Bible students are studying the Word and find verses that seem to refer to the same topic, they tend to weave those verses together in their minds to form a consistent picture. That is the way students can determine what the Bible teaches on any subject. What is most troubling to beginning students is when they encounter incompatible patterns that some other student has published. If several incompatible or contradictory patterns are happened upon, it is easy for the student to become discouraged, thinking he or she will never understand what the Bible says. Often, when enquiring students are introduced to the varying eschatological systems that have been put forth, not a few have come to believe they will never understand Bible prophecy.

To help keep students from becoming discouraged, it is important at this juncture to become acquainted with the general arrangement proposed by the major eschatological systems known as Postmillennialism, Historic Premillennialism, [8] Dispensational (or modern) Premillennialism, [9] and Amillennialism. The word "millennium" means a "thousand years" and each of the eschatological systems tries to relate the other prophecy verses they have studied (especially those that refer to Christ's second coming[10]) to the "thousand years" written about in Revelation 20. "Post-" (which means "after") in Postmillennialism reflects the view that Christ's second coming is *after* the thousand years.[11]   "Pre-" (which means "before") reflects the view that Christ's second coming is

---

[8] The adjective "historic" (in Historic Premillennialism) reflects the fact that some early church fathers taught Premillennialism.   They envisioned a future great tribulation (Revelation 7:14) just before Christ's second coming to inaugurate a future earthly millennium with Christians enjoying a thousand-year golden age with Christ.

[9] The adjectives "dispensational" or "modern" reflect the historical fact that this system was introduced in the 16th century by the Jesuit Ribera to relieve the Pope from the Protestant stigma of being the antichrist.   The system was made popular in some Protestant circles by J.N. Darby and the Plymouth Brethren.   This system has a Jewish emphasis, and it posits that had the Jews not rejected Him, Christ would have set up an earthly kingdom in which He and the Jews ruled the world.   Because they rejected Christ, the church age was introduced as a temporary arrangement until Christ comes again, at which time He will inaugurate a millennium in which Jewish people enjoy living and reigning with Christ.

[10] It must be kept in mind that both 1 Thessalonians 4,5 and 2 Thessalonians 2 are tied together with Christ's *parousia*.

[11] Revelation 20:7-10 is treated as being at the same time as Christ's second coming, so His coming is "post-millennial," since 20:1-6 tells of the thousand years.   About AD 1700 this system of eschatology was introduced by Daniel Whitby.   He copied some of the Jesuit Alcazar's ideas which had been set forth to defend the Pope against the Protestant affirmation that he was the man of lawlessness.

before the thousand years.[12] "A-" (from the Greek construction which negates what the rest of the word says) reflects the view that the "thousand years" plus the "little season" (Revelation 20:3) encompass the whole church age, and there is *no* literal future millennium to follow the close of this age.[13]

We have referenced the major eschatological systems in order to provide a basic framework for showing how advocates of each treat the prophecy in 2 Thessalonians.[14]

(1) Can *apostasia* be a reference to the rapture? Instead of translating the word "rebellion," some premillennialists have proposed the idea that *apostasia* should be translated "departure" and then advocate that it refers to the rapture of the church.[15] Then, since the "departure" comes "first" (2 Thessalonians 2:3), before the man of lawlessness comes onto the scene of history, in the premillennial system of eschatology the rapture is said to occur before the great tribulation,[16] the period of time when the man of lawlessness is active. While it can be correctly demonstrated that in classical Greek *apostasis* could have the meaning "departure,"[17] to separate the rapture from the *parousia* coming of Jesus (as premillennialism does) is certainly mistaken since 1 Thessalonians 4:15-17 ties the rapture together with Christ's *parousia*.

---

[12] When Premillennialists choose an outline for the book of Revelation, they treat chapter 19 (which in verses 11-21 describes Christ's second coming) as occurring in earth's history just before the "thousand years" of Revelation 20, and so Christ's coming is "pre-millennial."

[13] Because Amillennialists observe seven different passages in the book of Revelation that depict Christ's second coming, they understand that book to be presenting seven different surveys, or cycles, of earth's history from John's time to the second coming.   Since Revelation 19 describes the second coming, it is treated as the end of cycle six.   Chapter 20 starts a new cycle, which ends with Christ's coming and final judgment.   Revelation then closes this seventh cycle with a captivating description of the "new Jerusalem."   Some early church fathers taught this system of eschatology.

Representative Amillennial writers include Floyd Hamilton, *The Basis of Millennial Faith* (Grand Rapids: Wm. B. Eerdmans, 1942); J. Marcellus Kik, *Revelation Twenty* (Philadelphia: Presbyterian and Reformed Publishing Co., 1955); George L. Murray, *Millennial Studies* (Grand Rapids: Baker Book House, 1972); William Hendriksen, *More Than Conquerors* (Grand Rapids: Baker Book House, 1961); and G.K. Beale, *The Book of Revelation* in the New International Greek Testament Commentary (Grand Rapids: Wm. B. Eerdmans, 1998).

[14] How the prophecy in 2 Thessalonians has been interpreted through the ages will be covered in Special Study #3 in this volume, "The Man of Lawlessness."

[15] See Kenneth S. Wuest, "The Rapture – Precisely When?" in *Bib Sac* 114 (Jan-Mar 1957), p.69-70; E. Schuyler English, *Rethinking the Rapture* (Travelers Rest, SC: Southern Bible Book House, 1954), p.65; William W. Combs, "Is *apostasia* in 2 Thessalonians 2:3 a Reference to the Rapture?" in *Detroit Baptist Seminary Journal* 3 (Fall 1998), p.63-88; and John Sweigart, "Is There a Departure in 2 Thessalonians 2:3?" in *Conservative Theological Journal* 5 (Aug 2001), p.186-204.

[16] English, *op. cit.*, p.67-71; Wuest, *op. cit.*, p.63-67.   The great tribulation is spoken of in Revelation 7:14 and alluded to again in Revelation 20:7-9.

[17] H.G. Liddel and Robert Scott, *A Lexicon Abridged from Liddell and Scott's Greek-English Lexicon* (New York: American Book Company, 1881), p.93.

(2) If there is to be a brief, but worldwide, rebellion (or apostasy) at the end of the church age, where is this future *apostasia* to be inserted into one's eschatological system? The differing and often conflicting answers to this question cause prophecy students to almost despair as they try to match the paragraphs of Scripture like 2 Thessalonians 2 with the eschatological system being studied.

(a) Proponents of *postmillennialism* locate the final apostasy or rebellion at the end of the millennium, which, of course, would imply that the millennium ends in failure.[18] They do this because, after Revelation 20:1-6 speaks of a thousand year period of time (i.e., a millennium), verses 7 and 8 introduce us to Gog and Magog, whose activities are worldwide in scope since they affect "the nations which are in the four corners of the earth" (Revelation 20:8). Gog is the leader and Magog are his people. In order to position the *apostasia* at the close of the millennium, postmillennialists identify the "Gog" of Revelation with the "man of lawlessness" (2 Thessalonians 2:3). There is a slight problem harmonizing John and Paul, when we read that "fire comes down from heaven" and devours Gog and Magog, whereas Paul words it that the Lord will slay the man of lawlessness "with the breath of his mouth" (2 Thessalonians 2:8). However, recall that Paul also has declared that when the Lord Jesus is revealed from heaven with His mighty angels, He will deal out retribution "in flaming fire" to those who do not know God and to those who do not obey the gospel of our Lord Jesus (2 Thessalonians 1:8,9). It would appear that the flaming fire in Paul's writing refers to the same fire that John described in his writing. While there are some major difficulties with the whole postmillennial system of eschatology, perhaps they are correct when they insert the *apostasia* where they do in their system, just before the Lord's second coming occurs. Revelation 20:8 has Satan gathering Gog and his people together for "the war" (i.e., the same war previously introduced at Revelation 16:14 and 19:11), and they attack the saints who are still on earth (Revelation 20:9). If saints are still on earth, the *parousia* and the rapture have not occurred. Similarly, in 2 Thessalonians 2:1ff, the man of lawlessness appears before the rapture. It seems as though Paul and John are describing the same future event.

(b) Proponents of *historic premillennialism* treat the *apostasia* of 2 Thessalonians 2 as occurring during the great tribulation (Revelation 7:14).[19] In this system of eschatology, the great tribulation period is said to occur at the close of the church age, and the tribulation period is then ended by Christ's second coming and the rapture of the church (1 Thessalonians 4:17). The millennium follows Christ's *parousia*. Since

---

[18] Representative postmillennial writers include David Brown, *Christ's Second Coming: Will it be Premillennial?* (reprint Rosemead, CA: Old Paths Book Club, 1953) and Loraine Boettner, *The Millennium* (Grand Rapids: Baker Book House, 1957), p.69ff. Postmillennialists treat the "thousand years" of Revelation 20 as a literal span of time.

[19] Representative historic premillennial writers include Alexander Reese, *The Approaching Advent of Christ* (Grand Rapids: Grand Rapids International Publications, 1975) and George Eldon Ladd, *A Commentary on the Revelation of John* (Grand Rapids: Wm. B. Eerdmans, 1972).

the great tribulation occurs before the *parousia*, the *apostasia* of 2 Thessalonians 2 is believed to occur during the great tribulation period.   In addition, the great tribulation is treated as being something distinct from Satan's "little season" (Revelation 20:2) which occurs after the millennium.   This distinction, in turn, requires that the "man of lawlessness" must be treated as a figure who is distinct from Gog and Magog (Revelation 20:9).

(c) Proponents of *dispensational premillennialism* have the great tribulation happening after the *parousia* and rapture of the church.[20]   The great tribulation is judged to be 7 years long (after proponents of this system argue that Daniel's 70th week was postponed until the close of the church age).   Gog (Ezekiel 38 and 39) and antichrist (the "man of lawlessness") are identified as being a reference to the same person, who is supposedly active during the tribulation period.   The battle of Armageddon (Revelation 16:16 KJV) is explained as bringing the tribulation period to a close.   The tribulation period, in this system, is followed by a literal millennium and Satan's little season.   Since Revelation's Gog is active at the close of Satan's little season, Revelation's Gog is thought to be a different Gog than Ezekiel predicted.   In this system, the *apostasia* and the "man of lawlessness" are pictured as coming after Christ's *parousia*, a scenario which disregards the fact that 2 Thessalonians has both those events as happening before Christ returns.

If the best conclusion is to translate *apostasia* as "rebellion," where is this future rebellion against God and His rule to be inserted into one's eschatological system? A straightforward reading of 2 Thessalonians has this order:

- The rebellion occurs.
- The man of lawlessness takes advantage of it.
- The rebellion is then quashed as the man of lawlessness is slain at the very beginning of Jesus' *parousia* coming (2 Thessalonians 2:8).

---

[20] Representative dispensational premillennial writers include the footnotes in the *Scofield Reference Bible* (New York: Oxford University Press, 1909), p.1337; W.E. Blackstone, *Jesus is Coming* (New York: Fleming H. Revell, 1932); John Walvoord, *The Return of the Lord* (Findlay, OH: Dunham Publishing Co., 1955) and *The Rapture Question* (Findlay, OH: Dunham Publishing Co., 1957); Hal Lindsay, *The Late Great Planet Earth* (New York: Bantam Books, 1973); and Tim LaHaye and Jerry Jenkins, *Left Behind* series (Wheaton: Tyndale House, 1995).   For a refutation of this system see David Vaughn Elliott, *Nobody Left Behind* (published in Methuen, MA, 2004).

Special Study #3

THE MAN OF LAWLESSNESS

For two thousand years, Christians have been fascinated by this prophecy in 2 Thessalonians 2 about "the man of lawlessness." Some of the continuing interest in meaning and fulfillment of this prophecy may reflect a desire to know when the second coming of Christ is about to occur, since the activities of the man of lawlessness immediately precede Christ's *parousia*. In some instances, the language of the passage has been pressed into service in order to give the strongest possible castigation to a particular opposition group or individual. During the two millennia since the prediction was made, many a man or movement have been called the Antichrist or man of lawlessness, only to have succeeding history demonstrate that the proposed identifications of the man of lawlessness were patently mistaken. This special study seeks to give enough guidelines to satisfy a Bible reader's interest concerning the meaning of the prophecy, but without presenting another suggested interpretation that history will prove to be mistaken.

The Prominent Characteristics of the Man of Lawlessness[1]

2 Thessalonians 2 presents the following bits of information that help identify the man of lawlessness:

(1) From the wording in chapter 2, we may infer that the man of lawlessness will be *a single person*. In verse 3, he is called "the man of ..." – a single article, plainly a singular person. In verse 8, this man of lawlessness is styled as "the lawless one" – a single person. In verse 4, the expression "he exalts himself" points to a single person.

(2) Three times we read this brief description *"lawlessness"* (*anomia*). Since the Law of Moses has been abrogated (Hebrews 7:12), "lawlessness" means something other than merely opposition to the Law of Moses. When he presents himself as God (verse 4), the man of lawlessness is repudiating Jehovah God and any rules God may have made for the church age. The lawless one has no love for the truth. He makes rules in harmony with what Satan, that long-time opponent of God and godliness, would have him do. There is an absence of any respect whatsoever for authority except his own.

---

[1] Many of the older English versions, including the KJV and Douay-Rheims, read "man of sin" since *hamartias* ("sin") is the reading found in the manuscripts from the 6th century AD onward. The older uncials (Vaticanus and Sinaiticus) read "man of lawlessness" (*anomia*), and Bruce Metzger (*A Textual Commentary on the Greek New Testament* [London: United Bible Societies, 1975], p.675) has argued this is the preferred reading.

(3) The "mystery of lawlessness" (verse 7) is the milieu out of which the "man of lawlessness" arises. If "rebellion" is the meaning of *apostasia* in verse 3, then it appears that the lawless one will arise *after* the final rebellion has begun, and that he then encourages further rebellion. The lawlessness which grows until it permeates earth's society, and which eventually paves the way for the man of lawlessness to appear, is called a "mystery" in verse 7. The word "mystery" in the New Testament denotes something only dimly foreshadowed in the Old Testament, which it is the privilege of the New Testament apostles to disclose and make more fully known (Ephesians 3:3,4). Very likely the "little horn" of Daniel 7:8ff is one Old Testament passage where this mystery was dimly foreshadowed. The explanation of Daniel's vision found in Daniel 7:19-27, which pictures the "little horn" there described as a powerful political ruler who "wears down the saints," corresponds in many ways to the "man of lawlessness" described in 2 Thessalonians 2.[2]

(4) *Self-deification* is another characteristic displayed by the man of lawlessness. "He takes his seat in the temple" (*naos*, "sanctuary," the place where a deity dwells, verse 4) is a way of saying He declares himself to be God.

(5) The man of lawlessness is not Satan, but is *a servant of Satan*. The man of lawlessness is said to be energized by Satan (verse 9). Prompted and empowered by Satan, the lawless one uses deception and false miracles to trick people into giving their allegiance to him. He will use a deluding influence (verse 11, a "working of error," ASV) to cause those who are perishing to "believe what is false" ("believe a lie," ASV).

(6) *"Son of destruction"* (verse 3) is a Hebraism meaning the lawless one is characterized by the destruction he causes.[3] His policies are detrimental to men since they only leave behind utter waste and devastation in this life, and loss of eternal well-being in the life to come.

(7) Who the man of lawlessness is will be revealed *before* the *parousia* of the Lord happens (verse 8). The appearance of the man of lawlessness is now being restrained until his appointed time (verse 6). He is not in control; God is. It is not the coming of the man, but his "revelation," that is here emphasized. Once the man of lawlessness comes into power it will be revealed that this one actually is the long-predicted lawless one.

---

[2] It is doubtful that Daniel 2 (the image and the stone, which pictures the beginning of the church age), or Daniel 8's "little horn" (who comes out of Greece and is different from the "little horn" of Daniel 7), or Daniel 9 (Daniel's "seventy weeks" which Jesus said would be fulfilled in the AD 70 destruction of Jerusalem – Matthew 24:15 and Luke 21:20) or Daniel 11 (neither the persecuting king pictured in 11:26-32, nor the one pictured in 11:36ff) are passages where the "mystery" was foreshadowed. Perhaps Daniel 12:10 does picture the same personage named "man of lawlessness" by Paul.

[3] The NASB translation "son of destruction" is to be preferred to "son of perdition" found in the KJV and ASV.

(8) It is near *the end of the church age* when the man of lawlessness arises. Verse 8 specifically says he will be brought to an end when the "coming" of the Lord Jesus first becomes visible. That *parousia* coming ends the church age.

(9) The lawless one's whole program will be *brought to a stop* (verse 8) by the Lord when He appears. Very likely Revelation 19:19,20 is John's description of this same decisive overthrow of the man of lawlessness.

Possible New Testament Passages Likely Dealing with Same Lawless One

It is important to proceed cautiously and carefully at this point, for any conclusions reached about possible parallel passages will necessarily affect the rest of any attempt to gain a fuller understanding of the man of lawlessness, the rebellion, and the restrainer.[4]

Antichrist.   1 John 2:18-22

The person called "antichrist" in 1 John 2:18,22 appears to be identical with the person Paul referred to as "the man of lawlessness." "You heard that antichrist is coming" (verse 18) indicates John's readers were already familiar with that topic. That both Paul and John taught their readers about this personage implies that teaching about the future coming of the antichrist was a standard feature of Christian eschatology. Antichrist and the man of lawlessness are alike in that their appearance in history was something that would occur in the future. "Many antichrists have already appeared" suggests that the final antichrist has many forerunners. This is tantamount to Paul's "the mystery of lawlessness is already at work." The Gnostic teachers against whom John warned (calling them "many antichrists"), who were already in the world, were very similar to the future antichrist in their denial of "the Father and the Son." Such denials are likely comparable to the rebellion against God that is rampant when the lawless one comes.

The 8th Beast.   Revelation 17:7-18

Revelation 13:1-8 introduces a beast out of the sea, which has seven heads and ten horns. It is likely that what is symbolized is civil government which is anti-God and anti-

---

[4] A number of passages in the New Testament are sometimes said to have reference to the man of lawlessness, but it is doubtful that they should be inserted into this context.

- 1 Timothy 4:1 does have Christians falling away from the faith in the "latter times." However, "latter times" refers to the whole church age, not just events at the end of the age.
- 2 Peter 3:3 has "mockers" flourishing during "the last days." Peter's prophecy was a warning about the Gnostics who were just beginning to infiltrate the churches. Jude (written about AD 75) tells us that what Peter had predicted had actually happened by the time he wrote (Jude 17-19).
- In His eschatological discourse, Jesus spoke about many falling away (Matthew 24:10). But Special Study #2 has explained that, in this verse, He was giving signs of the approaching AD 70 destruction of Jerusalem, not of His second coming.

Christian. This beast, with the seven heads and ten horns, is reintroduced in Revelation 17. Revelation 17:10 tells us the seven heads are seven kings, five of whom have fallen before John wrote Revelation, one was ruling when John wrote,[5] and one was yet come. When the seventh ruler appears, John tells us in verse 10, his reign will be brief. Verse 11 introduces an eighth beast who is like the other seven. Verse 12 informs us that the ten horns on this beast symbolize "ten kings who have not yet received a kingdom, but they receive authority as kings with the beast for one hour." So, the 8th beast, who is like the seven, evidently is a government figure. The "one to come" (the 8th beast), about whom John wrote, has enough affinities with the man of lawlessness, about whom Paul wrote, to show the two books describe the same period of time. The "man of lawlessness" opposes God and exalts himself, proclaiming himself to be God (2 Thessalonians 2:4). Similarly, the "beast" opens his mouth for blasphemies against God, and welcomes the honor of being worshiped by a sinful world (Revelation 13:5-8). Revelation 19:19 informs us that "the beast and the kings of the earth and their armies assembled to make war against Him who sat on the horse and against His army." Like the man of lawlessness is brought to an end at the *parousia* of Christ (2 Thessalonians 2:8), it seems that the 8th beast is destroyed at the second coming (Revelation 17:14).

Daniel 7 has described a government leader. Revelation 17 has described a government leader. If it is granted that those passages deal with the same person whom Paul calls the man of lawlessness, it can be projected that the man of lawlessness also depicts a government leader.

A Brief History of the Interpretation of 2 Thessalonians 2

Throughout church history there has been a constant attempt on the part of Christians to apply the prophecy to their own day. Each writer's suggested identification of the man of lawlessness has tended to be influenced by the writer's contemporary historical situation or by the writer's own approach to Biblical criticism.[6] Time and again, these suggested identifications have proven to be mistaken. What is the reason for this? Perhaps those

---

[5] The "one who is," a ruler contemporary with John who is writing Revelation in AD 96, would have been the Roman government.

[6] A detailed overview of the history of the various interpretations given to this passage – those of the early church, the Middle Ages, and current – can be found in numerous commentaries: Henry Alford, "On the Prophetic Import of ch. 2:1-12," in *The Second Epistle to the Thessalonians* in Alford's Greek Testament (London: Rivingtons, 1871), p.55-69; C.H. Riggenbach, "Commentary on the Thessalonians" in *Lange's Commentary* (Grand Rapids: Zondervan Publishing Co., nd), p.133-140; G.G. Findlay, "The Man of Lawlessness" in *1 and 2 Thessalonians* in The Cambridge Bible for Schools and Colleges (Cambridge: University Press, 1898), p.170-180; P.J. Gloag, "Excursus on Man of Sin" in *2 Thessalonians* in the Pulpit Commentary (Grand Rapids: Wm. B. Eerdmans, 1950), vol.21, p.50-61; F.F. Bruce, "Excursus on Antichrist," in *1 & 2 Thessalonians* in the Word Biblical Commentary v.45 (Waco, TX: Word, 1982), p.179-188; Joel R. Beeke and Paul Smalley, "The Man of Sin: 2 Thessalonians 2:1-12," *PRJ* 10, 1 (2018), p.5-30.

writers making the identifications failed to take into account that a revelation from God (2 Thessalonians 2:8) will be needed before the man of lawlessness will be recognized. Until that revelation takes place, any identification of the man of lawlessness is problematic.

Early church fathers appear to have been on right track when they nominated this or that government ruler (rather than an apostate religious leader) as being the man of lawlessness, but those same early church fathers went too far when they named one of their contemporary emperors, however evil he happened to be, as being the lawless one. There was a natural tendency to identify any individual who seemed specially to threaten the existence of the church as being antichrist.

When the Roman empire fell (AD 476), the way was open for the Roman church to step into the power vacuum. Not long after, it began to be suggested that the pope, now one of the most powerful men in the world, was the antichrist. Pope Gregory the Great (AD 590) indignantly reproached the Patriarch of Constantinople, John the Faster, for calling himself the universal bishop as he had done at the Synod of Constantinople in 588, saying, "Whoever calls himself universal bishop, or desires this title, is, by his pride, the precursor to the antichrist."[7] Joachim (AD 1132-1202) did not name one particular pontiff as the antichrist, but suggested that the antichrist would be a *Universalis Pontifex*, and that he would occupy the Apostolic See.[8]

When Islam had begun sweeping the Mediterranean world, the Greek church pointed to Mohammed as being the man of lawlessness. In AD 1198, centuries after Mohammed's death, Pope Innocent III endeavored to promote a crusade aimed at delivering the Holy Land from Islamic rule by declaring that Mohammed was the man of lawlessness. There was a serious flaw in this identification. 2 Thessalonians 2:8 indicates the man of lawlessness will be brought to an end by the Lord's second coming. Mohammed's death 500 years earlier was not the result of the Lord's second coming.

In the Middle Ages, when opposition to the Roman hierarchy grew, the idea that the Pope might be the antichrist was adopted by Savonarola, the Algibenses, the Waldenses, Wycliffe, and the Hussites. Wycliffe (mid AD 1300's) wrote the treatise "Concerning Christ and his Adversary, Antichrist" in which he defended the proposition that the pope is an antichrist, giving 12 reasons. As the years passed, and several different men were named Pope, a slight change was made by the Protestants. Now it was the Papacy (not a single man but a series of Popes) that came to be identified as being the antichrist. Luther, Calvin, Zwingli, Melanchthon, and Beza all subscribed to this view. The Catholic church's rejoinder was that Luther was the man of sin.

---

[7] Letter of Pope Gregory I to John the Faster.

[8] Frederick Meyrick, "Antichrist" in *Smith's Dictionary of the Bible*, revised by H.B. Hackett (Grand Rapids: Baker, 1971 reprint), vol.1, p.106.

As the Reformation spread across Europe and into the new world, the idea that the Pope or the Papacy was the man of lawlessness remained the dominant Protestant view until the 19th century. This doctrine became an article in the creed of the Lutheran Church.[9] Many Protestants have followed Luther's lead, identifying the Pope as the Antichrist. The translators of the 1611 KJV included a dedicatory letter to James, king of England, in which he is given credit for having by means of his translation dealt "such a blow to that Man of Sin [meaning the Pope] as will not be healed."[10] The AD 1647 Westminster Confession of Faith, chapter 25, reads, "There is no other head of the church but the Lord Jesus Christ; nor can the Pope of Rome, in any sense, be head thereof, but is that Antichrist, the Man of Sin and Son of Perdition, that exalteth himself in the church against Christ and all that is called God." The Puritans held the view that the Pope was the man of lawlessness.[11]

When powerful national political leaders emerged in the 19th and 20th centuries, many were thought to be the antichrist. Napoleon, Kaiser Wilhelm III, Mussolini, Hitler, Stalin, and Saddam Hussein all, at one time or another, were accorded this dubious honor.

The preterist interpretation of Biblical prophecies, begun by Alcazar during the counter-reformation to defend the Papacy against the Reformation accusations that the Pope was the antichrist, has been revived by some teachers.[12] They interpret the Book of Daniel as referring to events that happened from the 7th century BC until the 1st century AD. They interpret the prophecies of Matthew 24, Thessalonians, and Revelation as being fulfilled in Nero as the man of lawlessness, and the rebellion as being fulfilled when the Jewish nation rebelled against Rome, leading to the AD 70 destruction of Jerusalem. When preterist interpreters affirm the *parousia* of Christ occurred in AD 70 it can be affirmed that the preterist view cannot be harmonized with what 1 Corinthians 15:22-28 and 1 and 2 Thessalonians say about the *parousia*.

---

[9] "Article IV: Of the Papacy" in *the Smalcald Articles*.

[10] Until the latter part of the 20th Century, "The Epistle Dedicatory" was always printed in the opening pages of the King James Bible.

[11] The view that the Pope was the man of lawlessness was advocated in the early years of the Restoration Movement in America. In his 1836 debate with Bishop Purcell, Alexander Campbell defended the proposition that the Roman Catholic Church "is the 'Babylon' of John, the 'Man of Sin' of Paul, and the Empire of the 'Youngest Horn' of Daniel's sea monster." (*A Debate on the Roman Catholic Religion* [Nashville: McQuiddy Printing Co., 1914], p.281-294.) B.W. Johnson's explanatory notes in *The People's New Testament* (Delight, AR: Gospel Light Publishing Co., 1950 reprint, vol.2, p.253) applied 2 Thessalonians 2 to the Papacy, and so did J.W. McGarvey and Philip Y. Pendleton, *Thessalonians, Corinthians, Galatians, and Romans* (Cincinnati, OH: Standard, 1916), p.41-43, who gave nine reasons to support this view.

[12] J. Stuart Russell, *The Parousia* (London: T. Fisher Unwin, 1887; republished Grand Rapids: Baker, 1983, 1999); Max King, *The Cross and The Parousia of Christ* (Warren, OH: Parkman Rd. Church of Christ, 1987).

Another method of prophetic interpretation known as modern premillennialism was introduced in the 16th century by the Jesuit Francisco Ribera to relieve the pressure on the Pope, whom the Reformers stigmatized as being the antichrist.   Ribera produced a commentary on the book of Revelation in which he made chapters 4-19 refer to a three-and-one-half year period of time just before the second coming of Christ.   Thus, they had no reference to the Pope in the Middle Ages.   These ideas were adopted and made popular both by J.N. Darby and by Cyrus Scofield in the footnotes in the *Scofield Reference Bible*.[13] These writers have produced an imaginary schedule of future events based on passages in Daniel 11, Ezekiel 38:8,9, and the middle chapters of Revelation.   However, "Not one single reference in Daniel or Ezekiel or Paul or the Book of Revelation which Premillennialists allege refers to Antichrist is connected in any way with the verses in the epistles of John that mention antichrist.   All is based on inference ... is pure fiction, without so much as one clear supporting verse in Scripture."[14]

This brief history of the interpretation of 2 Thessalonians 2 has helped us learn how mistaken men can be if, apart from divine revelation, we venture to suggest that any current powerful government leader may be the man of lawlessness.   21st century Bible students should recognize that, during the past 2000 years, the long list of individuals or institutions identified as the man of lawlessness has proven (as time passes) to be erroneous.   It appears the reason these identifications have proven to be erroneous is that interpreters have proposed this or that candidate as being the man of lawlessness without waiting for the revelation of the man of lawlessness about which 2 Thessalonians 2:8 speaks.

While awaiting that revelation to be made by God, we properly may draw a general conclusion about the meaning of the prophecy.   The man of lawlessness has not yet (it appears) been revealed.   Whether the time is getting close, we cannot say.   However, we do see things in our world – like society's growing anarchy against the Lord – that make us wonder.   In the meantime, Christians must stay ready, so the day of the Lord does not overtake us like a thief.

---

[13] More recent popularizers are Hal Lindsey, *The Late Great Planet Earth* (Grand Rapids, MI: Zondervan, 1970), and Tim LaHaye and Jerry Jenkins, *Left Behind, A Novel of the Earth's Last Days.* Volume #1 of a series (Wheaton, IL.:   Tyndale House, 1995).

[14] Loraine Boettner, *The Millennium* (Grand Rapids: Baker, 1958), p.210.

Special Study #4

THE RESTRAINER

To provide a believable identification of the restrainer that Paul references in 2 Thessalonians 2:6-8 has proven to be one of the most disputed topics in the study of the eschatology introduced in the Thessalonian letters.

Issues That Complicate Any Attempted Identification

One reason for the dispute is that few details are given concerning the restrainer. The Greek word translated "what restrains" (verse 6) is a present tense a neuter participle, while the Greek word translated "he who restrains" (verse 7) is a present tense masculine participle. The present tense as well as the adverb "now" in "he who now restrains" all indicate that the restraining power or person was already at work in Paul's day. Verses 7 and 8 show the restrainer will continue to be at work keeping the man of lawlessness from appearing on the scene of earth's history until nearly the time for the second coming of Christ.

Other reasons for the dispute lie in the fact that, before a discussion of the restrainer's identity even begins, several crucial interpretive decisions must be made, and these interpretive decisions have a profound effect on the task of identifying the restrainer.

- In most of our English versions there are nouns and verbs added to the sentences and clauses in verses 6 and 7. It must be determined whether or not the additions are justified since they necessarily affect the overall understanding of the passage.

- The choice of "apostasy" or "rebellion" in 2 Thessalonians 2:3 influences the decision about the identity of the restrainer.

- The decision made about the likely identity of the man of lawlessness in turn influences the decision about the identity of the restrainer.

- The choice of translation for the deponent Greek verb at the end of verse 7 ("taken out of the way" v. "until out of the midst he goes") influences the decision about the identity of the restrainer.

As an example of the difficulties inherent in these interpretive decisions, consider the debate engendered by the addition of certain nouns and verbs to the sentences and clauses in verses 6 and 7. Translators not infrequently make these kinds of additions in order to facilitate our understanding of the passage or to smooth broken sentences, implied thoughts, or incomplete constructions in the original Greek text.

The NASB is a typical example of the nouns and verbs added in our English translations. (a) Verse 6 in the NASB reads, "And you know what restrains him now, so that in his time he may be revealed." Usually when words are added by the translators, the words are printed in italics to warn the English reader that these words have been added, that these words do not exist in the original Greek text. However, at verse 6, the NASB translators do not italicize "him" even though there is no word for "him" in the Greek. The addition of "him" certainly affects the interpretation of the verse since it makes the man of lawlessness the one who is being restrained. (b) The last clause of verse 7 reads, "he who now restrains *will do so* until he is taken out of the way." The words "will do so" added in italics further reinforces the idea that it is a good restrainer who is holding back the evil man of lawlessness. (c) In the last part of verse 6, the NASB translators treat the clause "so that in his time he may be revealed" as being dependent on the participle "what restrains" rather than on the nearer antecedent "you know." This also affects our understanding of what the passage is trying to tell us since it advances the idea that the purpose of the restraint is to keep the man of lawlessness from being revealed before the appointed time for him to be revealed.

Objections to each of these translation (i.e., interpretive) decisions have been raised in various published studies of this difficult text[1]. In regard to (a) and (b), if the added words "him" and "will do so" are omitted from verses 6 and 7, the passage then may be understood to say that the mystery of lawlessness is the restraining power in place until the time arrives for the restraint to be removed.[2] However, this treatment, while possible, requires us to give the word "mystery" a peculiar meaning, unlike any used elsewhere in Scripture. Further, does this significant change truly help us to understand the identity of the restrainer? It seems difficult to understand how the mystery of lawlessness (treated as something evil) can keep something else that is evil (i.e., the rebellion or the apostasy) from happening.[3] In regard to (c), the Greek construction at the beginning of the last clause

---

[1] See Ernest Best, "The Katechon," in *The First and Second Epistles to the Thessalonians* in Black's New Testament Commentary (Peabody, MA.: Hendrickson Publishers, 1986), p.295-302; Paul S. Dixon, "The Evil Restraint in 2 Thessalonians 2:6," *JETS* 33/4 (December 1990), p.445-449; C.H. Giblin, *The Threat to Faith: An Exegetical and Theological Re-Examination of 2 Thessalonians 2* in Analecta Biblica 31 (Rome: Pontifical Biblical Institute, 1967).

[2] Dixon, *op. cit.*, p.447.

[3] The suggestion made by C.H. Giblin (*op. cit.*, p.230) does little to avoid this difficulty. His suggestion that the Greek participle *ho katechōn* should be translated "the Seizer" rather than "the restrainer" results in no advance in our understanding of the passage. Having correctly observed that the passive form of the verb *katechein* is used to mean "possessed" (by a demon), he then proposes that the "Seizer" (not "the restrainer") was a frenzied false prophet who upset the congregation at Thessalonica with his false message about the day of the Lord. Two things militate against this proposal. One, the participles translated "restrain" here in Thessalonians are in the active voice, not the passive; and, two, Giblin ignores the statements about the *parousia* of the Lord when he tries to locate the "Seizer" only in the 1st century church at Thessalonica.

in verse 6 is *eis* and an infinitive.   Since *eis* and an infinitive can express either purpose or result,[4] it makes little difference in the meaning of the final clause of verse 6 whether we make it dependent on the verb "you know" or on the participle "that which restrains."

All in all, it appears that those objecting to the added English words, or who have attempted translations and interpretations of the text which result in an evil restrainer, most often succeed in producing identifications for the restrainer that are even harder-to-believe than some of those offered across the centuries since 2 Thessalonians was written. Therefore, we conclude that the words added in our English translations do not negatively impact a correct understanding of the passage.

The decisions reached in the main body of the commentary concerning (2) the choice of "apostasy" or "rebellion" in 2 Thessalonians 2:3;   (3) the likely identity of the man of lawlessness;   and (4) the translation of the deponent Greek verb at the end of verse 7, were all made with full awareness of the impact those decisions have on identifying the restrainer.

Proposed Identifications to Be Rejected

Interpretations that present the whole of 2 Thessalonians 2 as mythological.

Beginning with Wilhelm Bousset in the late 1890's,[5] a number of commentators, having rejected the premise that either Paul or the Old Testament prophets (from whom Paul sometimes borrowed terminology) could have been inspired, then speculate about the source of the ideas Paul borrowed and included in 2 Thessalonians.   Perhaps, it is affirmed, Paul remolded, reworked, and elaborated some old uninspired Jewish apocalyptic ideas, the original source of which is lost in the dim prehistoric past.   During Paul's ministry, as he encountered different questions about his teaching, such commentators tell that us that Paul developed and modified his ideas more and more as the occasion demanded.

If modern commentators really believe that Paul simply wrote a highly imaginary prophecy about things that are never going to happen, Lenski has pointedly asked the right question, "Why do these commentators write their books and waste their learning on these words of Paul's?"[6] If 2 Thessalonians 2 is nothing but uninspired drivel, why bother to try

---

[4] H.E. Dana and Julius R. Mantey, *A Manual Grammar of the Greek New Testament* (New York: The Macmillan Co., 1954), p.284, 286.

[5] See the helpful summary of Wilhelm Bousset's, *Der Antichrist*, in M.R. James' article on "Man of Sin and Antichrist" in *Hasting's Dictionary of the Bible* (New York: Charles Scribner's Sons, 1908), vol. 3, p.226-228.

[6] R.C.H. Lenski, *The Interpretation of St. Paul's Epistles to the Colossians, to the Thessalonians, to Timothy, to Titus, and to Philemon* (Minneapolis: Augsburg Publishing House, 1961), p.413.

to explain it? If this is pure mythology, there is nothing worthwhile left that needs to be explained. If the words in 2 Thessalonians 2 cannot be taken seriously, can anything written in the Thessalonian letters be judged as being of any permanent value?

Interpretations that identify the restrainer as a then-existent civil government.

Some early church fathers interpreted the restrainer to be the Roman Empire and its ruler, and taught that when the Empire was gone then an apostasy from the Christian faith would occur, or that when the Empire was gone there would be widespread anarchy (rebellion) affecting society. It would seem that history has proven this early-attempted identification of the restrainer to be mistaken, for the supposed restrainer, the Roman Empire, has long since faded away, and the lawless one has not yet been revealed, nor has Christ's *parousia* yet occurred.

Interpretations that identify the restrainer as being the Holy Spirit.

Modern premillennial interpreters identify the Holy Spirit as being the restrainer. The Greek word for Spirit (*pneuma*) is neuter, but the Holy Spirit is a person. In this, it is urged, we have the change of gender in verses 6 and 7 explained. Modern premillennial interpreters also advance the scenario that when the church is raptured at Christ's *parousia*, the Holy Spirit also will leave the world. Then, with no more restraint on him by the Holy Spirit, the Antichrist will be revealed. A serious flaw in this attempted identification is the fact that there are no Scriptures to commend the theory that the appearance of antichrist follows the *parousia* and rapture. On the contrary, even this passage in Thessalonians has the man of lawlessness active before the *parousia* and destroyed at the *parousia*.

Interpretations that make Michael the archangel the restrainer.

In order to make this identification of the restrainer, several writers have called attention to the activity performed by Michael in the Old Testament, which is claimed to be similar to the activity of the restrainer in 2 Thessalonians 2.[7] For example, in Daniel 10, Michael is portrayed as a restrainer of the demonic enemies of Israel. In this passage, Daniel has been praying about the future of Israel now that the 70 years of her Babylonian captivity are at an end. When Daniel started his prayer, an angel was sent by God to give Daniel the answer to his prayer. However, that angel messenger was hindered in his journey for three weeks by a demon prince of the kingdom of Persia. Then it was that Michael came to help. He put a restraint on the demon prince of Persia, an action that finally allowed the angelic messenger from God to appear to Daniel. Michael then went to fight against another demon prince, this time the demon prince of Greece, for before long Greece would cause problems for Israel.

---

[7] See, Maarten J.J. Menken, *2 Thessalonians* (New York: Routledge, 1994), p.113; I. Howard Marshall, *1 and 2 Thessalonians* in the New Century Bible (Grand Rapids: Wm. B. Eerdmans, 1983), p.199-200; Marvin Rosenthal, *The Pre-Wrath Rapture of the Church* (Nashville: Nelson, 1990), p.256-61; and Colin Nicholl, "Michael, the Restrainer Removed (2 Thess. 2:6-7)," *Journal of Theological Studies* 51 (April 2000), p.27-53.

We find another reference to Michael in Daniel 12:1, which reads, "Now at that time Michael, the great prince who stands *guard* over the sons of your people, will arise. And there will be a time of distress such as never occurred since there was a nation until that time; and at that time your people, everyone who is found written in the book, will be rescued." "At that time" continues the future history of Israel described in Daniel 11. Daniel 11:20-35 is a prediction of what would happen in the intertestamental period when Antiochus Epiphanes would persecute Israel. It is almost certain that Daniel 11:36-45 predicts the fate of Israel when Herod the Great was king. The first verse of chapter 12 continues the prediction. It seems to make reference to not only the distress that would befall the city of Jerusalem in AD 70, but also predicts that the Jewish people whose names were written in the book of life would be kept safe. Daniel 12:2,3 then anticipates what happens when the final resurrection takes place at the end of time.

In this commentator's judgment, Colin Nicholl has made several wrong applications of the verses in Daniel 11 and 12 as he tries to show that Daniel's prophecy and 2 Thessalonians 2 are references to the same restrainer.[8] By treating Daniel 11:36ff as being a prediction of the future Antichrist he can then affirm that Michael is predicted to be active at the time the Antichrist arrives on the scene. By suggesting the verb translated "will arise" in Daniel 12:1 should read "will withdraw," Nicholl then has a parallel to the restrainer going out of the way in 2 Thessalonians 2:7. One other weakness of the interpretation that has Michael as the restrainer is that the neuter "what restrains" (2 Thessalonians 2:6) is not explained.[9]

The Most Likely Correct Identification of the Restrainer

Based on the studied decisions made in regard to each of the disputed matters, the view that is judged to be the better one is that "he who restrains" is God and "that which restrains" is the providential[10] outworking of His eternal plan.[11] Several lines of thought favoring this view can be marshaled:

---

[8] Nicholl, *op. cit.*, p.35,36.

[9] I.H. Marshall (*op. cit.*, p.199,200) has tried to supply this deficiency by suggesting that the "present opportunity for preaching the gospel" is "*that* which restrains," while "*he* who restrains" is the angelic figure Michael.

[10] "Providence" is defined as the care and preservation and government that God exercises over His creation so that it accomplishes the purposes for which it was made.

[11] According to 2 Timothy 1:9, before God ever began the work of creation described in Genesis 1, the members of the Godhead made a plan which they were going to put into operation. This "plan" or "resolve" or "purpose" is referred to in several New Testament texts. Romans 8:28 speaks of God working all things together for the spiritual good of folk on earth who are called or invited to become Christians in harmony with God's "eternal purpose." Ephesians 1:11 tells us that "according to His purpose [design, plan]" God works all things after the counsel of His will. Ephesians 3:11 indicates that the inclusion of Gentiles in His plan of salvation was in "accordance with the eternal purpose which He carried out in Christ Jesus our Lord."

(1) The strongest objection to this identification is removed when the deponent Greek verb *genētai* (verse 7) is given its active meaning.[12]

(2) That God Himself is involved in the restraint is favored by verse 6 ("in his time"), which almost certainly speaks of things happening on a divine timetable. If God does the "revealing" then it is likely God who is doing the restraining.

(3) Recall what is affirmed about God's hand in history in the words "God gave them up" (Romans 1:24,26,28 ASV). In those verses in Romans we not only see lawlessness growing worse and worse, but we also see how God withdraws His gracious providential aid as He removes restraints previously imposed against growing evil.

(4) This view that God is the restrainer is favored by Acts 17:26, which tells us that God determines when nations rise and fall, and how far their boundaries spread. He does have a hand in history, and that is precisely the idea being unfolded here in 2 Thessalonians 2:6,7.

(5) Verse 11 of 2 Thessalonians 2 also references God's hand in His world.

When we are told that the man of lawlessness opposes all that is called God, is it not implied that God is the One who is doing the restraining? God is in control. God is the One who knows the time of the second coming. He is working out His plan. God's plan is that the whole world should have an opportunity to hear and obey the gospel. Until that time is reached, it is not time for the events that will end earth's present history.

---

[12] See the explanatory notes in the commentary *supra,* or compare the reading in *The Living Bible*, "the one who is holding him back steps out of the way."

SELECTED BIBLIOGRAPHY

This annotated bibliography is intended for Bible students who wish to investigate further the letters to the Thessalonians to help them select volumes that will contribute to their growing knowledge and faith.

OLDER COMMENTARIES THAT ARE STILL VALUABLE

Some commentaries on Thessalonians that were produced near the end of the 19th century and the beginning of the 20th are still valuable tools. Since copies of these books have been reduced to digital format, they can easily be found on the web by searching these sites: BibleHub.com, or StudyLight.org, or Preceptaustin.org/1_Thessalonians_Commentaries.

Alford, Henry, *Alford's Greek Testament*, Vol. 3 (London: Rivingtons, 5th ed., 1871).
> Included in the introductory studies to the Thessalonian letters is a study entitled, "On the Prophetic Import of ch. 2:1-12," on pages 55-69.

Ellicott, Charles J., *Commentary on the Epistles of St. Paul to the Thessalonians* (Grand Rapids: Zondervan Publishing house, 1957).
> A highly technical exegetical study first published in 1861. Still ranked as one of the most scholarly treatments of these letters.

Findlay, George G., ed. "The Epistles of Paul the Apostle to the Thessalonians" in *The Cambridge Greek Testament* (Cambridge: University Press, 1904).
> This careful exposition of the epistles is based on the Greek text. There is a history of the interpretation of 2 Thessalonians 2 (the "Man of Sin") on pages 170-180.

P.J. Gloag, "1 Thessalonians," and "2 Thessalonians" in Vol. 21 of *The Pulpit Commentary* (Grand Rapids: Eerdmans, reprint 1950).
> Introductory studies and verse-by-verse comments. An "Excursus on Man of Sin" is included in the commentary on 2 Thessalonians, pages 50-61.

Plummer, Alfred, *A Commentary on St. Paul's First Epistle to the Thessalonians*, and *A Commentary on St. Paul's Second Epistle to the Thessalonians* (London: Robert Scott, 1908).
> A critical exegetical unfolding of these epistles. Greek words are often quoted but generally in parenthesis, so the non-Greek reader can readily understand what is written.

MODERN COMMENTARIES THAT REQUIRE CAUTIOUS READING

Although a few new commentaries on Paul's two letters to the Thessalonians did appear in the early part of the 20th century, the past four decades have witnessed the appearance of many significant commentaries in English. This flourish of new works follows a trend that has been well-documented: each time a new popular philosophy begins to influence culture, a whole new set of commentaries appears. The idea seems to be that the man in the street is more likely to pay attention to Bible books if the explanations of those books match the newly emerging philosophy.

When Kierkegaard's existentialism and Heidegger's existentialism were the prevailing philosophy, the methods of Bible study that became popular were form criticism and redaction criticism. These methods presume that our New Testament books contain three levels of material:

(1) What Jesus said and did, of which we actually know very little. (Just because one of the Gospels tells a story about Jesus, there is no reason to understand it actually happened the way the Gospel presented it.)
(2) What the apostles of Jesus said and did, of which we know very little.
(3) What the early church believed.

This third level, two generations removed from when the events actually happened, may differ considerably from what Jesus originally taught, and from what the apostles taught as they modified what they learned from Jesus as they encountered new situations in their ministries. The third generation also allegedly modified and adapted what they learned from the apostles. A few commentaries on Thessalonians in the German language attempted to show how the Thessalonian letters could be interpreted in this light.

The flood of new commentaries in recent years reflects the phenomena that existentialism has given way to postmodernism as the popular philosophy. Postmodern methods of interpreting Scripture include social-science criticism, rhetorical criticism, and reader-response criticism, among others. Social-science criticism focuses attention on social matters, such as haves versus have-nots, patron-client relationships, honor and shame. Rhetorical criticism attempts to identify what kind of ancient Greek or Roman rhetoric is embedded in the letters, whether it be epideictic rhetoric (or demonstrative, "to help people remember, understand, and learn") or deliberative rhetoric (designed to persuade). Ancient rhetoric had certain well-defined sections such as *exordium, narratio, propositio, probatio,* and *exhortatio.* Several of the newer commentaries use these names as the points of the outline when they offer an outline for the whole book. Reader-response criticism is interested in how the Thessalonian letters impact those who read and study them, without any judgment as to what might be true or false in the different responses.

It is the studied judgment of this author that none of these interpretive frameworks is very productive when one wants to know the message from God that is contained in the Thessalonian letters. So, modern commentaries that reflect the prevailing popular philosophy should be approached with extreme caution. The annotations that follow will identify the method of study employed in the commentary and some of the negative conclusions which these studies have produced.

Best, Ernest, *A Commentary on the First and Second Epistles to the Thessalonians.* Black's New Testament Commentary series (New York: Harper & Row, 1973; reprint, Peabody, MA: Hendrickson, 1987).

> A verse-by-verse critical commentary. A liberal British scholar who nonetheless favors the authenticity of the second letter, but who rejects the historical accuracy of the account of the mission work in Thessalonica found in Acts. He suggests we should view the letters in the light of a possible influence by Gnosticism.

Jewett, Robert, *The Thessalonian Correspondence: Pauline Rhetoric and Millenarian Piety* in Foundations & Facets: New Testament (Philadelphia: Fortress Press, 1986).

His interpretive methodology combines historical-critical research, rhetorical analysis, and social-scientific theory. Earlier hypotheses about elaborate redactional tinkering are critiqued and dismissed. Jewett argues that First Thessalonians is an instance of demonstrative/epideictic rhetoric and Second Thessalonians is demonstrative rhetoric, while also proposing that 2 Thessalonians was the first of the two letters to be written. His use of social-science criticism leads to the suggestion that the recipients of the letters had been strongly influenced by the utopian golden age ideas of the Cabiric cult which flourished in Thessalonica (p.127), and that the letters are intended to counteract those erroneous ideas.

Malherbe, Abraham, *Letters to the Thessalonians* in the Anchor Bible series, 32B (Garden City, NY: Doubleday, 2000).

Malherbe, a Restoration Movement scholar, staunchly defends the Pauline involvement in the authorship of both letters. Concerning the background of these two letters, he compellingly argues that both were written within a few months of each in the early AD 50s. He makes discriminating use of Acts, arguing for its historical accuracy (in opposition to several contemporary authors). He rejects the view held by some contemporary scholars that 1 Thessalonians 2:13-16 does not enjoy integrity. He makes use of rhetoric studies as he attempts to unfold what these letters say, and on matters of eschatology he is tentative in his conclusions.

Thiselton, Anthony C., *1 and 2 Thessalonians through the Centuries* in Blackwell Bible Commentaries (Chichester, West Sussex: Wiley-Blackwell, 2011).

The focus of this volume is on the reception history of the Thessalonian letters, not on what the text actually says. He cites Ulrich Luz's assertion that "the biblical texts do not have a simple fixed meaning." Thiselton makes no attempt to comment on the "truth" of any one interpretation, reflecting the editorial policy behind the Blackwell series.

Wanamaker, Charles A., *The Epistles to the Thessalonians: A Commentary on the Greek Text* in the New International Greek Testament Commentary series (Grand Rapids: Eerdmans and Exeter: Paternoster, 1990).

The publisher's book jacket identifies the areas of emphasis in the book – (1) an extensive discussion of introductory matters, (2) a strong argument for the priority of 2 Thessalonians, (3) the use of rhetorical analysis, and (4) an emphasis on the social dimensions of Christianity. Wanamaker starts with a premise that the eschatology in the two letters differs greatly. In an effort to explain these imagined differences, Wanamaker argues that 2 Thessalonians was actually written before 1 Thessalonians. He is heavily dependent on Jewett's rhetorical analysis, which provides the outline for his comments on the letters. Since the body of the commentary is based on the Greek text, it requires a knowledge of Greek to use this commentary.

Witherington III, Ben, *1 and 2 Thessalonians: A Socio-Rhetorical Commentary* (Grand Rapids: Eerdmans, 2006).

As the subtitle makes clear, he explores the letters through both a social (e.g., with abuse of patron-client relationships as the particular backdrop) and a rhetorical (i.e., structured according to the rhetorical conventions of the day) lens. Witherington tries to build a case that 1 Thessalonians is epideictic rhetoric, and 2 Thessalonians is deliberative rhetoric, with the writers using the rhetorical strategies for the maximum oral impact as the letters were read aloud in the public assembly of the church. There is heavy emphasis on identifying the anti-imperial and countercultural language in the letters. Witherington identifies the Restrainer (2 Thessalonians 2:6) as the archangel Michael (p.208-212). Noteworthy also is Witherington's thoroughgoing critique of Calvinistic and Dispensationalist readings of the Thessalonian letters. The collection of reasons he gathers in support of the Pauline authorship of 2 Thessalonians shows that the contemporary German view that this letter is pseudonymous is far less secure than is usually admitted by its proponents.

NEWER COMMENTARIES BIBLE BELIEVERS WILL FIND HELPFUL

The works listed in this section do not reflect post-modern emphases. Some were written before the newer emphases became the vogue, and some have been written in critique of the newer emphases.

Bruce, F.F., *1 & 2 Thessalonians* in the Word Biblical Commentary series, 45 (Waco, TX: Word, 1982).

> The "Word Biblical Commentary" series, resulting from the conviction that Christians need an underpinning of solid scholarship, aims to be evangelical in the sense of a commitment to Scripture as a divine revelation and critical in the sense of a careful and thorough scrutiny of evidence. Bible students will find a helpful resource for further study in the detailed bibliography sections that accompany the introductory studies, and each major paragraph of the letters. Most of Bruce's comments on the Greek text are theologically conservative. For example, Acts 16:6-18:5 may confidently be accepted as providing the historical framework within which 1 Thessalonians may be read. Both letters were written from Corinth about AD 50-51. A helpful feature of this volume is the 9-page excursus on the Antichrist figure (p.179-188). Readers who look for premillennial eschatological ideas will be disappointed, and Bible students will be given pause when they read Bruce's presentation that John's views about the Roman empire being the antichrist differ from Paul's view which has the Roman empire being the restrainer who keeps antichrist from appearing.

Morris, Leon, *The Epistles of Paul to the Thessalonians* in The Tyndale New Testament Commentaries (Grand Rapids: Eerdmans, 1957. Revised edition, 1984).

> Morris is also the author of the commentaries on Thessalonians in the New International Commentary on the New Testament series (Grand Rapids: Eerdmans, 1991). His comments at times reflect Reformed theology, and his eschatology is amillennial. His treatment of 2 Thessalonians 2 (the signs that must occur before the second coming of Christ) is well-worded. Concerning the man of lawlessness, he rejects the outmoded identifications of Antichrist with the Roman emperor or with Nero redivivus (since the Thessalonians letters are too early for that), and Morris observes that the once-popular identification of the papacy as being the antichrist "seems to have arisen more from hostility to the papacy than from exegetical considerations" (p.221). Since this antichrist figure appears just before the second coming of Christ, attempts through church history to identify him have proven futile and mistaken. The same caution should be observed by those who attempt to identify the restrainer. Such identification must await the time when it will be revealed.

Weima, Jeffrey A. D., *1-2 Thessalonians* in the Baker Exegetical Commentary on the New Testament series (Grand Rapids: Baker Academic, 2014).

> This detailed commentary includes 577 pages of exegetical material, which emphasize ancient letter-writing practices over rhetorical criticism as an aid to exegesis, and has mostly conservative theological conclusions. Rhetorical criticism is here defined as allowing Greco-Roman discussions of oral presentations to have a significant influence on the interpretation of these letters to the Thessalonians. Weima rarely mentions another recent interpretive trend – the implications of the patron-client relationship. As to introductory matters, Weima holds that Paul wrote both 1 and 2 Thessalonians from Corinth in AD 50-51. First Thessalonians was written first, and 1 Thessalonians 2:13-16 is not an interpolation. The "we" of the letters is to be taken "literarily rather than literally" (p.66). Weima's introductory arguments assume a high view of the historical accuracy of Acts. Weima has an extended discussion concerning the "restrainer" in which he concludes (based on Daniel 10-12) that the restrainer is the archangel Michael. His comments on the election/calling passages are compatible to a Reformed theological viewpoint.

INDEX

Cross-references to Scripture books cited in these comments on 1 and 2 Thessalonians are not included in the index. Roman numerals indicate page numbers.

Macedonian call – 137
Magistrates – see: Politarchs
Maintenance – 26
    of apostles – 26
    of ministers –
    Paul's refusal of –
    right of – 26
Man of lawlessness – 101,119,123,185,197,
    204,226,253
    identification of – 232,234,235,242
    revelation of – 128,129,134
    presents himself as God – 127,128
    supported by Satan – 126,133-136,238
    see also: Special Study #3, The Man
    of Lawlessness
Man of sin (KJV reading) – 125
Manifestation – 111,132
Marcion – 176,208
Mark, Gospel of – 190,196
Marriage – 57,72
Maternal figure of speech – 26,27,29
Matthew, Gospel of – 190
Meddlesomeness – 154
    prefer "busybodies"
Meeting (*apantesis*) – 69-71
Melanchthon –
    on Antichrist – 241
Messiah – 8,11,18,43,49,64,171,181,183
    long promised – 8,34,49,157,181,197,
    205
Michael (archangel) – 68,248,249,255,256
Middle ages – 192,240,241,243
Military metaphors –
    54,81,139,146,148,152, 154
Mind – 9-11,18,61,76,80,120-122,139,147,
    208
    God's – 35,89
Ministry (service) – 5,20,23,41,47,51,181
    continuing, of Paul and Silas – 173,178
    Jesus' earthly – 8,66,72,194,225
    of angels – 69
    mutual – 78
    Paul's, to the Gentiles – 7,21
Miracles – 13,87,133,134,224
    lying – 133,238
Missionary offerings, accepted by Paul –
    26,172,173,205
Modern dispensationalism – 30,232,248
Mohammedanism –
    and Antichrist – 241
Morals, Christian – 211

Muratorian Canon – 176,208
Mystery – 68,129,134,218,238,246
    of lawlessness – see: Lawlessness,
    mystery of

Name – 7,8,12,159,224
    four-letter sacred – 8,180,223
    in the, of the Lord – 118,148
Neapolis – 170
Nero (emperor) – 212
    a type of Antichrist – 242
    Redivivus Myth – 212
New birth – 90,138,197
New Jerusalem – 31,233
Newness of life – 76
Night – 27,28,34,48,63,71,74,75,150,151,
    171,187
    thief in the – see: Thief in the night
Non-Christians – 29,62,64,110,183
Nurse, nursing – 26,27,29,176

Obadiah, book of – 224
Obey, obedience – 10,13,18,33,112,113,129,
    135,136,148,155,156
    see also: Gospel, obey the
Octavian – 126,170
Offering for poor saints in Jerusalem – see:
    Jerusalem relief fund
Old Latin version – 176,208
Old Syriac version – 176,208
Old Testament – 51,63,68,112,132,180,223
    people – 8
    prophecy – 19,36,70,112,121,129
    prophets – 34,64,124,125,171,195,224,
    238,247
    Scriptures – 125,129,171,213
    use of – 177,213
Olivet discourse – see: Eschatological
    discourse
Olympian games – 39
Origen – 26

OTHER BOOKS BY GARETH L. REESE

New Testament History: Acts (097-176-5235)

New Testament Epistles: Romans (097-176-5200)

New Testament Epistles: 1 Corinthians (097-176-5251)

New Testament Epistles: 2 Corinthians & Galatians (097-176-5278)

New Testament Epistles: Paul's Prison Epistles (099-845-1800)

New Testament Epistles: 1 & 2 Timothy and Titus (097-176-5227)

New Testament Epistles: Hebrews (097-176-5219)

New Testament Epistles: 1 & 2 Peter and Jude (097-176-5243)

New Testament Epistles: James and 1,2,3 John (097-176-526X)

Order from:
Scripture Exposition Books
803 McKinsey Place
Moberly, MO, 65270
www.glreese@cccb.edu